The Priority of Events

Plateaus – New Directions in Deleuze Studies

'It's not a matter of bringing all sorts of things together under a single concept but rather of relating each concept to variables that explain its mutations.'
Gilles Deleuze, *Negotiations*

Series Editors

Ian Buchanan, Cardiff University
Claire Colebrook, Penn State University

Editorial Advisory Board

Titles available in the series

Visit the Plateaus website at www.euppublishing.com/series/plat

THE PRIORITY OF EVENTS
Deleuze's *Logic of Sense*

Sean Bowden

EDINBURGH UNIVERSITY PRESS

Edinburgh University Press Ltd
22 George Square, Edinburgh

www.euppublishing.com

Typeset in Sabon
by Servis Filmsetting Ltd, Stockport, Cheshire, and
printed and bound in Great Britain by
CPI Antony Rowe, Chippenham and Eastbourne

A CIP record for this book is available from the British Library

ISBN 978 0 7486 4359 2 (hardback)
ISBN 978 0 7486 4364 6 (paperback)

Contents

Acknowledgements

The following friends and colleagues all contributed to the realization of this work in various ways and at various times, through their comments, criticisms, linguistic advice and other kindnesses too numerous to list here: Alain Badiou, Alexandra Bourré, Hervé Bruneau, Ian Buchanan, Tim Clark, Rosalyn Diprose, Stéphane Douailler, Simon Duffy, Joanne Faulkner, Joe Hughes, Marc Jones, Simon Lumsden, Charles Ramond, Jack Reynolds, Florentin Roche, and Daniel W. Smith. I am particularly indebted to Paul Patton, who was a generous and judicious sounding board for many of the ideas developed herein. I am also very grateful to James Williams, for his enthusiasm for this work and for encouraging me to submit it to the Plateaus series. Carol Macdonald and the team at Edinburgh University Press made the publication process a very pleasant experience. A special mention is also due to my parents, Terry and Denise, for all their support.

Finally, and above all, I would like to thank Miriam Bankovsky for her generosity, encouragement, counsel and loving support over many years.

An early version of Chapter 1 was published as 'Deleuze et les Stoïciens: une logique de l'événement', *Le Bulletin de la société américaine de philosophie de langue française* 15: 1 (2005), pp. 72–97. A substantial portion of Chapter 2 also appears in the article 'Deleuze's Neo-Leibnizianism, Events and *The Logic of Sense*'s "Static Ontological Genesis"', *Deleuze Studies* 4: 3 (2010), pp. 301–28. I gratefully acknowledge the permission of these journals and their editors to republish this material.

Abbreviations

LS   Deleuze, Gilles, *The Logic of Sense*, trans. Mark Lester with Charles Stivale, ed. Constantin V. Boundas (New York: Colombia University Press, 1990).

DR   Deleuze, Gilles, *Difference and Repetition*, trans. Paul Patton (London: Athlone, 1994).

HRS   Deleuze, Gilles, 'How do We Recognize Structuralism?' in *Desert Islands and Other Texts 1953–1974*, trans. Michael Taormina, ed. David Lapoujade (New York: Semiotexte, 2004), pp. 170–92.

INFI Simondon, Gilbert, *L'individuation à la lumière des notions de forme et d'information* (Grenoble: Millon, 2005).

HP   Long, A.A. and D.N. Sedley, *The Hellenistic Philosophers: Volume 1: Translations of the Principal Sources, with Philosophical Commentary* (Cambridge: Cambridge University Press, 1987).

SVF   Arnim, Herman von, *Stoicorum Veterum Fragmenta*, 3 Vols (Leipzig: Teubner, 1903–1905).

Introduction: The Ontological Priority of Events in *The Logic of Sense*

The aim of this present study is above all to examine and clarify the complex way in which Deleuze asserts the ontological priority of events over substances in his 1969 work, *The Logic of Sense*. In particular, the book will analyze the way in which Deleuze grounds this assertion by establishing a relation, the precise nature of which will be seen below, between the works representative of several philosophers and intellectual movements, namely, the Stoics, Leibniz, Albert Lautman, Gilbert Simondon, structuralism and psychoanalysis. In short, it will be shown how Deleuze constructs a concept of the ontologically primitive event by extracting from the work of these thinkers and schools a number of event-related problems and a hybrid family of concepts which, with certain important qualifications, can be said to resolve these problems.

The question naturally arises as to why I have elected to focus on these particular figures and not others. Arguably, *The Logic of Sense* could profitably be explored in a number of different ways: through Deleuze's readings of Nietzsche and Husserl, for example, or through Lewis Carroll and Antonin Artaud. Indeed, several commentators have noted and analyzed the importance of these latter figures in *The Logic of Sense*.[1] The fact that they have already done so, of course, is reason enough for not duplicating their efforts. But it is also my belief that Deleuze's philosophy of events is most fruitfully examined in relation to the thinkers chosen for this present study. There are several reasons for holding this belief. First of all, Deleuze maintains in his 1988 work, *The Fold*, that the Stoics and Leibniz implemented, respectively, the first and second 'great logics' of the event.[2] These philosophers will thus be indispensable for any understanding of Deleuze's approach to events in 1969. Secondly, as will be seen in Chapters 3 and 4, Deleuze effectively reads the Stoics and Leibniz through several conceptual innovations developed by Lautman, Simondon and various structuralists. Finally, Deleuze's

1

engagement with psychoanalysis occupies the final quarter of the actual text of *The Logic of Sense*. It is in relation to psychoanalysis that Deleuze establishes his concept of the 'dynamic genesis' of sense and the event, which comes to complement the 'static genesis' of sense and the event developed primarily in relation to Leibniz, but also in relation to the other intellectual figures examined here. In sum, therefore, the decision to focus on the above-mentioned thinkers has been dictated by the very nature of the task that has been set, namely, to clarify Deleuze's claim for the ontological priority of events over substances in *The Logic of Sense*.[3]

In so far as the present study connects Deleuze's understanding of events to its explicitly acknowledged sources, it can be read as a work in the history of philosophy. By 'history of philosophy' is here meant, not an enumeration and comparison of philosophical opinions nor a Hegelian-style synthesis, but, more humbly, the crystallization of a number of ideas and problems which can be said to be common to several thinkers belonging to different historical periods, and which are capable of being connected to contemporary intellectual concerns. To undertake the history of philosophy in this way is to simultaneously engage in what Richard Rorty calls a context-bound, 'historical reconstruction' of what a particular thinker actually said; a 'rational reconstruction' of what these thinkers might say in a productive conversation with thinkers from different time periods, including our own; and a contingent, 'canon-forming reconstruction' of the problem which these thinkers share, and which is of contemporary interest.[4] Indeed, as will be seen, this present work examines the precise contributions made by Deleuze, as well as by each of the thinkers to whom he refers, in posing and resolving what will be called 'the problem of the event'.

It should be noted, however, that it is beyond the scope of this study to explore the ways in which contemporary thought concerns itself with events or processes. Here such interest in events will be taken for granted. Suffice it to say that the contemporary significance of events in Continental European philosophy is reflected, in very different ways, in the works of thinkers such as Alain Badiou and Michel Serres,[5] as well as in the works of those such as Bruno Latour and Bernard Stiegler, who are the inheritors of a philosophical tradition which includes Bergson, Bachelard, Simondon and Deleuze. In Anglo-American philosophy, events and processes have recently been examined, again in quite diverse ways, by philosophers such as Donald Davidson, Jaegwon Kim, Jonathan Bennett and Nicholas

Rescher.[6] Again, whilst it is beyond the scope of this project to analyze the conceptual proximity of Deleuze to these other philosophers, it is hoped that this book will be able to make such studies possible in the future, that is, precisely in so far as it is able to clarify Deleuze's own approach to events.

This volume also aims to contribute to the secondary literature on Deleuze. As Jean-Jacques Lecercle rightly notes, *The Logic of Sense* has until very recently been largely neglected by commentators. The reason for this, according to Lecercle, is that the text appears to be 'too structuralist' and 'too psychoanalytic' when read alongside the works which Deleuze co-authored with Félix Guattari.[7] As he writes, *The Logic of Sense* is generally regarded as

> the work of a structuralist Deleuze, still under the influence of Lacan and psychoanalysis, two unfortunate aspects which his meeting with Guattari enabled him to get rid of – the real Deleuze, before and after *Logic of Sense*, the vitalist Deleuze, herald of the Bergsonian virtual, of difference, becomings and haecceities, is not found in *Logic of Sense*, an accident in an otherwise distinguished career.[8]

The disproportionate focus in Deleuze scholarship on the two volumes of *Capitalism and Schizophrenia*, where Deleuze is highly critical of certain versions of structuralism and psychoanalysis, adds weight to Lecercle's argument. But one can also point to the complexity of *The Logic of Sense*, both in its form and in its content, as an obstacle to commentary. Indeed, in its form, this text is composed not of chapters but of relatively short 'series' which refer to one another in indirect, manifold and ultimately non-linear ways. The reader is, moreover, left to discover and establish the connections between these series for him or herself. Deleuze does provide an explanation of how this serial form 'works', but the reader must reconstruct this explanation with reference to several interrelated series. We shall return to a more ample discussion of Deleuze's concept of series below. In its content, the argument of *The Logic of Sense* is constructed with reference to thinkers who are themselves relatively unknown or comparatively 'minor' (the Stoics, Simondon, Lautman), or who are not, strictly speaking, considered to be philosophers (the various structuralists and psychoanalytic theorists to whom Deleuze refers). Furthermore, due to Deleuze's allusive writing style, it is often difficult to separate out precisely 'who' is speaking at any one time.[9] When, for example, Deleuze develops, in Series 16 and 17, his 'static ontological and logical geneses' in a vocabulary derived primarily from Leibniz, is it Deleuze who is speaking or Leibniz? Or, if it is a combination of the two, how can the line which divides Leibniz's thought from Deleuze's be characterized? These are questions which are not easily answered and present a real difficulty for any commentator.

But whatever the reason for this lacuna in Deleuze scholarship, it is incontestable that it exists. This book should thus be read, not only as a work in the history of philosophy, but also as an attempt to partially fill this gap in the secondary literature.

It should be noted, though, that as this book was nearing completion, a monograph devoted to *The Logic of Sense* was published by James Williams, entitled *Gilles Deleuze's* Logic of Sense: *A Critical Introduction and Guide*. This present study, however, differs from Williams' work in two ways. First of all, as his chapter headings make clear, Williams takes as his focus the way in which *The Logic of Sense* addresses, in various ways, several themes which are dear to philosophy, namely, language, the nature of philosophy itself, morality and thought. The present work, on the contrary, focuses exclusively on reading *The Logic of Sense* as a complex assertion of the ontological priority of events over substances. Secondly, while Williams is careful to cite the sources of Deleuze's thought and to indicate where Deleuze's philosophy of events overlaps with those of several contemporary philosophers, including Donald Davidson and Jaegwon Kim, his mode of presentation of Deleuze's arguments is to a large extent conversational, as befits a critical introduction, and makes use of many illuminating examples drawn from literature, film and everyday life. This present work, by contrast, attempts to explicate and analyze some of the more technical aspects of the philosophical and other works to which Deleuze refers in *The Logic of Sense*, and then juxtaposes this with detailed analyses of Deleuze's own way of talking about events. The two projects, therefore, are quite different in focus and approach, which accounts for the lack of citations to be found herein to Williams' work. This is not at all to say, however, that the two projects do not complement one another. Indeed, on the one hand, Williams' text addresses many issues which this present work cannot, due to its focus on the ontological priority of events over substances. On the other hand, the technical analyses to be found in this book shed light on some of Deleuze's more obscure claims and references in *The Logic of Sense*, claims and references which the nature of Williams' text precludes him from examining. Finally, it is clear that the present study will in any case be able to be understood much more easily by those having already read Williams' very clear introduction and guide. It thus benefits immeasurably from the prior publication of this latter.

Two other recent works dealing with *The Logic of Sense* also bear mentioning here, although neither is entirely devoted to this text. The first, Jean-Jacques Lecercle's *Deleuze and Language*, contains an excellent chapter-length analysis of *The Logic of Sense*, developed as part of the larger task of spelling out what a Deleuzian philosophy of language might look like. From the point of view of this larger task, Lecercle provides a clear overview of Deleuze's relation to the Stoics, structuralism and psychoanalysis, as well as a helpful comparison between Badiou's and Deleuze's respective understandings of the nature of events. What is missing from Lecercle's reading of *The Logic of Sense*, however, at least from the point of view of the task to be undertaken here, is a detailed analysis of the way in which Deleuze articulates his philosophy of the event with reference to Leibniz, Lautman and Simondon. Nevertheless, it is clear that it is the question of language and not that of the ontological priority of events which is Lecercle's primary focus, and it is precisely this focus which leads Lecercle to privilege certain of Deleuze's references at the expense of these latter philosophers who appear to us as crucial for any understanding of his philosophy of events.

The second text dealing with *The Logic of Sense* is a chapter of Alain Badiou's *Logics of Worlds*.[10] In several dense pages, Badiou extracts from *The Logic of Sense* what he calls the 'four Deleuzian axioms of the event', which he then contrasts with four axioms characterizing his own approach to events. These four Deleuzian axioms – (1) 'Unlimited-becoming becomes the event itself', (2) 'The event is always what has just happened, what will happen, but never what is happening', (3) 'The nature of the event is other than that of the actions and passions of the body. But it results from them', and (4) 'A life is composed of the same single Event, despite all the variety of what happens to it' – capture in a very precise way some of the essential aspects of Deleuze's understanding of the event. However, despite the inherent interest of Badiou's distillation of the essential 'axioms' of *The Logic of Sense*, and of the philosophical dispute between Deleuze's and Badiou's understanding of events more generally, it is clear that Badiou does not here go into the sort of detail usually expected of textual commentary. Indeed, such commentary is not at all his concern, and nor should we demand that it be so. There is thus much more to be said about *The Logic of Sense* if this present work is to fulfil its task of spelling out the precise way in which Deleuze affirms, with reference to the various thinkers and intellectual movements he privileges in this text, the ontological priority of events over substances.

The aim of the present work and its intellectual context thus outlined, what now can be said of the above-mentioned complex method which Deleuze uses in *The Logic of Sense* in order to ground his claims with regard to events? This question is of some importance, for its answer bears on the mode of presentation of Deleuze's philosophy of events to be used in what follows. It was remarked at the outset that Deleuze asserts the ontological priority of events by establishing a relation between the works of various thinkers in such a way that they can be said to collectively pose and resolve the 'problem of the event'. What, then, is the nature of this relation?

In his Preface, Deleuze indicates that the intellectual 'figures' he examines are related through the above-mentioned 'series' which compose the text of *The Logic of Sense*. He writes that 'to each series [of *The Logic of Sense*] there correspond figures which are not only historical but topological and logical as well. As on a pure surface, certain points of one figure in a series refer to the points of another figure: an entire galaxy of problems with their corresponding dice-throws, stories, and places, a complex place' (LS, xiv). We can thus see that three notions are here intertwined: figures, series and problems. What, then, are series, how do they bring the figures to refer to one another, and how does this determine an 'entire galaxy' of problems, dice-throws, and so on?

The precise nature of series will be examined in Chapters 2, 3 and, above all, Chapter 4. It can nevertheless be stated here that a series has, conceptually, three general conditions. First of all, a series is composed of terms which relate to one another 'reciprocally', which is simply to say that each term is what it is in the series because of its 'position' relative to all of the other terms of the series. Secondly, this 'positional relation' between the reciprocally determined terms constituting a series is itself determined with reference to (at least) a second series of reciprocally determined terms of a heterogeneous 'type'. Finally, the two series 'refer' to each other in this way through a 'paradoxical element'. This element cannot be defined as a term of either series. It is defined, rather, as that in relation to which the terms of one series are situated in their reciprocal relations, relative to the way in which the terms of the other series are situated in their own reciprocal relations.

6

In what way, then, can we understand what would normally be called the 'chapters' of *The Logic of Sense* as 'series' in the above sense? First of all, in abstract terms, we can say that the sentences which make up each of Deleuze's series are the 'terms' of that series. A series is thus composed of sentences which 'make sense' within that series, depending on their 'position' relative to all the other sentences making up that series. Secondly, the precise way in which the sentences constitutive of one series 'make sense' in relation to one another is itself determined with reference to the way in which the sentences composing each of the other series 'make sense' in relation to one another within their own series. Finally, the sentences of each series are situated in their particular relations relative to the sentences of each of the other series because of the particular relation each series has to a 'paradoxical element' which belongs to none of the series as such.

To put this in more concrete terms, I hope to show that *The Logic of Sense*'s paradoxical element is nothing other than the 'problem of the event', that is to say, the problem of affirming the ontological priority of events over substances 'all the way down'. Each series of the text can thus be said to relate to this overall problem in its own particular way. Indeed, each series takes the form of an examination of particular event-related problems and conceptual solutions. In fact, as will be seen, the 'problem of the event' can be analyzed into several sub-problems whose solutions, in turn, have various components. But what is more, the way in which each series is related, through the particular sub-problems and partial solutions they deal with, to the overall problem of the event, is ultimately determined by the way in which each of the other series relates to this same overall problem in its own way. The 34 series which compose *The Logic of Sense* will thus be said to 'set up' as well as 'resolve' the problem of the event. It is in this way, therefore, that the serial form of *The Logic of Sense* gives rise to 'an entire galaxy of problems', to which correspond various 'dice-throws', that is, various partial conceptual solutions to these problems.[11]

What now of the 'figures' which refer to one another across the different series of Deleuze's text? In short, Deleuze generates the particular event-related problems and solutions dealt with in each series by asking what this or that aspect of the works of the various intellectual figures he examines brings to the problem of the event. It thus amounts to the same thing to say that the sentences constitutive of the various series of *The Logic of Sense* collectively pose and resolve the problem of the event as it does to say that the 'points' (i.e., the event-related problems, arguments, conceptual solutions, and so on) of one figure in a series refer to the points of another figure in another series. In fact, as will be seen, these serial 'references' are quite complex, for as one progresses through the series of *The Logic of Sense*, from the work of one figure to another, the event-related problems and conceptual solutions developed in earlier series are being constantly refined, modified and even transformed.

As has already been noted, this complex 'serial method' used by Deleuze in asserting the ontological priority of events presents a real difficulty for the commentator. What he or she requires is a mode of presentation which is able to extricate itself from the subtleties of Deleuze's serial approach and take a birds-eye view of the precise ways in which the figures, problems and conceptual solutions found throughout *The Logic of Sense* contribute to the philosophy of events elaborated therein. The approach taken in this book will be, first of all, in each chapter, to examine in detail the works of one of the intellectual figures or movements to whom Deleuze refers. It will then be shown how and where they are used in the text of *The Logic of Sense*. The reason why we are obliged to enter so fully into the works of Deleuze's privileged references is in order to overcome Deleuze's allusive style and thus to show precisely 'who' is speaking at any one time. In light of these analyses, we will then be in a position to identify the event-related problems and conceptual solutions which Deleuze appropriates from each thinker, and distinguish these from the original notions which he brings to the table.

In the second place, from one chapter to another, and thus from one intellectual figure to another, it will be shown how the 'evental' problems and solutions developed in relation to the works of one thinker are refined, re-problematized and re-solved in relation to the works of another thinker. Once this process is complete, we shall finally be able to give a clear statement of Deleuze's philosophy of events such as this can be extracted from the complex way in which the historical sources examined in *The Logic of Sense* 'refer' to each other via the serial method employed in the text.

Two further issues should also be mentioned. First, one of the 'figures' in relation to which Deleuze constructs his philosophy of events is the contemporary intellectual movement know as structuralism. It should here be noted that several of the concepts which Deleuze develops in relation to structuralism, such as 'series' and 'paradoxical element', are not only crucial to his philosophy of events, they also allow us to understand, as indicated above, the way in which the text of *The Logic of Sense* 'functions'. In Chapter 4, we examine how these structuralist concepts contribute to Deleuze's philosophy of events, but we do not address therein how these concepts also capture what is essential to the textual machinery of *The Logic of Sense* itself. This is because, in line with what has just been said, these concepts also refer in complex ways to the problems and conceptual solutions examined in other chapters. In order not to confuse these different 'levels' of discourse, then, a discussion of the reflexive nature of *The Logic of Sense* has been left until the conclusion.

The second point which here bears addressing is the fact that, although I have attempted as much as is possible to treat *The Logic of Sense* uniquely on its own terms, I nevertheless refer to two of Deleuze's earlier works in order to clarify a number of issues. These earlier works are *Difference and Repetition* (1968) and 'How do We Recognize Structuralism?' (1967). The use of these texts in this present study is due only to the fact that they give very clear statements of Deleuze's understanding of several figures and concepts which, whilst crucial to the philosophy of events to be found in *The Logic of Sense*, are examined in a comparatively restrained way in this latter. I do not go so far as to claim that Deleuze is essentially writing about the 'same things' in these different texts. Rather, beginning with what is addressed in abridged form in *The Logic of Sense*, and keeping in mind the overall aim of this work, I show how an examination of Deleuze's more extensive treatment of certain figures and concepts in his earlier works enhances our understanding of this later text.

Let us now turn to a brief chapter-by-chapter overview of what is to come. Chapter 1 begins with an examination of the way that Deleuze initially sets up the problem of the event. He argues that events, picked out by 'verbs of becoming', are ideal entities upon which determined states of affairs are ontologically dependent. While they are not in themselves objectively present, events must nevertheless be 'posited' in order to account for the constitution of new states of affairs, as well as of those states of affairs which will be understood as past in relation to these new presents. Deleuze argues, furthermore, that our knowledge of 'things' depends on the way in which the events constituting them can be brought into relation in language. Language, however, is itself an event. The problem of the event is thus formulated in the following way: 'what are the evental conditions of the event if everything, including the very language in which events are ordered and related, is ultimately to be a well determined event?'

While undertaking a detailed exploration of Stoic philosophy, we consider Deleuze's 'Stoic solution' to this problem. In particular, we examine the way in which Deleuze understands events in terms of Stoic incorporeal *lekta* or sayables, which are at once the sense of propositions and the effect of causal relations between the bodies denoted by these propositions. The event, understood in this way, is then seen to unite the various aspects of Deleuze's problem of the event in so far as it is the juncture of a three-fold process involving: the analysis of causal relations between bodies in terms of their events-effects; the construction of concepts characterizing bodies in terms of their constitutive events; and the development of the Stoic sage's beliefs and desires with respect to these event-determined bodies. This three-fold process, each aspect of which is inseparable from the others, is thus said to be an ongoing 'sense-event', which determines the ideal events upon which things in general are ontologically dependent.

There are two further event-related problems which Deleuze initially attempts to resolve with reference to the Stoics. The first of these is the circularity of the definition of sense. Or again, the fact that, since each of the three dimensions of the proposition recognized by contemporary philosophy is called upon to ground the others in some way, sense cannot be said to reside exclusively in denotation, conceptual signification or personal manifestation. The second problem is that there appears to be an unbridgeable 'gap' between conceptual signification understood as the condition of a proposition's being true, and the truth of that conditioned proposition in relation to an objective state of affairs. As will be seen, however, for Deleuze, the Stoic 'sense-event' overcomes these problems. In short, Deleuze understands the ongoing sense-event as a 'fourth dimension' of the proposition which grounds the relations between the other three dimensions in an *a priori* manner, causal analysis being aligned with denotation, conceptual construction with signification, and the wise person's beliefs and desires with manifestation. Furthermore, because the sense-event grounds the relation between the processes of conceptual construction and causal analysis, it can be said that it establishes a relation between signification, understood as the condition of the truth of a proposition, and the possibility of that proposition's being true in relation to bodies situated in their causal relations.

For the Stoics, however, it appears that the ongoing sense-event is ultimately determinable in relation to a pre-given substance: Zeus. Such an affirmation obviously runs counter to Deleuze's philosophy of the ontologically primitive event. In Chapter 2, we thus see how Deleuze readdresses the problem of the event and its Stoic solution with reference to Leibniz, or rather, to a certain Leibnizianism without God. In particular, we explore the way in which Deleuze extends the Leibnizian notions of compossibility and incompossibility in order to re-describe the genesis of determined individuals, persons and concepts, as well as the relations between them, in terms of the 'ideal play' of events. This redetermination of the sense-event or 'fourth dimension' of the proposition in strictly evental terms has three aspects. First of all, individuals and persons will be held to be determined within a common world in so far as there is a convergent or law-like relation between the particular events which can be truly predicated of them. Secondly, in so far as one person's point of view may always diverge from another's with regard to the series of events and event-determined individuals making up a world, a knowledge of worldly individuals must ultimately depend on a 'disjunctive synthesis' of these divergent points of view. Thirdly, this disjunctive synthesis of a world of individuals 'common' to such divergent worlds will be able to be carried out under two conditions: firstly, an agreement must be reached between persons as to the events characterizing worldly individuals and the law-like relations between these events; and secondly, these events and their relations must come to be embodied in shared concepts of increasing and decreasing generality which worldly individuals will be said to exemplify precisely in so far as they are individuals belonging to the same world. As will be made clear, these three aspects of Deleuze's neo-Leibnizian re-description of the Stoic sense-event are encapsulated in what Deleuze calls the 'static ontological and logical geneses'.

In Chapters 3 and 4 we examine, with greater precision, the concepts Deleuze constructs in order to bypass Leibniz's God, that is, the substantial instance to which the play of events in Leibniz's system is reduced. Referring in various ways to the works of Lautman, Simondon and diverse structuralists, Deleuze effectively argues that the linguistic and intersubjective process of synthesizing events described in Chapter 2 is best talked about in terms of an underlying problem or structure, wherein the events which characterize things in general are themselves determined only by other events. Within this problem or structure, following Deleuze, series of events of all orders and types (physical, biological, psychological, social, linguistic, and so on) determine each other reciprocally, completely and progressively, and without reference to any substantial thing transcending this system. These processes of determination thus effectively re-describe the static ontological and logical geneses examined in Chapter 2. We will also argue that they constitute the 'evental-determination' of the events making up the 'lives' of things in general, and thus represent what is most essential to Deleuze's philosophy of events. Although the issues involved are extremely complex, as will be seen, the two ways in which Deleuze speaks of the evental-determination of events – in terms of problems (or problematic Ideas) and structures – are ultimately identical. In relation to 'problems' or problematic Ideas, Deleuze describes how a 'physics of surfaces' corresponds to a 'metaphysical surface' via the intermediary of a 'divided subject'. This metaphysical surface is nothing other than the ongoing articulation of a relation between, on the one hand, bodies (including the body of the divided subject), taken together as a whole and inside the limits of their physical surfaces, and, on the other hand, propositions in general. In precisely the same way, with respect to 'structures', Deleuze describes how series of events corresponding to the causal relations between series of bodies are determined in the series of propositions which denote these bodies, as well as in the series of further propositions bearing on the sense of these denoting propositions, and so on, indefinitely.

Finally, in Chapter 5, we examine the 'dynamism' underlying Chapter 2's static ontological and logical geneses, which is also to say, Chapter 3 and 4's problematic Idea or structure of events. Through a detailed reading of the way in which Deleuze appropriates various facets of Kleinian, Freudian and Lacanian psychoanalytic theory, we show how he understands the problem or structure of events to be itself dynamically produced as an event by persons, their changing social and corporeal relations, and their ever-evolving, intersubjective 'language of events'. Indeed, without such an 'evental-account' of the problem or structure of events, Deleuze could be accused of hypostatizing this latter, to the ruin of his affirmation of the ontological primacy of events in general. But it will also be shown that, even though Deleuze considers the problem or structure of sense to be an event, this in no way prevents him from continuing to maintain, as discussed in Chapters 3 and 4, that the problem or structure always produces persons, their relations and their language, as events. In light of this mutual evental-determination, then, the problem or structure of events will be held to be the evental-determination of the events on which individual 'things' in general ontologically depend 'all the way down'. Psychoanalytic concepts such as 'pregenital sexuality', 'the phallus', 'castration' and the 'phantasm' will thus here be seen to furnish Deleuze with the final, partial conceptual solutions to his underlying 'problem of the event'. And psychoanalysis in general will be seen to be absolutely essential to Deleuze's 1969 philosophy of events.

But let us now leave this general overview and examine the details of the philosophy of events to be found in *The Logic of Sense*, beginning with Deleuze's Stoicism.

Notes

1. On the importance of Husserl in *The Logic of Sense*, see Leonard Lawlor, *Thinking Through French Philosophy: The Being of the Question* (Bloomington and Indianapolis: Indiana University Press, 2003), pp. 84–5 and pp. 130–1; and James Williams, *Gilles Deleuze's Logic of Sense: A Critical Introduction and Guide* (Edinburgh: Edinburgh University Press, 2008), pp. 129–34. On the importance of Lewis Carroll, see Jean-Jacques Lecercle, *Philosophy Through the Looking-Glass: Language, Nonsense, Desire* (La Salle: Open Court, 1985). On the importance of Artaud and Nietzsche, see Michel Foucault, 'Theatrum Philosophicum', in *Language, Counter-Memory Practice*, trans. Donald F. Bouchard and Sherry Simon, ed. Donald F. Bouchard (Oxford: Basil Blackwell, 1977), pp. 171–2, pp. 179–80 and pp. 192–6.
2. Gilles Deleuze, *The Fold: Leibniz and the Baroque*, trans. Tom Conley (London: The Athlone Press, 1993), p. 53. According to Deleuze, a 'third great logic of the event will come with Whitehead', but since Whitehead's philosophy is not addressed in *The Logic of Sense*, we shall not deal with it here.
3. Indeed, as Paul Patton rightly remarks, '*The Logic of Sense* might equally well have been entitled "The Logic of the Event"'. See his 'Introduction' to Paul Patton (ed.), *Deleuze: A Critical Reader* (Oxford: Blackwell, 1996), p. 13.
4. See Richard Rorty, 'The Historiography of Philosophy', in *Truth and Progress: Philosophical Papers, Volume 3* (Cambridge: Cambridge University Press, 1998), pp. 247–73.
5. See Alain Badiou, *Being and Event*, trans. Oliver Feltham (London and New York: Continuum, 2005). On Michel Serres as a philosopher of events, see Jean Ladrière's 'Préface', in Anne Crahay, *Michel Serres: La mutation du cogito* (Bruxelles: De Boeck, 1988), p. 15.

6. Nicholas Rescher also identifies as philosophers of events or processes not only those working in the shadow of Whitehead, but also those working in the tradition of American pragmatism, inherited from Peirce, James and Dewey. While some of these latter philosophers may not explicitly talk about events or processes as such, their work is nevertheless typically processual in nature. See Nicholas Rescher, *Process Metaphysics: An Introduction to Process Philosophy* (New York: SUNY, 1996), pp. 1–26.

7. See Jean-Jacques Lecercle, *Deleuze and Language* (Basingstoke: Palgrave Macmillan, 2002), pp. 99–100.

8. Jean-Jacques Lecercle, 'Preface', in Williams, *Gilles Deleuze's* Logic of Sense, p. vii. The one exception to Lecercle's argument here is Slavoj Žižek who, precisely because of the psychoanalytic, structural and pre-Guattari nature of this text, understands *The Logic of Sense* as emblematic of the 'line of Deleuze proper'. See Slavoj Žižek, *Organs without Bodies: On Deleuze and Consequences* (New York: Routledge, 2004), p. 20.

9. On this point, see also François Zourabichvili, *Deleuze: Une philosophie de l'événement* (Paris: PUF, 1994), pp. 5–6.

10. See Alain Badiou, *Logics of Worlds: Being and Event II*, trans. Alberto Toscano (London and New York: Continuum, 2009), pp. 381–7.

11. On the 'dice-throw', see also Chapter 3.

1

The Stoics – Events and Sense

The Stoics are of central importance to Deleuze's project in *The Logic of Sense*. As he writes in the Preface, the 'privileged place assigned to the Stoics [in this text] is due to their having been the initiators of a new image of the philosopher which broke away from the pre-Socratics, Socratic philosophy and Platonism. This new image is already closely linked to the paradoxical constitution of the theory of sense' (LS, xiii–xiv). So what is this image and how is it linked to Deleuze's theory of sense and the event?

In the 'Eighteenth Series of the Three Images of Philosophers', Deleuze understands the 'image of the philosopher' to be connected to a response to the Kantian question: 'what is orientation in thinking? [*qu'est-ce que s'orienter dans la pensée?*]' (LS, 127, translation modified).[1] He distinguishes three such images – the Platonic, the pre-Socratic and the Hellenic – each of which has its own 'axes and orientations', its own 'geography' and 'dimensions' (LS, 127). In Plato, following Deleuze, the 'philosopher's work is always determined as an ascent and a conversion, that is, as the movement of turning toward the high principle (*principe d'en haut*) from which the movement proceeds, and also of being determined, fulfilled, and known in the guise of such a motion' (LS, 127). Indeed, it is well known that, for Plato, not only does knowledge of worldly things in general involve an apprehension of the transcendent Forms or Ideas in which these things 'participate',[2] but what is more, the 'philosopher' is distinguished and known *per se* precisely in so far as he or she contemplates the Ideas.[3] The orientation proper to Platonic thought is thus 'the heights' of the transcendent Idea (LS, 127). For Plato, in relation to sensible things, it is through combinations of supra-sensible Ideas that we are 'to define good and bad mixtures' (LS, 130–1). Corresponding to this orientation of thought, then, is the 'popular image of the philosopher with his head in the clouds . . . as well as the scientific image according to which the philosopher's heaven is an intelligible one, which nonetheless does not distract us from the earth since it includes its law' (LS, 127).

15

The orientation proper to the pre-Socratic philosopher, by contrast, is 'the depths' (LS, 128). Here, Deleuze is no doubt referring to the pre-Socratic 'physicists' or 'natural philosophers', among whom we can count Thales, Anaximander, Anaximenes, Heraclitus, Empedocles and Anaxagoras. For these philosophers, the fundamental principles of all things must be sought in physical nature itself: Empedocles' four elements and the forces of 'Love and Strife', for example.[4] Fundamental physical principles such as these were posited to provide an 'immanent measure . . . capable of fixing the order and the progression of a mixture in the depths of Nature (*Physis*)' (LS, 131). Heraclitus' 'fire ever-living', for example, 'kindling in measures and being extinguished in measures', produces the sea, the earth and all things.[5] As Deleuze puts it, these thoroughgoing materialists 'placed thought inside the caverns and life, in the deep. They sought the secret of water and fire . . . [T]hey philosophized with a hammer, the hammer of the geologist or speleologist' (LS, 128).

For Deleuze, the image of this philosopher whose orientation is the depths of nature – a physical nature of which the philosopher is also a part – is crystallized in one of the stories of the death of Empedocles, related to us by Diogenes Laertius.

> Hippobotus says that [Empedocles] got up and travelled to Mount Aetna; and that when he arrived he leapt into the craters of fire and disappeared, because he wished to confirm the story told about himself, that he had become a god; and that he was later recognized when one of his sandals was hurled back out – for he habitually wore bronze sandals.[6]

The significance of this anecdote, for Deleuze, lies in the contrast it provides between the image of the philosopher in and of the depths, and the image of the philosopher in and of the heights. As he writes, '[i]n a deluge of water and fire, the volcano spits up only a single reminder of Empedocles – his lead [*sic*] sandal. To the wings of the Platonic soul the sandal of Empedocles is opposed, proving that he was of the earth, under the earth, and autochthonous' (LS, 128).

In opposition to both of these figures, however, the Stoics, Megarians and Cynics bring about 'a reorientation of all thought and of what it means to think: *there is no longer any depth or height*' (LS, 130). For these philosophers, it

> is always a matter of unseating the Ideas, of showing that the incorporeal is not high above (*en hauteur*), but is rather at the surface, that it is not the highest cause but the superficial effect par excellence, and that it is

16

not Essence but event. On the other front, it will be argued that depth is a digestive illusion which complements the ideal optical illusion (LS, 130).

The 'surface' is thus the new dimension in which Hellenic philosophy operates, and corresponding to this new dimension is a new image of the philosopher. 'The philosopher is no longer the being of the caves, nor Plato's soul or bird, but rather the animal which is on a level with the surface – a tick or louse' (LS, 133). Or again, the image of the philosopher of the surface is Hercules, of the Stoic Seneca's tragedy *Hercules Furens* (*The Madness of Hercules*), in so far as he is engaged in a 'dual battle against both depth and height' (LS, 132).

The contrasts between these different 'images of the philosopher', whilst striking, are not absolutely essential to the present study. What is crucial, though, is the way in which Deleuze links the so-called 'surface orientation' of the Stoics to his theory of sense and the event. As he writes: 'the discovery of incorporeal *events, meanings, or effects*, which are *irreducible* to "deep" bodies and to "lofty" Ideas – these are the important Stoic discoveries against the pre-Socratics and Plato' (LS, 132, emphasis added). Following Deleuze, then, the Stoics appear to be the first philosophers to consider events as ontologically irreducible to fixed 'things', whether material or ideal. If, therefore, as we contend, *The Logic of Sense* is concerned above all to establish the claim that events have ontological priority over substances, we cannot avoid a thorough exploration of Deleuze's philosophical relation to the Stoics. Indeed, it is the task of this chapter to carry out this examination. Before doing so, however, and in accordance with our remarks in the Introduction, we must clarify the precise nature of the 'problem of events' to which the Stoic 'discoveries' will afford some of the elements of a solution.

1.1 The Problem of the 'Pure Event' and the Stoic Ontological Distinction Between Bodies and Incorporeal Sayables (Reference and Sense)

In the 'First Series of Paradoxes of Pure Becoming', Deleuze sets up in abridged form the overriding problem with which the entire text of *The Logic of Sense* will be concerned. The centrality of this problem for Deleuze will be brought out by our analyses throughout the present work, but it should be clearly stated here at the outset. The problem, of course, is one of accounting for the ontological priority of events over substances, but this priority must be understood in a very particular way.

Normally, an event is something which is said to happen to a thing or state of affairs. An event, in this sense, is a change in this thing – a change in its properties, for example, or the exemplification of a particular property at a particular time.[7] Indeed, it is generally held that there can be no changes without reference to underlying things which change. And yet it is also common to say that things depend on the events which bring them about or determine them to have this or that state at a particular moment in time.[8]

Deleuze, for his part, affirms this latter position in *The Logic of Sense*, arguing for the ontological dependence of substances on events. In fact, Deleuze's position is the somewhat more radical one which affirms that events are ontologically *primitive*, in the sense that so-called substances are entirely derived from them. This is clear from his analysis of the event of Alice's growing, taken from the works of Lewis Carroll (see LS, 1). Deleuze argues that when we employ the verb 'to grow' in the proposition, 'Alice grows', we mean that she becomes larger than she was. However, it also follows that, at precisely the same time that Alice becomes larger than she was, she becomes smaller than she will become. Thus, in so far as the event picked out by the verb 'to grow' is happening, as it were, Alice's nature or state cannot be precisely determined. And nor should the reference to time here mislead us into thinking that we can assign temporal moments to the event in order to determine it with reference to some underlying thing; that is, for example, by referring to the succession of determined states through which Alice, as a thing, passes: 'Alice smaller at t_1', 'Alice bigger at t_2', and so on. For the assignation of these temporal moments is *first of all* dependent on the event of growing in which Alice becomes smaller and bigger at the same time.[9] In other words, without the event or change there is no passage from t_1 to t_2. Indeed, without the event, t_1 would never be constituted as such, in its relation to t_2. In short, therefore, the event 'in itself' – that is, the 'pure' event which does not ultimately refer back but is rather ontologically prior to fixed and measured things – 'eludes the present' and appears as the 'infinite identity' of the two temporal directions implicated in the change (LS, 2–3). In this very 'elusiveness', however, in so far as it is this in relation to which a new state can be said to be constituted as present, and a former state can be said to be constituted as the past of this new present, the event is also the prior condition for the determination of the thing at whatever moment of its temporal existence we should care to single out.

Now, however, still following Deleuze, the event also has a particular relation to language. Indeed, Deleuze maintains that events, not being 'present' in the manner of fixed things and states of affairs, do not exist outside of the propositions which express them (LS, 23). What is more, whilst events always elude the present, we nevertheless *say* that events begin here, end there, and so on. As Deleuze writes, even if verbs seem to pick out pure becomings, it is also 'language which fixes the limits (the moment, for example, at which the excess begins)' (LS, 2–3). In other words, even though events have ontological priority over things, when it comes to the problem of our knowledge of the more or less durable things which make up our world (and everything which depends on this knowledge, such as our capacity to act effectively in and on the world), what is important is how the events which determine the states of the things we know are themselves to be determined, ordered and related using language.[10] Indeed, verbs of becoming can be conjugated into a network of persons, moods, voices and tenses (LS, 184). It appears, however, that we could never determine once and for all the order of events underlying all things with reference to some stated 'image of eternity'. For, as Deleuze makes clear throughout *The Logic of Sense*, and as we shall see, whilst language expresses events, language is itself also an event which is endlessly 'coming about' (see, for example, LS, 166–7). The fundamental problem which *The Logic of Sense* sets out to resolve is thus the following: given the ontological priority of events and their relation to language, what are the 'evental' conditions of the event if everything, including the very language in which events are ordered and related, is ultimately to be a well determined event?[11] Deleuze's turn to the Stoics – and in particular to the Stoic ontological distinction between bodies and incorporeals – is designed to provide a first response to this question.

1.1.1 Stoic Ontology

As Deleuze explains, the highest term in Stoic ontology is not 'Being' but 'Something', *ti*, which subsumes a division between real and existing bodies and four subsisting and objective 'incorporeals': sayable (*lekton*), void, place and time (LS, 7).[12] As will be seen, Deleuze analyzes these Stoic incorporeals – and in particular *lekta* and time – in such a way that they respond to the problem of the event such as we have set it up above.

A body, for the Stoics, is something which is capable of acting or being acted upon, and every body has its source in two eternal 'principles' which are themselves considered to be bodies: passive matter or unqualified substance, and god or reason which acts in this matter ('designing fire' or *logos*). Together, these two principles form a coherent whole: the world or *kosmos*.[13] Bodies of very different types make up this world. The soul is a body, for example, for it brings about effects in the body with which it interacts: 'when the soul feels shame and fear the body turns red and pale respectively . . . Therefore, the soul is a body.'[14] Qualities such as wisdom or virtue are bodies, or complex physical states, for their possession brings about a certain effect: the complex physical state of wisdom, for example, renders the one so disposed as 'being wise'.[15] From one cosmological 'conflagration' to another, then, all of these various bodies and their corresponding 'manners of being' develop and are unified, the ones thoroughly mixed or 'blended' with the others even as they preserve their individuality, by a divine 'fiery breath' or 'tensile movement' which pervades the entire universe.[16] In this way, the divine breath or the activity of god is said by the Stoics to be the 'sustaining cause' of each individual body in a universal sympathy – 'fate' or the cosmic present – wherein these bodies, according to their own natures and 'tensions', are the causes for each other of everything which happens (LS, 4). As Alexander puts it:

> They [the Stoics] say that since the world is a unity which includes all existing things in itself and is governed by a living, rational, intelligent nature, the government of existing things which it possesses is an everlasting one proceeding in a sequence and ordering. The things which happen first become causes to those which happen after them. In this way all things are bound together, and neither does anything happen in the world such that something else does not unconditionally follow from it and become causally attached to it . . . They say that the very fate, nature and rationale in accordance with which the all is governed is god. It is present in all things which exist and happen, and in this way uses the proper nature of all existing things for the government of all.[17]

As opposed to bodies, the four incorporeals neither act nor are acted upon.[18] In contrast to Platonic Ideas, the Stoic incorporeals have no causal efficacy. They are not physical beings, but they nevertheless objectively 'subsist' in relation to our thought.[19] In order to better understand the nature of these incorporeals and the reasons why the Stoics proposed an ontological division between incorporeals and bodies, let us examine the types of problems to which they appear to respond.

Let us first of all turn to the incorporeals 'void' and 'place'. The void, following the commentary of Goldschmidt, responds to the problem of thinking the event of the *kosmos* itself, before each conflagration. The idea here is that to conceive of the development of the world implies being able 'to conceive this place, before the world is brought into existence . . . [and] devoid of all quality. And about which one can say that it "is simply capable of receiving body", or being "occupied by an existent"'.[20] Place is defined, by contrast, as this which an existent effectively does occupy, or which can be partially occupied and partially unoccupied with respect to a particular body, though without being itself a body.[21] As Jean Brun has put it, place is like 'a theatre, forever full, where bodies succeed and interpenetrate one another'.[22] In short, void and place are subsisting, non-physical incorporeals in the sense that they respond to the objective problem of *thinking* the spatial changes and relations of everything that exists.

Let us now examine the incorporeal which is time. As reported by Arius Didymus, for the Stoic Chrysippus, time is the 'interval of motion according to which the measure of speed and slowness is spoken of; or, time is the interval which accompanies the motion of the cosmos. And each and every thing is said to move and to exist in accordance with time.' In other words, Chrysippus appears here to identify time with the total movement of the physical world or the cosmic present. As has been seen, this present is equivalent to the activity of Zeus, which is the 'sustaining cause' of all individual bodies being the causes for each other of everything that happens. Chrysippus also argues, however, that 'no time is present in the strictest sense, but only loosely speaking. He says that only the present exists, whereas the past and future subsist but do not at all exist.'[23] So how is one to resolve this seeming contradiction? Deleuze, following Goldschmidt, insists that we must distinguish between the present that actually exists and the present as a pure being of reason. We must distinguish, in other words, between the total movement of the physical *kosmos* and a type of durationless limit or pure instant of becoming between an incorporeal past and future subsisting in accordance with our thought (LS, 164).[24] On the one hand, then, for the Stoics, only the motion of the cosmos is real and exists, it being coextensive with the rational and providential activity of Zeus.

Deleuze calls this physical dimension of time 'Chronos': a 'vast present which . . . is an encasement, a coiling up of relative presents' (LS, 162). Every relative present or movement – every relative speed or slowness – is in reality only a part of Chronos' all-embracing and total movement. On the other hand, however, we worldly creatures are only finite beings and the cosmic perspective escapes us.[25] From our point of view, then, as reported by Stobaeus, what happens is thinkable only in relation to an ideal temporal instant which is divisible into an unlimited, incorporeal and subsisting past and future, and where every instant of this past and future is also so divisible.[26] Now, it is clear that this ideal instant, to the extent that it comprises the 'difference' between the past and the future, is a pure 'moment of becoming'. But what is more, in so far as every instant of this past and future is also such a pure moment of becoming, it must be said that every instant becomes only in relation to every other. In distinction to Chronos, Deleuze calls this unlimited and infinitely divisible dimension of time 'Aion'. To what kind of problem did this distinction respond? Deleuze suggests that without the ontological distinction between the dimensions of physical Chronos and incorporeal Aion, the Stoics would have been unable to affirm that everything that appears to us to happen, from the point of view of our finite knowledge of the world, is reducible to the one, providential and causal order. Indeed, impressions of what happens, taken at random or at different moments in time, could come into conflict and thereby threaten our view of the 'good and wise measure' of the physical universe.[27] We must thus conceive of these temporal moments which we have isolated from the whole as incorporeal, that is, as merely ideal instants divisible into relative pasts and futures, every instant of which is also so divisible. Such an approach to the temporal order will then allow us to bring new connections between events to light and gradually modify our apprehension of what happens so as, perhaps, to approach an understanding of the unique cosmic present. Or again, as Deleuze puts it in a much more literary fashion:

> Chronos must . . . express the revenge taken by future and past on the present in terms of the present, because these are the only terms it comprehends and the only terms that affect it. This is its own way of wanting to die . . . Chronos wants to die, but has it not already given way to another reading of time? . . . In accordance with Aion, only the past and future inhere or subsist in time. Instead of a present which absorbs past and future, a future and past divide the present at every instant and subdivide it ad infinitum into past and future, in both directions at once.

22

Or rather, it is the instant without thickness and without extension, which subdivides each present into past and future, rather than vast and thick presents which comprehend both future and past in relation to one another ... Whereas Chronos expressed the action of bodies and the creation of corporeal qualities, Aion is the locus of incorporeal events, and of attributes which are distinct from qualities. Whereas Chronos was inseparable from the bodies which filled it out entirely as causes and matter, Aion is populated by effects which haunt it without ever filling it up ... Aion is the eternal truth of time: *pure empty form of time* ... (LS, 164–5)[28]

Finally, let us turn to the notion of incorporeal sayables or *lekta*. Deleuze in fact identifies a strong relation between the sayable and time. Indeed, in the citation above, when Deleuze writes that 'Aion is the locus of incorporeal events, and of attributes which are distinct from qualities', the incorporeal events or attributes referred to are *lekta*. How should this be understood? For the Stoics, when a physical body acts upon another such body, it produces an effect or event which is not itself a body but an incorporeal predicate or sayable, corresponding to the verb of the proposition (LS, 4–5). 'For instance the scalpel, a body, becomes the cause to the flesh, a body, of the incorporeal predicate "being cut". And again, the fire, a body, becomes the cause to the wood, a body, of the incorporeal predicate "being burnt".'[29] As Long and Sedley suggest, the problem to which this division between bodies and incorporeal predicates or events appears to respond is that of thinking changes in otherwise enduring bodies.

> The alternative was presumably to say that thanks to the scalpel one body, uncut flesh, ceases to exist and is replaced by a new body, cut flesh. But that would imply that *no* body persists through the process, so that there is no body in which we can say that the change has been brought about. Since the object changed, must, normally speaking, persist through the change ... it proved more palatable for them to say that the effect is not a new body but the incorporeal predicate 'is cut' (or 'being cut'), which comes to be true of the persisting flesh. The predicate should perhaps be thought of less as an extra entity that appears on the scene than as an aspect of the cut flesh which we abstract in order to present a proper causal analysis.[30]

We shall return to examine this notion of a 'proper causal analysis' of bodies and the essential role of the incorporeal event in this process. It should nevertheless begin to be clear how Deleuze will utilize the Stoic ontological distinction between the incorporeal sayables of Aion and the corporeal dimension of Chronos in his philosophy of events. For it will be by 'posing' the relations between infinitely divisible incorporeal events-effects or predicates-effects at various times that the Stoic 'sage' will be able to effectively determine for him or herself what produces these effects: the cosmic present which is said to be composed entirely of bodies and their causal relations. In other words, a determinate body or state of affairs, for the Stoic sage, will be determined as such within a network of events.

This role of the sayable in Stoic physics is, however, only one of its aspects, for it is also an important element of Stoic logic, which examines everything related to reason, language and argument, including speech, truth and knowledge. The precise role *lekta* play in this part of the Stoic system will be examined more fully below. What is crucial to examine at this point is the way in which the ontological division between bodies and incorporeals carries over into Stoic logic, and to examine some of the consequences of this division.

As Sextus Empiricus relates, when considering 'what is true and false' in their logical discussions, the Stoics argued that three things are linked together: 'the signification', 'the signifier' and 'the name-bearer'.

> The signifier is an utterance, for instance 'Dion'; the signification is the actual state of affairs revealed by an utterance, and which we apprehend as it subsists in accordance with our thought, whereas it is not understood by those whose language is different although they hear the utterance; the name-bearer is the external object, for instance, Dion himself. Of these, two are bodies – the utterance and the name-bearer; but one is incorporeal – the state of affairs signified and sayable, which is true or false.[31]

Two important points which bear mentioning follow from these distinctions. First of all, it appears that the utterance-sayable-name-bearer distinction corresponds in many respects with Frege's *Zeichen-Sinn-Bedeutung* distinction (as well as Carnap's designator-intension-extension distinction).[32] In other words, the Stoics, like Frege, distinguish between the reference or object of an utterance, the utterance itself, and that by which an utterance is 'related to an object', which is the 'sayable' or 'sense' of the utterance.[33] That is to say that the Stoic sayable, which is 'the actual state of affairs revealed by an utterance, and which we apprehend as it subsists in accordance with our thought', is comparable to Frege's sense (*Sinn*), which contains the 'mode of presentation' of the referent,[34] or provides the expressible '"conditions" that something must meet to be the referent of a given name'.[35]

The second and related point is that even though the Stoics understand the utterance to 'express' an incorporeal sense, they nevertheless place the utterance itself at the same ontological level as the referent or object. As recounted by Sextus above, the sense of an utterance is, for the Stoics, never identical to the utterance itself. What this means, following Deleuze, is that whilst an utterance in a given language has a sense which is understood by speakers of that language, one never actually utters the sense of what one is saying when one says it (LS, 28). Sense is something 'extra' – an altogether different type of entity – added on to or extracted from the actual utterance. It thus follows that in order to explicitly state the sense of what I say, the sense of my utterance must be taken as the object of a second utterance. But this second utterance also expresses a sense which is, in turn, not identical with that utterance. The sense of this second utterance must then be taken as the object of a third utterance, having its sense, and so on, ad infinitum. Deleuze calls this regress 'Frege's paradox' whereby, if I am to state the sense of what I actually say, for each one of the 'names' I employ, 'language must contain a name for the sense of this name' (LS, 29).[36]

So how are these two points with regard to the logical dimension of incorporeal sense to be related to the physical notion of the incorporeal event-effect? In short, it appears that in order to think the physical cosmic present through its infinitely divisible and temporal events-effects, the Stoics believed it necessary to relate these events-effects to incorporeal *sense-effects*, that is, to the kinds of effects produced by *bringing language to bear upon itself*. Indeed, this relation between causal events-effects and sense-events appears to have been the 'glue' of the Stoic system, in as much as the different parts of this system – physics, logic and ethics – are articulated around this relation. We shall examine these systematic relations below. Before turning to them, however, let us first try to state, in a more precise way, how Deleuze takes up the Stoic ontological division between bodies and incorporeals (or reference and sense) in order to resolve the problem which was formulated above as: given the ontological priority of events and their relation to language, what are the 'evental' conditions of the event if everything, including the very language in which events are ordered and related, is ultimately to be a well determined event?

It was noted that, for Deleuze, determined states of affairs appear to be ontologically dependent on events. These events are picked out by the verbs of propositions and, as such, events may be ordered and related using language. However, the capacity of language and language speakers to do this, at a given moment in time, also depends upon the ongoing event of language. Now, in relation to the Stoic division between bodies and incorporeals – the reference and sense of the proposition – Deleuze can say that the event ultimately corresponds to the 'sense' of the proposition, understood as a 'sense-event', that is, as an effect of the way in which language is effectively brought to bear on itself. In other words, the ontological division between bodies and events-effects – reference and sense – allows the event to 'subsist' (as opposed to 'exist', which applies only to bodies) in the proposition which expresses it, without being confused either with the state of affairs designated by the proposition or, importantly, with the actual proposition itself. The event will thus be an 'objective' ontological ideality for the determination of states of affairs in language, but only in so far as it is also the 'sense to come' of this language. As Deleuze formulates it:

> *Sense is both the expressible or the expressed of the proposition, and the attribute of the state of affairs.* It turns one side toward things and one side toward propositions. But it does not merge with the proposition which expresses it any more than with the state of affairs or the quality which the proposition denotes . . . It is in this sense that it is an 'event': *on the condition that the event is not confused with its spatio-temporal realization in a state of affairs.* We will not ask therefore what is the sense of the event: the event is sense itself. (LS, 22)

1.2 *The Fourth Dimension of the Proposition: the Sense-Event and the Stoic 'Comprehensive Representation'*

We have seen above that, thanks to the Stoic ontological division between bodies and incorporeals – the reference and the sense of the proposition – the pure event can be said to subsist in the proposition which expresses it as the 'sense' or 'sense-event' of that proposition. The question demands to be asked, however: is this sense ultimately determinable or grounded in relation to something else? As Deleuze analyses it following Russell, the proposition has three dimensions or relations: denotation (the proposition's relation to individuated states of affairs), manifestation (its relation to the psychological person's beliefs and desires) and signification (its relation to concep-

26

tual or logical implication).[37] So is sense grounded in one of these dimensions?

This problem in fact involves two sub-problems. First of all, following Deleuze's analysis, it appears that in relation to the question of sense, the three dimensions of denotation, manifestation and signification presuppose one another in a circular manner, and so sense or the event cannot, strictly speaking, be isolated in any one of them. Secondly, it appears that the dimension of signification nevertheless does resemble sense in one important respect, namely, in as much as it is defined as the *condition of possibility* for a proposition being true in relation to an objective state of affairs. Indeed, a proposition devoid of signification can be neither true nor false: it is, rather, absurd. At the same time, however, when we ask about the truth or falsity of the proposition, it is generally agreed that it is, quite straightforwardly, a question of denotation, that is, of the proposition's 'correspondence' (or lack thereof) with a factual state of affairs.[38] There is thus always a hiatus between sense or signification understood as the 'condition of truth', and the truth of the conditioned proposition in relation to the world. Putting these two sub-problems together, Deleuze thus asks: can we determine a 'fourth dimension' of the proposition which would be coextensive with the event itself and which would allow the tri-dimensional model of the proposition to function entirely from within, generating the sense of the proposition, its objective correlates (individuals, persons and general concepts) and thus its truth in relation to 'evental' states of affairs? Let us unpack this further.

How do the three dimensions of the proposition all presuppose one another? First of all, *denotation* is the relation of the proposition to an external state of affairs. It functions through the 'association' of the words used in the proposition with particular 'images' which are supposed to 'represent' the state of affairs. With respect to denotation, a proposition will be said to be 'true' if it corresponds to the state of affairs, if it is effectively 'filled' by the state of affairs, or if the correct image has been selected. 'False' signifies that the denotation does not correspond to the state of affairs (LS, 12–13).

Manifestation concerns the relation of the proposition to the person who speaks. In other words, manifestation appears as a statement of beliefs or desires which corresponds to the proposition. The association of words and images in denotation is thus made possible by manifestation (LS, 13).

Signification is 'the relation of the word to *universal or general* concepts, and of syntactic connections to the implications of the concept' (LS, 14). In terms of this dimension, in other words, the elements of a proposition are considered to 'signify' conceptual implications capable of referring to other propositions serving as the 'premises' of the first. In relation to signification, a proposition is only ever a part of a larger 'demonstration' (in the most general sense of the word) in which it serves as a premise or a conclusion. For example, 'x is a bachelor' if and only if 'x is unmarried' and 'x is a man'; 'x is a man' if and only if . . .; and so on. Thus, while denotations may be true or false in relation to states of affairs, signification is rather the '*condition of truth*': the aggregate of conditions under which the denoting proposition, considered from the point of view of its signifying elements, 'would be' true (LS, 14).

So in what way do these three dimensions all presuppose one another? As noted above, the process of associating words and 'representative' images in the denoting proposition is made possible by the dimension of personal manifestation. Furthermore, the dimension of manifestation also has a role to play in the development of conceptual signification, for when the 'I' speaks, it is presumed to be capable of stating the meaning of what it says: the 'I' implicitly envelops the significations which it may later develop.[39] From another point of view, however, this primacy of manifestation is only apparent, for the conceptual signification of the words used in the denoting proposition may also be developed independently of any particular speaking person. As Deleuze writes

> the possibility of causing particular images associated with the word to vary, of substituting one image for another in the form 'it is not this, it's that', can be explained only by the constancy of the signified concept. Similarly, desires would not form an order of demands and even of duties, distinct from a simple urgency of needs, and beliefs would not form an order of inferences distinct from simple opinions, if the words in which they were manifested did not refer first to concepts and conceptual implications rendering these desires and beliefs significant. (LS, 16, translation modified)

However, from yet another point of view, denotation has primacy over signification (and thus, by extension, manifestation). Indeed, in order to be able to affirm the 'conclusion' of a demonstration, it is first of all necessary that the premises of this demonstration be true or 'fulfilled' denotations. Furthermore, in order to be able to affirm as true a conclusion, Z, from the true premises, A and B, another proposition – call it C – must be given within the dimension of conceptual implication which states that 'Z is true if A and B are true'. This proposition, however, refers to another proposition, D, which states that 'Z is true if A, B and C are true', and so on, *ad infinitum*.[40] As Deleuze interprets it, this 'amounts to saying that . . . implication never succeeds in grounding denotation except by giving itself a ready-made denotation, once in the premises and again in the conclusion' (LS, 16).[41]

Having asked, therefore, in what dimension the sense of the proposition could reside, we have been led in a circle from denotation to manifestation, then to signification and finally back to denotation. In other words, whilst it has been argued that the event is inseparable from the sense to come of the proposition expressing it, this sense is displaced throughout the dimensions normally associated with the proposition and hence cannot finally be grounded in any of them. The question that ensues for Deleuze is thus: can a fourth dimension of the proposition be determined which would be coextensive with sense or the event (LS, 17)?

Following Deleuze's initial attempt to answer this question, it appears that the dimension of signification does in fact share an important characteristic with what we are looking for in this 'fourth dimension', namely, in so far as it is the 'condition of truth' of the proposition. As has been noted, the dimension of conceptual implication ought to provide the totality of conditions under which a denoting proposition 'would be' true. Strictly speaking, however, signification is only the *formal condition of possibility* for a proposition to be true, for, as has been seen, it is generally accepted that truth and falsity concern the relation between the proposition and concrete states of affairs. As Deleuze then writes,

> For the condition of truth to avoid this defect, it ought to have an element of its own, distinct from the form of the conditioned. It ought to have *something unconditioned* capable of assuring a *real genesis* of denotation and of the other dimensions of the proposition. Thus the condition of truth would be defined no longer as the form of conceptual possibility, but rather as an ideational material or 'stratum', that is to say, no longer as signification, but rather as sense. (LS, 19, emphasis added)

To sum up: the event, having ontological priority with respect to determined things and states of affairs, subsists in the proposition which expresses it as the sense to come or sense-event of that proposition (the result of the way in which language is brought to bear on itself). This sense cannot be said to entirely reside in any of the three dimensions normally associated with the proposition, for, with respect to sense, all of these dimensions presuppose one another in various ways. Nevertheless, the dimension of signification does share an important feature with sense in so far as it is a condition of possibility for a proposition to be true in relation to a state of affairs. If, however, the event is ontologically prior to things, we must attribute to it a reality which is altogether different from the type of formal possibility attached to conceptual signification. So the question for Deleuze becomes: can we determine a fourth dimension of the proposition which would be coextensive with the ontological reality of the event itself, that is, in so far as it brings about the 'real genesis' of sense and the event with respect to the objective correlates associated with the tri-dimensional model of the proposition (individuals, persons and general concepts)? And again, it is with reference to the Stoics that Deleuze attempts a first answer to this question. As he writes towards the end of his analysis of the problems involved in the tri-dimensional model of the proposition, in relation to sense or the event, the 'Stoics said it all: neither word nor body, neither sensible representation nor *rational representation*' (LS, 19). It is to unpack that to which Deleuze here alludes that we must now turn. We shall see in what follows how, for Deleuze, the Stoics affirm a network of relations between the different parts of their system – physics, logic and ethics – in order to account for the functioning of this 'fourth dimension' of the proposition which is sense or the event.[42] As will be seen, these relations are articulated around the notoriously difficult Stoic epistemological notion of the 'comprehensive representation' (*phantasia kataléptiké*) which, following Deleuze's analyses, envelops an event which it cannot represent, but which also *cannot not* be represented if it is to be 'comprehensive'. We shall show that this event which the comprehensive representation envelops stands for the effective unfolding of the circle of the proposition and the exposure of its 'fourth dimension' which is nothing other than the 'pure event' itself, namely, the ongoing, problematic articulation of the relation between the sense of the proposition and its truth with respect to a thoroughly processual world.

1.2.1 STOIC PHYSICS

'Physics', for the Stoics, 'is practiced whenever we investigate the world and its contents'.[43] As noted above while examining the notion of 'body', Stoic physics, which can be compared to what we would today call a 'metaphysics of nature',[44] affirms the existence of a single and unified world, a living *kosmos* which is composed entirely of bodies which act, suffer and are causes 'to' each other of everything that happens.[45] The two principles (god and matter), the four elements, plants and animals, souls and qualities such as hardness and wisdom are all causes to each other of everything that comes to pass. In short, Stoic physics explains how the universe functions according to a divine, rational plan. The physicist 'gives an account of the universe by means of metaphysical concepts which, returning to the origin of things, that is, in the final analysis, to the Agent, have the power to explain everything'.[46] What interests Deleuze, however, is not so much the rational theology of the Stoics, as the division within their physics between bodies and incorporeal events.

As noted, the Stoics only attribute existence to bodies, but then distinguish these latter from their 'manners of being' which are rather abstractions or 'signs', that is, both the incorporeal effects of the actions and passions of bodies and the material of Stoic logic.[47] It is thanks to these incorporeal effects, which themselves have no causal efficacy but only a certain 'subsistence' in relation to our thought, that the Stoic physicist can seek the immanent reason of things (god) in things themselves.[48] For the Stoics, whilst events-effects have their own, logical laws of combination, because they are inseparable from the dimension of physics, they also 'express in each case the relative unity or mixture of bodies on which they depend for their real causes' (LS, 6).

It is important to note, however, that within their physics the Stoics distinguish not only between cause and effect, but also between various types of cause: sustaining, complete, proximate, auxiliary, preliminary, joint, and so on.[49] As Michael Frede has shown, however, from among all these causes, the Stoics will single out the cause *stricto sensu*, that is, the perfect (*autoteles*) or sustaining (*sunektikon*) cause.[50] And this complete or sustaining cause must always be *a* body. Indeed, since they did not possess the notion of inertia – with regard to which a change in the movement of a body is held to be the result of a force applied to it by another, external body – the Stoics placed all force and all activity entirely within individual bodies.[51] What this implies is that, for each event, the Stoics want to identify 'the thing responsible' (*aition*): the body which, through its own force and activity, produces the event.[52] This event, which is produced by the cause, as has been said, is not another body, but a predicate, a sayable, which comes to be true of the body whose effect it is. To return to an example given above, it will be because of the nature of wood that the wood 'is burnt'. The wood will be the complete cause of the predicate 'being burnt' which is true of the wood.

We are faced here with an apparent contradiction, however, for the Stoics also believed that the canonical representation of the causal relation is not between a body and a predicate, but between a body, a second body, and a predicate which is true of the latter. It must be said, therefore, following Sextus, that the fire, a body, becomes to the wood, another body, the cause of the incorporeal predicate 'being burnt'. But how must we understand this three-place relation, given that the Stoics must thereby affirm the existence of external causes, an affirmation which would contradict their thesis that force and activity are entirely internal to individual bodies?

In fact, the Stoics did affirm the existence of prior causes. For them, as was noted above, nothing is separated from what has previously occurred, for otherwise 'the world would be wrenched apart and divided, and no longer remain a unity'.[53] Following Frede, then, the causal relation must be analyzed into at least two relations, each of them between a complete cause and its effect. In this way it will be said that every prior cause will be a prior cause of something, p, by being a complete cause for a complete cause, s, of a passive affection, q, in such a manner that the complete cause s in state q is the complete cause of p.[54] To take an example attributed to Chrysippus, a cylinder, once pushed, will roll through its own force and nature. However, since it is the person pushing the cylinder who gives it 'its beginning of motion', it must be said that the cylinder is the complete and active cause of the predicate 'rolling' only in so far as it has a particular passive affection with respect to the pushing person. This person is thus the complete cause for the cylinder's being the complete cause, through its own force and nature, of the predicate 'rolling'.[55]

It is precisely in this way that Deleuze appears to analyze Stoic physics (although this is not immediately evident, given the literary style of the text in question). As he writes, a body's passion – what it undergoes – always refers to the action of a more powerful body, right up to the action of the greatest of bodies, Zeus or the cosmic present, which is in the final analysis the active and sustaining cause of everything that happens (LS, 163). Physically speaking, the Stoic understanding of the capacity of bodies in their various causal relations to bring about this or that effect must ultimately refer to a body which is characterized as *causa sui*. It is not the case, however, that Zeus is the *direct* cause of every event. It is rather that Zeus is the perfect cause of the fact that individual bodies in general are, according to their own natures, the complete causes to each other of everything that comes to pass. As Deleuze puts it, the cosmic present in this way can be said to be the 'limit' or 'measure' of the actions and passions of bodies in relation to one another (LS, 163).

But now, as Deleuze goes on to ask, 'from where exactly does it [i.e., Zeus or the cosmic present] draw *its* measure?' (LS, 163, emphasis added). We should be careful to recognize here, however, that this question is no longer related to physical concerns, but to logical ones. Why? For the same reasons offered above in relation to the necessity of distinguishing between the dimensions of Chronos and Aion: we must distinguish between the unique causal order to which our physical analyses must ultimately refer and the thought of that order and of the bodies which compose it. The thought of this causal order, as noted above, involves incorporeal events or sayables which have their own logical laws of combination. And so it is to an examination of Stoic logic that we must now turn.

1.2.2 STOIC LOGIC

The foundation of Stoic logic, the knowledge of the functions of *logos* or rational discourse,[56] is a theory of sayables or *lekta*. As has been seen, sayables are events, that is, incorporeal predicates that one body causes for another body, such as 'being burnt' or 'being cut'. The sayable is thus not itself a body; it is rather something which is said *about* a body.[57] Sayables are 'states of affairs which are said'[58] and which subsist in accordance with a rational representation, a rational representation being one whose content can be exhibited in language.[59] As has also been noted, the sayable, in so far as it is said 'about' a body, is distinguished not only from the 'name-bearer' or referent, but also from the utterance, which is itself a body.[60] It is thus clear that the sayable is something like the sense of what is said about bodies, a sense which can itself be spoken about or determined in various ways.

To be more precise, the Stoics divide sayables into two classes. On the one hand, there are 'incomplete' or unfinished sayables, which are predicates or verbs without a subject (or an object in the case of transitive verbs) which may be asserted. On the other hand, there are complete or finished sayables in which the predicate is attached to a subject – the nominative case which the referent is said to 'bear' – in order to generate both simple and complex propositions which may be true or false in relation to factual states of affairs.[61] Stoic logic is thus essentially an attempt to acquire knowledge about when a predicate can, in truth, be attached to its subject, or about how sayables or events can be logically combined in order to generate true propositions. In its systematic relation to physics, then, Stoic logic examines how one is to think the body which 'bears' the nominative case, as well the other bodies to which this first body is causally related, by combining the events attributable to them in logically appropriate ways. Indeed, as will be seen, Stoic logic specifies the conditions under which one event can be said to be logically compatible or incompatible with another, as well as elaborates a theory of knowledge which implies a certain 'use of representations' which has consequences not only for their physics, but also for their ethics.

So, for the Stoics, a simple, complete sayable – such as 'It is day' or 'Dion is walking' – denotes a physical state of affairs and may be true or false in relation to that state of affairs. But such simple propositions can also have different kinds of relation with one other, thereby forming complex propositions. A conditional proposition, for example, has the form: 'If it is day, it is light'; a conjunctive proposition is of the form: 'Both it is day, and it is light'; and a disjunctive proposition is of the form: 'Either it is day, or it is night'.[62] A conjunction is truth-functional in so far as a conjunctive proposition will be true if all of its conjoined elements are true in relation to existing states of affairs.[63] A disjunction is also truth-functional in so far as a disjunctive proposition, which is always interpreted by the Stoics as an exclusive disjunction, will be true if one and only one of its disjuncts is true in relation to existing states of affairs.[64] The conditional connective, however, is non-truth-functional. A true conditional is rather 'one the contradictory of whose consequent conflicts with its antecedent':

> For example, 'If it is day, it is light'. This is true, since 'Not: it is light', the contradictory of the consequent, conflicts with 'It is day'. A false conditional is one the contradictory of whose consequent does not conflict with its antecedent. For example, 'If it is day, Dion is walking'. For 'Not: Dion is walking' does not conflict with 'It is day'.[65]

Now, the problem here is one of understanding what is meant by 'conflict': is it empirical (causal), analytical, or formal logical conflict? Deleuze argues that 'commentators are certainly right to recall that the question here is not about a relation of physical consequence or of causality in the modern sense of the word. But they are perhaps wrong to see in them a simple logical consequence in the form of identity' (LS, 69).[66] He then goes on to interpret the Stoic conditional in terms of a kind of 'theory of types'. This move, Deleuze argues, is justified by the fact that, in arguments, the Stoics number the members of their hypothetical propositions.[67] 'If this woman has milk, this woman has conceived', for example, is rendered as: 'If the first, the second'. Deleuze thus considers the event-predicate, 'having conceived', as signifying a property of a higher type than that over which it presides, 'having milk' (LS, 69). Following Deleuze's reading of the theory of types, each 'name' receives a 'determination of signification' thanks to two 'laws'. According to a first, 'regressive law', the sense of each name must be denoted by another name of a higher degree. Indeed, Deleuze explicitly aligns this 'regressive law' with the infinite regress of sense examined above, which Deleuze called 'Frege's Paradox' (whereby, for each name employed, language must contain a name for the sense of this name). But now, following Deleuze, from the point of view of the propositional dimension of signification rather than sense, these names of different degrees refer to classes or properties of different 'types'. As he writes:

> Any normal name has a sense which must be denoted by another name and which must determine the disjunctions filled by other names. In so far as these names, which are endowed with sense, are subject to these laws, they receive *determinations of signification*. The determination of signification and the law are not the same thing; the former derives from the latter and relates names, that is, words and propositions, to concepts, properties, or classes. Thus, when the regressive law states that the sense of a name must be denoted by another name, these names of different degrees refer, from the point of view of signification, to classes or properties of different 'types'. Every property must belong to a type higher than the properties or individuals over which it presides, and every class must belong to a type higher than the objects which it contains. It follows that a class cannot be a member of itself, nor may it contain members of different types. (LS, 68)[68]

Correlatively, according to a second, 'disjunctive law', each 'term in relation to which a classification is made cannot belong to any of the groups of the same type which are classified in relation to it' (LS, 68–9).[69] It thus follows that if these two laws adequately capture what is at stake in the different 'levels' of the Stoic conditional, the 'conflict' characterizing a true conditional must be understood, not in the relation of a term to its opposite on a 'single level' (as is the case with formal logical conflict), but rather 'in the relation of the opposite of a term with the *other* term', that is, 'between the antecedent itself and the negation of the consequent' (LS, 69, 170, translation modified). As Deleuze speculates, the proposition, 'If it is day, it is light', implies that it is not possible that it be day and *not* light, perhaps because 'being day' would have to be an element of a set classified in relation to 'being light' (LS, 69).

Deleuze's interest in the logic of the Stoics is not limited to the way in which their propositional connectives express relations between events. He is also interested in their theory of modality or, more precisely, in the Stoic thesis which affirms physical 'fate' but denies 'necessity' (LS, 33–4, 169). Indeed, despite the Stoics' deterministic physical theory, Chrysippus claimed that there are things which are possible which will nevertheless not happen.[70] Reconstructing Deleuze's reading of this point, it appears that Chrysippus was able to make this claim precisely in so far as the Stoics affirm a difference between, on the one hand, conjunctive and disjunctive propositions which are either true or false depending on the truth or falsity of their component propositions in relation to existing states of affairs, and, on the other hand, conditional propositions, whose truth or falsity is rather a matter of 'compatibility' or 'incompatibility' (or conflict) between different 'levels' of sayables-events, but without any reference to a totalizing instance (a 'set of all sets'). As Deleuze notes, this difference can be seen in the way in which Chrysippus insists on the transformation of the propositions of the Chaldean astrologers, which purport to assert the necessity of certain future events based on past and hence necessary truths about certain other events, from the form of conditionals into (negated) conjunctions (LS, 170). The Chaldean proposition, 'If someone was born at the rising of the Dogstar, he will not die at sea', is thus transformed by Chrysippus into 'Not both: someone was born at the rising of the Dogstar, and he will die at sea.'[71] This transformation makes it clear that, for Chrysippus, the Chaldean conditional cannot express the necessity of a future event based on a necessary truth about a past event; for whilst a true simple proposition about a past event is a necessary truth because past facts are immutable,[72] the truth of a conditional depends on the 'determinations of signification' brought about by an open-ended regress of sense. In other words, for Chrysippus, it is not, strictly speaking, contradictory to deny in this case that someone will not die at sea if he was born at the rising of the Dogstar: his dying at sea is 'possible' in this minimal sense, even if he is causally fated to die on land as much as he was fated to be born at the rising of the Dogstar. The transformation of 'divinatory' conditionals into conjunctions is, on the other hand, entirely appropriate if one is concerned with understanding and predicting the workings of immutable fate, for, as has been seen, the truth or falsity of the conjunctive proposition, for the Stoics, depends on whether its component propositions are true or false in relation to factual states of affairs or the cosmic present.

Following the arguments examined in the preceding two paragraphs, it should be emphasized here that Deleuze distinguishes quite clearly between the notions of 'incompatibility' ('conflict') and 'contradiction'. The relation of incompatibility between sayables-events, as has just been seen, cannot be derived from the thoroughly deterministic causal order, for whilst events maintain a relation of causality with physical bodies, they are nevertheless incorporeal predicates which have their own 'logical' laws of combination. But what is more, the relation of incompatibility is distinct from the relation of contradiction which could be derived from a closed system of inter-defined concepts. Indeed, the idea that there is an in-principle infinite regress of 'levels' in the 'determinations of signification' would seem to preclude the very possibility of such a closed system. This is not to say, however, that Deleuze dispenses with the notion of contradiction. It is to say, rather, that the relation of contradiction is derived from and contingent upon the relations of compatibility and incompatibility established by the regressive law and the determinations of signification it brings about.[73] As Deleuze puts it:

> In virtue of what is an event compatible or incompatible with another? We cannot appeal to causality, since it is a question of a relation of effects among themselves ... Would two events be incompatible because they were contradictory? ... Even with respect to hypothetical propositions (if it is day, it is light), the Stoics noted that contradiction cannot be defined on a single level. Rather, contradiction must be defined between the antecedent itself and the negation of the consequent (if it is day, it is not light). This difference of levels in the contradiction, we have seen, assures that contradiction results always from a process of a different nature. Events are not like concepts; it is their supposed contradiction (manifested in the concept) which results from their incompatibility, and not the converse ... [T]here is first of all a relation of primary, 'evental' incompatibility, which physical causality inscribes only secondarily in the depth of the body, and which logical

contradiction then only translates in the content of the concept. (LS, 170–1, translation modified)

It would appear, then, that we are now in a position to understand Deleuze's enigmatic assertion that 'astrology' – that is, no doubt, Chaldean astrology tempered by Stoic logic – 'was perhaps the first important attempt to establish a theory of alogical incompatibilities and noncausal correspondences' (LS, 171). For divinatory interpretation is a question of producing, multiplying and orienting relations of compatibility and incompatibility between sayables-events in discourse, beyond any physically necessary connection or finally determinable conceptual order (hence the 'noncausal' and 'alogical' nature of the relation), in order to follow, nevertheless, the movement of the cosmic present as it unfolds (LS, 143).

But now, it appears that there is no essential difference between this divinatory interpretation of the world and the Stoic interpretation of physical 'signs' in general. According to Sextus, the form of the sign is precisely that of the conditional: 'If this, then that'.[74] It is necessary, however, to transform this conditional (whether empirical or logical) into a conjunctive proposition in order to approach an understanding of the cosmic present, for signs are concerned with sayables-events which have been brought about by causal relations between present things.[75] As Deleuze notes, this is precisely why 'the Stoics say that signs are always present, that they are signs of present things'. For example, one 'cannot *say* of someone mortally wounded that he has been wounded and that he will die, but that he *is* having been wounded (*il est ayant blessé*), and that he *is* due to die (*il est devant mourir*)' (LS, 63).[76] In other words, it is always a question of translating what appears to us to be causal or temporal succession into simultaneity, or again to interpret logical consequence as conceptual coexistence, in order to follow the movement of the cosmic present and approach an understanding of it.[77] But in fact, this is precisely the relation, examined above, between the dimensions of Aion and Chronos. Indeed, we can recall that Chronos is the cosmic present, the total 'conjunctive' causal order: that in virtue of which signs are signs of present things. And Aion is the infinitely divisible abstract line composed of relations between incorporeal events which are both causal effects and sense-effects.

The importance of the foregoing for Deleuze is that it now becomes possible to define a relation between two propositional relations: the relation between the proposition and existing states of affairs (denotation), and the relation of implication between various sayables-events (signification). On the one hand, signification, expressed here by the Stoic conditional, presents various possibilities for relations between sayables-events. On the other hand, denotation, expressed here by the conjunctive proposition, indicates material instances which may 'realize' these possibilities (LS, 118). What is the relation between these two propositional relations? If, for the Stoics, it is a practical matter of the utmost importance to *know* with what other events a given event is 'co-fated' (and indeed, Stoic philosophy was always conceived of as a practical *ars vitae*), perhaps the more precise question to ask is: what are the criteria for this knowledge?[78] We must here turn to an examination of Stoic epistemology.

1.2.3 STOIC EPISTEMOLOGY

Strictly speaking, Stoic epistemology is a part of their logic, for logic is the study of everything related to rational discourse, including thought, judgement and the 'yardsticks and criteria' which are the 'means to the discovery of the truth'.[79] Of particular interest to us here is the Stoic notion of the 'comprehensive representation'.[80] The comprehensive representation, for the Stoics, was the 'criterion of truth' and the foundation of knowledge in the sense that, if one assents only to comprehensive representations (which, by their nature, are infallibly true), one's knowledge will be infallible.[81]

The Stoics in fact distinguished between several different types of representation. First of all, a 'sensory representation' is an affection or modification which, by means of the sense organs, is produced in the corporeal soul, and which 'reveals itself and its cause', that is, the 'impressor'.[82] Subsequently, 'thought, which has the power of utterance, expresses in language what it experiences by the agency of the impression'.[83] It is in this sense that Deleuze calls sensory representations 'denotations' (LS, 145). Strictly speaking, however, sensory representations are not identical with the propositions which express them, for a proposition can be the same for diverse sensory representations: impressions which are received from far away, from close up, and so on.[84]

A 'rational representation', by contrast, while still corporeal, is formed in the corporeal soul by means of thought and has a content which can be exhibited in language in the form 'p is q', that is to say, corresponding to the form of a complete sayable.[85] Deleuze calls these rational representations 'significations' (LS, 145). The reason given by the Stoics for the existence of this second type of corporeal representation is that, following a providentialist conception of human nature, human beings are so designed as to think by 'inference and combination', that is, in precisely the manner examined above in relation to sayables or signs.[86]

Now, in so far as it is formed by the 'commanding-faculty' of the soul or mind, the rational representation is necessarily sensitive to the particular characteristics of the soul in question: to the network of its other representations or beliefs, for example, whether these are sensory or rational.[87] Rational representations, in other words, depend on experience, that is, the accumulation of sensory representations.[88] But they also depend on the kind of thought for which Stoic logic studies the rules, for the content of the representation is propositional and is formed by inference and combination. We have yet to understand, however, how we can recognize that our representations are true in relation to existing states of affairs.

Thus we come to the problem of the 'cognitive' or 'comprehensive representation' which, for the Stoics, is infallibly true. A comprehensive representation, it is reported, has three conditions: it 'arises from what is and is stamped and impressed exactly in accordance with what is, of such a kind as could not arise from what is not'.[89] How is it that we can recognize that a given representation is comprehensive in this sense? The well-known difficulty is that of understanding precisely what is meant by 'what is' (*huparchon*) in the above definition. Following Michael Frede, it appears that it is necessary to interpret 'what is', not as the real object, but as the incorporeal *fact* or true proposition that this object 'is such and such'. If the representation '*p* is *q*' is comprehensive, this must be because '*p* is *q*' obtains.[90] However, what is the point in saying that the comprehensive representation is to arise from and be imprinted exactly in accordance with 'what is' if 'what is' – the fact – is precisely what we seek to know by means of the comprehensive representation?[91] The appropriate response to this problem, as Frede has shown, is to point to the Stoic thesis of the 'identity of indiscernibles', which implies that the comprehensive representation can in principle distinguish one object from any other, and thus the facts or events truly attributable to it.[92] In this case, then, the 'mark' of a comprehensive representation will be nothing over and above its representing a particular fact in a certain way, and thus in relation to a network of other rational and sensory representations.[93] In short, for the Stoics, starting from a given set of sensory and rational representations, the comprehensive representation must bring together in thought, in a 'craftsmanlike way',[94] all the particular features characterizing a given state of affairs, that is, all the predicate-events which the various bodies implicated in this state of affairs bring about for each other in their own unique ways. As Frede puts it, emphasizing a certain holism:

> Since it is the mind which forms even sensory representations, and since the mind in forming representations is influenced by its state, including its beliefs, its false beliefs may make it difficult for it to form comprehensive representations. In any case, its representations will reflect its false beliefs. So it is obvious how we can improve and perfect our sensitivity to comprehensive representations. We have to attend to our representations, we have to eliminate our false beliefs, and we have to learn what the things we are concerned with are like and how they differ from other things, and look at our representations carefully in the light of this. In the end we will have a reliable sense for whether a representation is comprehensive and give assent to precisely those representations which are comprehensive. This is what Boethus had in mind, when he said that right reason is the criterion. If we have a perfected reason we will have a reliable sense for which representations are comprehensive.[95]

Now, it appears that this holism with regard to belief and representation has a precise parallel with one of the major theses of Stoic physics. Indeed, we can recall from our above discussion of causality that the events attributable to a particular body always refer to the action of more powerful bodies right up to the action of the greatest of bodies (Zeus), and that a proper causal analysis of a given event must involve reference to these further bodies. It follows from this point, then, that the comprehensive representation, in order to accurately represent a given physical state of affairs, must in the final analysis be able to represent (or at least cohere with the representation of) the total 'conjunctive' cosmic order. Here, however, following Deleuze, it appears that the comprehensive representation must 'envelop an expression' – sense or the event – which it cannot, strictly speaking, represent (LS, 145). In other words, and in line with our above analyses, the immense conjunctive proposition (arrived at by 'inference and combination') which purports to represent the cosmic present insofar as it purports to consist of the totality of all true propositions, could only be such a totality in relation to an 'expression' of a higher degree which is not itself one of the totality. As Deleuze writes

> We have encountered this difference of nature between the expression and the representation at every turn, each time we noted the specificity of sense or of the event, its irreducibility to the denotatum and to the signified ... This difference culminates in the opposition between the object = x as the identitarian instance of the representation in common sense [the cosmic present], and the thing = x as the nonidentifiable element of expression in the paradox [the 'set of all sets' or the 'barber of the regiment']. (LS, 145)[96]

This is not to say, however, that this expression or event of a 'higher degree' does not have a role to play in representation. Indeed, a representation could be 'comprehensive' only in so far as it envelops this expression which it cannot, strictly speaking, represent. In other words, the expression of sense or the event appears here as an ideal instance in relation to which 'conjunctive truth' and 'rational signification' *could* be articulated in relation to one another. This is what Deleuze means when he says that sense or the event – the fourth dimension of the proposition – is neither a 'sensible representation' or denotation, nor a 'rational representation' or signification (LS, 19). Rather, it is an *ongoing* sense-event: an ongoing sense-event that governs the articulation of the relation between the dimensions of denotation and signification, that is to say, between conjunctive truth and its condition. But the question now is what is it that grounds the 'ongoing' nature of this sense-event for the Stoics? We must here turn to Deleuze's analysis of Stoic ethics.

1.2.4 STOIC ETHICS

In *The Logic of Sense*, Deleuze does not appear to be overly interested in Stoic ethics as such, that is, in the particular objects of its study: the 'virtues', 'proper function', what is 'good, bad and indifferent', and so on. Rather, he is interested in the Stoic 'moral imperative' and its consequences for his theory of events. Diogenes Laertius, following Zeno and then Chrysippus, formulates this imperative in the following manner: 'living in agreement with nature', or 'living in accordance with experience of what happens by nature ... for our own natures are parts of the nature of the whole'.[97]

Given Stoic determinism, it would initially seem that one has no choice but to live in passive accordance with nature. On the one hand, however, as was seen above, Stoic physics affirms that each body is essentially responsible for what happens to it, that is, for the events which come to be truly predicated of it, even if these events always also refer to the actions of more powerful bodies. Moral responsibility is thus fully compatible with physical 'fate', for each body is in some way (that is, depending on its passive affection in relation to other bodies) the 'complete cause' of its actions. On the other hand, because human beings as rational creatures have an in-built capacity to think by 'inference and combination' with regard to relations between 'co-fated' events, our understanding of 'right actions' (the actions-events we ought to perform) will be closely bound up with our knowledge of the physical world.[98] Thus, actions attributable to moral agents embody the two aspects of incorporeal events which we examined above: they are causal-effects entirely brought about by bodies, but also, being incorporeal sayables, they are the 'alogical' and 'noncausal' sense-effects of rational discourse. As Deleuze puts it, emphasizing the idea of freedom in its connection with moral responsibility:

> The wise person is free in two ways which conform to the two poles of ethics: free in the first instance because one's soul can attain to the interiority of perfect physical causes [she is the perfect cause of the events which depend on her]; and again because one's mind may enjoy very special relations established between effects in a situation of pure exteriority [i.e., in relation to the pure sense-event]. (LS, 169)

Stoic ethics, then, for Deleuze, concerns itself with the experience of what happens in and for one's body, a body which acts and suffers and is the perfect cause of the events which depend on it. Yet it is also a question, following Epictetus, of a certain living 'use of representations', that is, of an ongoing interpretation of one's experience with respect to the whole: nature or the *kosmos*.[99] As has just been seen, however, this 'whole' can only be enveloped within a comprehensive representation in relation to a sense-event which is not represented as such. The Stoic moral imperative, then, 'living in accordance with the experience of what happens by nature', must be transformed into something like 'living in accordance with the event which never finishes coming about'. As Deleuze puts it, 'Stoic ethics . . . consists of willing the event as such, that is, of willing that which occurs *in so far as it does occur*' (LS, 143, emphasis added). Or again, it consists in willing 'not exactly what occurs, but something *in* that which occurs, something yet to come which would be consistent with what occurs . . . : the Event' (LS, 149).

Victor Goldschmidt, whom Deleuze follows here, reconstructs the reasoning behind this Stoic conception of ethics which is above all an *ars vitae* in relation to the pure sense-event. First of all, it must be recalled that only Zeus perceives the whole: the entire causal chain whose movement is coextensive with his intelligence. Human intelligence, by contrast, can never manage to reconstruct all of the relations in relation to which a particular incorporeal event, ideally isolated from the whole, finds its ultimate place.[100] Secondly, however, the Stoics affirm that Zeus has given to every man a 'portion of himself to guard and guide him', which is his 'mind and reason'.[101] In other words, not only are we physical parts of the cosmos and responsible for the events which depend on us, we may also attain to Zeus's vision of things in accordance with the form of thought he has given us, which operates by inference and combination. But since, as has been seen, a 'comprehensive representation' of the cosmos must envelop an expression or event which cannot itself be represented, it is not so much a question of the Stoic 'sage' understanding the causal order through the total conjunction of its effects, as it is of *giving her body to the ongoing determination of the event in which she participates* (LS, 147). The Stoic sage, in other words, in his liberty, *'understands the pure event* in its eternal truth, independently of its spatio-temporal actualization ... But at the same time, the sage also *wills the embodiment* and the actualization of the pure incorporeal event in a state of affairs and in his or her own body and flesh' (LS, 146). Following Goldschmidt's analysis, it is thanks to the 'portion' which Zeus bequeaths us, the 'commanding-faculty' of the soul, that we corporealize the incorporeal event. The event of 'walking', for example, for Chrysippus, 'acquires a body under the effect of the hegemonic principle [i.e., the commanding-faculty] which is manifested in it' (LS, 147).[102]

On the one hand, then, it is a question of the events which the body of the moral agent brings about as their perfect cause. On the other hand, it is a question of the representations to which the soul could assent in so far as it is obliged by its very nature to interpret the relations between these events of which the agent is the complete cause and the rest of the cosmic present. Thus, the sage 'not only comprehends and wills the event, but also *represents it and, by this, selects it*' (LS, 147). Deleuze's preferred example for illustrating this Stoic 'double causality' is the event of 'to die'. The agent is thus said to give a body to this event, not only in so far as it is actualized within him, but also in so far as this event is represented in propositions connecting it to other events emerging as effects from the movement of the cosmos, but without reference to any physical totality or 'set of all sets'. An event such as 'to die', therefore, has 'an always open problematic structure (where and when?)' in so far as the sense of this event and its 'place' in the greater scheme of things remains to be expressed (LS, 145). Or again, as Deleuze puts it with reference to the two dimensions of time, namely, physical Chronos and the locus of infinitely divisible and incorporeal events which is Aion:

> With every event, there is indeed the present moment of its actualization, the moment in which the event is embodied in a state of affairs, an individual or a person, the moment we designate by saying '*here*, the moment has come'. The future and the past of the event are evaluated only with respect to this definitive present, and from the point of view of that which embodies it. But on the other hand, there is the future and the past of the event considered in itself, sidestepping each present, being free of the limitations of a state of affairs . . . It has no other present than that of the mobile instant which represents it, always divided into past-future . . . There are thus two accomplishments [of the event], which are like actualization and counter-actualization. (LS, 151–2)

As the sage corporealizes the pure event, he or she participates in what Deleuze calls the 'quasi-cause' of the event, which is another word for the ongoing determination of sense or the event (the ongoing sense-event). Why quasi-*cause*? In short, although the quasi-cause is irreducible to both physical causality and particular representations of the causal order, it is that which nevertheless *must* be represented if the causal order is, for us, to be complete.[103] As Deleuze writes:

> What is excessive in the event [i.e., its sense 'to come'] must be accomplished . . . [T]he instant as the paradoxical element or the quasi-cause which runs through the entire straight line [of Aion] must itself be represented. It is even in this sense that representation can envelop an expression on its edges, although the expression itself may be of another nature; and that the sage can 'identify' with the quasi-cause, although the quasi-cause itself is missing from its own identity. This present of the Aion representing the instant is not at all like the vast and deep present of Chronos: it is the present . . . of the pure operation. (LS, 168)

We can now return to the problem left over from our examination of Stoic epistemology. In short, it has just been seen that it is through the living 'use of representations' in Stoic ethics that the pure sense-event enveloped by the comprehensive representation can be determined in an ongoing way. Or again, it is by living in accordance with the event which never finishes coming about that the sage finds him or herself caught up in open-ended articulation of the relation between sensible and rational representation, that is, between denotation and signification or, finally, conjunctive truth and its condition.

*   *   *

We are now in a position to see how Deleuze understands Stoic philosophy to be a response to the problem of the event such as this was outlined above. First of all, the Stoic ontological distinction between bodies and incorporeals (reference and sense) allows Deleuze to say that the events upon which substantial things ontologically depend and which make up their lives, subsist in the propositions which express them as the 'sense to come' of these propositions. The event, in other words, is an objective ontological ideality for the determination of states of affairs, but only in so far as it is also understood to be an ongoing sense-event. Secondly, the way in which this ontological distinction between bodies and incorporeal events determines the relation between the different parts of the Stoic system – physics, logic and ethics – allows Deleuze to establish the sense-event as the 'fourth dimension' of the proposition, distinct from denotation, manifestation and conceptual signification, yet also grounding their relation. Indeed, we have just seen how the Stoics understand the pure sense-event, necessarily enveloped by the comprehensive representation, to govern in an ongoing and rigorous manner the relations between the causal analyses of individual things (in terms of their events-effects), conceptual development, and the manifestation of the wise person's beliefs and desires (the 'ethical' use of representations). It is precisely in this movement or process that the event can be said to allow the tri-dimensional model of the proposition 'to function a priori from within', progressively determining the sense of the proposition, its objective correlates (individuals, persons and concepts) and thus the truth of the proposition in relation to evental states of affairs (LS, 17). The event is thus not, like signification, the condition of *possibility* for a proposition to be true in relation to a factual state of affairs, but the *real* condition for the production of the sense and truth of propositions in relation to their corresponding evental states of affairs.

To reformulate the above in terms of Chronos and Aion, it can be said that while Aion (which can now be understood as the 'fourth' dimension of the ongoing determination of the pure event) can never correspond to Chronos (the realm of bodies), we can nevertheless conceive of it as a 'unique event', determinant of all other events. On this reading, the particular events making up the lives of bodies will be the 'signs' of this unique event, in so far as they both compose Aion and are determined by it. As Deleuze puts it, each 'event is adequate to the entire Aion; each event communicates with all others, and they all form one and the same Event, an event of the Aion where they have an eternal truth' (LS, 64). Speaking in the structuralist vocabulary which will be the focus of Chapter 4, Deleuze also calls Aion the line traced by a mobile 'paradoxical instance', which runs through and gathers together the differential series of events which make up the structure of the universe. As he writes, 'the paradoxical instance is the Event in which all events communicate and are distributed. It is the Unique event, and all other events are its bits and pieces' (LS, 56).

Why, however, does Deleuze not simply affirm Stoic philosophy as *the* philosophy of the event? As he writes, it appears, 'if we follow the surviving partial and deceiving texts, that the Stoics may not have been able to resist the double temptation of returning to the simple physical causality or to the logical contradiction' (LS, 171). In other words, and although Deleuze offers us no textual proof of this, it would appear that the Stoics ultimately determine the unique event of the Aion as Zeus, a substantial, totalizing instance which creates a unity on both sides of the ontological divide. On the one hand, then, evental quasi-causality was replaced by pure physical causality founded on Zeus as *causa sui*; and on the other hand, Zeus, as the 'set of all sets' or 'name of names', brought the ongoing determination of the event to an end by anchoring the 'determinations of signification', and thereby also engendering a strong principle of logical contradiction (at the expense of the much looser, experimental relations of evental compatibility and incompatibility). Deleuze must therefore look for a way of determining the event in its 'ideal play' only, in accordance with the above stated problematic: what are the (evental) conditions of the event if everything is to be an event? We shall see how Deleuze does this in the coming chapters. Nevertheless, Deleuze will retain: the Stoic ontological division between bodies and incorporeals (between reference and sense); the differences in nature and the relations between the sense-event, the 'sensory representation' (denotation) and the 'rational representation' (signification); and finally, the Stoic idea of a personal responsibility for the (counter-) actualization of events.

Notes

1. Immanuel Kant, 'What is Orientation in Thinking?', in *Kant: Political Writings*, trans. H. B. Nisbet, ed. H. S. Reiss (Cambridge: Cambridge

University Press, 1991), pp. 237–49. This text is generally translated in French as *Qu'est-ce que s'orienter dans la pensée?* See, for example, Philonenko's translation, published by Vrin.

2. See, for example, on the Idea of 'equality' (but also of beauty, goodness, uprightness, holiness, etc.) and the knowledge of equal things (beautiful, good, upright, holy, etc., things), Plato, *Phaedo*, in *Plato: The Collected Dialogues*, ed. E. Hamilton and H. Cairns (Princeton: Princeton University Press, 1961), 74a–75d.

3. See on this Plato, *Republic*, in *Plato: The Collected Dialogues*, V475e–480b, and particularly 480b: 'the philosophers are those who are capable of apprehending that which is eternal and unchanging, while those who are incapable of this, but lose themselves and wander amid the multiplicities of multifarious things, are not philosophers'.

4. See, for example, Hippolytus, *Refutatio*, 7.29.9–7.30.4 (211.17–215.12), in Brad Inwood, *The Poem of Empedocles: A Text and Translation* (Toronto: University of Toronto Press, 1992), pp. 80–2.

5. See Clement, *Miscellanies* 5.14.104.1–5, in Jonathan Barnes, *Early Greek Philosophy* (London: Penguin, 2001), pp. 59–60.

6. Diogenes Laertius, *The Lives of the Philosophers*, 8.69, cited in Inwood, *The Poem of Empedocles*, pp. 150–1.

7. See, for example, Lawrence Brian Lombard, 'Ontologies of Events', in Stephen Laurence and Cynthia Macdonald (eds), *Contemporary Readings in the Foundations of Metaphysics* (Oxford: Blackwell Publishers, 1998), p. 289. Lombard's article also provides an overview of the work of several important philosophers of the event in the Anglo-American tradition.

8. 'Objects are prime actors in events; objectless events are uncommon. But so are eventless objects; events make up the lives of objects.' Roberto Casati and Achille Varzi, 'Events', in Edward N. Zalta (ed.) *The Stanford Encyclopaedia of Philosophy* (Summer 2006 Edition) http://plato.stanford.edu/archives/sum2006/entries/events. This article by Casati and Varzi provides an excellent overview of the various philosophical positions taken with respect to events in Anglo-American philosophy.

9. Deleuze puts this point very clearly in *Difference and Repetition*: 'one does not become "harder" (or taller) than one was without at the same time becoming "softer" (or smaller) than one is in the process of becoming. We cannot avoid this by distinguishing times, since the distinction between times is subsequent to the becoming which interposes the one in the other and, at the same time, posits both the movement by which the new present is constituted and the movement by which the former present is constituted as past' (DR, 236).

10. Although this particular point will only be explored in detail in *The Logic of Sense*'s later series, it is already clear from the text of this

first series that the ontological priority of events poses a problem for knowledge, as well as for the knowing and acting subject. As Deleuze writes: 'the proper or singular name is guaranteed by the permanence of *savoir*. The latter is embodied in general names designating pauses and rests, in substantives and adjectives, with which the proper name maintains a constant connection . . . But when substantives and adjectives begin to dissolve, when the names of pause and rest are carried away by the verbs of pure becoming and slide into the language of events, all identity disappears from the self, the world and God. This is the test of *savoir* and recitation which strips Alice of her identity . . . It is as if events enjoyed an irreality which is communicated through language to the *savoir* and to persons. For personal uncertainty is not a doubt foreign to what is happening, but rather an objective structure of the event itself, in so far as it moves in two directions at once, and in so far as it fragments the subject following this double direction' (LS, 3).

11. When we use expressions such as 'everything is an event' or 'things and persons are themselves events', we are not confusing what Deleuze sees as categorically distinct items. For, in *The Logic of Sense*, things in general are ultimately *nothing but* relations between events, and where these relations are themselves determined by further events. 'Things', in other words, are simply more or less stable relations between events, these latter having ontological priority 'all the way down'.

12. See on this Sextus Empiricus, *Against the professors* 10.218, in *HP*, §27D (*SVF* 2.331, part).

13. See Diogenes Laertius 7.134 and 7.137, in *HP*, §44B and F (*SVF* 2.300, part, 2.299 and 2.526, part). See also Calcidius 293, in *HP*, §44E; Cicero, *Academica* 1.39, in *HP*, §45A (*SVF* 1.90); and Aetius 1.7.33, in *HP*, §46A (*SVF* 2.1027, part).

14. Nemesius 78,7–79,2, in *HP*, §45C (*SVF* 1.518, part).

15. See Seneca, *Letters* 117.13 and 117.2, in *HP*, §33E and §60S; Simplicius, *On Aristotle's Categories* 214,24-27, in *HP*, §28M (*SVF* 2.391, part); Plutarch, *On moral virtue* 440E–441D, in *HP*, §61B.

16. Alexander, *On mixture* 216,14–218,6 and 223,25–36, in *HP*, §48C and §47L (*SVF* 2.473 and 2.441, part). On the 'conflagration' or 'the world's periodic destruction into fire [and subsequent reconstitution] at very long intervals', see Eusebius, *Evangelical preparation* 15.14.2 and 15.18.2, in *HP*, §46G and K (*SVF* 1.98, part and 2.596, part).

17. Alexander, *On fate* 191,30–192,28, in *HP*, §55N (*SVF* 2.945). See also Aetius 1.11.5, in *HP*, §55G (*SVF* 2.340).

18. Sextus Empiricus, *Against the professors* 8.263, in *HP*, §45B (*SVF* 2.363).

19. On the relation of incorporeals to thought, see Sextus Empiricus,

Against the professors 8.409, in *HP*, §27E (*SVF* 2.85, part). On the 'subsisting' nature of the void, for example, see Cleomedes 8,10–14, in *HP*, §49C (*SVF* 2.541).

20. Victor Goldschmidt, *Le système stoïcien et l'idée du temps* (Paris: Vrin, 1953), p. 28. All translations from this text are my own. Goldschmidt is here citing Cleomedes 8,10–14 and Sextus Empiricus, *Against the professors* 10.3–4, in *HP*, §49C and B (*SVF* 2.541 and 2.505, part).

21. Sextus Empiricus, *Against the professors* 10.3–4, in *HP*, §49B (*SVF* 2.505, part).

22. Jean Brun, *Le stoïcisme* (Paris: PUF, 1958), p. 56, my translation.

23. Arius Didymus 26 (*SVF* 2.509), in Brad Inwood and L.P. Gerson (eds), *Hellenistic Philosophy: Introductory Readings* (Indianapolis and Cambridge: Hackett Publishing Company, second edition, 1997), p. 167. See also Simplicius, *On Aristotle's Categories* 350,15–16 and Stobaeus 1.106,5–23, in *HP*, §51A–B (*SVF* 2.510, part and 2.509).

24. See on this, Goldschmidt, *Le système stoïcien*, pp. 43–4.

25. See Cicero, *On divination* 1.127, in *HP*, §55O (*SVF* 2.944): 'since all things happen by fate ... if there were some human being who could see with his mind the connection of all causes, he would certainly never be deceived ... But since no one but god can do this, man must be left to gain his foreknowledge from various signs'. We shall examine below the relation between 'signs' and time.

26. See Stobaeus 1.105,17–106,4, in *HP*, §51E: Posidonius 'holds that the time which is thought of in terms of "when" is partly past, partly future, and partly present. The last consists of a part of the past and a part of the future, encompassing the actual division. But the division is point-like'.

27. As Deleuze puts it, drawing on Marcus Aurelius' reflections on the merely apparent injustices of fate, '[t]he physical mixture is exact only at the level of the whole, in the full circle of the divine present. But with respect to each part, there are many injustices and ignominies, many parasitic and cannibalistic processes which inspire our terror at what happens to us, and our resentment at what occurs' (LS, 151). It is for this reason that we must attempt to see things from the point of view of Nature as a whole. On Marcus Aurelius' cultivation of the cosmic perspective, see John Sellars, *Stoicism* (Berkeley and Los Angeles: University of California Press, 2006), pp. 126–8.

28. See also on this, John Sellars, 'An Ethics of the Event: Deleuze's Stoicism', *Angelaki* 11: 3 (2006), pp. 161–2 and n.35. Sellars argues, however, that Deleuze's account of the difference between Chronos and Aion is not altogether Stoic, and is rather derived from Goldschmidt's 'highly speculative and synthetic reconstruction that draws upon fragmentary and inconclusive reports of Chrysippus and the *Meditations* of Marcus [Aurelius]'.

29. Sextus Empiricus, *Against the professors* 9.211, in *HP*, §55B (*SVF* 2.341).

30. *HP*, §55, commentary.

31. Sextus Empiricus, *Against the professors* 8.11–12, in *HP*, §33B (*SVF* 2.166, part).

32. For an excellent account of these parallels, see also Benson Mates, *Stoic Logic* (Berkeley and Los Angeles: University of California Press, 1961), pp. 21–2. For Gottlob Frege, the reference is 'On *Sinn* and *Bedeutung* [1892]' and 'Comments on *Sinn* and *Bedeutung* [1892]', in Michael Beaney (ed.), *The Frege Reader* (Oxford: Blackwell Publishers, 1997). For Rudolf Carnap, see *Meaning and Necessity: A Study in Semantics and Modal Logic* (Chicago and London: University of Chicago Press, 1947). Deleuze cites these two latter texts in the 'Fifth Series of Sense', n.1, in relation to the infinite regress of the sense of denoting terms, whereby each denoting term has a sense which may be denoted by another such term, and so on ad infinitum (LS, 337–8).

33. See Frege, 'Comments on *Sinn* and *Bedeutung*', p. 180.

34. Frege, 'On *Sinn* and *Bedeutung*', p. 152.

35. Beaney, 'Introduction', *The Frege Reader*, p. 23.

36. On this infinite regress in Frege, see Beaney, ibid., pp. 24–6.

37. See, for example, Bertrand Russell, *An Inquiry into Meaning and Truth* (Harmondsworth: Penguin, 1962), pp. 158–9.

38. Ibid. p. 201.

39. Deleuze here follows the linguist Benveniste who argues that the 'I' or the indicator of person 'is this property that establishes the basis for individual discourse, in which each speaker takes over all the resources of language for its own behalf'. See Émile Benveniste, *Problems in General Linguistics*, trans. Mary Elizabeth Smith (Coral Gables, FL: University of Miami Press: 1971), pp. 218–20.

40. See on this, Lewis Carroll, 'What the Tortoise said to Achilles', *Mind* 4: 14 (1895), pp. 278–80.

41. Deleuze seems to be alluding to Bertrand Russell's discussion of Carroll's paradox in *The Principles of Mathematics* (Cambridge: Cambridge University Press, 1903), §38. Russell argues that in order to overcome this paradox, one must distinguish between, on the one hand, the notion of 'implies' which concerns only the dimension of signification and a relation between *unasserted* propositions; and on the other hand, the notion of 'therefore' which concerns the dimension of denotation and states a relation between *asserted* propositions 'whereby the hypothesis may be dropped and the conclusion asserted by itself'.

42. The Stoics divide the discipline of philosophy into three parts which are systematically coordinated with one another: physics, logic and

ethics. Each of these parts is effectively founded on theses belonging to the other parts. See Diogenes Laertius 7.39–41, in *HP*, §26B.

43. Aetius 1, Preface 2, in *HP*, §26A (*SVF* 2.35).
44. Jean-Joël Duhot, *La conception stoïcienne de la causalité* (Paris: Vrin, 1989), p. 54.
45. 'Causes are not *of* each other, but there are causes *to* each other. For the pre-existing condition of the spleen is the cause, not of fever, but of the fever's coming about . . . In the same way . . . the stones in the vault are causes to each other of the predicate "remaining", but they are not causes of each other. And the teacher and the pupil are causes to each other of the predicate "making progress"'. See Clement, *Miscellanies* 8.9.30.1–3, in *HP*, §55D (*SVF* 2.349).
46. Duhot, *La conception stoïcienne de la causalité*, p. 61, my translation.
47. On the one hand, speaking 'physically', a sign is always 'a present sign of a present [physical] thing'. On the other hand, speaking 'logically', the sign is always of the form 'if this, then that'. See Sextus Empiricus, *Against the professors* 8.254–5 and 8.275–6, in *HP*, §51H and §53T (*SVF* 2.221, part and 2.223, part). The logical dimension of the sign or sayable will be examined more closely below.
48. See also on this, Goldschmidt, *Le système stoïcien*, pp. 15–16; and Émile Bréhier, *La théorie des incorporels dans l'ancien stoïcisme* (Paris: Vrin, 1928), pp. 11–13.
49. See Alexander, *On fate* 191,30–192,28, and Cicero, *On fate* 39–43, in *HP*, §55N and §62C (*SVF* 2.945 and 2.974).
50. Michael Frede, 'The Original Notion of Cause', in *Essays in Ancient Philosophy* (Minneapolis: University of Minnesota Press, 1987), p. 128.
51. Bréhier, *La théorie des incorporels*, p. 6.
52. See, for example, Stobaeus 1.138,14–139,4, in *HP*, §55A (*SVF* 1.89 and 2.336).
53. Alexander, *On fate* 191,30–192,28, in *HP*, §55N (*SVF* 2.945).
54. Frede, 'The Original Notion of Cause', p. 149.
55. See Cicero, *On fate* 39–43 and Gellius 7.2.6–13, in *HP*, §62C and D (*SVF* 2.974 and 2.1000, part).
56. See Diogenes Laertius 7.83, in *HP*, §31C (*SVF* 2.130).
57. Seneca, *Letters* 117.13, in *HP*, §33E.
58. Diogenes Laertius 7.57, in *HP*, §33A (*SVF* 3 Diogenes 20, part).
59. Sextus Empiricus, *Against the professors* 8.70, in *HP*, §33C (*SVF* 2.187, part). We shall return to examine the nature of the rational representation below.
60. Sextus Empiricus, *Against the professors* 8.11–12, in *HP*, §33B (*SVF* 2.166, part).
61. Diogenes Laertius 7.63–4, in *HP*, §33F–G and §34A (*SVF* 2.183, part and 2.193, part).

62. Diogenes Laertius 7.71–4, in *HP*, §35A.
63. Gellius 16.8.10–11, in *HP*, §35D. See also Jacques Brunschwig, 'Le modèle conjonctif', in *Études sur les philosophies hellénistiques: Épicurisme, stoïcisme, scepticisme* (Paris: PUF, 1995), pp. 161–87.
64. Gellius 16.8.12–14, in *HP*, §35E.
65. Diogenes Laertius 7.71–4, in *HP*, §35A. See also Sextus Empiricus, *Outlines of Pyrrhonism* 2.110–13, in *HP*, §35B: 'Those who introduce "cohesion" [i.e., Chrysippus] say that a conditional is sound whenever the contradictory of its consequent conflicts with its antecedent.'
66. Susanne Bobzien argues that it is in fact 'historically inappropriate to ask whether Chrysippus intended empirical, analytical, or formal logical conflict, given that a conceptual framework which could accommodate such distinctions is absent in Hellenistic logic'. See Susanne Bobzien, 'Logic', in Brad Inwood (ed.), *The Cambridge Companion to the Stoics* (Cambridge: Cambridge University Press, 2003), p. 95.
67. See on this, Diogenes Laertius 7.76–81, in *HP*, §36A. The example which follows comes from Sextus Empiricus, *Outlines of Pyrrhonism* 2.104–6, in *HP*, §35C.
68. From the point of view of sense, on the other hand, as opposed to signification, 'the regressive law no longer relates the names of different degrees to classes or properties, but rather distributes them in a heterogeneous series of events' (LS, 69–70). We shall return to this notion of series in its relation to the production of sense in later chapters.
69. Russell, of course, introduced the theory of types in order to resolve paradoxes such as the 'set of all sets' and the 'barber of the regiment'. See Bertrand Russell, 'Appendix B: The Doctrine of Types', in *Principles of Mathematics*, pp. 523–8.
70. See Cicero, *On fate* 12–15, in *HP*, §38E.
71. Ibid.
72. Ibid. With regard to past truths being necessary truths, Cicero writes in this passage that 'all past truths are necessary, as Chrysippus holds . . . because past facts are immutable and cannot change from true to false'.
73. 'The interest of the determinations of signification lies in the fact that they engender the principles of non-contradiction and the excluded middle, instead of these principles being given ready made' (LS, 69).
74. Sextus Empiricus, *Against the professors* 8.275–6, in *HP*, §53T (*SVF* 2.223, part).
75. See also on this Frédérique Ildefonce, *Les Stoïciens I: Zénon, Cléanthe, Chrysippse* (Paris: Les Belles Lettres, 2000), p. 199; and Goldschmidt, *Le système stoïcien*, pp. 82–3.
76. See Sextus Empiricus, *Against the professors* 8.254–5, in *HP*, §51H

(*SVF* 2.221, part). See also on this Goldschmidt, *Le système stoïcien*, pp. 43–4.

77. On the Stoic representation of truth and science as 'integral sums of true propositions, that is, as immense conjunctive propositions without any flaws', see Brunschwig, 'Le modèle conjonctif', p. 174.

78. On the co-fatedness of events, see Cicero, *On fate* 28–30, in *HP*, §55S. On Stoic philosophy as a practical 'art of living', see Seneca, *Letters from a Roman Stoic*, trans. Robin Campbell (London: Penguin, 1969), XVI, pp. 63–5. See also Sellars' discussion of this point in his *Stoicism*, pp. 26–9 and 31–6.

79. See Diogenes Laertius 7.41–4, in *HP*, §31A.

80. What we are here calling the 'comprehensive representation' is a translation of *phantasia katalēptikē*, more often translated in English as 'cognitive impression'. Our use of 'comprehensive representation', however, is in line with the English translation of *The Logic of Sense*, and follows Goldschmidt's French translation of *phantasia katalēptikē*, which Deleuze also uses, as *la représentation compréhensive*. It is also important to remember that, despite its translation here as 'representation', *phantasiai* are all corporeal.

81. Diogenes Laertius 7.54, in *HP*, §40A (including *SVF* 2.105, Posidonius fr. 42); Cicero, *Academica* 2.145, in *HP*, §41A (*SVF* 1.66).

82. Aetius 4.12.1–5, in *HP*, §39B (*SVF* 2.54, part).

83. Diogenes Laertius 7.49–51, in *HP*, §39A (*SVF* 2.52, 55, 61).

84. See on this, Michael Frede, 'Stoic Epistemology', in Keimpe Algra, et al. (eds), *The Cambridge History of Hellenistic Philosophy* (Cambridge: Cambridge University Press, 1999), pp. 304–5.

85. See Sextus Empiricus, *Against the professors* 8.70, in *HP*, §33C (*SVF* 2.187, part): 'They [the Stoics] say that a "sayable" is what subsists in accordance with a rational impression, and a rational impression is one in which the content of the impression can be exhibited in language'.

86. Sextus Empiricus, *Against the professors* 8.275–6, in *HP*, §53T (*SVF* 2.223, part); Diogenes Laertius 7.53, in *HP*, §39D (*SVF* 2.87, part); Epictetus, *Discourses* 1.6.12–22, in *HP*, §63E.

87. Frede, 'Stoic Epistemology', pp. 306–7.

88. Aetius 4.11.1–4, in *HP*, §39E (*SVF* 2.83).

89. Sextus Empiricus, *Against the professors* 7.247–52, in *HP*, §40E (*SVF* 2.65, part).

90. See Frede, 'Stoic Epistemology', pp. 302–3.

91. See Sextus Empiricus, *Against the professors* 8.85–6, in *HP*, §34D.

92. On the Stoic principle of the 'identity of indiscernibles', see Cicero, *Academica* 2.83–5, in *HP*, §40J.

93. See Frede, 'Stoic Epistemology', pp. 308–10 and pp. 314–16.

94. Sextus Empiricus, *Against the professors* 7.247–52, in *HP*, §40E (*SVF* 2.65, part).

95. Frede, 'Stoic Epistemology', p. 316. For the reference to Boethus, see Diogenes Laertius 7.54, in *HP*, §40A (including *SVF* 2.105, Posidonius fr. 42).

96. On 'common sense', see LS, 78: 'Objectively, common sense subsumes under itself the given diversity and relates it to the unity of a particular form of object or an individualized form of a world.'

97. Diogenes Laertius 7.87–9, in *HP*, §63C.

98. On the 'co-fated' nature of events, see Chrysippus' response to the 'Lazy Argument', such as this is reported by Cicero in *On fate*, 28–30, in *HP*, §55S. '"You will recover, regardless of whether or not you call the doctor" is fallacious. For it is just as much fated for you to call the doctor as for you to recover.'

99. See Epictetus, *Discourses* 1.1.7–12 and 1.6.12–22, in *HP*, §62K and §63E.

100. Goldschmidt, *Le système stoïcien*, pp. 97–8.

101. Marcus Aurelius, *Meditations*, trans. A.D.L. Farquharson (Oxford: Oxford University Press, 1944), V, 27.

102. Goldschmidt, *Le système stoïcien*, p. 107. See also Seneca, *Letters* 113.23, in *HP*, §53L (*SVF* 2.836, part): 'Cleanthes and his pupil Chrysippus did not agree on what walking is. Cleanthes said it was breath extending from the commanding-faculty to the feet, Chrysippus that it was the commanding-faculty itself.' It is the position of Chrysippus that Deleuze and Goldschmidt are here following.

103. See also on this point, Žižek, *Organs without Bodies*, p. 27.

2

Leibniz –The Static Ontological and Logical Geneses

Deleuze's philosophical relation to Leibniz has in general been down-played in the secondary literature.[1] Deleuze's major, pre-*Difference and Repetition* influences are frequently cited as Nietzsche, Bergson and Spinoza, and that these figures are constant touchstones for Deleuze is undeniable.[2] Nevertheless, in his 1968 Spinoza book it is clear that, in certain respects, Deleuze reads Spinoza through Leibniz.[3] It is also clear that Leibniz is a major reference in 'The Method of Dramatization', which is an early summary of the major themes of *Difference and Repetition*. In the text of *The Logic of Sense*, which was published one year after *Difference and Repetition*, Spinoza is not mentioned at all, and Bergson is cited only once. Leibniz, on the other hand, features prominently in the highly impor-tant 'Sixteenth Series of the Static Ontological Genesis', as well as in the 'Twenty-Fourth Series of the Communication of Events' where he is heralded as 'the first important theoretician of the event' (LS, 171). Similarly, in the much later text, *The Fold: Leibniz and The Baroque*, Leibniz is affirmed as having implemented 'the second great logic of the event', after the Stoics and before Whitehead.[4] It is thus not unlikely that Deleuze sees himself as a direct, philosophical descendent of Leibniz when he maintains in a 1988 interview that he has tried in all his books to discover the nature of events.[5]

This is not to say, however, that Deleuze accepts all of the premises on which Leibniz bases his philosophy. On the contrary, Deleuze's constant criticism is that Leibniz ultimately subordinates the ideal play of events to a principle of converging differences under the hypothesis of a God who calculates and chooses for exist-ence the 'best' or maximally convergent series of possible events. In *The Logic of Sense*, Deleuze suggests that Leibniz's God perhaps responds to a 'theological exigency', or again to an 'economic prin-ciple' for the determination of causes and effects, or means and ends (LS, 172, 59).[6] Nevertheless, according to Deleuze's own testimony in *Difference and Repetition*, this subordination of events to a principle of convergence was Leibniz's 'only error' (DR, 51). In this work, Deleuze writes that 'no one has gone further than Leibniz in the exploration of sufficient reason . . . [and] the element of difference' (DR, 213). Similarly, in *The Logic of Sense*, Deleuze writes that Leibniz went a long way (although not 'all the way') in establishing 'a theory of singular points' and their 'ideal play' (LS, 116), that is to say, a theory of the relations of alogical compatibility and incompatibility between predicate-events which would be irreducible to the identical and the contradictory (LS, 171).

Now, as was seen in the previous chapter, the Stoic ontological distinction between bodies and incorporeals – or reference and sense – allowed Deleuze to affirm that the events which make up the lives of substantial things, and upon which they ontologically depend, 'subsist' in the propositions which express them as the 'sense to come' of those propositions (hence the 'sense-event'). What is more, the way in which this ontological distinction between bodies and incorporeals determines the relation between the different parts of the Stoic system – physics, logic and ethics – allowed Deleuze to affirm that the ongoing sense-event is the 'fourth dimension' of the proposition which makes the tri-dimensional model of the proposition function entirely from within by determining the objective correlates of these dimensions and the relations between them: denoted things, manifested persons and signified concepts. In particular, it was seen that the problematic 'envelopment' of the sense-event in the Stoic comprehensive representation – the event that it cannot not represent if it is to be comprehensive – governs the ongoing articulation of a relation between the causal analysis of things, conceptual development and the ethical 'manifestation' of the Stoic sage's beliefs and desires. In the final analysis, however, the Stoics brought to a halt this ongoing determination of the sense-event by returning to a doctrine of pure physical causality and a strong principle of logical contradiction, that is, by determining the event with reference to the body and 'name' of Zeus. The question for Deleuze thus remained: how are individuals, persons, general concepts, and the relations between them, to be generated by the event without reference to any underlying, substantial unity?

Deleuze now turns to Leibniz in order to argue, from the perspective of a different system of philosophical concepts, that two types of relation between events govern their 'ideal play' and underlie the determination and relation of denoted things, manifested persons and general concepts. Leibniz calls these relations 'compossibility' and 'incompossibility'.[7] Deleuze, for his part, calls these relations 'convergence' and 'divergence' (LS, 111) or 'compatibility' and 'incompatibility' (LS, 177). Before examining how Deleuze takes up Leibniz's philosophy, however, it will be useful to explicate certain elements of the latter's system, and the role of compossibility and incompossibility therein.

2.1 Leibniz's System in Outline

For Leibniz, before the creation of the world, God has an understanding of all of the 'possibles', that is, of all possible individual concepts.[8] What is possible, at this level, is anything whose concept does not, in itself, violate the 'principle of contradiction'.[9] In other words, in so far as the concept of an individual does not in itself involve a contradiction, it is possible in the minimal sense that there is no inherent reason why it cannot be thought: it is, as Leibniz writes, 'perfectly conceivable'.[10]

Not all of these possibles, however, can be thought together without contradiction, for what is possible in itself is not necessarily 'compossible' with other such possibles.[11] Using one of Leibniz's preferred examples in his correspondence with the theologian and philosopher Antoine Arnauld, whilst it can be said that an Adam who does not sin is possible in itself, the concept of such an individual is nevertheless 'incompossible' with other possible individuals such as, for example, a Christ who redeems Adam's original sin.[12]

Now, in God's understanding, possibles which are compossible with one another in various ways form 'an infinite number of possible worlds'.[13] Or again, the possible world of any given individual concept is the totality of all individual concepts compossible with it.[14] As Leibniz writes, in 'every possible world everything is linked together (*tout est lié*). The universe – however it might be constituted – is a unified whole'.[15] It follows, therefore, that possibles which are 'incompossible' with one another must belong to different possible worlds.

From among all of these possible worlds, God will bring only one into existence: the 'best' of all possible worlds, that is, the one which is maximally compossible, displaying the most perfection, which is to say, the most variety and order with respect to the series of individual concepts.[16] This act of creation follows from the very nature of God, whose concept includes the primary perfections: power, wisdom, goodness and, of course, existence.[17] Following Leibniz, it is the existence of this necessary and perfect being 'which causes the existence of the best [of all possible worlds], which God knows through his wisdom, chooses through his goodness, and produces through his power'.[18] In other words, given that he is a necessary and all perfect being, to not bring into existence the best of all of the possible worlds would contradict the very nature of God.[19]

The existing world, our actual world, is thus entirely composed of individual substances, or 'monads', which 'realize' the maximally compossible series of possible individual concepts in their own unique way. Indeed, for Leibniz, no two monads are exactly alike, differing only in number. For if two things shared exactly the same properties then they could not be distinguished, that is to say, they would, for all intents and purposes, be the same, one thing.[20] Being compossible with the entire series of existing monads, then, each individual monad is said to 'express' or 'mirror' the entire universe of monads,[21] one thing 'expressing' another 'when there is a constant and regular relation between what can be said [that is, predicated] about one and about the other'.[22] It is due to this relation of compossibility or expression that each monad is said to carry 'traces of everything that happens in the universe'.[23] In short, Leibniz argues that each existing monad or 'singular substance expresses the whole universe in its own way, and that all its events, together with all their circumstances and the whole sequence of external things, are included in its notion' or concept in a particular way.[24] Another way of putting this is to say that each monad has a 'complete individual concept' which is capable of distinguishing it from every other such monad, and in which God is able to read, from a particular 'point of view', not only everything that happens to it, but also everything that happens in the entire universe.[25]

Now, the monads for Leibniz are simple, unified substances: '*simple*, that is to say, without parts'; and 'where there are no parts, there neither extension, nor shape, nor divisibility is possible'.[26] Being simple, they can neither be generated nor perish in the course of nature, as is the case with compounds.[27] Indeed, monads are said to 'last as long as the universe, which will be changed but not destroyed'.[28] They are the 'true atoms of nature', but there are no causal relations between them.[29] They rather have, as has been seen, expressive relations of predication. In other words, what 'we call causes are only concurrent requisites' whose agreement or 'harmony' has been regulated by God from all eternity.[30] Nevertheless, in this non-causal relation of expression, a monad is said to be '*active* in so far as what is distinctly known in it [that is, in its concept] explains what occurs in another, and *passive* in so far as the reason for what occurs in it is found in what is distinctly known in another'.[31]

Imperishable and extensionless 'points of view' on the universe, monads are necessarily souls or minds (a mind being a 'reasonable' soul);[32] but it is thereby also clear that there are souls and minds 'in the least part of matter'.[33] As Leibniz poetically expresses it, each 'portion of matter may be conceived as a garden full of plants, and as a pond full of fish. But every branch of each plant, every member of each animal, and every drop of their liquid parts is itself likewise a similar garden or pond.'[34] Even in the case of 'rational souls' such as ourselves – that is, souls endowed with memory, reason and capable of acts of reflection – our 'bodies' are teeming with 'bare monads', 'sensitive souls' or 'little spermatic animals' having between them particularly well coordinated and direct relations of expression.[35]

As thinking substances, monads or souls are essentially characterized by their perceptions and appetitions, perception being a 'passing state, which involves and represents a plurality within the unity or simple substance', and appetition being 'the passage from one perception to another'.[36] It is important to note that this characterization of monads is perfectly compatible with the idea that monads are distinguished by the way in which they realize, in their own particular way, the maximally compossible series of possible individual concepts conceived of by God, for God himself is a monad, having as his attributes the primary perfections. In other words, what God perfectly and all at once perceives, the created monads perceive only imperfectly, in related, though varying and changing, degrees of clarity and confusion depending on their 'point of view' on the universe. Indeed, Leibniz argues that each monad perceives the entire universe, but confusedly for the most part, in minute, unconscious perceptions.[37] What the monad perceives or represents most distinctly, on the other hand, are those monads 'nearest' to them and which compose its 'body'. As Deleuze puts it, 'the individual monad expresses a world according to the relation of other bodies with its own, as much as it expresses this relation according to the relation of the parts of its own body' (LS, 110).[38] Or again, as Leibniz writes:

> although each created monad represents the whole universe, it represents more distinctly the body which is particularly affected by it, and whose entelechy it is: and as this body expresses the whole universe by the connexion of all matter in the plenum, the soul represents the whole universe also in representing the body which belongs to it in a particular way.[39]

Every body, then, has a 'dominant' monad which is 'active' in the sense examined above: its concept explains more distinctly what happens in and for the monads composing its body. The 'dominated' monads, for their part, represent this dominant monad confusedly or passively, but they in turn are dominant or active in relation to other monads, representing them clearly, and so on, to infinity.[40] The body is in this sense 'not a substance, but a phenomenon resulting from simple substances', the 'reality of which is situated in the harmony of the perceivers with themselves (at different times) and with other perceivers'.[41] In other words, a 'body is ... an aggregate of substances', these latter being understood, not as parts which make up a whole, but as the body's 'essential, internal requisites'.[42] As Deleuze describes it, since 'all the individual monads express the totality of their world – although they express clearly only a select part – their bodies form mixtures and aggregates, variable associations with zones of clarity and obscurity' (LS, 112).

Monads, then, are simple, unified or 'closed', imperishable substances which have non-causal, expressive relations between one another, and which fall under complete individual concepts which express the entire universe from a particular point of view. If monads are simple or 'closed', however, what is the status of relations between existing individual substances? It is clear that compossibility and incompossibility are relations, but these relations only govern the formation of worlds, the best of which is subsequently realized by simple substances which alone exist. The relations between existing individuals must, therefore, be 'out of the subjects; but being neither a substance nor an accident, it must be a mere ideal thing'.[43] Nevertheless, relations are *well founded* in the sense that they '*inhere in the nonrelational properties of the relata at issue*' which, as has been seen, are ultimately grounded in relations of compossibility and incompossibility.[44] As Leibniz summarizes it in an example, '[m]y judgment about relations is that paternity in David is one thing, sonship in Solomon another, but that the relation common to both is a merely mental thing whose basis is the modifications of the individuals'.[45] In other words, even though the substances David and Solomon are 'closed over' their complete list of nonrelational properties, as it were, the relation between them nevertheless inheres in these properties. This is not to say that the relation of 'kinship' binds them, for this relation, not being included in either substance, is only imaginary. Rather, the basis of the relation between paternity in David and sonship in Solomon is to be found in the regulated 'modifications of the individuals' which has been decreed by God from all eternity according to the laws of compossibility and incompossibility.

Another important consequence of monadic 'closure' and the 'completeness' of its concept is that the infinite number of predicates which define each monad's unique point of view on the universe are, as Leibniz says, analytically 'contained' or 'included' in its concept.[46] It does not follow from these notions of analyticity and inclusion, however, that the opposite of a true proposition denoting an existing monad implies a logical contradiction strictly speaking. For, as seen above, such a proposition about existing monads is always possible or perfectly conceivable in so far as it does not in itself involve a contradiction.[47] The opposite of a true proposition denoting an existing monad is not contradictory in itself, but rather incompossible with the set of true propositions characterizing the world of created monads. As Deleuze explains by way of an example, the apparent contradiction between Adam-the-sinner and Adam-non-sinner in fact *results from* the incompossibility of worlds in which Adam sins or does not sin (LS, 111).

Truths of 'fact' are thus of a different nature than truths of reason, even if both are 'analytic'. Indeed, for Leibniz, if the principle of contradiction governs truths of reason or necessary truths (formal possibilities or essences), then the 'principle of sufficient reason' governs contingent truths or truths of fact.[48] Leibniz formulates the principle of sufficient reason in the following way: 'nothing happens without its being possible for one who has enough knowledge of things to give a reason sufficient to determine why it is thus and not otherwise'.[49] What this means is that, following our exposition above, the sufficient reason why something is true of a given simple substance must be able to be seen in an analysis of the way in which something is true of another monad whose concept is apt to explain the nature of the former. Furthermore, since a sufficient reason must also be found for this latter monad's being such and such, this analysis must be continued into that of the 'concurrent requisites' of a third monad, and so on, right across the infinite series of created things, and finally into an analysis of the concept of a God who, in line with his perfections, grants existence to that series of monads which realizes the maximally compossible series of possible individual concepts which he conceives of in his understanding. God, in the final analysis, is thus the sufficient reason for the entire series of created things. Leibniz puts this point in the following way, complementing his ontological proof of the existence of God through the principle of contradiction[50] with an 'existential proof' through the principle of sufficient reason:

> [I]n the case of the series of things spread over the universe of created things ... resolution into particular reasons might go on into endless detail on account of the immense variety of things in the nature and the division of bodies *ad infinitum* ... [A]ll this differentiation involves only other prior or more differentiated contingent things, all of which need a similar analysis to explain them ... This is why the ultimate reason must lie in a necessary substance, in which the differentiation of the changes only exists eminently as in their source; and this is what we call *God*.[51]

For Leibniz, therefore, all 'true predication has some basis in the nature of things', up to and including the nature of that thing called God.[52] And the difference between these truths of fact and truths of reason is that the latter can be analyzed in a finite number of steps while an analysis of the former requires an infinite number of steps. Of course, no created monad can carry out an infinite analysis. God, however, sees the entire series 'at the same time' or knows it 'intuitively'.[53] This is still not to say, however, that at the end of the analysis, true propositions of fact can be reduced to simple, primitive terms. For if they were so reducible, the world would have to have been created according to an absolute, logical or metaphysical necessity, thereby contradicting the concept of God who, in his perfect power, wisdom and goodness, must be *free* to choose and bring into existence the best of all possible worlds.[54] Since God must nevertheless be said to be the sufficient reason for the series of created things and their expressive relations, rather than arguing that contingent truths can be reduced to identical propositions, we must say that the infinite analysis of contingent truths is 'asymptotic' to certain necessary truths: those concerning God's essential attributes, the relation between which was established by the ontological proof of his existence.[55] As Leibniz writes:

> true contingent propositions cannot be reduced to identical propositions, but is proved by showing that if the analysis is continued further and further, it constantly approaches identical propositions, but never reaches them. Therefore it is God alone, who grasps the entire infinite in his mind, who knows all contingent truths with certainty. So the distinction between necessary and contingent truths is the same as that between lines which meet and asymptotes, or between commensurable and incommensurable numbers.[56]

Now, our argument here is that it is in accordance with the problem of finding a coherent means of speaking about the onto-logical primacy of events in relation to things that Deleuze turns to Leibniz. Having explicated the major lines of Leibniz's philosophical system, let us now examine what Deleuze takes from it.

2.2 Deleuze and Leibniz: The 'Static Genesis' of Individuals, Persons and General Concepts and the Ideal Play of Events

Central to Deleuze's philosophy of the event is a certain appropria-tion of the Leibnizian relations of compossibility and incompossibil-ity between events, in so far as these are understood to ontologically precede and govern the constitution of worldly individuals and persons. As he writes:

> Compossibility does not . . . presuppose the inherence of predicates in an individual subject or monad. It is rather the inverse; inherent predicates are those which correspond to events from the beginning compossible (the monad of Adam the sinner includes in predicative form only future and past events which are compossible with the sin of Adam) . . . Convergence and divergence are entirely original relations which cover the rich domain of alogical compatibilities and incompatibilities, and therefore form an essential component of the theory of sense. (LS, 171–2)

It should be noted, however, as a point of terminological clarifica-tion, that when Deleuze speaks of compossibility and incompossibil-ity between events, he does so, more often than not, by speaking of them in terms of the convergence and divergence of *singularities* (LS, 172). It is thus not uncommon for Deleuze to talk of 'singularities-events' (LS, 103, 112, 116). The precise reason why Deleuze speaks of events and their relations by means of these quasi-mathematical concepts will become clear in Chapter 3.[57] What is important to understand at this stage is that singularities-events and their relations of convergence and divergence have several characteristics which map quite precisely onto those of their correlates in the Leibnizian system: predicate-events and their relations of compossibility and incompossibility.

Now, the first of these characteristics is that singularities-events are 'impersonal and preindividual' (LS, 109). For Deleuze, in other words, just as for Leibniz, events and their relations *precede* the constitution of individuals and persons. As Deleuze argues, relations between events form 'worlds', and the 'individual is inseparable from a world' (LS, 109).

Secondly, as Deleuze describes it, singularities-events may be either convergent or divergent (LS, 109, 111, 172), or as Leibniz would say, compossible or incompossible. Deleuze explicitly ties together the notions of compossibility and convergence when he writes that 'compossibility is . . . defined as a *continuum* of singularities, whereby continuity has the convergence of series as its ideational criterion' (LS, 111).

It is important to note here, however, that Deleuze speaks of the convergence of 'series' rather than of singularities-events *per se*, for, as he writes, the 'nature' of a singularity is determined in so far as it is 'analytically prolonged over a *series of ordinary points* up to the vicinity of another singularity' (LS, 109, emphasis added and translation modified). We shall see more precisely in Chapter 3 what this distinction between the singular and the ordinary means for Deleuze, but for now we must find the precise correlate in Leibniz's system.

It was said above that, for Leibniz, within a possible world, a given individual substance is active or dominant with respect to another in so far as its concept *distinctly* expresses what occurs in relation to this other. And this latter substance is, correspondingly, passive or dominated in relation to the former: its concept expresses what happens only *obscurely*. 'Distinctly' here thus means: more economically, more simply, with greater explanatory force relative to a differentiated system of concepts. Thus, to take one of Leibniz's examples, we cannot explain the motion of a ship in terms of it being caused by its wake, for, given the connection between our concepts of these individuals (which are themselves bound up with our more general concepts of water, displacement, ships, wind propulsion, and so on), this would lead us to have a very confused or indeed 'obscure' representation of what is going on.[58] But distinctly or otherwise, what are known in individuals are precisely the events which ground their expressive relations to other individuals over time.[59] For Leibniz, therefore, within a world of compossible individuals, there can be said to be both distinct events and obscure events. Now, Leibniz's 'distinct and obscure' events map quite precisely onto Deleuze's 'singular and ordinary' events. Indeed, when Deleuze says that singular events are 'analytically prolonged' over ordinary events, this must be understood in terms of the Leibnizian principle of sufficient reason which governs truths of fact in relation to worldly individuals. Thus, the sufficient reason why a first, obscure or ordinary event can be truly predicated of a given simple substance must be able to be seen in an analysis of the way in which a second, distinct or singular event can be truly predicated of another monad, and in such a way that the concept of this latter is apt to explain why the first event is included in the concept of the former. And of course, for Leibniz as well as Deleuze, the reason why this second event can be truly predicated of this second simple substance must be able to be seen in an analysis of the way in which a third event can be truly predicated of a third simple substance, and so on, *ad infinitum*.

The third point of correspondence between the Leibnizian and Deleuzian systems is thus that, in so far as singularities-events are analytically prolonged over series of ordinary events, and in so far as these series converge with series which depend on other singularities-events, a possible world is formed (LS, 109, 111). Conversely, therefore, another world, incompossible with the first, would begin 'in the neighbourhood' of those singularities-events whose series diverge (LS, 109, translation modified).

Now (and this is our fourth point), within such a compossible world, 'individuals are constituted which select and envelop a finite number of the singularities of the system. They combine them with the singularities that their own body incarnates . . . [and] spread them out over their own ordinary lines' (LS, 109). For Deleuze, therefore, just as for Leibniz, the individual 'parts' of an individual's body are related in precisely the same way as individuals in general, that is, through the way in which the events which define them can be analytically prolonged over one another within a compossible world. As Deleuze writes, Leibniz 'was right to say that the individual expresses a world according to the relation of other bodies with its own, as much as it expresses this relation according to the relation of the parts of its own body' (LS, 110).

Now, in accordance with the Leibnizian system, Deleuze proceeds to argue that, to the extent that existing individuals are said to envelop singularities-events which have been 'analytically prolonged' over ordinary events within a possible world, these convergent events must be said to have become, within this world, 'the analytic predicates of constituted subjects' (LS, 112). This, then, is a fifth point of correspondence: singularities-events are effectively 'realized' or 'actualized' as the predicates or 'concurrent requisites' of existing individuals. The analyticity of the individual's predicates follows from the idea that the individual simply is its realization of a particular, determined slice of the continuum of singular and ordinary events

66

which have been analytically prolonged over one another within a compossible world. Each 'expressing' the entire world-series in a unique way, each determined individual thus expresses every other, but in 'variable and complementary degrees of clarity' depending on the particular slice of the continuum of singularities-events they actualize (LS, 111). Viewed together severally, therefore, 'their bodies form mixtures and aggregates, variable associations with zones of clarity and obscurity' (LS, 112). What is more, it follows from the analytic nature of the continuum of singularities-events that we can consider the 'relations' between bodies as the analytic predicates of the mixtures they form (LS, 112).

Deleuze, however, goes on to argue that

> contrary to certain aspects of the Leibnizian theory, it is necessary to assert that the analytic order of predicates is an order of coexistence or succession, with neither logical hierarchy nor the character of generality; having a colour is no more general than being green ... The increasing or decreasing generalities appear only when a predicate is determined in a proposition to function as the subject of another predicate. As long as predicates are brought to bear upon individuals, we must recognize in them equal immediacy which blends with their analytic character. To have a colour is no more general than to be green, since it is only this colour that is green, and this green that has this shade, that is related to the individual subject. This rose is not red without having the red colour of this rose. This red is not a colour without having the colour of this red ... (LS, 112)

Although Deleuze does not cite which 'aspects of the Leibnizian theory' he is criticizing, we may reconstruct the problem in the following way. In the *Discourse on Metaphysics*, §8, for example, Leibniz claims that, even though it is not determinate enough to constitute an individual, the concept of 'king' is nevertheless contained in the concept of Alexander the Great. Now, it is true that we can consider 'king' to be a general concept which is composed of simpler concepts spelling out the necessary and sufficient conditions for something to be a king. However, because the predicates-events which determine each unique individual in its expressive relations with other such individuals are derived from the world-continuum of singular and ordinary events, the predicates-events of these individuals must be brought to bear on them with 'equal immediacy'. It thus cannot be said, at this level of worldly existences, that the concept 'king' is contained in the complete individual concept of Alexander the Great in so far as Alexander the Great 'is the sovereign ruler of an independent state', 'acquired his title by heredity or conquest', and so on. Rather, we must say that 'being king', such as this is predicated of Alexander, is no more general than predicates such as 'vanquishes Darius and Porus', and so on, for it is only this individual who is king of Macedon between 336 and 323 BC, this king which vanquishes Darius and Porus, this vanquisher of Darius and Porus who dies of poison in 323 BC, and so on, through the infinite number of predicates (and their relations of simultaneity and succession) which determine the complete individual concept of Alexander the Great and his relation to other individuals over time (variable mixtures and aggregates). At this level, in other words, the analytic predicates of existence are akin to what are now called 'tropes' or 'abstract particulars': 'abstract' because they only ever concern a 'part' of the individual concerned, but 'particular' because they are wholly and completely localizable.[60]

This criticism notwithstanding, Deleuze concludes this section of his analysis and extension of certain Leibnizian concepts by writing that he 'identifies', following Leibniz, 'the domain of intuitions as immediate representations, the analytic predicates of existence, and the *descriptions* of mixtures or aggregates' (LS, 113). And we have seen what these 'identifications' amount to: the domain of intuitions refers to the 'harmoniousness' of the world-series of convergent singularities-events (which is to say, for Leibniz, God's intuitive knowledge thereof); the analytic predicates of existence are the determinations in relation to which individuals 'actualize' particular 'slices' of this world-series; and the description of mixtures or aggregates refers to the way in which relations of coexistence and succession between individuals and their bodies can be understood as a function of the analytic predicates of existence. What will also be essential to retain from the above is that Deleuze follows Leibniz in arguing that the continuum of singularities-events must be distinguished from the individuals who envelop or express 'clearly' only a certain number of these singularities-events. In other words, while the expressed world 'does not exist outside of the monads which express it', the world cannot be identified with the way in which it exists in the monads, for the world is defined, prior to the constitution of worldly individuals, as the convergence of singularities as they extend themselves over series of ordinary points (LS, 110–11). As Deleuze writes, while the world exists in the individual as a predicate, it 'subsists in an entirely different manner, as an event or a verb, in the singularities which preside over the constitution of individuals' (LS, 111). We have spoken of the predicates which determine individual things as such (for example, Adam is a sinner), but these predicates are themselves determined in relation to convergent series of pre-individual events (to sin, to be redeemed, and so on) which are only subsequently realized in determined, existing individuals (Adam, Christ, and so on).

The next question Deleuze addresses in the 'Sixteenth Series', still following Leibniz in certain respects, is how the individual can transcend the world of compossible singularities-events in which it is determined in order to confront this world and constitute itself as a 'knowing subject' in relation to objects of experience, as well as in relation to other such knowing subjects. Indeed, as was made clear in the previous chapter, the problem of understanding how events are ontologically primitive in relation to 'things' is prolonged in the problem of how we are to have knowledge of these things through their events. In fact, there is in Deleuze's reading of Leibniz, as there is throughout *The Logic of Sense*, a fertile relation between these ontological and epistemological problems. They find their common denominator, as has already been seen in relation to the Stoics, in the idea that the ontologically primary pure event does not exist outside of the propositions constitutive of knowledge, be this a knowledge which, like sense, is forever being actualized. We might even say that Deleuze's ontology of events in *The Logic of Sense* is a transcendental ontology, in the sense that the world of events, which has ontological priority over worldly individuals, is not something external to the conditions of knowledge. And as will be seen, for Deleuze, this 'world of events' is itself an event which results from another, prior event, which is a synthesis of divergent worlds or divergent points of view in an intersubjective and linguistic context.

Now, we do not say that one individual knows another simply because they ontologically 'express' one another within a compossible world. We would not say, for example, that a rock knows the hammer which breaks it apart, simply because of a law-like or expressive relation between their 'concurrent requisites' (to use the Leibnizian vocabulary). Rather, when we speak of knowledge, we speak of an individual's knowledge that x, where x has propositional content which may be exhibited in language in an intersubjective context. In other words, knowledge necessarily implies a relation between 'persons', and a relation between these persons and the world, which transcends their relations within a compossible world. Indeed, this is precisely why Deleuze, in the first instance, emphasizes relations between *incompossible* worlds for the determination of knowing subjects and the 'things' they know. As he writes,

> the Ego as knowing subject appears when something is *identified* inside worlds which are nevertheless incompossible, and across series which are nevertheless divergent ... Only when something is identified between divergent series or between incompossible worlds, an object = x appears transcending individuated worlds, and the Ego which thinks it transcends worldly individuals, giving thereby to the world a new value in view of the new value of the subject which is being established. (LS, 113)

As examined above, a world is said to be incompossible with another when series of ordinary events, which depend upon a given singularity-event (analytic prolongation), diverge with series depending on another. Now, for Leibniz, since the created world is characterized by the universal convergence of series of events, such divergences must be only apparent: a by-product of the fact that no existing individual, save God, can carry out an infinite analysis of the convergent world-series of events. Indeed, Leibniz often tells us that various 'evils' – that is, events such as Christ's dying, Judas' betraying Christ, Sextus Tarquin's raping of Lucretia, and so on – can appear to us to diverge with the world created by an omnipotent, omniscient and perfectly benevolent God.[61] This divergence, however, is only apparent, for it is based on the inability to appreciate that everything is of the highest perfection there can be, either because we lack God's vision of the convergent world-series, or because we cannot perform the calculations necessary to see that a world devoid of a given evil would be a comparatively less perfect world.[62] For Leibniz, in short, because divinely conceived worlds are defined by the convergence of series of events, the relation between incompossible worlds is ultimately one of *exclusion*: either this world or another world but not both (LS, 172).

For Deleuze, however, taking up some of Leibniz's texts in a very non-Leibnizian way, we can establish a *positive* relation – that is, a relation which would no longer be, strictly speaking, one of exclusion – between incompossible worlds in terms of a *problem* which refers to certain conditions which constitute it *as* a problem (LS, 113). As he writes, a 'problem ... has conditions which necessarily include "ambiguous signs", or aleatory points, that is, diverse distributions of singularities to which different cases of solution correspond' (LS, 114, translation modified). In spelling out the nature of these 'ambiguous signs', Deleuze's main references are Leibniz's *Theodicy*, one of Leibniz's letters to Arnauld, and a much earlier mathematical text, 'On the Method of Universality' (1674).[63] In relation to this latter work, Deleuze examines the way in which, in relation to conic sections, Leibniz attempts to find the 'formula, rule, equation or construction' for which the equations of the various curves (circle, ellipse, hyperbola, parabola, straight line) are only particular cases.[64] What is crucial is that this 'universal equation' has 'ambiguous signs' or 'characters' which allow for the 'inclusion' of the different cases of conic sections. These ambiguous characters are here of two forms: a *sign*, which may be either an addition, subtraction, or a series of such operations; and a *letter*, which may be a finite, an infinitely large or an infinitely small line or number. These characters, which are ambiguous or indeterminate in the general formula, may then be 'filled in' by unambiguous signs, thereby generating the finite number of cases corresponding to the cases of conic sections. In other words, the universal equation unifies and exhibits, within an objective 'problem', the relations among the series of apparently discontinuous cases of conic sections. As Emily Grosholz concludes, 'this equation, by exhibiting the conic sections as limit cases of one general equation ... displays their mutual relations as a coherent system'.[65] Or again, as Deleuze puts it:

> the equation of conic sections expresses one and the same Event that its ambiguous sign subdivides into diverse events – circle, ellipse, hyperbola, parabola, straight line. These diverse events form so many cases corresponding to the problem and determining the genesis of the solutions. We must therefore understand that incompossible worlds, despite their incompossibility, have something in common – something objectively in common – which represents the ambiguous sign of the genetic element in relation to which several worlds appear as cases of solution for one and the same problem. (LS, 114, translation modified)

Now, although Leibniz did not explicitly treat such 'ambiguous signs' with respect to the relation between possible existences belonging to incompossible worlds, Deleuze finds several indications of such an operator in Leibniz's works. In particular, Deleuze understands the figure of Adam in one of the letters to Arnauld, as well as the figure of Sextus in the *Theodicy*, to be examples of such ambiguous signs. In other words, these figures are considered to be 'objectively indeterminate' operators within an inter-worldly 'problem' which is 'resolved' by the way in which these operators take on particular, determinate values within the incompossible worlds forming the cases of solution to the problem. Thus, in his letter to Arnauld of July 14, 1686, Leibniz responds to Arnauld's criticism that 'it is no more possible to conceive of several possible Adams, if Adam be taken as a singular nature, than it is to conceive of several "myselves"', by writing that:

> when I speak of several [possible] Adams, I do not take Adam for a determined individual but for some person conceived in a relation of generality (*sub ratione generalitatis*), under circumstances which seem to us to determine Adam to be an individual but which do not truly do so sufficiently; as for instance, when we mean by Adam the first man, whom God puts in a pleasure garden, which he leaves through sin, and from whose side God makes a woman. But all this does not sufficiently determine him, and so there might be several other disjunctively possible Adams ... But that concept which determines a certain Adam must include, absolutely, all his predicates, and it is this complete concept which determines the relation of generality in such a way as to reach an individual (*rationem generalitatis ad individuum*).[66]

As Deleuze extrapolates:

> Within these [incompossible] worlds, there is, for example, an objectively indeterminate Adam, that is, an Adam positively defined *solely* through a few singularities which can be combined and can complement each other in a very different fashion in different worlds (to be the first man, to live in a garden, to give birth to a woman from himself, etc.). The incompossible worlds [thus] become the variants of the same story. (LS, 114)

As Deleuze notes, however, in the letter to Arnauld, such a 'vague Adam has no existence; he exists only in connection with our finite understanding, and his predicates are only generalities' (LS, 346, n.4). In other words, Leibniz's primary aim here is to make a distinction between how finite individuals can conceive of a 'vague Adam' (that is, in relation to a few predicates of a general nature), and how God conceives of the complete individual concept of the existing Adam, with his infinity of determinate predicates. Deleuze, however, is more interested in defining the 'ambiguous sign' common to incompossible worlds without passing through the distinction between God and his finite creatures. He thus turns to the figure of Sextus in Leibniz's *Theodicy*.

At the end of the *Theodicy* (§§413–17), Leibniz presents us with a story of the historical figure, Sextus Tarquin. Sextus goes one day to find the God, Jupiter, whom he beseeches to change his fate. Jupiter replies that were he to renounce the then kingdom of Rome, he would be given other destinies. Sextus, however, not being able to reconcile himself to the sacrifice of the crown, leaves Jupiter's temple in a rage and abandons himself to his destiny such as we know it: to the rape of Lucretia which will bring about the collapse of the kingdom of Rome. Theodorus, the high priest, who has been watching this scene, asks Jupiter why he has not given Sextus another will. The God replies that Theodorus should go and see his daughter Pallas, who will show him what he, Jupiter, was obliged to do in order to create the world. Theodorus then finds himself transported with the goddess to the palace of destinies, where he sees representations not only of the real world but of all other possible worlds. What he sees in effect is a series of apartments organized in the form of a pyramid. In each apartment there is a possible world filled with all of the individuals of that world including, each time, a different Sextus: a Sextus happy but mediocre in Corinth, a Sextus king of Thrace, and so on. As Theodorus climbs the pyramid, these worlds with their various Sextuses become more and more beautiful, indeed, they become 'better', until finally at the summit he sees a representation of the real world, the most perfect of all, where Sextus leaves the temple, goes to Rome, rapes Lucretia, brings about the downfall of the kingdom, and so on.

For Leibniz, of course, these pages function as a kind of counterfactual proof of the goodness of God, designed to show why he could not *not* have chosen for existence the Sextus which we know, along with his evil deeds. For it is in comparing all of the possible worlds and their different Sextuses that we come to realize that the existence of the historical Sextus is an integral condition of the best of all possible worlds.[67] Deleuze's interpretation of these passages, however, is that Leibniz is inviting us to consider the pyramid with its incompossible worlds as a 'problem' which is susceptible to various orders or states. Within this problem, then, Sextus functions as an 'ambiguous sign' common to all the incompossible worlds making up the pyramid, in so far as these different worlds 'appear' depending on the different ways in which he is determined. As Deleuze writes, we

> are no longer faced with an individuated world constituted by means of already fixed singularities, organized into convergent series, nor are we faced with determined individuals which express this world. We are now faced with the aleatory point of singular points, with the ambiguous sign of singularities, or rather with that which represents this sign, and which holds good for many of these worlds, or, in the last analysis, for all

worlds, despite their divergences and the individuals which inhabit them. (LS, 114)

There is thus, following Deleuze's reading of Leibniz, a Sextus = x – or, more generally, an 'object = x' (LS, 114–15) – which is common to a number of incompossible worlds, and which forms part of the objective conditions of the 'problem' defining the positive or non-exclusionary relation between these worlds. These objects = x are thus no longer thought of as individuals determined in relation to an analytic continuum of singularities-events within a single compossible world, but rather as 'ambiguous signs' which express a non-exclusionary relation between worlds perceived as incompossible.

Now, this shift from the determined individual to the object = x also signals the necessity to rethink the nature of the predicates which would define such objects. As Deleuze explains, in relation to objects = x, predicates are no longer the analytic predicates of individuals determined within a world and carrying out the *description* of these individuals. They are rather predicates which *define* objects = x synthetically, and open different worlds and individualities to them as so many variables or possibilities. In other words, instead of each world being the analytic predicate of individuals described in series, it is rather the incompossible worlds which are the synthetic predicates of objects = x, in so far as these latter must be defined in relation to what Deleuze calls a 'disjunctive synthesis' of these incompossible worlds (LS, 115).

How then do these considerations respond to the problem of knowledge such as this was characterized above? First of all, in so far as it forms part of the conditions of the problematic relation between perceived incompossibilities, it is clear that the object = x transcends any particular individuated world. Furthermore, the individual which 'thinks', 'identifies', or synthetically defines this object = x in relation to these incompossible worlds, must itself transcend worldly individuals. Indeed, it must be at precisely the same instant that the individual gives to the world a 'new value' through the synthetic determination ('identification') of an object = x in relation to variables belonging to incompossible worlds, that it must itself be given a new value within this world. For, if individuals are relationally determined within a world in the way examined above (analytic continuum), then a world which is being supplemented with new values must entail corresponding new definitions for all of its related individuals. In other words, the individual which has become a 'knowing subject' must also be said to be synthetically defined by the kind of 'incompossible predicates' to which the object = x has exposed it.

This is not, however, the end of the story. Deleuze proceeds to argue that all objects = x are 'persons'. As he writes: 'There is thus a "vague Adam", that is, a vagabond, a nomad, an Adam = x common to several worlds, just as there is a Sextus = x or a Fang = x. In the end, there is something = x common to all worlds. All objects = x are "persons" and are [synthetically] defined by predicates' (LS, 114–15).

The reason why objects = x are 'persons' must be approached from two points of view. First of all, Deleuze writes that we are not so much concerned with the ambiguous sign *per se*, as with what *represents* this sign (LS, 114),[68] and that which represents this sign could only be a person or an 'I'. As examined in Chapter 1 in relation to the propositional dimension of manifestation, at least in the order of speech, 'it is the I which begins, and begins absolutely ... the I is primary, not only in relation to all possible denotations which are founded upon it, but also in relation to the significations which it envelops' (LS, 15). In this sense, persons correspond with what Leibniz calls 'minds' or 'spirits', that is, rational and conscious monads capable of thinking, willing and conversing among themselves. They not only perceive or represent the world relatively clearly and have memory, they are also capable of inference and reflexive self-consciousness and may approach God's understanding of the world of which they are a part, though only with respect to a limited portion of it.[69] Limited in this way, of course, as argued above, a particular person's perception of the world of which they are a part may diverge from the perceptions of others. But for Deleuze, it appears, it will be by positing an object = x open to different possible worlds that the person will be able to formulate the 'problem' corresponding to the positive, non-exclusionary relation between these worlds, and then resolve that problem by representing that object = x in a particular way.

On the other hand, however, Deleuze writes that objects = x simply *are* persons. So what could it mean to say that a person synthesizes incompossible worlds by representing an object = x, if this object = x is itself a person? In short, and although Leibniz never puts it in quite this way, it appears that Deleuze wants to argue that there is at work here what Donald Davidson calls a process of 'triangulation', whereby knowledge of the world cannot be separated from knowledge of oneself (that is, of the contents of one's beliefs) as well as knowledge of other persons or minds.

Now, 'triangulation' in Davidson's work is designed to respond to the problem of correlating a concept with some as yet unknown object, but without presupposing the concept as already given. As he writes:

> It takes [at least] two points of view to give a location to the cause of a thought [i.e., perception], and thus to define its content. We may think of it as a form of triangulation: each of two people is reacting differentially to sensory stimuli streaming in from a certain direction. Projecting the incoming lines outward, the common cause is at their intersection. If the two people now note each other's reactions (in the case of language, verbal reactions), each can correlate these observed reactions with his or her stimuli from the world. A common cause has been determined. The triangle which gives content to thought and speech is complete. But it takes two to triangulate.[70]

How can this concept of triangulation be translated back into the Deleuzian-Leibnizian vocabulary we have here been employing? It is by arguing that the reason why objects = x are to be understood as persons is that the 'unknowns' which condition the positive relation between incompossible worlds refer to a problematic relation between persons or knowing subjects. In other words, the knowing subject does not *directly* represent some unknown thing (object = x) which defines a problematic but non-exclusionary relation between incompossible worlds. Rather, the knowing subject stands in a problematic relation to another such subject in an intersubjective and linguistic context, which is to say that inter-worldly problems are interpersonal problems. It thus follows that both subjects' mutual 'identification' of one another (that is, of their behaviour, the meaning of their verbal activity, the contents of their beliefs, their behaviour *vis-à-vis* further persons, and so on) is a necessary condition for resolving a problematic but positive or non-exclusionary relation between different ways in which the world can be perceived. The problem of the relation between incompossible worlds will thus be resolved to the extent that a three-fold determination takes place: that of the beliefs of a knowing subject, that of the beliefs of another knowing subject, and that of a common world of individuals corresponding to these beliefs. And this three-fold determination conforms quite precisely to Deleuze's resolution of the problem of knowledge, such as this was cited above: when something is identified between divergent series or between incompossible worlds, an object = x or person appears transcending individuated worlds, and the person which thinks it transcends worldly individuals, thereby giving to the world a new value in view of the new value of the subject which is being established. And as was also examined above, for Deleuze, these persons are defined by predicates: no longer the analytic predicates which carry out the description of individuals determined within a world, but predicates which define persons synthetically in relation to disjunctive syntheses of incompossible worlds, opening these divergent worlds and their corresponding individuals to them as so many variables or possibilities.

Of course, in Leibniz, there is a 'person' who is common to *all* possible worlds: God. As Deleuze writes, as

> far as the absolutely common object in general is concerned, with respect to which all worlds are variables, its predicates are the first possibles [*premiers possibles*] or the categories ... The universal Ego is, precisely, the person corresponding to something = x common to all worlds, just as the other egos are the persons corresponding to a particular thing = x common to several worlds. (LS, 115, translation modified)

The 'first possibles', in this citation, refer of course to the 'irreducible concepts' or 'absolute attributes of God'.[71] As has been seen, for Leibniz, it is because God is ontologically determined by his attributes or perfections that he brings into existence a unique and maximally compossible world of singularities-events: the best of all possible worlds. Indeed, it is for this precise reason that any incompossibilities perceived by the individual substances belonging to the created world are merely apparent. But now, if we also take into account the Leibnizian idea that whatever the created monads perceive has always-already been included by God in their concepts, it can be said that God, as a determined object = x, is absolutely common to all perceptions of apparently incompossible worlds. Conversely, if finite, created individuals *were* able to show that perceived incompossibilities such as various 'evil' events are in fact integral parts of the same, maximally compossible world – the best of all possible worlds – then these individuals would have effectively proved that God, in choosing this world for existence, evils and all, is all wise, all powerful, all good, and so on.[72] Leibniz's God, therefore, can be thought of in this sense as a 'person', determined in a triangular structure along with other persons and worldly individuals.

Nevertheless, it is also clear that Leibniz's 'ontological proof' for the nature and existence of God requires no recourse to such triangulation, relying as it does only on the principle of contradiction.[73] As was seen, it is precisely because the nature of God can be determined independently in this way that the convergence of the world-series of singularities-events is guaranteed and that perceived incompossibilities are merely apparent. Crucially, then, for the problem which guides our work in this chapter, Leibniz ultimately determines the 'ideal play' of singularities-events with reference to an underlying substance: God. In other words, individuals and persons, for Leibniz, are not determined by singularities-events 'all the way down'. Rather, the events which determine individuals and persons are themselves determined with reference to God.

How, then, must the Leibnizian system be modified such that it can be said that events, considered only from the point of view of their ideal play, govern the genesis of worldly things? In short, following Deleuze, two requirements must be met: divergences must be 'affirmed' *as* divergences, and the persons who are 'common' to these divergences must always be considered as 'produced forms', brought about only by the play of converging and diverging events (LS, 113, 116, 172). Indeed, these two requirements are interrelated, for if persons are always derived from the play of events, there can be no original or divine point of view from which it can be said that divergent worlds are reducible to the same world which is in principle identifiable. And conversely, if incompossible worlds are affirmed *as* incompossible (as opposed to 'apparently' incompossible), then persons, unable to finally resolve divergences, remain forever 'open' to further (re-)determinations within the above analyzed structure of 'triangulation'.[74]

With regard to the first requirement of affirming divergences, Deleuze writes that 'Leibniz did not attain the free character of this play [of singularities-events], since he neither wanted nor knew how to breathe enough chance into it, or to make of divergence an object of affirmation as such' (LS, 113–14).[75] What, then, does it mean to affirm divergences? We shall return to this question at greater length in Chapter 3, but Deleuze does expand upon this idea in the 'Twenty-Fourth Series of the Communication of Events', immediately after his critique of the Stoics and his heralding of Leibniz as the 'first' (though obviously not the last) 'important theoretician of the event' (LS, 171). In this series, Deleuze argues that to affirm divergences means that different 'things' must be affirmed through difference rather than through identity. In other words, instead of a 'form of identity' determining things in their differences, it must be difference itself which relates things together in so far as they are different (LS, 172–3). What this implies is that, instead of a certain number of predicates being excluded from a thing in so far as this would contradict the form of identity guaranteed by the existence of God (maximally compossible world), each 'thing' must be open to the infinity of predicates through which it passes (LS, 174). Or to put it another way, as Deleuze does somewhat poetically, we must speak of the communication of series of singularities-events, no longer with reference to a world (cosmos), but within a 'chaosmos' (chaos-cosmos) (LS, 174). What then causes events to communicate within this 'affirmative synthetic disjunction' is 'the erection of a paradoxi-cal instance . . . which traverses the divergent series as divergent and causes them to resonate' (LS, 174). But in fact, we have shown that this paradoxical instance is an object = x or 'person' common to incompossible worlds, but never 'given' independently of a rela-tion to other such persons within a process of triangulation. This is what Deleuze means when he writes that, in affirming divergences, 'the ideational centre of convergence [the object = x or person] is by nature perpetually decentred, it serves only to affirm divergence' (LS, 174–5).

This leads us to our second point: that of understanding this para-doxical instance – this person – as always produced and never origi-nary. Indeed, Deleuze writes that, in 'truth, the person is Ulysses, no one [*elle n'est personne*] properly speaking, but a produced form, derived from this impersonal transcendental field' (LS, 116). Deleuze is here playing on the homophony between the French noun *per-sonne* or 'person' and the pronoun *personne* or 'nobody', but there is also a deeper, philosophical transformation at stake. Indeed, we have seen how the person is determined or identified as such (with respect to their beliefs, behaviours, and so on) within a triangular structure involving another person and an object of experience, and such that each 'point' of the triangle must be determined only in relation to the other two. Within such a structure, therefore, there is no unproduced 'point of view': every point of view could only be a 'result' of triangulation. If, however, there are no unproduced points of view, then there is no guarantee that perceived divergences could be reduced to a convergence, from which it also follows that persons remain 'open' to further determinations. In this sense, the person is never an underlying substance but itself an event, produced entirely by syntheses of singularities-events within processes of triangulation.

Deleuze confirms this productive relation of triangulation in the 'Twenty-Fifth Series of Univocity' when he writes that it is

> necessary for the individual to grasp himself as an event; and that he also grasp the event actualized within him as another individual grafted onto him. In this case, he would not understand, want, or represent this event without also understanding and wanting all other events as individuals, and without representing all other individuals as events ... [T]he individual, born of what comes to pass, affirm[s] his distance [i.e., difference] with respect to every other event. As the individual affirms the distance, he follows and joins it, passing through all the other individuals implied by the other events, and extracts from it a unique Event which is once again himself. (LS, 178, translation modified)[76]

Or again, more poetically, in the 'Twenty-Fourth Series of the Communication of Events':

> Leibniz ... subjected the points of view to exclusive rules such that each opened itself onto the others only in so far as they converged: the points of view on the same town ... [O]n the contrary, the point of view is opened onto a divergence which it affirms: another town corresponds to each point of view, each point of view is another town, the towns are linked only by their distance and resonate only through the divergence of their series, their houses and their streets. There is always another town within the town ... [D]ivergence is no longer a principle of exclusion, and disjunction no longer a means of separation. Incompossibility is now a means of communication. (LS, 173–4)[77]

But now a question arises: if, for Deleuze, persons are always produced – if, in other words, there is no uncreated creator – what brings about the convergence of singularities-events which determine worldly *individuals* in the first place? Deleuze does not address this point directly, even though he continues to maintain that '[i]ndividuals are infinite analytic propositions' even after affirming that the person is 'nobody' (LS, 118). So how must the individual and its analytic predicates of existence now be understood, in the absence of God's divine ordering of them? It appears that Deleuze wants to argue, relatively uncontroversially, that the individual concepts which make up the actual world must, quite simply, be consistent with one another. In other words, if something is an individual in a given world, its concept must be consistent with those of the other individuals in that world. Indeed, this is only another way of saying that the world in question, if it is to be a world, must be law-like. Therefore, in so far as it is necessary for the definition of worldly individuals as such, the notion of consistency – or rather, of convergence – will be an integral part of the Deleuzian system. Thus, even if worldly consistency is no longer grounded in a divine act as it is for Leibniz, convergence will still be understood as the 'analytic prolongation' of singular events over series of ordinary events, up to the neighbourhood of another singularity-event; and this convergence of series of events will still be ontologically prior to the way in which determined individuals 'express' the world-series in their variably distinct and obscure 'concurrent requisites'.

Now, if consistency or convergence is a necessary requirement for the determination of a world and the individuals which express it in law-like ways, how must we understand the further idea, examined above, that individuals are determined by relations between persons who are common to *divergent* worlds? First of all, it has been said that divergent worlds appear as a consequence of the fact that persons are, like any worldly thing, 'finite with respect to their clear expression', that is, with respect to the 'corporeal zone of expression' or perceptual apparatus in terms of which they express their relations with the world (LS, 118). And again, that knowing subjects are 'finite' in this way is a relatively uncontroversial claim. Nevertheless, as has also been seen, persons transcend their immediate worldly determinations in so far as they bring about syntheses of divergent worlds within a triangular structure simultaneously implicating other persons and a world of determined individuals corresponding to the beliefs of these persons. As Deleuze puts it, persons are grounded on individuals and, conversely, individuals are grounded by the person (LS, 118). With respect to these syntheses, then, the person as a knowing subject will be said to have been synthetically defined in relation to the divergent worlds. On the other hand, in accordance with the requirement noted above, the world of individuals synthesized out of the incompossible worlds will still be said to have resulted from a continuum of converging singularities-events; *but now, this convergence must be considered to have been generated by the same synthesis of incompossible worlds which defined the knowing subject*. In other words, even though convergence is a necessary relation with respect to determined worlds and worldly individuals, this must here be seen to be generated by prior divergences and 'disjunctive syntheses' in relation to persons. So it is in this sense that, as was said earlier, the law-like 'world' of events – which has priority over determined, worldly individuals – is not something external to the conditions of knowledge. The world and, by consequence, its individuals and persons, are rather constituted, as events, by these conditions. In other words, Deleuze's ontology of events, whereby events are ontologically prior to substances 'all the way down', is a transcendental ontology.

Several other important points must be borne in mind in relation to syntheses of incompossible worlds. First of all, because these syntheses are brought about by persons having a finite zone of clear expression, these syntheses must themselves be considered to be finite. Secondly, as has been seen, since there is no 'original' substance which would guarantee the reducibility of divergences to an underlying convergence, persons and individuals will always remain *open* to further determinations. Indeed, Deleuze puts these two points together when he argues that persons 'are finite synthetic propositions: finite with respect to their definition, indefinite with respect to their application' (LS, 118). Thirdly and finally, because the continuum of converging singularities-events is, on the one hand, a necessary relation for the determination of worlds and worldly individuals, and on the other hand, effectively generated by any number of prior syntheses of divergent worlds, it must be considered to be at once basic *and* infinitely divisible. In relation to this infinitely divisible continuum, then, individuals must correspondingly be understood to be 'infinite analytic propositions', that is, infinite with respect to what they 'obscurely' express, but 'finite with respect to their clear expression' (LS, 118). In other words, while in Leibniz individuals were held to be infinite analytic propositions because they expressed in various and complementary degrees of clarity and obscurity the same infinite world brought into existence by God, in Deleuze they are infinite analytic propositions because they express a 'chaosmos' which is infinitely divisible in relation to persons understood as 'nobody': the aleatory points of singular points (LS, 114, 176). As Deleuze poetically expresses it:

> Everything [now] happens through the resonance of disparates, point of view on a point of view, displacement of perspective, differentiation of difference . . . It is true that the form of the self ordinarily guarantees the connection of a series; that the form of the world guarantees the convergence of continuous and prolongable series; and that the form of God, as Kant had clearly seen, guarantees disjunction in its exclusive or limitative sense. But when disjunction accedes to the principle which gives to it a synthetic and affirmative value, the self, the world, and God share in a common death, to the advantage of divergent series as such . . . The divergence of the affirmed series forms a 'chaosmos' and no longer a world; the

aleatory point which traverses them forms a counter-self, and no longer a self; the disjunction posed as a synthesis exchanges its theological principle for a diabolic principle . . . Nothing other than the Event subsists, the Event alone . . . which communicates with itself through its own distance and resonates across all of its disjuncts. (LS, 175–6, translation modified)

So, in accordance with the problem with which we began this chapter, it can now be seen how denoted individuals and manifested persons are reciprocally determined, and in an ongoing way, by relations of convergence and divergence between singularities-events and without any reference to an underlying, substantial unity. This is precisely what Deleuze means by the 'static ontological genesis'. But now, what about the dimension of conceptual signification? How can general concepts be said to be determined by this ideal play of events? It should be noted that Deleuze addresses this issue in very sparing terms. Nevertheless, in light of our above analyses, several highly condensed passages in the Sixteenth and Seventeenth Series provide us with a sufficient number of signposts to reconstruct this 'static logical genesis'.

Deleuze writes that 'the variables which realize the possibilities of a person' must be treated as 'concepts which necessarily signify classes and properties, and therefore as essentially affected by an increasing or decreasing generality' (LS, 115). What does this mean? The first point that should be made is that these 'properties and classes are quite distinct from the individual aggregates of the first level' (LS, 115). Indeed, we saw that the analytic predicates of existence at this first level were akin to tropes or 'completely localizable' abstract particulars. In so far as they translate actual structures of trope-like events, then, determined individuals and persons considered in relation to these predicates of existence are 'ontological propositions' (LS, 118). Generalities, on the contrary, 'appear only when [such] a predicate is determined in a [logical] proposition to function as the subject of another predicate' (LS, 112). In other words, generalities appear to be, in Deleuze, founded upon structured classes of tropes or actual events.[78] But the whole question is: what grounds this structuring operation?

In fact, Deleuze posits *a relation of mutual determination between logical and ontological propositions*, a relation which is itself grounded on the person. As Deleuze explains, whilst on the one hand, the variables which effectively come to realize the possibilities of a person must be treated as general concepts which necessarily signify classes and properties, on the other hand, these properties and classes are themselves

> grounded in the order of the person. This is because persons themselves are primarily *classes having one single member*, and their predicates are *properties having one constant*. Each person is the sole member of his or her class, a class which is, nevertheless, constituted by the worlds, possibilities, and individuals which pertain to it. Classes as multiples, and properties as variables, derive from these classes with one single member and these properties with one constant. (LS, 115)

Now, it is common for trope theorists to say that an individual is strictly equivalent to its set of 'compresent' tropes.[79] Deleuze, however, wants to extend this idea to persons who, as has been seen, are understood as synthetically defined in relation to incompossible worlds within a triangular structure implicating other such persons. What is interesting here is thus that the incompossible worlds implicated in the process of triangulation or disjunctive synthesis are structurally or virtually 'compresent' with the person who is helping to bring about this synthesis. It thus follows that in order to define persons and describe individuals within a world which would be synthesized out of incompossible worlds, relations must be sought between the individual 'tropes' constitutive of the entities expressing these different possible worlds. These relations will thus effectively be realized by means of variable and overlapping classes of tropes, that is to say, in relation to the logical proposition, in concepts of increasing and decreasing generality. As Deleuze puts it with his characteristic (and often frustrating) brevity, whilst a particular world or 'garden may contain a red rose . . . there are in other worlds or in other gardens roses which are not red and flowers which are not roses' (LS, 115). What Deleuze is gesturing at with this example is a synthesis of related and overlapping classes of tropes at different levels of generality: a trope of redness → the class of all rednesses → the class of all colours; a trope of roseness → the class of all rosenesses → the class of all flowers, and so on. These general classes allow us to determine a world of individuals common to incompossible worlds, that is to say, a world of differently coloured types of flower which had initially belonged to divergent gardens. What is more, at the same time that these classes and properties are determined, it will be able to be said that the individuals and persons which have been synthesized out of the divergent worlds 'exemplify' them, precisely because these overlapping classes of tropes were established by the process of triangulation whose very aim was the determination of these persons and individuals.[80] Again, it is by exemplifying in various ways the properties resulting from synthesized classes of tropes that individuals and persons will be said to share one and the same world.

Deleuze sums up this relation of mutual determination between the logical and ontological propositions when he writes that, even though classes and properties ontologically depend on a relation between persons in an intersubjective and linguistic context (triangulation), these classes are also embodied in the logical proposition. Or, put another way, being ontologically dependent on a relation between persons, structured classes of tropes constitute the condition or form of possibility of the logical proposition. But at the same time, within the logical proposition, they constitute this form of possibility only in so far as the individuals and persons on which they depend 'realize' the relations constitutive of the logical proposition: denotation (relation to the individual), manifestation (relation to the person's beliefs and desires) and signification (relation to general concepts and conceptual relations bearing on individuals and persons). In Deleuze's own words:

The third element of the ontological genesis ... namely the multiple classes and variable properties which in turn depend on persons, is not embodied in a third proposition which would again be ontological. Rather, this element sends us over [*nous fait passer*] to another order of the proposition. It constitutes the condition or the form of possibility of the logical proposition in general. In relation to this condition and simultaneously within it, individuals and persons no longer play the role of ontological propositions. They act now as material instances which realize the possibility and determine within the logical proposition the relations necessary to the existence of the conditioned (*conditionné*): the relation of denotation as the relation to the individual (the world, the state of affairs, the aggregate, individuated bodies); the relation of manifestation as the relation to the personal; and the relation of signification defined by the form of possibility. We are thus better able to understand the complexity of the question: what is primary in the order of the logical proposition? For, if signification is primary as the condition or form of possibility, it nevertheless refers to manifestation, to the extent that the multiple classes and variable properties defining signification are grounded, in the ontological order, upon the person; as for the manifestation, it refers to denotation to the extent that the person is grounded upon the individual. (LS, 118–19, translation modified)

After laying out the 'static logical genesis' in this way, Deleuze goes on to emphasize that, although individuals, persons and general concepts are produced by disjunctive syntheses in an intersubjective and linguistic context – that is, in a relation of mutual determination between the ontological and the logical propositions – these two types of proposition remain irreducible to one another. As he writes, reiterating the essential aspects of what we have called the process of triangulation:

> between the logical genesis and the ontological genesis there is no parallelism. There is rather a relay which permits every sort of shifting and jamming. It is therefore too simple to argue for the correspondence between the individual and denotation, the person and manifestation, multiple classes or variable properties and signification. It is true that the relation of denotation may only be established in a world which is subject to the various aspects of individuation, but this is not sufficient. Besides continuity, denotation requires that an identity be posited and made dependent upon the manifest order of the person. This is what we previously indicated when we said that denotation presupposes manifestation. Conversely, when the person is manifested or expressed in the proposition, this does not occur independently of individuals, states of affairs, or states of bodies, which, not content with being denoted, form so many cases and possibilities in relation to the person's desires, beliefs, or constitutive projects. Finally, signification presupposes the formation of a good sense which comes about with individuation, just as the formation of a common sense finds its source in the person. It implicates an entire play of denotation and manifestation both in the power to affirm premises and in the power to state the conclusion. There is therefore, as we have seen, a very complex structure in view of which each of the three relations of the logical proposition is, in turn, primary. This structure as a whole forms the tertiary arrangement of language. (LS, 119)

We can thus finally see what we wanted to show in this chapter, namely, that the 'tertiary arrangement of language', and the circular relation between its dimensions, is entirely produced by relations of convergence and divergence between singularities-events, and without any reference to any underlying, substantial unity such as Leibniz's God or the Stoics' Zeus. In other words, Deleuze has effectively re-described, in neo-Leibnizian terms, the 'unconditioned' 'fourth dimension of sense' which makes the tri-dimensional model of the proposition function entirely from within. Indeed, not only does this play of singularities-events 'engender the logical proposition with its determinate dimensions (denotation, manifestation, and signification); it engenders also the objective correlates of this proposition which were themselves first produced as ontological propositions (the denoted, the manifested and the signified)' (LS, 120).[81] This 'fourth dimension of sense' is thus nothing other than the 'static genesis' itself, taken in both its ontological and logical aspects.

*   *   *

It has thus been seen in this chapter how Deleuze initially follows Leibniz in arguing that the determination of individuals and persons – or 'monads' in the Leibnizian vocabulary – presupposes relations of convergence and divergence between singularities-events. However, for Deleuze, Leibniz was not able to reach the point of affirming the full ontological priority of events over substances, since, for him, relations between events are ultimately determined with reference to a given, divine substance. Leibniz, let us recall, only made a *negative* use of divergence, in so far as his God brings into existence a single, maximally compossible world, and excludes from existence anything incompossible with this world. Deleuze, however, extending certain Leibnizian concepts such as the 'ambiguous sign', argues that divergence must rather be affirmed as such. This affirmation of divergence effectively consists of the erection of a paradoxical instance – the object = x or person understood as 'nobody' – which causes all of the divergent series of events to communicate through their differences. Within a 'triangular' structure implicating persons and their beliefs, a chaosmos of incompossible world-series, and language, disjunctive syntheses are then carried out which generate determined individuals, persons, concepts and the relations between them.

Now, in order to explain Deleuze's relation to and critique of Leibniz, we have imported several philosophical concepts which cannot, strictly speaking, be found in *The Logic of Sense*: triangulation and tropes, in particular. We believe that these concepts capture, in a very precise way, what is at stake in Deleuze's *dépassement* of Leibniz. Nevertheless, Deleuze himself refers to other concepts and philosophical figures in order to develop his neo-Leibnizian take on the ontological priority of events. These concepts and figures will be the subject of Chapter 3.

Notes

1. There are only a few works devoted to Deleuze's philosophical relation to Leibniz, and all of these concern Deleuze's 1988 work on Leibniz,

The Fold. See Alain Badiou, 'G. Deleuze, Leibniz: Le Pli et le baroque', *Annuaire philosophique 1988–1989* (Paris: Seuil, 1989), pp. 161–84; Lang Baker, 'The Cry of the Identicals: The Problem of Inclusion in Deleuze's Reading of Leibniz', *Philosophy Today* 39: 2 (1995), pp. 198–211; Elie During, 'Leibniz selon Deleuze: une folle création de concepts', *Magazine Littéraire* 416 (2003), pp. 36–7; Christiane Frémont, 'Complication et Singularité', *Revue de métaphysique et de moral* 1 (1991), pp. 105–20; Keith Robinson, 'Events of Difference: The Fold in Between Deleuze's Reading of Leibniz', *Epoché* 8: 1 (2003), pp. 141–64. There is also a recently published collection on *The Fold*: Niamh McDonnell and Sjoerd van Tuinen (eds), *Deleuze and The Fold: A Critical Reader* (Hampshire: Palgrave Macmillan, 2010).

2. See, for example, Todd May, *Gilles Deleuze: An Introduction* (Cambridge: Cambridge University Press, 2005); Michael Hardt, *Gilles Deleuze: An Apprenticeship in Philosophy* (Minneapolis: University of Minnesota Press, 1993).

3. See Gilles Deleuze, *Expressionism in Philosophy: Spinoza*, trans. Martin Joughin (New York: Zone Books, 1990), p. 11: 'What interested me most in Spinoza wasn't his Substance, but the composition of finite modes. I consider this one of the most original aspects of my book. That is: the hope of making substance turn on finite modes, or at least of seeing in substance a *plane of immanence* in which finite modes operate, already appears in this book. What I needed was both (1) the expressive character of particular individuals, and (2) an immanence of being. Leibniz, in a way, goes still further than Spinoza on the first point. But on the second, Spinoza stands alone. One finds it only in him. This is why I consider myself a Spinozist, rather than a Leibnizian, although I owe a lot to Leibniz'. In fact, with regard to the concept of 'expression', Deleuze goes even further when he writes that 'no explicit definition or demonstration of expression is to be found in Spinoza (even though such a definition and such a demonstration are implicit throughout his work). In Leibniz, on the other hand, one finds passages that deal explicitly with what is comprised in the category of expression, and how far it extends' (ibid., pp. 327–8).

4. Deleuze, *The Fold*, p. 53. Although Deleuze here seems to revise his argument from *The Logic of Sense* that Leibniz was the first important theoretician of the event, it should be noted that the above citation from *The Logic of Sense* occurs immediately after Deleuze's critique of the Stoics, examined in Chapter 1, which shows how they ultimately failed to think the 'ideal play of events'.

5. Gilles Deleuze, *Negotiations 1972–1990*, trans. Martin Joughin (New York: Columbia University Press, 1995), p. 141.

6. On the 'principle of economy', see also Frémont, 'Complication et Singularité', n. 10.

7. On the concepts of 'compossibility' and 'incompossibility', see G.W. Leibniz, 'Letter to Louis Bourguet, December 1714', in *Gottfried Wilhelm Leibniz: Philosophical Papers and Letters*, trans. and ed. Leroy E. Loemker (Dordrecht: D. Reidel Publishing, 1969), pp. 661–2. See also G.W. Leibniz, *New Essays on Human Understanding*, trans. and ed. Peter Remnant and Jonathan Bennett (Cambridge: Cambridge University Press, 1996), III, vi, §12. This concept of compossibility is fundamental to all of Leibniz's most important works, even if it is not always mentioned by name. See, for example, G.W. Leibniz, *Monadology*, in *Leibniz: Philosophical Writings*, ed. G.H.R. Parkinson, trans. Mary Morris and G.H.R. Parkinson (London and Toronto: J.M. Dent and Sons, 1973), §56; *Principles of Nature and Grace, Founded on Reason*, in *Philosophical Writings*, §10; *Discourse on Metaphysics*, in *G.W. Leibniz: Philosophical Essays*, trans. and ed. Roger Ariew and Daniel Garber (Indianapolis and Cambridge: Hackett Publishing Company, 1989), §9 and §14; *Theodicy: Essays on the Goodness of God, the Freedom of Man and the Origin of Evil*, trans. E.M. Huggard (London: Routledge and Kegan Paul Ltd, 1951), §201.

8. Leibniz, *Monadology*, §43; *Principles of Nature and Grace*, §10.

9. Leibniz, *Monadology*, §31. See also G.W. Leibniz, 'On Freedom and Possibility', in *Philosophical Essays*, p. 19: 'all truths that concern possibles or essences and the impossibility of a thing or its necessity (that is, the impossibility of its contrary) rest on the principle of contradiction'.

10. Leibniz, 'Letter to Bourguet, December 1714', p. 662. See also G.W. Leibniz, 'General Inquiries about the Analysis of Concepts and of Truths', in *Leibniz: Logical Papers*, trans. and ed. G.H.R. Parkinson (Oxford: Clarendon Press, 1966), p. 54.

11. 'The compossible is that which, with another, does not imply a contradiction.' G.W. Leibniz, *Textes inédits d'après de la bibliothèque provinciale de Hanover, 2 volumes*, trans. and ed. Gaston Grua (Paris, 1948), p. 325. Cited in Benson Mates, *The Philosophy of Leibniz: Metaphysics and Language* (Oxford: Oxford University Press, 1986), p. 75, n. 36.

12. See generally, Leibniz, 'Correspondence with Arnauld', in *Philosophical Papers and Letters*, pp. 331–50.

13. Leibniz, *Monadology*, §53.

14. Nicholas Rescher, *The Philosophy of Leibniz* (Englewood Cliffs, NJ: Prentice-Hall, 1967), p. 17.

15. C.I. Gerhardt, *Die philosophischen Schriften von G.W. Leibniz*, 7 vols (Berlin: Weidmann, 1850–1863), VI, p. 107. Cited in Nicholas Rescher, *Leibniz: An Introduction to his Philosophy* (Oxford: Basil Blackwell, 1979), p. 49.

16. Leibniz, *Monadology*, §55 and §58; *Principles of Nature and Grace*, §10.

17. Leibniz, *Discourse on Metaphysics*, §1.
18. Leibniz, *Monadology*, §55.
19. Leibniz's argument that the existence of God *necessarily* follows from his concept is a recasting of Descartes' 'Ontological Argument' in relation to the principle of contradiction. In short, Leibniz supplements the argument that if we conceive of God as a being having all perfections to the highest possible degree, and if existence is such a perfection, then God exists by definition, by showing that the idea of a being having all conceivable perfections is not contradictory. God is thus a necessary, existing being and this can be known *a priori* or by reason alone. See Leibniz, *Monadology*, §41 and §45; and 'Letter to Countess Elizabeth, On God and Formal Logic', in *Philosophical Essays*, pp. 237–8.
20. On Leibniz's 'principle of the identity of indiscernibles', see, *Discourse on Metaphysics*, §9; and 'Primary Truths', in *Philosophical Essays*, p. 32. See also Leibniz's 'Fourth Letter to Clarke', in *Philosophical Essays*, p. 328: 'To suppose two things indiscernible is to suppose the same thing under two names.'
21. Leibniz, *Monadology*, §56.
22. G.W. Leibniz, 'Letter to Arnauld, October 9, 1687', in *Philosophical Papers and Letters*, p. 339.
23. Leibniz, *Discourse on Metaphysics*, §8.
24. Ibid., §9.
25. Ibid., §8 and §14.
26. Leibniz, *Monadology*, §1 and §3.
27. Ibid., §§4–6.
28. Leibniz, *Principles of Nature and Grace*, §2.
29. Leibniz, *Monadology*, §3 and §7.
30. Leibniz, 'Primary Truths', p. 33.
31. Leibniz, *Monadology*, §52.
32. G.W. Leibniz, 'Letter to Arnauld, 28 November/8 December, 1686', in *Philosophical Essays*, p. 79; and 'Primary Truths', p. 34.
33. Leibniz, *Monadology*, §66; and *Principles of Nature and Grace*, §1.
34. Leibniz, *Monadology*, §67.
35. Ibid., §§28–30 and §82.
36. Ibid., §§14–15; and *Principles of Nature and Grace*, §2.
37. Leibniz, *Principles of Nature and Grace*, §13; *New Essays*, pp. 53–4.
38. Speaking of events as 'singularities' – and we shall see more closely what this means in Chapter 3 – Deleuze also writes that in 'each world, the individual monads express all the singularities of this world – an infinity – as though in a murmur or a swoon; but each monad envelops or expresses "clearly" a certain number of singularities only, that is, *those in the vicinity of which it is constituted and which link up with its own body*' (LS, 111).

39. Leibniz, *Monadology*, §62.
40. Ibid., §70; *Principles of Nature and Grace*, §4.
41. G.W. Leibniz, 'Letter to de Volder, 30 June, 1704', and 'Letter to de Volder, 1704 or 1705', in *Philosophical Essays*, p. 181.
42. G.W. Leibniz, 'Notes on Some Comments by Michel Angelo Fardella', in *Philosophical Essays*, p. 103.
43. Leibniz, 'Fifth Letter to Clarke', in *Philosophical Essays*, p. 339.
44. Rescher, *Leibniz: An Introduction to his Philosophy*, p. 56.
45. Leibniz, 'Letter to Des Bosses, April 21, 1714', in *Philosophical Papers and Letters*, p. 609.
46. Leibniz, *Discourse on Metaphysics*, §8 and §13.
47. See also Leibniz, *Monadology*, §33.
48. Ibid., §§31–6.
49. Leibniz, *Principles of Nature and Grace*, §7.
50. For Leibniz's ontological proof, see n. 19 above.
51. Leibniz, *Monadology*, §§36–8.
52. Leibniz, *Discourse on Metaphysics*, §8.
53. See G.W. Leibniz, 'The Source of Contingent Truths' and 'Meditations on Knowledge, Truth and Ideas', in *Philosophical Essays*, p. 99 and p. 25.
54. See, on this, Leibniz, *Discourse on Metaphysics*, §13; and 'Letter to Landgraf Ernst von Hessen-Rheinfels, 12 April, 1686', in *Philosophical Writings*, p. 49.
55. See also on this, n. 19 above.
56. Leibniz, 'General Inquiries about the Analysis of Concepts and of Truths', p. 77.
57. See also on this Simon Duffy, 'Leibniz, Mathematics and the Monad', in McDonnell and van Tuinen (eds), *Deleuze and The Fold: A Critical Reader*, pp. 89–111.
58. See G.W. Leibniz, 'Draft of a Letter to Arnauld, 8 December, 1686), in *Philosophical Writings*, pp. 63–4. On the distinct and obscure, see also Leibniz, 'Meditations on Knowledge, Truth, and Ideas'.
59. The 'notion of an individual includes considered as possible what, in fact, is true, that is, considerations related to the existence of things and to time'. See Leibniz, 'Letter to Arnauld, May, 1686', in *Philosophical Essays*, p. 70.
60. For a classic account of trope theory, see Donald C. Williams, 'On the Elements of Being', *Review of Metaphysics* 7 (1953–1954), pp. 3–18 and pp. 171–92. For a more contemporary account, see Cynthia Macdonald, 'Tropes and Other Things', in Laurence and Macdonald (eds), *Contemporary Readings in the Foundations of Metaphysics*, pp. 329–50.
61. See, for example, Leibniz, *Discourse on Metaphysics*, §3; *Theodicy*, §§414–16.

62. See particularly on this, G.W. Leibniz, *On the Ultimate Origination of Things*, in *Philosophical Essays*, pp. 153–4.

63. G.W. Leibniz, 'De la méthode de l'universalité', in *Opuscules et fragments inédits de Leibniz*, ed. Louis Couturat (Hildesheim: Georg Olms, 1961), pp. 97–122, partially translated as 'On the Method of Universality', in *Leibniz: Selections*, ed. Philip P. Wiener (New York: Charles Scribner's Sons, 1951), pp. 3–4.

64. See 'De la méthode de l'universalité', pp. 115–17. See also on this Laurence Bouquiaux, 'La notion de *point de vue* dans l'élaboration de la métaphysique leibnizienne', in Benoît Timmermans (ed.), *Perspective Leibniz, Whitehead, Deleuze* (Paris: Vrin, 2006), pp. 34–5.

65. Emily R. Grosholz, 'Studies for the Infinitesimal Calculus', in *Representation and Productive Ambiguity in Mathematics and the Sciences* (Oxford: Oxford University Press, 2007), p. 212.

66. Leibniz, 'Letter to Arnauld, July 14, 1686', in *Philosophical Papers and Letters*, p. 335.

67. See also on this, Christiane Frémont, *Singularités, individus et relations dans le système de Leibniz* (Paris: Vrin, 2003), pp. 79–103; and Sean Bowden, 'Deleuze, Leibniz and the Jurisprudence of Being', in *Pli (The Warwick Journal of Philosophy)* 17 (2006), pp. 108–9.

68. '[I]ncompossible worlds, despite their incompossibility, have something in common – something objectively in common – which *represents* the ambiguous sign of the genetic element in relation to which several worlds appear as instances of solution for one and the same problem … We are now faced with the aleatory point of singular points, with the ambiguous sign of singularities, *or rather with that which represents this sign*' (LS, 114, emphasis added).

69. Leibniz, *Principles of Nature and Grace*, §5 and §§14–15: 'As regards the rational soul or *mind*, there is in it something more than in monads, or even in simple souls. It is not only a mirror of the universe of created things, but also an image of the Deity. The mind not only has a perception of the works of God, but is even capable of producing something like them, though on a small scale … For this reason all minds … entering as they do by virtue of reason and the eternal verities into a kind of society with God, are members of the City of God.' See also Leibniz, *Monadology*, §29 and §§83–4 and *Discourse on Metaphysics*, §§34–6.

70. Donald Davidson, 'Three Varieties of Knowledge', in *Subjective, Intersubjective, Objective* (Oxford: Clarendon Press, 2001), pp. 212–13.

71. Leibniz uses these terms as synonyms in 'Meditations on Knowledge, Truth, and Ideas', in *Philosophical Papers and Letters*, p. 293. The 'categories' mentioned in this citation, on the other hand, refer to the synthetic *a priori* concepts which define the 'unity of apperception'

in Kant, in so far as these allow diverse appearances to be brought together in a law-like manner for the knowing subject. However, we shall not here deal with Deleuze's critique of Kant, except to say that Kant treats the knowing subject as an origin rather than as a produced form in accordance with the ontological priority of events over substances (see LS, 97–8, 105).

72. See also on this Bowden, 'Deleuze, Leibniz and the Jurisprudence of Being', pp. 110–11; and Frémont, *Singularités, individus et relations*, p. 86. Frémont argues that the story of Sextus Tarquin is designed to illustrate how we must understand – that is, by comparing, for example, the effects which ensue from differently determined Sextuses – how historical evils are not divergences from, but rather the conditions of, the best of all possible worlds. It follows from such a 'juridical proof' that God must be all good, all wise, all powerful, and so on. As she writes, 'one only justifies God by showing how evil is necessary'.

73. See note 19, above.

74. As Deleuze puts it in *The Fold*, p. 137: 'Leibniz's monads submit to two conditions, one of closure and the other of selection. On the one hand, they include an entire world that does not exist outside of them; on the other, this world takes for granted a first selection, of convergence, since it is distinguished from other possible but divergent worlds, excluded by the monads in question . . . Now the selection is what tends to be disappearing, first of all and in every way . . . [N]ot only are dissonances excused from being "resolved", divergences can be affirmed . . . But when the monad is in tune with divergent series that belong to incompossible worlds, then the other condition is what disappears: it could be said that the monad, straddling several worlds, is kept half open as if by a pair of pliers' (translation modified).

75. When, later on in *The Logic of Sense*, Deleuze writes that Leibniz 'makes use of this rule of incompossibility in order to exclude events from one another', this should be understood at the level of the different worlds – compossible in themselves but incompossible with one another – in the understanding of God. In other words, God will choose only one of these worlds for existence, thereby excluding a relation between incompossible events *in reality*. In this sense, Leibniz makes a negative use of divergence. As Deleuze writes, however, this 'is justified . . . only to the extent that events are already grasped under the hypothesis of a God who calculates and chooses, and from the point of view of their actualization in distinct worlds or individuals. It is no longer justified, however, if we consider the pure events and the ideal play whose principle Leibniz was unable to grasp, hindered as he was by theological exigencies' (LS, 172).

76. It is clear from the context here that for 'individual' in this citation, we should read either 'person' or 'individual or person', but only in so far

as, by 'person', we understand 'nobody', a 'produced form'. The idea of grasping the event being actualized within me as another individual or person '*grafted*' onto me is no doubt a means of recalling this passage from the 'Sixteenth Series of the Static Ontological Genesis': 'In truth, the person is Ulysses, no one [*elle n'est personne*] properly speaking, but a produced form . . . And the individual is always anyone [i.e., any individual, *quelconque*], born, *like Eve from Adam's rib*, from a singularity prolonged [*prolongée*] over a line of ordinary points' (LS, 116, emphasis added and translation modified).

77. This citation is related to a comparison of Leibniz's 'point of view' and Nietzsche's 'perspectivism'. While Deleuze affirms that Nietzsche's perspectivism affirms divergence in the way in which we have analyzed it here, he does not show how Nietzsche provides the conceptual machinery necessary for such an affirmation. As such, we have chosen to focus on other figures in developing our argument: not only Leibniz, but also, as will be seen in Chapters 3 and 4, Lautman, Simondon and various structuralists.

78. On properties as classes of tropes, compare Macdonald, 'Tropes and Other Things', p. 334; John Bacon, *Universals and Property Instances* (Oxford and Cambridge: Blackwell, 1995), pp. 13–19; and Keith Campbell, *Abstract Particulars* (Oxford and Cambridge: Blackwell, 1990), pp. 81–5. For these authors, such classes are determined by variable and overlapping relations of similarity or resemblance.

79. See on this, Macdonald, 'Tropes and Other Things', p. 335; and Williams, 'On the Elements of Being', p. 9.

80. This, then, is the Deleuzian 'evental' solution to the problem of the relation between general properties and particular objects of experience, as much as it is to the problem of 'the fundamental link between the concept and the Ego' (LS, 115).

81. In fact, there arises here a further problem which will not be dealt with until we examine Deleuze's relation to psychoanalysis in Chapter 5. This problem can be formulated in the following way (see LS, 124): if relations of convergence and divergence between singularities-events entirely produce '[i]ndividuation in bodies, the measure in their mixtures, the play of persons and concepts in their variations', what does it now mean to say, as we did in Chapter 1, that the event is produced by bodies? In short, it must be in a different way that the event is produced by bodies. The question for Chapter 5 will thus be: how can 'bodies taken in their undifferentiated depth' themselves produce the events which individuate them and engender the logical proposition with its determinate dimensions?

3

Lautman and Simondon – Problematic Ideas and Singularities

Let us review the ground covered thus far. First of all, we examined how, after analyzing verbs of becoming such as 'to grow', Deleuze contends that events must be understood as ideal changes which are ontologically prior to individuated states of affairs. While they are not themselves objectively 'present' in the same way as fixed things and states of affairs, Deleuze maintains that events are nevertheless the prior condition for the constitution of new, present states of affairs, as well as for the simultaneous constitution of those presents which are determined as past with respect to these new presents. In other words, events picked out by verbs of becoming both express problematic relations between present states of affairs ('problematic' because these relations 'elude the present'), and determine these states in their temporal relations (past present, present present).

It was also seen that events have a necessary relation to language. Indeed, not being present in the manner of fixed things and states of affairs, Deleuze claims that events do not exist outside of the propositions which express them. What is more, it appears that when it comes to our knowledge of worldly things and their relations, what is crucial is how the events which determine their states are themselves determined, ordered and related using language. The major question, then, for Deleuze's philosophy of the event, is thus: given the ontological priority of events and their relation to language, what are the conditions of the event if everything, including the very language in which events are determined, must ultimately be reducible to events?

We then saw how Deleuze turns to the Stoics in order to approach an answer to this problem. In particular, we observed that he takes up the Stoic ontological distinction between bodies and incorporeals, which itself implies a distinction within Stoic logic between the reference and sense of propositions. By comparing the event with the Stoic incorporeal 'sayable', which is both an 'effect' of causal relations between bodies and the 'sense' of propositions, Deleuze was able to affirm that events occurring in and for physical states of affairs ('Chronos') must themselves be determined in relation to an ideal 'sense-event' ('Aion') which is nothing other than the ongoing articulation of a relation between the causal analysis of bodies, conceptual development, and the ethical 'manifestation' of the wise person's beliefs and desires.

It was also seen how this Stoic understanding of sense or the event resolved two further problems. The first of these problems was described as the circularity of the definition of sense, or rather, the fact that the sense of the proposition is only ever deferred in a circular manner between the three dimensions of the proposition commonly identified in contemporary philosophy: denotation, manifestation and signification. The second problem was identified as the conflict – also apparent in contemporary theories of the proposition – between understanding the dimension of signification as the condition of possibility for a proposition to be true, and maintaining that the truth or falsity of a proposition is a matter of its correspondence (or lack thereof) with an objective state of affairs. With reference to the Stoics, Deleuze attempted to resolve these problems by arguing, first of all, that the ongoing sense-event should be seen as a 'fourth dimension' of the proposition which determines the other three in their various relations: causal analysis being aligned with denotation, the sage's beliefs and desires with manifestation, and conceptual development with signification. But it also follows from this that, in so far as the ongoing sense-event generates the relation between the dimensions of signification and denotation, a relation is established *within* sense between the condition of truth and the truth of propositions in relation to their corresponding, determined objects. Nevertheless, because the Stoics ultimately determined the sense-event, not with reference to the infinitely divisible Aion or 'unique Event', but with reference to an underlying substance (the body and name of Zeus), Deleuze was obliged to look elsewhere for the conceptual tools needed to develop his philosophy of the event.

Turning to Leibniz, Deleuze was then able to affirm from a different perspective how relations of convergence and divergence between series of singularities-events precede and generate the individuals, persons and general concepts with which we are ordinarily familiar. In particular, it was seen how individuals and persons must initially be considered as 'ontological propositions' in relation to the trope-like events which determine them in their expressive relations with one another within a world-series of compossible or convergent events.

It was also observed that, because they clearly express only a finite portion of this world, persons perceive divergences between series of events. In relation to disjunctive syntheses of such divergences, then, persons were seen to transcend their 'original' worldly relations and bring new 'values' to the world. These disjunctive syntheses were held to be akin to 'events of knowing' within a triangular structure implying the simultaneous and related determinations of: the beliefs of a knowing subject, the beliefs of another knowing subject, and a common world of individuals corresponding to these beliefs. Whilst for Leibniz such syntheses are carried out in relation to an uncreated creator (God), to whose coherent vision of things all divergences must be reduced, for Deleuze, on the contrary, there is no such primary and substantial form. Rather, the persons implicated in processes of triangulation are always 'produced' and remain open to divergences or differences which, in the absence of any guarantee of an underlying convergence, must be affirmed as such. Finally, it was seen how general concepts are determined in this synthesis of diverging series of events compresent with the person, that is, in relation to the genesis of variable and overlapping classes of tropes corresponding to properties of increasing and decreasing specificity exemplified by the individuals and persons synthesized out of the initially incompossible worlds.

In this and the following chapter, we shall examine how Deleuze once again takes up these event-related issues, but goes beyond the above-analyzed Stoic and Leibnizian responses, by speaking of events as 'singularities' which are inseparable from 'problems' or 'problematic Ideas'. These singularities-events both define the conditions of these problems as problems, and are implicated in the generation of the solutions to them, in the form of determined individuals, persons and concepts (LS, 52, 54). As Deleuze writes, we 'can speak of events only as singularities deployed in a problematic field, in the vicinity of which the solutions are organized' (LS, 56). We shall see how, with reference to the philosophical concepts of singularity and problem, Deleuze completely revisits and re-solves the event-related puzzles examined in Chapters 1 and 2. In particular, we shall see how Deleuze develops his concept of the problem in such a way that it accounts for the internal genesis of both the sense and the truth of propositions, along with the object which realizes this truth, and without reference to anything transcending the problem and determining it from the outside. For Deleuze, every true proposition will express a sense or a singularity-event, but this sense or singularity-event will itself be determined in relation to a sub-representative problem for which such propositions collectively function as elements of response or cases of solution. A true proposition, in other words, will 'make sense', in both the active and passive senses of this phrase, in relation to a sub-representative problem: it will be made sense of by the other elements constitutive of the problem, just as it will contribute to making sense of these elements. As he writes, sense or the event is 'expressed as the problem to which propositions correspond in so far as they indicate particular responses, signify instances of a general solution, and manifest subjective acts of resolution' (LS, 121). In other words, sense expressed as a problem is equivalent to what was called the 'fourth dimension' of the proposition, underlying and engendering the other three dimensions of the proposition. And as for the nature of the objective correlates of these three dimensions – that is, the objects or states of affairs to which the sense of particular propositions will apply and which will realize the truth of these propositions – these will be 'engendered at precisely the same time that the problem [internally] determines *itself*' (LS, 121). The truth of a proposition will thus be a matter of the proposition's correspondence to an 'evental' state of affairs determined within the problem, rather than an external state of affairs existing independently of the problem. This internal determination of the problem must, therefore, be understood to be equivalent to the neo-Leibnizian static ontological and logical geneses which were the focus of Chapter 2.

Now, as will be seen in detail, Deleuze speaks of the problem as the reciprocal, complete and progressive determination of purely 'differential elements' by means of the 'adjunction' and 'transformation' of singularities-events, where singularities-events are understood to correspond to the 'values' of relations between differential elements, and where differential elements are in turn determined by syntheses of singularities-events. In other words, the process of determining the elements of the problem is carried out in relation to singularities-events and, as an ongoing process, must itself be considered to be the 'evental-determination' of these events. By conceiving of the problem in this manner, Deleuze effectively revisits two other event-related issues examined above. First of all, in so far as the problem is fully 'evental' in the way just mentioned, it accounts for the ontological priority of events over things 'all the way down'. In the second place, by means of the concepts of singularity and problem, Deleuze is able avoid treating the 'person' as a substantial thing to which the play of events must be reduced, in the manner of Leibniz, but also, in different ways, in the manner of Kant and Husserl (see LS, 99). Indeed, it was noted at the end of Chapter 2 that in order to explicate Deleuze's extension of certain aspects of the Leibnizian system, and in particular with respect to 'persons', we were obliged to consider a concept which does not itself appear in *The Logic of Sense*, namely, that of triangulation. Although this concept clearly encapsulates what is at stake in Deleuze's neo-Leibnizianism, Deleuze himself moves beyond Leibniz by elaborating the concepts of singularity and the problem (also called variously the 'problematic Idea', 'problematic field', 'metaphysical surface', 'transcendental field', 'unconscious surface', the 'problematic' and, as will be seen in Chapter 4, 'structure'). As Deleuze writes:

> We seek to determine an impersonal and pre-individual transcendental field, which does not resemble the corresponding empirical fields, and which nevertheless is not confused with an undifferentiated depth. This field can not be determined as that of a consciousness ... What is neither individual nor personal are, on the contrary, emissions of singularities in so far as they occur on an unconscious surface and possess a mobile, immanent principle of auto-unification through a *nomadic distribution*, radically distinct from fixed and sedentary distributions as conditions of the syntheses of consciousness. Singularities are the true transcendental events ... Far from being individual or personal, singularities preside over the genesis of individuals and persons; they are distributed in a 'potential' which admits neither Self nor I, but which produces them by actualizing or realizing itself, although the figures of this actualization do not at all resemble the realized potential. Only a theory of singular points is capable of transcending the synthesis of the person and the analysis of the individual as these are (or are made) in consciousness ... Only when the world, teeming with anonymous and nomadic, impersonal and pre-individual singularities, opens up, do we tread at last on the field of the transcendental. (LS, 102–3)

It is clear from this, then, that 'the subject of this new discourse' of problems and singularities is no longer, strictly speaking, the 'person'. Rather, as Deleuze writes, and as we shall come to understand, the true 'subject is this free, anonymous, and nomadic singularity which traverses men as well as plants and animals independently of the matter of their individuation and the forms of their personality' (LS, 107). Let us now turn to examine this new discourse which, as has just been shown, promises so much in the way of understanding Deleuze's philosophy of the event in *The Logic of Sense*.

* * *

The most important series for our examination of the concepts of singularities and problems are the 'Ninth Series of the Problematic', the 'Fifteenth Series of Singularities', and the 'Seventeenth Series of the Static Logical Genesis'. But in fact it is in *Difference and Repetition*, published a year before *The Logic of Sense*, that one finds the full, technical elaboration of these concepts.[1] Indeed, in the later text, Deleuze appears only to state the conclusions of his detailed work in the earlier text. In what follows, we shall thus primarily examine Deleuze's arguments in *Difference and Repetition* while noting the corresponding passages in *The Logic of Sense*.

In point of fact, in *Difference and Repetition*, Deleuze's elaboration of the concept of the problem or the 'problematic Idea' (along with the concept of singularity) arises, as it does in *The Logic of Sense*, in the context of an examination of the notion of sense. Or more precisely, it arises in the context of a critique of a certain 'image of thought' for which the privileging of the propositional dimension of 'designation' over that of 'sense' is one of the postulates. Deleuze's critique here can be outlined as follows (for what follows, see DR, 153–4).

Sense is commonly defined as the condition of the true. Indeed, a proposition devoid of sense can be neither true nor false. Thus we ordinarily distinguish two dimensions of a proposition: 'expression', whereby a proposition says or expresses an idea or something ideal; and 'designation', whereby a proposition indicates the objects to which what is expressed applies. However, it is generally agreed that truth and falsity have to do with what words and sentences indicate or designate and not with what they express. Sense thus appears as the condition of the truth of the proposition, and yet at the same time it must remain indifferent or exterior to what it conditions. The dimension of sense is thus reduced to psychological flair or logical formalism and, in as much as it remains external to the dimension of designation, presents us with an unbridgeable divide between words and things.[2]

It is thus in response to this problem that Deleuze sets out to show how the relation between the sense of a proposition and what it designates can be internally established within sense itself. As he will argue, the designated object whose nature determines the truth or falsity of the proposition cannot be posited in reality exterior to sense, 'but only at the limit of its process'. The 'proposition's relation to what it designates, in so far as this relation is established, is constituted within the unity of sense, along with the object which realizes this unity' (DR, 154).

Our primary interest here is that Deleuze first introduces his concept of the 'problem' (and, as will be seen, his concept of 'singularity') in order to establish the conditions for this internal genesis. In short, for Deleuze, every designating proposition has a sense, but this sense will itself be located in a sub-representative problem in relation to which these propositions in turn function as elements of response or cases of solution (DR, 157). Or again, as Deleuze puts it in *The Logic of Sense*, '[s]ense is ... expressed as the problem to which propositions correspond in so far as they indicate particular responses, signify instances of a general solution, and manifest subjective acts of resolution' (LS, 121). In other words, a proposition will be endowed with sense in so far as it is determined, with respect to at least one of its dimensions, as the solution to a problem. But it also follows from this – at least, if Deleuze is to remain consistent – that even philosophical propositions which treat the 'objective' nature of the problem must emerge as solutions to what we can thus call 'the problem of the problem'. In *The Logic of Sense*, Deleuze indicates this self-reflexive nature of the problem when he writes that the problem determines '*its* own conditions', or when he speaks of the 'self-determination of the problem' (LS, 122).

Now, if all representations, up to and including propositions with regard to the nature of the problem itself, must find their sense and truth value within the problem, it is clear that the problem must ultimately be 'sub-representative' or 'non-propositional'. But whilst it '*is not* propositional', the problem nevertheless 'does not exist outside of the propositions which express it' (LS, 122). Or to put it another way, the problem is both transcendent and immanent in relation to its 'propositional solutions' (DR, 163).[3] As a form of shorthand, therefore, we will say that it is in relation to the problem that true propositions 'make sense' – in both the active and passive senses of 'make sense' – as elements of response or cases of solution.

As regards the precise nature of the object to which the sense of a given proposition applies and which will realize the truth of this proposition, this will be determined at the same time that the problem itself is completely determined or 'solved'. In *Difference and Repetition*, Deleuze likens this object to the Kantian object = x. For Deleuze, however, this object is determinable not so much in relation to the already given categories of the understanding as in relation to those dialectical or problematic 'Ideas' which would provide the conditions under which objects of experience can be represented with a maximum of synthetic unity. It should come as no surprise, therefore, that in *Difference and Repetition* Deleuze refers to problems as 'Ideas', and that to solve such a problem means to fully determine the problem as a problem: a sub-representative problem in relation to which all meaningful and true propositions would be determined, up to and including propositions with regard to the objective nature of the problem itself.[4] Or again, as Deleuze puts it in *The Logic of Sense*, the 'synthesis of the problem with *its* own conditions constitutes something ideational or unconditioned, determining at once the condition and the conditioned, that is, the domain of resolvability and the solutions present in this domain' (LS, 122).

How, then, does Deleuze construct his philosophical concept of the problem or problematic Idea? He does so in two moments. First of all, with reference to the differential calculus (as well as group theory and Riemannian differential geometry) and some of the meta-mathematical theses of Albert Lautman, Deleuze outlines a highly abstract concept of the problematic Idea in terms of the reciprocal, complete and progressive 'differential' determination of elements which themselves have no prior signification, sensible form or function, by means of the 'adjunction' and 'transformation' of 'singularities'. Then, following the work of Gilbert Simondon, Deleuze develops a general theory of intensive individuation which relates this problematic Idea to actual things in so far as it is necessary to posit it as an ideal 'pre-individual field', with respect to which both knowledge embodied in propositions and known things can be thought of as being individuated in an ongoing and related way, and without reference to any determining instance falling outside the system. How are these two moments of the problem related such that the problem is determined or 'solved' as the kind of problem in relation to which all propositions which are endowed with sense and true in relation to their corresponding objects are determined? In short, they determine each other mutually. On the one hand, intensive individuation necessarily presupposes a pre-individual field which takes the same form as the problematic Idea. On the other hand, the theory of intensive individuation shows how the problematic Idea is the problem for its various solutions, that is, for the determined individuals, persons and concepts characteristic of diverse fields of knowledge. In other words, emerging as solutions to the sub-representative 'problem of the problem', the philosophical propositions constitutive of the general theory of intensive individuation make sense of, and are made sense of by, the philosophical propositions constitutive of the theory of problematic Ideas. But let us now turn to the detail of this complex argument.

3.1 Problematic Ideas and Singularities in Difference and Repetition: From Kant to the Calculus

Following Deleuze, a first resource for developing a philosophical concept of problems is Kant, since the objects of Kant's dialectical Ideas have a number of features characteristic of 'sub-representative' problems in general. Indeed, the objects of Kant's Ideas are at once:

1. objectively necessary (they allow us to represent objects of experience with maximum synthetic unity);
2. undetermined (the object of an Idea is an object which can be neither given nor known, but must be represented without being able to be directly determined);
3. determinable (the object of an Idea is determinable 'by analogy' with those objects of experience upon which it confers unity);
4. and finally they carry with them the ideal of a complete and infinite determination (the object of the Idea ensures a specification of the concepts of the understanding, by means of which the latter comprise more and more differences on the basis of a properly infinite field of continuity) (DR, 169).

For Kant, however, Ideas are subject to external constraints: the Ideas of the faculty of reason are determinable only in relation to the objects of experience given or giveable in intuition, and bear the ideal of complete determination only in relation to the *a priori* concepts of the understanding (DR, 170).[5] And we have already seen that, for Deleuze, problems or problematic Ideas could only be subject to internal constraints, since they alone are supposed to account for the internal genesis of the sense and truth of propositions in general, along with the objects to which these senses apply and which realize these truths. So how could the problematic Idea and its elements be entirely internally determined? Deleuze's solution is to characterize the problem in purely differential terms, whereby the elements of the problematic Idea are considered as differences which are united and determined by difference alone. In order to do this, as will be seen, he first of all 'models' the problematic Idea in terms derived from the differential calculus, group theory and differential geometry. He then shows how these mathematical theories to which he refers emerge or 'make sense' as solutions to a more general 'dialectic of problematic

Ideas' which nevertheless has the same abstract form as the problematic Idea described in mathematical terms. Finally, he develops a theory of intensive individuation which shows how the problematic Idea thus characterized 'makes sense' as the problem for which the determined individuals, persons and concepts characteristic of diverse fields of knowledge are the solutions.

The first mathematical resource to which Deleuze refers in developing his philosophical concept of problematic Ideas is the differential calculus, or more precisely, the 'barbarous or pre-scientific' interpretations of the calculus (DR, 170). In these interpretations, according to Deleuze, the 'symbol dx', just like the objects of Kantian Ideas, 'appears as simultaneously undetermined, determinable and determination'. What is more, corresponding to these three aspects of the symbol dx are three principles which together form a 'sufficient reason' for problems: 'a principle of determinability corresponds to the undetermined as such (dx, dy); a principle of reciprocal determination corresponds to the really determinable (dy/dx); a principle of complete determination corresponds to the effectively determined (values of dy/dx)' (DR, 171). Let us firstly examine the 'undetermined' dx which, in the history of the calculus, essentially concerns the problem of the status of the 'infinitesimal' or 'differential'.

Following Deleuze, and just as in the modern interpretations of the calculus, the differential dx is in no way equal to zero, and nor does it imply the actual existence of the infinitely small. Rather, citing the philosopher Jean Bordas-Demoulin, whose work came some years before the final, 'rigorous formulation' of the calculus, Deleuze argues that dx represents only the cancellation of quantity in general: 'dx is strictly nothing in relation to x, as dy is in relation to y'.[6] At the same time, however, while the 'zeros involved in dx and dy express the annihilation of the quantum and the quantitas, of the general as well as the particular', they serve also to express 'the universal and its appearance' (DR, 171). In other words, while dy/dx expresses the cancellation of individual values and the variation of individual relations within the function, it also elevates the differential relation itself to the status of a universal which remains the same with respect to changing values and relations. Or again, as Duffy writes, citing Deleuze's seminars on Spinoza, even though, as vanishing, the terms of the differential relation are unassignable, the differential relation itself, dy/dx, nevertheless subsists as a 'pure relation'.[7]

Thus, even though dx is totally undetermined with respect to x, as is dy to y, since the relation subsists, they are in principle determinable with respect to each other. But in what form, precisely? As Deleuze writes, a principle of 'reciprocal determination' corresponds to the determinability of the relation. By reciprocal determination, we take it that Deleuze means not only that dx and dy exist absolutely only in relation to each other at a point on a curve (the point of tangency), but also that the successive derivatives taken at this point are determinable only in relation to each other, and that the reciprocal relation or synthesis of these derivatives thereby characterizes a part of the curve or generates the primitive function (integration here being understood as summation in the form of a series).[8] Indeed, the crux of the matter for Deleuze appears to be that the problematic differential relation dy/dx is logically and ontologically prior to the 'primitive' function whose slope the differential relation is normally said to represent. As Aden Evans puts it, in 'Deleuze's rereading of the calculus, the primitive function does not precede the differential relation, but is only the ultimate result or byproduct of the progressive determination of that relation. The differential is a problem, and its solution leads to the primitive function.'[9] Indeed, for Deleuze, following Wronski's 'pre-scientific' ideas on the calculus, this process of the determination of the primitive function from the reciprocal synthesis of differential relations of different 'local' orders takes place in an element of 'pure potentiality' wherein the differential dx is essentially a problematic or 'ideal difference' which is 'associated with the generation of magnitude' rather than being implicated in 'the laws of quantities already formed'.[10] We take it that Deleuze is referring to this process whereby the primitive function is generated from summing or integrating the power series of derivatives taken at a particular point when he writes:

The whole question, then, is: in what form is the differential relation determinable? It is determinable first in qualitative form, and in this connection it expresses a function which differs in kind from the so-called primitive function. When the primitive function expresses the curve, $dy/dx = - (x/y)$ expresses the trigonometric tangent of the angle made by the tangent of the curve and the axis of the abscissae . . . This is only a first aspect, however, for in so far as it expresses another quality, the differential relation remains tied to the individual values or to the quantitative variations corresponding to that quality (for example, tangent). It is therefore differentiable in turn . . . In this sense the Idea has the differential relation as its object: it then integrates variation, not as a variable determination of a supposedly constant relation ('variability') but, on the contrary, as a degree of variation of the relation itself ('variety') to which corresponds, for example, the qualified series of curves. (DR, 172–3)[11]

Now, to this process of reciprocal determination in the element of pure potentiality there corresponds a principle of 'complete determination', by which Deleuze means the composition of a form, or the complete determination of the curve or object. For, in the process of taking successive differentiations – in the manner of Weierstrass' analytic continuation of the function – and integrating them, the overall behaviour of the curve becomes apparent through the discovery of the precise number and distribution of 'singular points' which are then used to determine the type or species of the primitive function in question.[12] Singular points are points on the curve where the curve changes behaviour – such as turning and inflection points, local maxima and minima, and points of discontinuity – and where the value of the differential relation becomes, for example, 0 or ∞. And in fact, as Deleuze writes, it is only in relation to such singular points 'that the serial form within potentiality assumes its full meaning' (DR, 175–6), for it is precisely from these singular points that the 'ordinary points' of the function can be determined by power series expansions:

> The interest and necessity of the serial form appear in the plurality of series subsumed by it, in their dependence upon singular points, and in the manner in which we can pass from one part of the object where the function is represented by a series to another where it is expressed in a different series ... Just as determinability pointed toward reciprocal determination, so the latter points towards complete determination. (DR, 176)

Or again, as Duffy elaborates, the

> power series determines not only the specific qualitative nature of the function at the distinctive point in question but also the specific qualitative nature of all of the regular points in the neighbourhood of that distinctive point ... By examining the relation between the differently distributed distinctive points determined by the differential relation, the regular points which are continuous between the distinctive points, that is, in geometrical terms, the branches of the curve, can be determined ... To the extent that all of the regular points are continuous across all of the different branches generated by the power series of the other distinctive points, the entire complex curve or the whole analytic function is generated.[13]

So we have seen how, in the determination of species of curves, the differential dx symbolizes the object of the problematic Idea: while entirely undetermined in itself, it is reciprocally, differentially determinable with other differentials (in series of derivatives), leading in this way, via the discovery and investigation of singular points and their 'neighbourhoods', to the complete determination of the function of the curve under consideration.[14] As Deleuze says, the solution emerges the more the problem is determined.

Strictly speaking, however, the above-analyzed Weierstrassian 'local' method of integration only leads to the primitive function if the series obtained at singular points converge with the function. In general, the analytic continuation of power series expansions can be continued in all directions up to the points in the immediate neighbourhood of certain types of singularities, called 'poles', where the series obtained diverge. In the case of divergence, therefore, the 'effective domain of an analytic function determined by the process of the analytic continuation of power series expansions is . . . limited to that between its poles'.[15] What this implies, therefore, for our particular concerns here, is that our 'differential problem' – that is, the problem of the differential – still remains to be explored for series that diverge. However, it is precisely in the context of this problem of divergent series that Deleuze turns in *Difference and Repetition* to Albert Lautman's analysis of Henri Poincaré's 'qualitative theory' of differential equations (DR, 177). Indeed, Poincaré famously devised a method for considering, via the study of certain 'essential' singularities, discontinuous local functions in relation to one another. In short, it can be said that if the local discovery of the existence and distribution of singular points in general (including poles) can be said to provide the conditions for the complete determination of, and thus eventual solution to, a differential problem, then Poincaré's global approach to the role of singularities effectively extends this local method in order to obtain the conditions for solutions to nonlinear differential equations. Let us turn to a very brief sketch of Poincaré's theory.[16]

Under the impetus of the 'three body problem' (the problem of modelling the mutual interactions of three solar system bodies such as the sun, earth and moon) which cannot be solved in a closed form by means of elementary functions, Poincaré set out to examine the global properties of certain nonlinear differential equations. Or more exactly, he set out to geometrically examine the global properties of the solution curves to these nonlinear differential equations, as opposed to confining himself strictly to the local analysis of given points by means of power series. He did, however, employ the local method in order to establish the existence and distribution of the 'poles' of discontinuous local functions from which he in turn created differential 'composite functions'. Then, in the analysis of the kinds of solution curves that such nonlinear differential equations can have, what Poincaré discovered was that certain 'essential' singular points played a key role in organizing the space of the solutions. These essential singularities were effectively determined in relation to the poles of the local functions from which the composite function was composed, by the periodic fluctuations of the values that solutions to the composite function could receive. Poincaré distinguished four recurring types of such singular points according to the geometrical 'look' of the solution curves – focus points, saddle points, nodes and centres (*foyer, col, nœud, centre*) – and described the behaviour of the solution curves around such points (Deleuze names these points explicitly at DR, 177 and LS, 52 and 104). In brief, as DeLanda has put it, the existence, number and distribution of these singularities were found to organize the space of solutions by acting as what we would now call 'attractors' for the different trajectories in the system.[17]

Technical details aside, Deleuze's primary concern here (quite apart from the nonlinear physics to which Poincaré's ideas would lead, and which is the focus of DeLanda's work in this area),[18] following the work of the philosopher of mathematics Albert Lautman, is to show how singular points both refer to the complete determination of the conditions of a differential problem, and are immanent in the solutions to that problem.[19] In other words, if the differential dx can be said to symbolize the various aspects of the problematic Idea in its relation to its object (determinability, reciprocal determination, complete determination), singularities can in turn be said to symbolize how this problem is both transcendent to and immanent in its solutions. As Deleuze writes,

> No doubt the specification of the singular points (for example, dips, nodes, focal points, centres) is undertaken by means of the form of integral curves, which refer back to the solutions for differential equations. There is nevertheless a complete determination with regard to the existence and distribution of these points which depends upon a completely different instance – namely, the field of vectors defined by the equation itself. (DR, 177)[20]

Or again, in a long note in *The Logic of Sense*, citing Lautman:

> The geometrical interpretation of the theory of differential equations clearly places in evidence two absolutely distinct realities: there is the field

of directions [i.e., vectors] and the topological accidents which may sud-
denly crop up in it, as for example the existence of the place of *singular
points to which no direction has been attached*; and there are the integral
curves with the form they take on in the vicinity of the singularities of the
field of directions . . . *The existence and distribution* of singularities are
notions relative to the field of vectors defined by the differential equation.
The form of the integral curves is relative to the solution of this equation. The two problems are assuredly complementary, since the *nature*
of the singularities of the field [of vectors] is defined by the form of the
curves in their neighbourhood [*voisinage*]. But it is no less true that the
field of vectors on one hand and the integral curves on the other are two
essentially distinct mathematical realities. (LS, 344–5, n.4, translation
modified)[21]

We can see that these considerations correspond, in an analogous
way, to our problem of sense. Every true designating proposition has
a sense (just as a solution curve has its singularity), but this sense is
itself located in a sub-representative (purely differential) problem
in relation to which such propositions serve or 'make sense' as elements of response or cases of solution (solution curves specifying the
nature of the singularity). Singularities carry out the complete determination of the problem as such, in so far as they both direct and are
specified by the solution curves.

It is clear, however, that the task of conceptualizing the internal
genesis of sense precludes Deleuze from using the differential calculus as a model or paradigm which would analogously determine
the sense of sense. Deleuze must, therefore, show how this particular, 'differential model of sense' emerges as a solution to a more
general problem, or what he will call a dialectic of problems. The
way that Deleuze goes about this task occurs over three moments:
first of all, he will invoke some of the theses of Albert Lautman in
order to show how mathematical theories such as the differential
calculus necessarily participate in problematic Ideas which take the
same abstract form as the one modelled by the calculus;[22] secondly,
he will briefly examine some other mathematical expressions of the
problem-solution complex (group theory and differential geometry)
and reattach some of their characteristics to this meta-mathematical
dialectic of problems; finally, he will outline the relation that this
theory of problems has with a general theory of intensive individuation, which can be shown to be at work in various scientific domains
(not only mathematics but also physics, biology, psychology,
linguistics etc.).

3.2 Albert Lautman and the Dialectic of Problematic Ideas

For Deleuze, Lautman's meta-mathematical theses and concrete analyses of certain mathematical theories are essential in two respects. We have already seen the first: Deleuze essentially follows Lautman's analyses of Poincaré's qualitative theory of differential equations in order to show how the solutions to a differential problem are dictated by certain salient traits of the problem itself, that is, by the singularities of this problem and the way in which they are distributed in a system.[23] Strictly speaking however, Lautman's interest in his analysis of Poincaré is to show how – and we shall see what this means – certain dialectical couples such as 'the local and the global' and 'the discrete and the continuous' are posed and resolved in Poincaré's work. And indeed, this is precisely the second aspect of Lautman's work that Deleuze takes on board: his general meta-mathematical theory of dialectical Ideas or problems which govern the development of mathematics. As Deleuze explains it, following

> Lautman's general theses, a problem has three aspects: its difference in kind from solutions; its transcendence in relation to the solutions that it engenders on the basis of its own determinant conditions; and its immanence in the solutions which cover it, the problem *being* the better resolved the more *it is* determined. Thus the ideal connections constitutive of the problematic (dialectical) Idea are incarnated in the real relations which are constituted by mathematical theories and carried over into problems in the form of solutions. (DR, 178–9)[24]

In order to better understand the importance of Lautman for Deleuze, we will here briefly explicate the general lines of Lautman's project.

Lautman distinguished several layers of mathematical reality. Apart from mathematical facts, entities and theories, Lautman also argued for the existence of a 'dialectic of Ideas' which governs the development of theories and provides them with their unity, meaning and philosophical value.[25] This dialectic, following Lautman, is constituted by pairs of opposites (same and other, whole and part, continuous and discontinuous, essence and existence, etc.), and the Ideas of this dialectic present themselves as the problem of establishing relationships between these opposed notions.[26] As prior 'questions' or 'logical concerns' relative to possible affirmations of existence within mathematical discourse, these problematic Ideas are thus transcendent with respect to mathematics and can be posed outside of mathematics. Indeed, many of the pairs of opposites analyzed by Lautman can be found in the history of philosophy. However, since the Ideas, in order to be thought concretely, require an appropriate 'matter' in which they can be thought, any effort to respond to the problems that they pose is to effectively constitute mathematical theory. In this sense, therefore, the dialectic must equally be said to be immanent to mathematics (as Lautman then goes on to argue, the link between this transcendence and this immanence is established by the notion of 'genesis').[27] Thus, for example,

> The question of knowing whether forms of solidarity exist between space and matter is in itself a philosophical problem which lies at the heart of Cartesian metaphysics. But any effort to resolve this problem necessarily leads the mind to constitute an analytical mechanics wherein a relationship between geometry and dynamics can be affirmed.[28]

In order to avoid the charge of a naive idealism (indeed, Lautman's affirmed 'Platonism' bears little resemblance to that which is ordinarily labelled Platonism in mathematics), Lautman is careful to qualify the transcendence of Ideas as simply the 'possibility' of experiencing concern for a mode of connection between two ideas.[29] The anteriority of Ideas is here rational, logical or ontological as opposed to psychological or historical.[30] And this is precisely why Lautman argues that mathematics not only incarnates traditional metaphysical problems; it can also give birth to problems which could not have been previously posed. The philosophy of mathematics does not, therefore, consist so much in finding a classical metaphysical problem within a mathematical theory, as grasping the overall structure of a theory in order to extract the logical problem which is at once defined and resolved by the very existence of this theory.[31] Nevertheless, as Lautman goes on to argue, just as, in the very meaning of these terms, 'intention' precedes 'design' and the 'question' the 'response', the existence of established mathematical relations necessarily refers to the prior, positive Idea of the search for such relations.[32] Or to put it another way, because the 'sufficient reason' for the diversity and development of mathematical theories, along with their progressive integrations and interferences, cannot be found within mathematics itself,[33] we are obliged to affirm the prior existence of something like the dialectic of Ideas. In short, to conceive of the historical development of mathematical theories and their 'mixes' as responses or solutions to problematic Ideas is to give unity and meaning to these theories.[34]

So what does Deleuze draw from this work? In short, Lautman's work allows Deleuze to generalize, at a meta-mathematical level, his concept of the problem such as this was developed in relation to the differential calculus. As we have already noted in relation to his analysis of the calculus, for Deleuze, a problem has in general three moments: undetermined, reciprocal determination and complete determination. Or again, as undetermined, the problem is transcendent to its solutions, and yet it does not exist outside of its solutions, thanks to the singularities which both express the complete conditions of the problem as a problem, and are immanent in the solutions. But now, are these not precisely Lautman's theses, generalized and repeated at a meta-mathematical level? Indeed, the terms of Lautman's 'pairs of opposites' subsist in undetermined differential relations. These relations constitute the problematic or dialectical Idea which is transcendent (universal) with respect to the different mathematical theories in which they can be incarnated. Concrete mathematical theories then carry out the immanent definition and resolution of this problematic Idea, and the couples constitutive of it, in relation to the development of a characteristic symbolic field which will have adequately expressed the differential conditions of the problematic Idea. As in the example cited above, the conditions of the undetermined relation between space and matter are themselves expressed in the development of a relation between geometry and dynamics, which is in turn specified and resolved by the existence of an analytical mechanics and its solutions to concrete problems.

It is thus a generalized dialectic of problems that Lautman's work allows Deleuze to formulate. As he writes,

> Differential calculus . . . is an entirely mathematical instrument. It would therefore seem difficult to see in it the Platonic [that is, in Lautman's sense] evidence of a dialectic superior to mathematics. At least, it would be difficult if the immanent aspect of problems did not offer an adequate explanation. *Problems are always dialectical*: the dialectic has no other sense, nor do problems have any other sense. What is mathematical (or physical, biological, psychical or sociological) are the solutions . . . That is why the differential calculus belongs entirely to mathematics, even at the very moment when it finds its sense in the revelation of a dialectic which points beyond mathematics. (DR, 179)

Now, given this 'superiority' of the problematic Idea, it is clear that for both Lautman and Deleuze the differential calculus is only one possible concrete mathematical expression of it. Deleuze in fact

maintains that other procedures, and in particular the development
of group theory, have better expressed the concept of the problem.
Indeed, for Deleuze, group theory allows the specification of a final
figure of the sufficient reason of the problem-solution complex: to
reciprocal and complete determination is now added a principle
of 'progressive determination'.[35] What is important for Deleuze in
group theory, and in particular in the work of Abel and Galois, is
that it spells out how the conditions of a mathematical problem can
be determined in such a way as to progressively specify its solvability
(DR, 179–80). In particular, following the work of Jules Vuillemin,
Deleuze emphasizes the procedure of 'adjunction' in the work of
Galois:

> Starting from a basic 'field' (R), successive adjunctions to this field (R′,
> R″, R‴ . . .) allow a progressively more precise distinction of the roots of
> an equation, by the progressive limitation of possible substitutions. There
> is thus a succession of 'partial resolvants' or an embedding of 'groups'
> which make the solution follow from the very conditions of the problem.
> (DR, 180)

These mathematical developments with respect to groups came
about as a means of approaching the problem of the quintic, that is
to say, the problem of providing a general solution, via a formula,
to equations raised to the fifth power. In short, Galois developed a
general theory of transformations (permutations or substitutions)
of the solutions to quadratic, cubic and quartic equations, concen-
trating on those permutations that preserve all algebraic relations
between the solutions. He then noted that a certain relation held
between these permutations: if two of them are performed in turn,
then the result is always another permutation in the same system.
Such a system is called a 'group' of permutations. Within a group of
permutations, when a given permutation of one solution by another
leaves the equation valid, the two solutions become, in a sense,
indistinguishable as far as this validity is concerned. The equation
is, as it were, indifferent to the switch. Following this, the solutions
to the equation then become increasingly more accurately defined as
the original group gives rise to sub-groups which progressively limit
the substitutions which leave the relations invariant. In other words,
with the successive adjunctions of these sub-groups, the problem
itself becomes progressively better specified and, as a by-product,
individual solutions emerge. As the culmination of his work, Galois
then showed that equations that can be solved by a formula must

have groups of a particular type, and that the quintic has the wrong sort of group.[36]

The importance of Galois' work for Deleuze is twofold. In the first place, it allows him to specify a final aspect of his concept of the problem, namely, progressive determination. As he writes, 'Galois' "progressive discernibility" unites in the same continuous movement the processes of reciprocal determination and complete determination (pairs of roots and the distinction between roots within a pair). It constitutes the total figure of sufficient reason, into which it introduces *time*' (DR, 180). But what is more, by his very use of Abel and Galois' work, Deleuze is able to illustrate how 'progressive determination' is also at work in his Lautman-inspired dialectic of problematic Ideas. Indeed, as Deleuze notes, Abel's work on group theory 'concerned above all the integration of *differential formulae*' (DR, 180, emphasis added), indicating thereby that, just as for Lautman's mathematical *mixtes*, the 'same' transcendent dialectic of problematic Ideas is governing the progressive development of mathematics even in the apparent fragmentation of the discipline (differential calculus, group theory, etc.). This is what Deleuze means when he writes that:

> What matters to us is less the determination of this or that break [*coupure*] in the history of mathematics (analytic geometry, differential calculus, group theory . . .) than the manner in which, at each moment of that history, dialectical problems, their mathematical expression and the simultaneous origin of their fields of solvability are interrelated. From this point of view, there is a continuity and a teleology in the development of mathematics which make the differences in kind between differential calculus and other instruments merely secondary. (DR, 180–1)

Thus, following Deleuze, we can speak generally about problems and say that 'Ideas always have an element of quantitability, qualitability and potentiality; there are always processes of determinability, of reciprocal determination and complete determination, always distributions of singular and ordinary points; always adjunct fields which form the synthetic progression of a sufficient reason' (DR, 181). Indeed, given this enlarged concept of the problematic Idea, we are in a better position to understand why Deleuze also takes up the vocabulary of Riemannian differential geometry in order to announce that 'Ideas are multiplicities'. In brief, it is in order to 'adjoin' to our generalized concept of the dialectical or problematic Idea its appropriate mathematical expression: that of an intrinsic geometry – that is, one which requires no supplementary dimension – for the reciprocal, complete and progressive determination of any space whatsoever.[37] And indeed, that Deleuze is here continuing to follow the historical development of mathematics in relation to a dialectic of problematic Ideas which governs it is clear when we consider that differential geometry has its roots in the differential and integral calculus, and that the notion of 'groups' is essential to it (in relation to the so-called 'differential invariants', for example).[38] In any case, it is clear that certain general characteristics of Riemannian differential geometry provide Deleuze with his final definition of the problematic Idea. As he writes,

An Idea is an *n*-dimensional, continuous, defined multiplicity ... By dimensions, we mean the variables or co-ordinates upon which a phenomenon depends; by continuity, we mean the set of relations between changes in these variables ...; by definition, we mean the elements reciprocally determined by these relations, elements which cannot change unless the multiplicity changes its order and its metric. (DR, 182–3)[39]

He then concludes that there are three conditions that allow us to define the problematic Idea in general:

(1) the elements of the multiplicity must have neither sensible form nor conceptual signification, nor, therefore, any assignable function. (2) These elements must in effect be determined, but reciprocally, by reciprocal relations which allow no independence whatsoever to subsist. Such relations are precisely non-localizable ideal connections [i.e., singularities], whether they characterize the multiplicity globally or proceed by the juxtaposition of neighbouring regions. In all cases the multiplicity is intrinsically defined, without external reference or recourse to a uniform space in which it would be submerged ... (3) A multiple ideal connection, a differential *relation*, must be actualized in diverse spatio-temporal *relationships*, at the same time as its *elements* are actually incarnated in a variety of *terms* and forms. (DR, 183)

Here, then, we can see how these three conditions for a multiplicity or problematic Idea are a restatement of Deleuze's four principles which together form a sufficient reason for problems: (1) corresponds to the principle of 'mere determinability'; (2) corresponds not only to the principle of reciprocal determination, but also to complete and progressive determination, in so far as the reciprocal determination of merely determinable elements cannot not imply completion even over discontinuous domains, and in so far as such a complete, internal determination could only be carried out progressively from one series of determinations to another and back again; and finally (3) corresponds to the principle of progressive determination, in this same sense that the reciprocal and complete determination of merely determinable elements immediately implies the ongoing, intrinsic and step by step securing of terms or forms and their relations.[40] It should also be noted that Deleuze tends to abbreviate talk of this complex process of reciprocal, complete and progressive determination by speaking of the determination of differential relations with respect to the adjunction (or 'apprehension') and condensation (or 'transformation') of singularities (for example: DR, 187, 188–90, 192, 197–9, 201, 210–11, 220, 258–9). Indeed, as we have seen, singularities are capable of determining series of differences by being prolonged over ordinary points up to the vicinity of another 'apprehended' singularity, as much as 'essential' singularities are capable of differentially 'condensing' and 'transforming' (that is, 'specifying') discontinuous singular 'poles', thereby prolonging discontinuous series the ones into the others.

The question now is how we go from the problematic Idea thus characterized to the propositions, objects and states of affairs which, as was said, are the concrete solutions to this problem. For Deleuze, every 'thing' is a solution to a problem.[41] He will therefore show how, beneath the qualities and extensities that we ordinarily perceive in various systems (physical, biological, psychic, social, linguistic, etc.), there are what he calls 'spatio-temporal dynamisms' – or 'dramatizations', or, our preferred term, 'intensive individuations' – which progressively 'actualize' virtual or problematic differences in such a way that these qualities and extensities appear as the 'resolution' of these virtual differences (DR, 214). However, what could it mean for virtual differences to be actualized in things if the formless, functionless and asignifying elements of a problematic multiplicity must be of an entirely different nature than the constituted qualities and extensities that we ordinarily perceive? We already know what this process of actualization cannot be: it cannot be modelled on the form of an analogy which would hold between the mathematical expression of the problem-solution complex and the resolution of problems in these other systems; nor can it take the form of a direct application of the mathematical expression of problems to these other domains; nor, finally, can the above-analyzed concept of the problem function as the general concept for which these other domains would be particular instantiations. Rather, in accordance with the task announced at the outset, we must show how the problem such as it has been characterized above is determined as the problem for which things in general 'make sense', in both the active and passive senses of 'make sense'. As will be seen, Deleuze is able to think things in general as the actualization of virtual differences by turning to a general theory of 'intensive individuation'. In relation to this latter, the problematic or differential Idea is understood as a 'pre-individual field' which individuals will be said to structure and resolve through their various and related becomings (spatio-temporal dynamisms). Let us then turn to look at Deleuze's theory of intensive individuation. Or rather, let us examine the work of Gilbert Simondon, since this is the basis of Deleuze's theory of intensive individuation in *Difference and Repetition*, and since Simondon is one of the major references in *The Logic of Sense* as regards the concepts of singularity and the problem. As Deleuze writes in this latter text, Simondon's *L'individu et sa genèse physico-biologique*, 'has special importance, since it presents the first thought-out theory of impersonal and pre-individual singularities. It proposes explicitly, beginning with these singularities, to work out the genesis of the living individual and the knowing subject' (LS, 344, n. 3).

3.3 *Gilbert Simondon and the Theory of Individuation*

Simondon's *L'individu et sa genèse* is an attempt to think the individual as the result of ontologically prior 'processes of individuation', as opposed to thinking individuation with reference to already constituted individuals.[42] According to Simondon, such a project runs counter to the Western philosophical tradition which has traditionally always taken one of two paths: the substantialist path or the hylomorphic path (see on this INFI, 23–5). On the one hand, metaphysicians of substance tend to begin with the already constituted individual and subsequently ask about its coming to be, thereby thinking the nature of individuation uniquely in terms of the characteristics of this already given individual. But as Simondon asks, what if processes of individuation 'overflow' what we ordinarily think of as individuals? What if processes of individuation are not exhausted in the production of individuals and simultaneously produce something more than the individual? If this were the case, then by beginning their investigation on the basis of the already constituted individual metaphysicians of substance risk masking a more fundamental reality.

On the other hand, taking their inspiration from Aristotle,

philosophers have tended to begin with a 'principle of individua-tion' whose function is to explain that the individual is an individual because, for example, it is a particular combination of matter and form (or sensation and *a priori* spatio-temporal and conceptual form, etc.). In this case, while it is a principle of individuation and not the individual itself which is presupposed, the principle is nevertheless a 'first term', that is to say, an individual which the philosopher gives him or herself, in thought, in order to explain individuation. Once again, then, philosophy fails to think individuals in general as the result of prior processes of individuation.

In order to avoid presupposing anything already individuated, either in reality or in thought, Simondon proposes to think individu-ation through a simultaneous and corresponding individuation of the thought of individuation. As he puts it, this task 'consists in *fol-lowing being in its genesis*, in accomplishing the genesis of thought at the same time that the genesis of the object is carried out' (INFI, 34). So how is this 'immanent double genesis' of being and thought to be carried out?[43]

First of all, in order to account for individuation without recourse to an already constituted individual, Simondon hypothesizes the existence of what he calls the 'pre-individual' and a correspond-ing operation of individuation which will be carried out in relation to it (INFI, 149). As will be examined more fully below, the pre-individual internalizes a difference or potential which the individual will be said to have structured or resolved, although not without remainder, through a process of individuation (INFI, 25). Now, at first glance, it appears that Simondon has once again postulated an individual 'thing' with certain determinate characteristics – a type of dynamized 'primordial soup' – in order to think individuation, thereby failing once more to think the ontological priority of indi-viduation with respect individuals in general. But in fact, Simondon bases his hypothesis of the pre-individual and its corresponding operation of individuation on an 'encyclopedic', but in principle open, series of investigations into the processes of individuation of entities in different domains: physical entities, but also biological, psycho-social and technological.[44] As will be seen below, he will then argue that his concept of 'transduction', which picks out the charac-teristic general features of processes of individuation in these diverse domains, also characterizes the individuation of the very thought of individuation in these domains (INFI, 36). In other words, individu-ation will be 'known' through transduction understood as a process which generates both individuals and the thought of their individuation, rather than by means of a fixed concept of transduction.[45]

In the second place, Simondon affirms what he calls a 'realism of relations', whereby a relation is not an accident with respect to a substance but rather a prior and constitutive condition of substance (INFI, 82–3).[46] As he puts it, the 'individual is the reality of a constitutive relation', a constitutive relation which does not depend for its existence upon already given terms, but rather refers only to other relations (INFI, 62).[47] Granting primacy to relations over individuals 'all the way down' is a consequence of Simondon's commitment to an anti-substantialist approach to individuation. Indeed, it is for this reason that, for Simondon, being is not a unified 'one', identical to itself. As he writes, a

> relation must be grasped as a relation in being, a relation of being, a manner of being and not a simple relationship between two terms that could be adequately known by means of concepts because they would have effectively separate existences . . . If substance is no longer the model of being, it is possible to think of relations as the non-identity of being with respect to itself, the inclusion in being of a reality which is not identical with it, with the result that being as being, before individuation, can be grasped as more than a unity and more than an identity. (INFI, 32)

So what is the link between pre-individual processes of individuation and this realism of relations? Simondon argues that the first characteristic of the pre-individual is that it is distributed according to different 'orders of magnitude' (INFI, 31–2). These orders of magnitude take a variety of different forms depending on the domain under consideration, for example: the different inter-elemental forces in the clay and in the mould in the operation of casting a brick (INFI, 43–4); the different potential energies corresponding to two different structures such as a supersaturated solution and a seed crystal (INFI, 76–7); the difference between, on the one hand, different species of chemicals in the earth and atmosphere and, on the other hand, solar energy, in the case of the individuation of a plant (INFI, 34, n.12); the difference between an organism's internal organization and its external environment in the case of the individuation of an animal (INFI, 28, 225–6), and so on. Following Simondon, what we are dealing with in each of these cases is a pre-individual which is comprised only of disparate orders of magnitude which are, primitively, without communication (INFI, 34). What is crucial, then, is that relations are established between these orders by processes of individuation (INFI, 26). In other words, following Simondon, the pre-individual will form a system of relations governing the genesis of the individual, but only in so far as the individual, in its coming to be, actualizes or structures these relations.[48] Indeed, this manner of conceiving the pre-individual both allows us to think the individual in terms of relations, and prevents us from postulating Simondon's 'orders of magnitude' as themselves the types of already individuated things between which there could be relations.[49]

Now, Simondon talks about pre-individual relations between different orders of magnitude in a variety of ways. In thermodynamic terms, he speaks of a 'metastable' system wherein there is a 'potential energy' between different orders of magnitude and where the process of individuation corresponds to the progressive degradation of this potential energy through a series of transformations (a potential energy is said to be actualized by these transformations) (INFI, 26). In terms of the theory of vision, Simondon speaks of a 'disparation' between two orders of magnitude, whereby two twin sets which are not totally super-imposable, such as left and right retinal images, are seized together in a system and allow the formation of a single set of a higher degree which integrates all their elements (INFI, 205–6, n.15). Indeed, it is in light of these various characterizations that Deleuze says that we may, in speaking of individuation, speak of the establishment of interactive communication between different orders of magnitude or disparate realities, as much as of the actualization of a potential energy or the integration of singularities, as much as of the resolution of the problem posed by disparate realities by the organization of a new dimension of a higher degree.[50] In any case, what is important is that a pre-individual relation between different orders of magnitude is both established by and governs a process of individuation which actualizes or structures these relations.

But now, what brings these orders of magnitude into communication if it cannot, strictly speaking, be the individual? To be sure, since the individual does not exist prior to the relation that it will have been said to actualize, it cannot be what initially establishes the relation. For Simondon, then, it is a 'singularity' which begins individuation (INFI, 62, 97). As he writes, concretely, a singularity may be 'the stone that begins the dune, the gravel which is the seed for an island in a river carrying sediment' (INFI, 44, n.5); or again, it may be the 'information' contained in a seed crystal such that it induces further crystallization when added to a supersaturated solution (INFI, 78).[51] In Simondon's words, the individual which is coming about 'prolongs' a singularity (INFI, 63, 82). But interestingly, it also appears that an already constituted individual may play the role of a singularity when it enters into another system in a state of metastable equilibrium and brings about a transformation (INFI, 82, n. 9). As Deleuze notes in this regard, however, it is important to carefully distinguish between singularity and individual, for singularities are by definition pre-individual.[52] Indeed, it appears that the capacity of an individual to function as a singularity for a pre-individual metastable system ultimately depends on the nature of the metastable system in question. In other words, a singularity is simply whatever is capable of bringing about a 'break' in a metastable system and of causing its heterogeneous orders to communicate in a process of individuation which actualizes the system's potentials and transforms it in the production of new individuals (INFI, 78). A singularity is thus 'pre-individual' in the sense that it has a local and functional definition which is strictly relative to the different pre-individual orders between which it brings about communication.[53]

It is in this manner that, for Simondon, a singularity is also 'information' (INFI, 48, n.8, 97), in a sense that can be generalized from cybernetics and information theory. In the theory of information, information is what 'passes' between an emitter and a receptor (or a cascade of such emitters and receptors) when the receptor can be said to make a 'decision' with respect to the state of the emitter (whether this decision be a reaction, an adaptation, a decoding or some other transformation, depending on whether one is dealing with physical, biological, technological, etc., systems). However, it is essential to note that information must not here be equated with a 'message'. Information rather depends upon relations between the natures of the emitter and the receptor, that is, upon relations between the 'possible states' or 'events' which define each of them, and factors such as the background interference or 'noise' due to the nature of the information channel. In this sense, then, information is essentially, in the words of one early Cybernetician, a 'set of possibilities', and the problem which cybernetics and information theory were originally designed to deal with is that of formalizing the probabilistic conditions under which the correct or intended message can be reliably selected from a set of possible messages.[54] Technical details aside, what is important for Simondon's philosophical concept of information or singularities is that it must obey certain purely relational (or again, 'purely operational' – INFI, 220) conditions with respect to the different orders between which it functions. On the one hand, information must be in some sense 'unforeseeable' for the receptor if it is not to be received as the simple external repetition of an already existing internal state or simply confused with background 'noise' (in information theory, the total probability for the receptor of a particular state of the emitter, as much as the non-distinction of the information signal due to noise, means no information, that is, no 'decision' or transformation on the part of the receptor with respect to the emitter). On the other hand, information must be in some sense 'foreseeable' if it is to be meaningful for and capable of being integrated by the receptor, since the receptor already has its own possible states and mode of functioning with which to make a 'decision' with respect to the state of the emitter (or again, more technically, if all states of the emitter are equiprobable for the receptor, then there is no information) (INFI, 221–3). It is thus clear that there is information only when what emits the signal and what receives it can form a differential system in relation to something 'non-immanent' to, but 'almost entirely' coinciding with, that particular system (INFI, 79, 223). As Simondon writes, 'information is *between* the two halves of a system in a relation of disparation' (INFI, 223, n.30), meaning thereby that, if there is information, a system is formed which integrates the elements of the two disparate realities in a common process. In other words, 'information is *this through which the incompatibility of the non-resolved system becomes the organizing dimension in its resolution*' (INFI, 31, emphasis in the original). And indeed, extrapolating from this, in so far as it refers to the system's constitutive difference, information is something like the sense or meaning (Simondon typically writes, 'signification') of this system, provided that one also adds that this 'sense' only emerges in the concrete transformations that actually take place in the system.[55] Sense, for Simondon, is relational (INFI, 223).

But precisely how does the individual emerge from such communication between heterogeneous orders? The concept that Simondon introduces in order to account for the emergence of the individual is that of 'transduction'.[56] As he writes,

We understand by transduction an operation – physical, biological, mental, social – through which an activity spreads step by step within a domain, this propagation being founded on a structuring of the domain which is carried out from place to place: each region of the constituted structure serves as the principle for the constitution of the following region, in such a way that a modification is thus progressively extended at the same time as this structuring operation . . . A crystal which, from a tiny germ, grows and spreads in all directions in its solution furnishes the simplest image of the operation of transduction: each constituted molecular layer serves as the structuring basis for the layer which is currently being formed. (INFI, 32–3)

In effect, then, transduction is the name given to the ongoing actualization or structuring of the potentials of a metastable system whose constitutive, heterogeneous orders have been brought into communication by a singularity functioning as a 'structural germ'. It is in this way that, as mentioned above, the structured individual which emerges from this process is said to 'prolong' this singularity. For Simondon, a 'complete individuation' would correspond to the total use of potential energy contained in the metastable system before structuring. 'Incomplete individuation', on the other hand, corresponds to a structuring which has not absorbed all of its potential energy (INFI, 79–80). But in fact, incomplete individuation is the general case, since the individual always tends to emerge at the same time as a characteristic 'milieu' or environment (such as a crystal and its solution) (INFI, 24–5). This milieu emerges precisely because the individual is not capable of exhausting all of the potentials of the pre-individual reality from which it emerges. And indeed, this is why Simondon says that the milieu is itself a system, synthetically grouping together two or more levels of reality (INFI, 30, n.6). It can thus be considered the individual's 'reserve' of pre-individual charge (INFI, 62–3). In any case, the picture that emerges here is of a world composed of heterogeneous orders between which there exists a 'potential energy' which may be actualized in various ways by appropriately structured singularities. The individuals produced by these transductive operations may in turn serve as singularities for other systems or even as relatively amorphous structures (in themselves, or in relation to their milieus) which may be re-structured in encounters with other singularities. As Simondon writes, a being

is genetically constituted by a relation between an energetic condition and a structural condition which prolong their existence in the individual, an individual which can at any moment behave like a structural germ or like an energetic continuum; its relation differs depending on whether it enters into a relation with a milieu which is equivalent to a continuum or with a milieu which has already been structured. (INFI, 110–11)

Of course, these processes of individuation may be more or less complex, depending on the number of systems and subsystems involved. For example, transduction is direct and at a single level in physical systems, and indirect and hierarchized in the living being (INFI, 160).[57] And things are even more complex when we consider the relation between the physical and the biological, or again, the biological and the psychic. At the limit, such a conception of transduction would 'consider the energetic regimes and the structural states as convertible into each other through the becoming of the whole' of Nature (INFI, 148–9). It should be noted, however, that this 'whole' does not dissolve the difference between, and the specificity of, the different domains of individuation. The individual does not have a direct relationship with the whole of Nature (INFI, 65). On the contrary, each regime, as we have seen, is characterized by the type and number of relations and processes it implicates or in which it is implicated. This is precisely what allows Simondon to specify the difference between, for example, the biological and the physical in terms of information and transduction:

[T]here is *physical* information when the system is capable of receiving information just once, then develops and amplifies this initial singularity. If the system is capable of successively receiving several contributions of information, of compatibilizing several singularities instead of repeating the initial singularity, the individuation is vital. (INFI, 152)

So we have our characterization of processes of individuation via the concept of transduction. However, Simondon also gives us another and at first sight unrelated definition of transduction:

Transduction is a mental process [*procédé*] and, even more than a process, a movement [*démarche*] of the mind which discovers. This movement consists in *following being in its genesis*, in accomplishing the genesis of thought at the same time that the genesis of the object is carried out ... Transduction is thus not only movement of the mind; it is also intuition, since it is through transduction that, within a problematic domain, a structure appears as bringing about the resolution of the problems posed. (INFI, 34)

So how is this second definition of transduction to be reconciled with the first? We have already examined two features of Simondon's thought which allow us to see how these two aspects of transduction are to be thought together. The first is Simondon's anti-substantialist assertion that being is through and through relational. In other words, if relations virtually precede their terms in all domains, then not only will we have to characterize concrete processes of individuation in physical, biological, etc., systems in a relational way, the very thought of these processes, and thus the determination of the terms

124

in which these processes are characterized, must also emerge in a relational way. It can thus be said that Simondon's dual definition of transduction as both objective and mental is in line with this requirement for a relational description of processes of all kinds. Indeed, even the relation between the objective and the mental – the relation typically called knowledge – must be described in relational terms. What this means is that, as Simondon writes, 'knowledge is not a relation between a substance object and a substance subject, but the *relation between two relations*, one of which is in the domain of the object and the other in the domain of the subject' (INFI, 82–3).[58]

The second and related feature of Simondon's thought which shows us precisely what he means by 'transduction' is the method he employs in *L'individu et sa genèse*, that is, as has been seen, his encyclopaedic if in principle open investigation of processes of individuation in diverse domains. This method incorporates both the objective and the mental aspects of transduction in a single, speculative philosophy. Indeed, as a number of commentators have noted, Simondon's initial analysis of the formation of crystals through transduction functions as the 'elementary paradigm' for the individuation of the thought of individuation. In other words, the use of this paradigm in different and increasingly complex, 'problematic' domains of knowledge acts as a 'structural germ' for the gradual transformation of our understanding of transductive processes of individuation in these other domains, and in turn leads to an ongoing individuation of our knowledge of individuation (INFI, 33, 83–4, 555).[59] As Simondon describes his method:

> Having thus attempted to seize, on the one hand, the epistemological role of the notion of the individual in this domain, and on the other hand the phenomenological contents to which this notion refers, we will try to transfer the results of this first test to domains which are logically and ontologically subsequent ... [This method] is founded ... on the search for a structure and an operation which is characteristic of the reality that one may name the individual; if this reality exists, it can be applicable to different forms and levels, but must authorize the intellectual transfer from one domain to another, by means of necessary conversions; the notions that it will be necessary to add in order to pass from one domain to the next will thus be characteristic of the order of reality which makes up the content of these domains. (INFI, 555)[60]

Or more simply, as Jean-Hugues Barthélémy has put it, if we are dealing with relations 'all the way down', as it were, then 'to pass from the polarization of the *crystal* to that of the living being, is *to pass from one degree of individuality to an other by a multiplication of the relation*.[61] In short, transduction thus describes, at once, 'real processes of individuation in their analogically connected diversity *and* the kind of thought which allows them to be understood'.[62]

But what now of Deleuze's relation to the philosophical system that Simondon establishes in *L'individu et sa genèse physico-biologique*?

3.4 Deleuze, Simondon and Lautman: Singularity and Problem

There are a number of points at which Simondon's influence on Deleuze's *Difference and Repetition* can clearly be felt. First of all, in terms of general aims, Deleuze, like Simondon, wants to think of 'identities' as ontologically derived entities. What Deleuze calls 'identities', here, have traditionally been understood to be onto-logically primary, self-identical individuals, differing from all others, and whose differential 'criteria of identity' can be conceptually specified using an appropriate means (Platonic division and dialectic, Aristotelian generic and specific difference, Leibnizian compossibil-ity or 'vice-diction', Hegelian contradiction, and so on).[63] Deleuze, however, wants to think identity in terms of difference rather than difference in terms of identity. In other words, as opposed to think-ing difference as a relation between two, already given, self-identical individuals, Deleuze wants to think a differential difference from which all apparently self-identical individuals would ultimately be derived. As he writes, '[d]ifference is the state in which one can speak of determination *as such*' (DR, 28). The task is thus to show how this differential determination or individuating difference ontologically precedes constituted individuals 'all the way down' (DR, 38).

In relation to this aim, Deleuze posits two, intimately related 'halves' of difference. On the one hand, as we have seen, Deleuze speaks of a purely differential, problematic or virtual Idea made up only of differential relations and singularities. On the other hand, this Idea is actualized or differenciated by 'spatio-temporal dyna-misms' or 'intensive processes of individuation' (DR, 279–80). This parallels quite precisely the way in which Simondon posits trans-ductive processes of individuation as actualizing a purely relational pre-individual, made up only of different orders of magnitude and singularities. Indeed, Deleuze himself makes this parallel explicit when he writes that:

Gilbert Simondon has shown recently that individuation presupposes a prior metastable state – in other words, the existence of a 'disparateness' such as at least two orders of magnitude or two scales of heterogeneous reality between which potentials are distributed. Such a pre-individual field nevertheless does not lack singularities: the distinctive or singular points are defined by the existence and distribution of potentials. An 'objective' problematic field thus appears, determined by the distance between two heterogeneous orders. Individuation emerges like the act of solving a problem, or – what amounts to the same thing – like the actualization of a potential and the establishing of communication between disparates. The act of individuation consists ... in integrating the elements of the disparateness into a state of coupling which ensures its internal resonance. The individual thus finds itself attached to a pre-individual half which is not the impersonal within it so much as the reservoir of its singularities. In all these respects, we believe that individuation is essentially intensive, and that the pre-individual field is a virtual-ideal field, made up of differential relations ... Individuation is the act by which intensity determines differential relations to become actualized, along the lines of differenciation and within the qualities and extensities it creates. (DR, 246)

This, then, is Simondon's second influence on Deleuze. In short, Simondon provides Deleuze with a means of speaking about the concrete actualization of those purely problematic Ideas through which every difference can be determined as a difference of difference. Indeed, it appears from the above exposition that Simondon's work directly inspired two of Deleuze's philosophical concepts bound up with his conception of the actualization of problematic Ideas: 'intensity' or 'intensive magnitude', and 'singularities'. To speak, first of all, about the concept of intensity, we do not think it is a coincidence that both Simondon and, subsequently, Deleuze make use of a thermodynamic vocabulary in order to speak about the way in which relations or differences are primary in relation to 'things'. As was seen above, Simondon speaks of 'orders of magnitude', 'metastable systems' and 'potential energy' in order to characterize the pre-individual and defend his commitment to an anti-substantialist 'realism of relations'. Similarly, Deleuze employs the concept of 'intensive quantity' precisely in order to talk about the purely differential basis of 'what happens' and 'what appears'. As he writes:

Everything which happens and everything which appears is correlated with orders of differences: differences of level, temperature, pressure, tension, potential, *difference of intensity* ... Every intensity is $E - E'$, where E itself refers to an $e - e'$, and e to $\varepsilon - \varepsilon'$, etc.: each intensity is already a coupling (in which each element of the couple refers in turn to other elements of another order). (DR, 222)[64]

In terms of the concept of 'singularity', it is again clear that Deleuze's concept resembles Simondon's in many respects. We know that while Simondon privileges an 'informational' model for his concept, Deleuze refers primarily to Weierstrassian analysis (at least implicitly) and Albert Lautman's analysis of Henri Poincaré's 'qualitative theory' of differential equations. However, what both of these models have in common is that they define the concept of singularity entirely in relational terms, that is, as that which allows for the communication and actualization of a purely differential or problematic relation within a new form or individual. More precisely, for both thinkers, a singularity refers to the differential conditions of a purely problematic instance: for Simondon, as has been seen, a singularity is defined by the way in which it 'almost coincides' with the different pre-individual orders between which it establishes communication, just as for Deleuze singularities correspond to the 'values' of the relations between the purely differential elements of the problematic Idea. Furthermore, this same singularity is immanent in the real solutions which 'resolve' this problematic or differential instance: for Simondon, the individual resolving or structuring the relation between different orders of magnitude is said to 'prolong' the singularity which brought them into communication and initiated a transformation, while for Deleuze singularities are said to be 'enveloped' by the intensive series of individuating factors which determine the differential relations of the Idea to be 'actualized' in new forms (DR, 246, 279).[65] In other words, for both philosophers, the singularity refers to both pre-individual relations and to the real forms and individuals which specify the 'actual' nature of these pre-individual relations.

A third point of convergence between Simondon's and Deleuze's respective projects is the claim that intensive processes of individuation concern all of the domains of being: physical, biological, social, psychological, perceptual, linguistic, and so on.[66] In Chapter 5 of *Difference and Repetition*, Deleuze discusses a number of 'intensive systems' belonging to diverse domains, and the various ways in which they have been and ought to be thought. He discusses, for example, classical thermodynamics (DR, 222–4, 228–9, 240–1), Curie's work on symmetry (DR, 222–3; 234),[67] the visual perception of space (DR, 229–31), number theory and order theory (DR, 232–3; 237–8), embryogenesis (DR, 249–52), biological evolution (DR, 255–6), and the relation between self and other in psycho-social systems (DR, 256–61). In Chapter 2, Deleuze also analyzes language in intensive terms, in particular in relation to literary systems (DR, 121–4), psychic systems (DR, 122–6), and psycho-social systems (DR, 261).[68] In fact, Chapter 2's discussion of the passive synthesis of habit in terms of the contemplations and contractions of elementary 'repetitions' is a discussion of the way in which individuals are constituted by syntheses of series of intensive differences, wherein each element of a contracted couple refers to (or 'repeats') coupled elements from other orders:

> What we call wheat is a contraction of the earth and humidity . . . What organism is not made of elements and cases of repetition, of contemplated and contracted water, nitrogen, carbon, chlorides and sulphates, thereby intertwining all the habits of which it is composed? . . . [E]verything is contemplation, even rocks and words, animals and men . . . even our actions and our needs. (DR, 75)

Now, Deleuze further argues (as does Simondon, it can be recalled, when he argues that the individual does not have a direct relationship with the whole of Nature), that even though all the systems and domains of being he discusses have a common 'intensive character', this 'should not prejudice them being characterized as mechanical, physical, biological, psychic, social, aesthetic or philosophical, etc. Each type of system undoubtedly has its own particular conditions' (DR, 117–18). It is nevertheless clear that, for Deleuze as much as for Simondon, a number of systems from different domains can be conjoined in the production of certain individuals. For example, biological, social, psychic and linguistic intensive processes combine to produce modern human beings. What is more, it is evident that if, as Deleuze claims, difference must account for 'determination as such', the relation between these different systems must also be thought 'differentially', that is to say, in relation to purely differential or problematic Ideas (the Simondonian pre-individual).[69]

Of particular relevance with respect to this question of the relation between different intensive systems is the question of the relation between those systems implicated in the production of the individual human being and those systems producing the individuals making up this being's 'world'. Indeed, it is clear that the determination of this relation will have some bearing on how we are to think about 'knowledge'. The question is, in other words: how are we to determine the relation between the development of knowledge embodied in concepts, the intensive constitution of the individuals which are known in various domains, and the intensively constituted knowing subject along with its associated beliefs and desires? We saw that, for Simondon, knowledge is the structuring of a relation between two relations in pre-individual tension, one of which is in the object and the other in the subject. Similarly, Deleuze speaks of a complex differential relation between knowledge, the known and the knowing subject.[70] He argues that intensive processes of individuation progressively determine the actualization of virtual Ideas within concepts corresponding to the resulting individuals, through the intermediary of a 'divided subject' who, while thoroughly dissolved in intensive processes, thinks itself, its world, and the relations between them, in purely differential terms. With respect to the actualization of Ideas by processes of intensive individuation, Deleuze writes that 'the role of dramas [i.e., intensive processes of individuation] is to specify concepts by incarnating the differential relations and singularities of an Idea' (DR, 218). Or again:

> It is because of the action of the field of individuation that such and such differential relations and such and such distinctive points (pre-individual fields) are actualized – in other words, organized within intuition along lines differenciated in relation to other lines. As a result, they then form the quality, number, species and parts of an individual, in short, its generality. (DR, 247)[71]

As for the 'divided subject', it is on the one hand a 'dissolved self', which is to say 'an event which takes place in pre-existing fields of [intensive] individuation: it contemplates and contracts the individuating factors of such fields, and constitutes itself at the points of resonance of their series' (DR, 276). On the other hand, it is a 'fractured I' who does not so much actively and spontaneously think (since psychic systems are, properly speaking, systems of intensive individuation), as stand in a relation to those pre-individual and impersonal problematic Ideas wherein the psychological self, its intensive world, and the relations between them, can progressively be thought, that is to say, differentially determined 'all the way down' (DR, 86).[72] As Deleuze writes,

> the individual in intensity finds its psychic image . . . in the correlation of the fractured I with the dissolved self . . . [W]hat swarms around the edges of the fracture are Ideas in the form of problems – in other words,

in the form of multiplicities made up of differential relations and variations of relations, distinctive points and transformations of points. These
ideas, however, are expressed in individuating factors, in the implicated
world of intensive quantities which constitute the universal concrete
individuality of the thinker or the system of the dissolved Self. (DR, 259)

Or again:

> Every body, every thing, thinks and is a thought to the extent that,
> reduced to its intensive reasons, it expresses an Idea the actualization of
> which it determines. However, the thinker himself makes his individual
> differences from all manner of things: it is in this sense that he is laden
> with stones and diamonds, plants 'and even animals'. The thinker . . .
> is he who makes use of all the power of the clear and the confused, of
> the clear-confused [i.e., of implicated and implicating intensities], in
> order to think Ideas in all their power as distinct-obscure [i.e., as fully
> differen*t*iated but not yet differen*c*iated or actualized]. (DR, 254)

As with Simondon, then, Deleuze understands 'knowing' to be the
actualization of a relation, in pre-individual or differential 'tension',
between two systems of differential relations, one constitutive of the
known individual and the other of the knowing subject. More precisely, knowing is an ongoing, open-ended and differential process
involving the simultaneous actualization of ideal, pre-individual relations in persons, individual things, and the concepts corresponding
to these persons and individuals.

Now, let us recall that the original aim of the above analyses was
to examine Deleuze's contention that the sense and truth value of
propositions in relation to their corresponding objects are located
in a sub-representative problematic Idea in relation to which these
propositions 'make sense', in both the passive and active senses of
'make sense', as cases of solution. In particular, it was argued that
philosophical propositions with respect to the objective nature of this
sub-representative problematic Idea must also find their sense and
truth value in relation to the problem. And we have seen Deleuze's
philosophical solution to this 'problem of the problem': it 'makes
sense' to characterize the problematic Idea by the reciprocal, complete
and progressive determination of differential elements in relation to
the adjunction and transformation of singularities, precisely in so far
as it also 'makes sense' to say that everything that happens and everything that appears is due to differential intensive processes (along
with their corresponding potentials for transformation) which, via
the intermediary of the intensive individuation of a 'divided subject',

actualize this Idea for this subject in the qualities and extensities which 'make sense' of the things populating our world.

However, two questions still remain for us to consider. First of all, in what form do we find these considerations from *Difference and Repetition* expressed in *The Logic of Sense*? Secondly, how are these considerations with regard to the philosophical concepts of the problem and singularity supposed to apply to particular, non-philosophical propositions constitutive of diverse domains of knowledge and bearing on states of affairs which, as Deleuze contends, are constituted by events? Indeed, we can at this stage only affirm in a general way, following Deleuze's alignment of Simondon's work with the Lautmanian problematic Idea, that in so far as intensive processes actualize the problematic Idea and thereby generate knowledge and the known in diverse domains, then propositions constitutive of knowledge and bearing on the known must find their sense and truth value within the problem. But in fact, to affirm this presupposes that we can speak of the language in which these propositions are formulated in differential and intensive terms and, therefore, as determined or 'making sense' within the problematic Idea.

We shall leave this second question for Chapter 4, when we examine Deleuze's use of structuralism in *The Logic of Sense*. Even though, as will be seen, Deleuze views structuralism through the lens of his philosophical concepts of singularity and the problem, most of his pronouncements with regard to the serial or differential organization of objective things and events on the one hand, and propositional denotations and expressions on the other, are formulated using a structuralist vocabulary. So, in light of the above analyses of *Difference and Repetition*, let us now rather answer the first question by examining Deleuze's account of the problem and singularity in *The Logic of Sense*.

As noted above, the most important series for our examination of the concepts of singularity and the problem are the 'Ninth Series of the Problematic', the 'Fifteenth Series of Singularities', and the 'Seventeenth Series of the Static Logical Genesis'. In particular, in the 'Fifteenth Series', Deleuze outlines five characteristics of the world of singularities and the problem which coincide with the above analyses. The first characteristic is that

> singularities-events correspond to heterogeneous series which are organized into a system which is neither stable nor unstable, but rather 'metastable', endowed with a potential energy wherein the differences between series are distributed. (Potential energy is the energy of the pure event,

whereas forms of actualization correspond to the realization of the event).
(LS, 103)

Now, there are in fact two points packed into this first characteristic. With regard to the first point (that singularities-events correspond to heterogeneous series . . .), Deleuze omits a minor detail discussed elsewhere in *The Logic of Sense*, namely, that series are composed of 'ordinary points' or 'terms which exist only through the relations they maintain with one another' (LS, 50). To be precise, then, singularities-events correspond, not simply to heterogeneous series, but to the 'values' of the 'relations' between the terms or ordinary points constituting the series (LS, 50). What is essential for our purposes here, of course, is to understand that this 'metastable system' comprised of singularities and series of ordinary points is identical to what was called above the problematic Idea. Indeed, as was said, the problem is composed of merely determinable elements which are reciprocally determined in relation to each other with reference to singularities corresponding to the values of the relations between these elements.

The second point at stake in the above citation concerns the notion of 'potential energy' and its actualization. It is clear that Deleuze is here following, at least to some extent, Simondon's use of this term to describe the potential for transformation which exists in the relation between different orders of magnitude, whatever these may be. However, it should be emphasized that Deleuze here speaks of 'potential energy' only with reference to the 'pure event' and not a physical state of affairs. By 'pure event', of course, Deleuze means the Unique Event, Aion or problematic Idea, that is to say, the 'evental-determination' of singularities-events and the purely differential elements which depend on them. The potential energy of the pure event thus refers to the serial distribution of difference within the problematic Idea. As Deleuze puts it in *Difference and Repetition*, 'the differential relation is a pure element of potentiality' (DR, 175).

Now, corresponding to the realization of the potential energy of the problem – or of the differences constitutive of this potential – are 'forms of actualization'. And this maps equally neatly onto the discussion of the problematic Idea above, since the progressive determination of the problematic Idea automatically entails the genesis of determined individuals. In other words, the problematic Idea is a differential 'pre-individual field' which will have been said to be (reciprocally, completely and progressively) determined in so far as it is actualized in the qualities and extensities characterizing worldly individuals. In fact, it should be noted that this is precisely what was meant in Chapter 2 when it was argued that worldly individuals will be determined in their related differences in so far as each of the singularity-events which characterize them is 'analytically prolonged over a series of ordinary points up to the neighbourhood of another singularity' (LS, 109, translation modified). Indeed, let us recall that for Leibniz, and Deleuze following him, there are within a world both distinct (or singular) events and obscure (or ordinary) events making up the lives of the individuals belonging to this world. Following a principle of sufficient reason, singular events are said to be 'analytically prolonged' over series of ordinary events in so far as the reason why these series of ordinary events are attributable to a series of related individuals is explained by a relation between individuals characterized by the distinct or singular events. In other words, the 'analytic prolongation' of singularities-events over series of ordinary events up to the 'neighbourhood' of other such singularities determines these ordinary events in their relations, and thereby also determines the law-like relations between those worldly individuals which are inter-defined by these events, whether ordinary or singular. As Deleuze puts it in his work on Leibniz in the 'Sixteenth Series of Ontological Genesis', returning to the notion of 'potential energy': 'it is in the same way that a singularity is prolonged over a line of ordinary points and that a potential energy is actualized and falls to its lowest level' (LS, 110).

Now, following once again the 'Fifteenth Series of Singularities', Deleuze states that the second characteristic of the world of singularities and the problem is that 'singularities possess a process of auto-unification, always mobile and displaced to the extent that a paradoxical element traverses the series and makes them resonate, enveloping the corresponding singular points in a single aleatory point and all the emissions, all dice throws, in a single cast' (LS, 103). To what aspect or aspects of the problematic Idea does this characteristic correspond? As was seen above, the problematic Idea is not only reciprocally determined, but also completely and progressively determined. As was argued, the reciprocal determination of merely determinable elements cannot not imply completion even over divergent series, and what is more, such a complete, internal determination could only ever be carried out progressively and 'experimentally', from one series of determinations to another and back again.[73] In other words, the reciprocal and complete determination of merely determinable elements implies the ongoing, intrinsic, and step by step securing of terms or forms, by means of the 'adjunction' and 'transformation' of the singularities-events corresponding to the values of the relations between these elements. As Deleuze puts it in the 'Seventeenth Series':

> As for the determination of the conditions [of the problem], it implies, on the one hand, a space of nomad distribution in which singularities are distributed (*Topos*); on the other hand, it implies a time of decomposition whereby this space is subdivided into sub-spaces. Each one of these sub-spaces is successively defined by the adjunction of new points ensuring the progressive and complete determination of the domain under consideration (Aion). There is always a space which condenses and precipitates singularities, just as there is always a time which progressively completes the event through fragments of future and past events. Thus, there is a spatio-temporal self-determination of the problem, in the sequence of which the problem advances . . . Solutions are engendered at precisely the time that the problem determines *itself*. (LS, 121, emphasis added)

So we now understand the idea of a mobile and displaced – that is to say, progressive and experimental – process of the auto-unification (complete determination) of singularities-events. But what about the 'paradoxical element' on which this process depends? Let us recall that in Chapter 1 it was suggested that the paradoxical element could be understood in terms of the incorporeal 'instant' which not only traces the line of Aion (that is to say, gathers together all of the incorporeal events making up the cosmos), but is also represented and actualized by the Stoic sage who wills and 'identifies' with it (by giving his or her body to the ongoing determination of the event in which he or she participates). In Chapter 2, the paradoxical element was characterized as the person understood as 'nobody'. Because it is common to divergent worlds, the person was said to be an 'operator' in the disjunctive synthesis – or, we might say, the 'differential determination' – of divergent series of events. But what is more, the person was also said to be a 'produced form' derived from such syntheses and thus inseparable from relations to other persons, worlds and event-determined individuals. The person, then, as a general 'operator', was said to be by nature perpetually displaced or decentred. Now, taking up the vocabulary of singularities and problems in the 'Ninth Series of the Problematic', Deleuze writes that:

> If the distributions of singularities corresponding to each series form fields of problems, how are we to characterize the paradoxical element which runs through the series, makes them resonate, communicate and branch

out, and which exercises command over all the repetitions, transformations and redistributions? This element must itself be defined as the locus
of a question. The *problem* is determined by *singular points* corresponding to the series, but the *question* is determined by an *aleatory point* corresponding to the empty square or mobile element. The metamorphoses
or redistributions of singularities form a history; each combination and
each distribution is an event. But the paradoxical element is the Event in
which all events communicate and are distributed. It is the Unique event,
and all other events are its bits and pieces . . . The question is developed
in problems, and the problems are enveloped in a fundamental question.
(LS, 56)

We thus see that in this new vocabulary the paradoxical element
once again implies both a personal moment, in so far as the 'question' necessarily implies a 'questioner', and an impersonal moment
in so far as the question is 'developed' in problems which, as we
know, are ontologically prior to any determined form. And here,
it is important to recall that in *Difference and Repetition* Deleuze
explains how these two aspects of the question are related by speaking of questions as 'imperative questions' (see, for what follows,
DR, 195–200). In short, that a question is 'imperative' means that
the question is forced upon or experienced as a 'problem' by a
questioner. The experience of a problem (the divergence of series
of events within a world, for example) puts the worldly questioner
'into question', as it were, and forces him or her to answer. On the
other hand, problems are said to emanate from questions, for the
distribution of the singularities-events which condition the problem,
along with the solutions in which this problem is incarnated, will
depend on the answer forced from the questioner (which is to say,
in Deleuze's neo-Leibnizian vocabulary, that they will depend on
the disjunctive synthesis of the divergent series which the questioner experienced as a problem). Furthermore, it follows from the
above that the questioner is never the ultimate source of problems
and questions, for in so far as the questioner is itself a 'solution' or
derived form, its capacity to be affected by problems could only be
the result of prior distributions of singularities-events. And nor is the
question an original instance, for it refers only to the infinite power
of problems to put questioners into question. Finally, it follows that
the problem itself is always derived, for the determination of the
conditions of the problem as a problem refers back to imperative
questions and thus to questioners. Comparing this situation to a
'throw of the dice', Deleuze writes:

The singular points are on the die; the questions are the dice themselves; the imperative is to throw. Ideas are the problematic combinations which result from the throws ... The throw of the dice carries out the calculation of problems, the determination of differential elements or the distribution of singular points which constitute a structure. The circular relation between imperatives and the problems which proceed from them is formed in this manner. (DR, 198)

Or again, as Deleuze puts it in *The Logic of Sense*:

Each throw operates a distribution of singularities, a constellation. But instead of dividing a closed space between fixed results which correspond to hypotheses, the mobile results are distributed in the open space of the unique and undivided cast. This is a *nomadic* and non-sedentary *distribution*, wherein each system of singularities communicates and resonates with the others, being at once implicated by the others and implicating them in the most important cast. It is the game of problems and of the question. (LS, 60)

So now we see how Deleuze understands singularities to possess a process of auto-unification or complete determination, which itself refers to a progressive and experimental determination which is always-already 'underway'. What is more, it is clear that this process implies a subject or 'questioner' (or rather an open series of such subjects) who, while never the ultimate source of problems and questions, is a necessary operator in their open, 'circular' relation. As was argued above, this questioner is the 'divided subject' who is thoroughly 'dissolved' in the (biological, psycho-social, etc.) intensive processes constituting it, and who, in the absence of some underlying substance, is forced by such processes to think their differential co-existence, along with the relations between the worldly individuals to which they give rise, in the form of the ongoing determination of the problematic Idea. Or again, in Deleuze's neo-Leibnizian vocabulary, the questioner is *personne*, that is, nobody: a produced form who is also an operator in the disjunctive syntheses of divergent series of ordinary events and the singularities-events upon which they depend. Finally, the questioner is also the Stoic sage who, willing, representing and actualizing the event, gives his or her body to its ongoing determination. But now we also know that if it is the sage who throws the dice, as it were, it is nevertheless the Aion which is 'the ideal player of the game ... the unique cast from which all throws are qualitatively distinguished' (LS, 64).

The 'third characteristic' of the world of singularities and the problem is that 'singularities or potentials haunt the surface' (LS, 103). The two examples which Deleuze here provides of singularities and surfaces are, following Simondon's work, the development of a crystal at the surface (or, rather, at its 'edges', no doubt in relation to a seed crystal acting as a singularity in relation to the structuring of tensions in a super-saturated solution), and mucous membranes, which put the entire internal organization of an organism in contact with its external environment at the level of the skin. Now, I want to argue with respect to this 'third characteristic' that Deleuze is essentially talking about those intensive processes (here, physical and biological) which are bound up with the actualization of the problematic Idea. Although Deleuze does not use the term 'intensive' or 'intensive processes' in *The Logic of Sense*, in the Seventeenth Series he does talk in very general terms about a 'physics of surfaces'; and this physics of surfaces, it appears, is by nature intensive. He writes that bodies, their mixtures and their actions and passions contribute to the production of sense 'at the surface' because the 'depth' in which they are enveloped

> acts in an original way, *by means of its power to organize surfaces and to envelop itself within surfaces*. This pulsation sometimes acts through the formation of a minimum amount of surface for a maximum amount of matter (thus the spherical form), and sometimes through the growth of surfaces and their multiplication in accordance with diverse processes (stretching, fragmenting, crushing, drying and moistening, absorbing, foaming, emulsifying, etc.) . . . The surface is neither active nor passive, it is the product of the actions and passions of mixed bodies . . . Being a theatre for sudden condensations, fusions, changes in the states of extended layers and for distributions and reshufflings of singularities, the surface may indefinitely increase, as in the case of two liquids dissolving into each other. There is therefore an entire physics of surfaces as the effect of deep mixtures – a physics which endlessly assembles the variations and the pulsations of the entire universe, enveloping them inside these mobile limits. (LS, 124–5)[74]

This Deleuzian 'physics of surfaces' has been explicitly analyzed by DeLanda in intensive terms. He argues that a large number of different physical structures form spontaneously when 'their components try to meet certain energetic requirements' or 'seek a point of minimal free energy'. Thus, for example, the soap bubble 'acquires its spherical form by minimizing surface tension' and the salt crystal 'adopts the form of a cube by minimizing bonding energy'.[75] In other words 'soap bubbles and salt crystals . . . are equilibrium structures which emerge from a process driven by intensive gradients, or more exactly, from the spontaneous tendency of the molecular components of bubbles or crystals to minimize a potential (or minimize an intensive difference)'.[76] Following DeLanda's analyses, then, it would appear that Deleuze's 'physics of surfaces' is indeed intensive, in the sense this latter term has in *Difference and Repetition*. It would also appear that it is due to this intensive physics of surfaces that, as was said above, 'potentials for transformation' – that is to say, singularities corresponding to the values of the differences constitutive of this potential – 'haunt the surface' (third characteristic of the world of singularities and the problem).

Now, it should also be noted that Deleuze immediately connects this talk of an intensive physics of surfaces to the notion of a metaphysical surface (transcendental or problematic field, etc.) which is the locus of sense. To continue the previous citation from the Seventeenth Series:

And to the physics of surfaces a metaphysical surface necessarily corresponds. Metaphysical surface (*transcendental field*) is the name that will be given to the frontier established, on one hand, between bodies taken together as a whole and inside the limits [of the physical surfaces] which envelop them, and on the other, propositions in general ... In all these respects, the surface is the transcendental field itself, and the locus of sense and expression. Sense is that which is formed and developed at the surface. Even the frontier is not a separation, but rather the element of an articulation, so that sense is presented both as that which happens to bodies and that which insists in propositions. (LS, 125)

But in fact, this is precisely the 'fourth characteristic' of the world of singularities and the problem which Deleuze spells out in the 'Fifteenth Series of Singularities': not only do singularities or potentials haunt the surface, as illustrated by processes of crystallization and the development of biological organisms, this 'surface is the locus of *sense*', and 'signs [i.e., singularities-events] remain deprived of sense as long as they do not enter into the surface organization which assures the resonance of two series (two images-signs, two photographs, two tracks, etc.)' (LS, 104).[77] So it would appear that if the metaphysical surface is the frontier between bodies and propositions in general, haunted by singularities-events corresponding to series of differences which will be subject to processes of reciprocal, complete and progressive determination, then it is nothing other than that problem or problematic Idea whose concept Deleuze introduced in order to speak of the internal genesis of the sense and truth of propositions, along with the objects to which these senses apply and which realize these truths. Apart from mentioning 'the resonance of two series', however, Deleuze does not at this point spell out exactly how 'that which happens to bodies' and 'that which insists in propositions' are supposed to 'correspond' within the problem. We must rather examine Deleuze's work on structuralism and, finally, psychoanalysis to appreciate this point, and this will form part of the subject matter of Chapters 4 and 5 respectively.

This then leads us to Deleuze's fifth and final characteristic of the world of singularities and the problem, namely, that

> this world of sense has a properly *problematic* status: singularities are distributed in a properly problematic field and crop up in this field as topological events to which no direction is attached . . . This allows us, as we have seen, to give an entirely objective definition to the term 'problematic' and to the indetermination which it carries along, since the nature of directed singularities and their existence and directionless distribution depend on objectively distinct instances. (LS, 104–5)

What Deleuze is signalling with the above is not only, as we have just established, that the 'world of sense' is by nature thoroughly problematic (in the sense this latter term has in *Difference and Repetition*). What is more, the fully differential and objective problem characterizing the world of sense is distinct from the propositions and objective correlates of these propositions which will appear as its resolutions. In other words, in relation to these latter, the problem is sub-representative or virtual, and will persist in the solutions which express it.

In relation to these five characteristics set out in the Fifteenth Series, we can now see that the full definition of the problem or problematic Idea such as this can be found in *Difference and Repetition* is applicable to the world of sense, Aion or the 'static genesis' found in *The Logic of Sense*. The problem will thus be said to be composed of merely determinable, fully differential elements which are reciprocally, completely and progressively determined in relation to the adjunction and transformation of singularities-events corresponding to the values of the relations between these elements. What is more, these processes of determination are carried out in relation to a 'divided subject' (*personne*, questioner, dice-thrower, etc.) – or, rather, to an open series of such subjects – who, without reference to some underlying substance to which the play of difference could be reduced, must progressively and experimentally think its intensive world, and its own self therein, by actualizing the fully differential elements and singularities (potential energy) of the ultimately inexhaustible problem.

But now, what more can be said of that aspect of the problem which concerns the sense and truth of propositions in relation to their corresponding objects? In fact, there are three further characteristics of singularities and the problem that are not discussed by Deleuze in the Fifteenth Series, but which are discussed elsewhere in *The Logic of Sense*, and which correspond to this final aspect of the problematic Idea. First of all, Deleuze writes in the Seventeenth Series that the problem '*is not* propositional, although it does not exist outside of the propositions which express it' (LS, 122). However, because we are leaving a discussion of language and propositions until Chapter 4, when we address Deleuze's relation to structuralism, we shall deal with this point then.

The second and related point is that singularities-events are expressed in propositions. Indeed, as we have already seen, Deleuze argues that the verb of the proposition expresses an event (see, for example, LS, 24). But once again, because further consideration of this point necessitates an examination of Deleuze's treatment of language and propositions, we shall return to it in Chapter 4.

The third and final point is that the world of the problem and singularities-events both engenders 'the logical proposition with its determinate dimensions (denotation, manifestation, and signification)' and 'engenders also the objective correlates of this proposition which were themselves first produced as ontological propositions (the denoted, the manifested, and the signified)' (LS, 120). Indeed, Deleuze elsewhere writes that singularities-events 'characterize' each of the objective correlates of the three dimensions of the proposition: concepts, states of affairs and persons. As he puts it:

> an ideal event ... is a singularity – or rather a set of singularities or of singular points characterizing a mathematical curve, a physical state of affairs, a psychological and moral person. Singularities are turning points and points of inflection; saddle points, nodes, focus points, and centres [*des cols, des nœuds, des foyers, des centres*]; points of fusion, condensation and boiling; points of tears and joy, sickness and health, hope and anxiety, 'sensitive' points. (LS, 52, translation modified)

And in fact, in Chapter 2, we analyzed this genetic role that singularities-events play in relation to the determination of concepts, individuals and persons. We said that disjunctive syntheses of divergent series of singularities-events imply the simultaneous and related determinations of: (at least two) persons, a world of individuals corresponding to the beliefs of these persons, and variable and overlapping classes of trope-like events corresponding to properties of increasing and decreasing generality which are exemplified by these individuals and persons synthesized out of the initially incompossible worlds. But again, we must ask, what is the role of language in these disjunctive syntheses? Surely the relation between persons established in these disjunctive syntheses – along with the relation between these persons, the determined concepts which they share, and the determined individuals falling under these concepts – must be mediated by language? Again, then, we will be obliged to return to this point in Chapter 4.

Notes

1. It is interesting to note that the doctoral thesis which would later become *Difference and Repetition* was originally conceived as a project dealing with 'the idea of the problem'. See François Dosse, *Gilles Deleuze et Félix Guattari: Biographie Croisée* (Paris: La Découverte, 2007), p. 147.
2. The corresponding sections in *The Logic of Sense* are: LS, 18–19 and 96.
3. In *The Logic of Sense*, following Lautman, Deleuze maintains both that 'the instance-problem and instance-solution differ in nature', and that the singularities which constitute the conditions of the problem also 'preside over the genesis of the solution' (LS, 54. See also LS, 104–5 and n.4, 344–5).
4. On solutions necessarily following 'from the complete conditions under which the problem is determined as a problem', see DR, 159 and LS, 54. With regard to problems-Ideas, Deleuze writes that Ideas are 'essentially "problematic"' and, conversely, 'problems are Ideas' (DR, 168). In *The Logic of Sense*, Deleuze speaks of problems as Ideas only once, when he writes: 'Even if the problem is concealed by its solution, it subsists nonetheless in the Idea which relates it to its conditions and organizes the genesis of the solutions. Without this Idea, the solution would have no *sense*. The problematic is both an objective category of knowledge and a perfectly objective kind of being. "Problematic" qualifies precisely the ideal objectivities. Kant was without doubt the first to accept the problematic not as a fleeting uncertainty but as the very object of the Idea, and thereby as an indispensable horizon of all that occurs or appears' (LS, 54).
5. See also on this James Williams, *Gilles Deleuze's* Difference and

Repetition: *A Critical Introduction and Guide* (Edinburgh: Edinburgh University Press, 2003), pp. 142–3.

6. On the 'rigorous formulation' see Carl B. Boyer, *The History of the Calculus and its Conceptual Development* (New York: Dover, 1959), pp. 267–98. Deleuze's reference to Jean Bordas-Demoulin is to his work, *Le Cartésianisme ou la véritable rénovation des sciences* (Paris: Hetzel, 1843), pp. 133–5.

7. See Simon Duffy, *The Logic of Expression: Quality, Quantity and Intensity in Spinoza, Hegel and Deleuze* (Aldershot: Ashgate, 2006), pp. 49–50; and 'The Mathematics of Deleuze's Differential Logic and Metaphysics', in Simon Duffy (ed.), *Virtual Mathematics: The Logic of Difference* (Manchester: Clinamen, 2006), pp. 119–20. See also Daniel W. Smith's analysis of this point in relation to an example drawn from Leibniz in 'The Conditions of the New', *Deleuze Studies* 1: 1 (2007), pp. 10–11.

8. As Duffy has clearly shown, Deleuze is almost certainly here following certain aspects of Weierstrassian analysis from 'the local point of view'. On Deleuze and Weierstrass see Duffy, *The Logic of Expression*, pp. 69–75; 'The Mathematics of Deleuze's Differential Logic and Metaphysics', pp. 127–32; and 'Schizo-Math: The Logic of Different/ciation and the Philosophy of Difference', *Angelaki* 9: 3 (2004), pp. 204–5.

9. Aden Evens, 'Math Anxiety', *Angelaki* 5: 3 (2000), p. 111. See also Duffy, 'The Mathematics of Deleuze's Differential Logic and Metaphysics', pp. 126–32.

10. On Wronski, see Boyer, *The History of the Calculus*, pp. 261–3.

11. Further on, when Deleuze writes that '[p]ower is the form of reciprocal determination according to which variable magnitudes are taken to be functions of one another' (DR, 174, emphasis added), we must remember that as a power series expands by means of the repeated differentiation of the differential relation at a given point, the exponent, or 'power', of each successive term increases. Indeed, given a function $f(x)$, the general formula for a power series is $a_0 + a_1x + a_2x^2 + a_3x^3 + \ldots a_nx^n + \ldots$ (where a is a distinct constant).

12. See Evens, 'Math Anxiety', p. 112. For elementary examples of various species of function and their singularities in the early period of the calculus, see Morris Kline, *Mathematical Thought from Ancient to Modern Times* (New York: Oxford University Press, 1972), pp. 547–54; on Weierstrass see pp. 642–4; for more advanced considerations on singularities, see pp. 721–38.

13. Duffy, 'Schizo-Math', pp. 204–5. See also LS, 52–3: 'the singular point is opposed to the ordinary . . . each singularity is the source of a series [of ordinary points] extending in a determined direction right up to the vicinity of another singularity'.

14. In speaking of 'differential series' and 'singularities' in relation to the 'minimal conditions for a *structure*' – which, as will be seen in Chapter 4, is another term for the problem or problematic Idea – Deleuze writes that each 'series is constituted by terms which exist only through the relations they maintain with one another. To these relations, or rather to the values of these relations, there correspond very particular events, that is, *singularities* which are assignable within the structure. The situation is very similar to that of the differential calculus, where distributions of singularities correspond to the values of differential relations ... Moreover, it seems that the singularities attached to a series determine in a complex manner the terms of the other series' (LS, 50).

15. With regard to the convergence and divergence of series in the neighbourhood of singularities, that is to say, with regard to the differences between 'removable singularities' and 'poles', see Duffy, 'The Mathematics of Deleuze's Differential Logic and Metaphysics', pp. 130–1. In this paragraph, we are following the general lines of Duffy's work, in particular his 'Mathematics of Deleuze's Differential Logic and Metaphysics', and 'Schizo-Math'.

16. For a full examination of the topic, see June Barrow-Green, *Poincaré and the Three Body Problem* (Rhode Island: The American Mathematical Society, 1997), in particular pp. 29–33. See also Kline, *Mathematical Thought*, pp. 732–8.

17. Manuel DeLanda, *Intensive Science and Virtual Philosophy* (London and New York: Continuum, 2002), p. 15.

18. Not only DeLanda but also Jean-Michel Salanskis and Jean Petitot have pointed out the proximity of Deleuze's work to dynamical systems theory. See Jean-Michel Salanskis, 'Mathematics, Metaphysics, Philosophy', in Duffy (ed.), *Virtual Mathematics: The Logic of Difference*, pp. 46–64; and Jean Petitot, *Morphogenèse du sens* (Paris: PUF, 1985).

19. On this, see also Daniel W. Smith, 'Axiomatics and Problematics as Two Modes of Formalization: Deleuze's Epistemology of Mathematics', in Duffy (ed.), *Virtual Mathematics: The Logic of Difference*, pp. 161–2.

20. Similarly, in *The Logic of Sense*: 'A problem is determined only by the singular points which express its conditions. We do not say that the problem is thereby resolved; on the contrary, it is determined as a problem. For example, in the theory of differential equations, the existence and distribution of singularities are relative to a problematic field defined by the equation as such. As for the solution, it appears only with the integral curves and the form they taken in the neighbourhood [*voisinage*] of singularities inside the field of vectors. It seems, therefore, that a problem always finds the solution it merits, according to the conditions which determine it as a problem. In fact, the singularities preside over the genesis of the solutions of the equation. Nonetheless,

it is still the case, as Lautman said, that the instance-problem and the instance-solution differ in nature – as they represent the ideal event and its spatio-temporal realization' (LS, 54, translation modified).

21. See the collection of Albert Lautman's works, *Les mathématiques, les idées et le réel physique* (Paris: Vrin, 2006), pp. 295–6.

22. Indeed, even in an early presentation of the major themes of *Difference and Repetition*, when Deleuze is questioned over his 'use' of mathematics, he immediately invokes Lautman's thesis that mathematics necessarily participates in a dialectic of Ideas which surpasses it. See Gilles Deleuze, 'The Method of Dramatization', in *Desert Islands and Other Texts 1953–1974*, trans. Michael Taormina, ed. David Lapoujade (New York: Semiotexte, 2004), p. 107.

23. See also on this, Jean-Michel Salanskis, 'Pour une épistémologie de la lecture', *Alliage* 35–36 (1998), http://www.tribunes.com/tribune/alliage/accueil.htm. See also his 'Idea and Destination', in Patton (ed.), *Deleuze: A Critical Reader*, p. 61.

24. It is clear that it is a discussion of problematic or dialectical Ideas which is missing from Deleuze's references to Lautman in *The Logic of Sense*. As seen above, Deleuze refers directly in *The Logic of Sense* to Lautman's discussion of the qualitative theory of differential equations in order to talk about the difference in nature between the problem and the solution, as well as about the transcendence/immanence of the problem in relation to its solutions. He does not, however, mention the Lautmanian thesis, defended in *Difference and Repetition*, that the constitution of such mathematical theory itself presupposes the problem or problematic Idea.

25. Lautman, *Les mathématiques*, p. 223. On the question of the 'meaning' that the dialectic of Ideas imparts to the theories, see in particular Jean Petitot, 'Refaire le "Timée" – Introduction à la philosophie mathématique d'Albert Lautman', *Revue d'histoire des sciences* 40: 1 (1987), pp. 79–115. For an introduction to the work of Lautman in English, see Charles Alunni, 'Continental Genealogies. Mathematical Confrontations in Albert Lautman and Gaston Bachelard', in Duffy (ed.), *Virtual Mathematics: The Logic of Difference*, pp. 65–80; and Simon Duffy, 'Albert Lautman', in Graham Jones and Jon Roffe (eds), *Deleuze's Philosophical Lineage* (Edinburgh: Edinburgh University Press, 2009), pp. 356–79.

26. Lautman, *Les mathématiques*, p. 229, p. 243, p. 260 and p. 276.

27. Ibid., p. 66, p. 229, pp. 243–4 and p. 262.

28. Ibid., p. 262 (my translation).

29. Ibid., p. 229.

30. Ibid., p. 260.

31. Ibid., p. 229.

32. Ibid., p. 242.

33. Nor, evidently, can we find this sufficient reason in the theories' greater or lesser abilities to appropriate an already given empirical real. See Catherine Chevalley, 'Albert Lautman et le souci logique', *Revue d'histoire des sciences* 40: 1 (1987), p. 61.

34. The terms *mixtes* is Lautman's. See *Les mathématiques*, pp. 197–210.

35. Deleuze takes up these notions of complete and progressive determination (as well as the group-theoretical concept of 'adjunction') in his discussion of the 'problem' in *The Logic of Sense*: 'The relation between the problem and its conditions defines sense as the truth of the problem as such . . . As for the determination of conditions, it implies, one the one hand, a space of nomad distribution in which singularities are distributed (*Topos*); on the other hand, it implies a time of decomposition whereby this space is subdivided into sub-spaces. Each one of these sub-spaces is successively defined by the adjunction of new points ensuring *the progressive and complete determination* of the domain under consideration (Aion)' (LS, 120–1, emphasis added). Although Deleuze does not speak of 'determinability' or 'reciprocal determination' in *The Logic of Sense*, he does say, in line with the discussion above, that the series constitutive of a structure or problem are 'constituted by terms which exist only through the relations they maintain with one another' (LS, 50). On the systematic and serial distribution of differences in the problem, see also LS, 103.

36. See on this, Ian Stewart and Martin Golubitsky, *Fearful Symmetry* (Oxford: Blackwell, 1992), p. 42; and DeLanda, *Intensive Science*, pp. 182–4. For more advanced considerations, see Kline, *Mathematical Thought*, pp. 755–63. On Deleuze and group theory see Daniel W. Smith, 'Mathematics and the Theory of Multiplicities', *The Southern Journal of Philosophy* 45 (2003), p. 427; and Salanskis, 'Mathematics, Metaphysics, Philosophy', pp. 52–3.

37. On the importance of Riemann's work (and its extensions) for Deleuze, see Arkady Plotnitsky, 'Manifolds: On the Concept of Space in Riemann and Deleuze', in Duffy (ed.), *Virtual Mathematics: The Logic of Difference*, pp. 187–208.

38. On 'differential invariants', see Kline, *Mathematical Thought*, p. 900. The way in which all of the above-mentioned branches of mathematics (the differential calculus, singularity theory, group theory and differential geometry) converge in dynamical systems theory, and the relation of this latter to Deleuze's philosophy, is the subject of DeLanda's *Intensive Science*.

39. While discussing 'manifolds', Kline writes: 'Riemann developed an intrinsic geometry for any space. He . . . speaks of n-dimensional space as a manifold. A point in a manifold of n dimensions is represented by assigning special values to n variable parameters, $x_1, x_2, \ldots x_n$, and the aggregate of all such possible points constitutes the n-dimensional

manifold itself . . . The *n* variable parameters are called coordinates of the manifold. When the *xi*'s vary continuously, the points range over the manifold. . . .' See his *Mathematical Thought*, p. 890.

40. '[T]he essential aspects of sufficient reason – determinability, reciprocal determination, complete determination – find their systematic unity in progressive determination. In effect, the reciprocity of determination does not signify a regression, nor a marking time, but a veritable progression in which the reciprocal terms must be secured step by step, and the relations themselves established between them. The completeness of the determination also implies the progressivity of the adjunct fields . . . In this sense, by virtue of this progressivity, every structure has a purely logical, ideal or dialectical time. However, this virtual time itself determines a time of differenciation, or rather rhythms or different times of actualization which correspond to the relations and singularities of the structure and, for their part, measure the passage from virtual to actual . . . Each differenciation is a local integration or a local solution which then connects with others in the overall solution or the global integration' (DR, 210–11).

41. As Salanskis puts it, 'a plural game of singularities . . . generates a proper space of the problem, an internal topology of the virtual, through a process which Deleuze called *differentiation*. But this process cannot avoid simultaneously being the process of the concrete formation of real individuals, and the design of actual areas in the world, occupied by these individuals: such an effective and actual process Deleuze calls *differenciation* . . . This description, or, better said, this matrix-story, is supposed to hold for the individuation of every being in the universe', whether natural or cultural. See his 'Mathematics, Metaphysics, Philosophy', p. 51.

42. Originally published at Presses Universitaires de France in 1964, *L'individu et sa genèse physico-biologique*, the first part of Simondon's 1958 *doctorat d'état*, was reprinted in 1989 with Aubier, and in 1995 with Krisis. It can now be found reunited with the second part of Simondon's *doctorat d'état*, *L'individuation psychique et collective*, in *L'individuation à la lumière des notions de forme et d'information* (Grenoble: Millon, 2005). All translations of this work, as well as of the other French-language texts in the remainder of this chapter, are my own.

43. On this 'immanent double genesis of being and thought', see Jacques Gareli, 'Transduction et information', in Gilles Châtelet (ed.), *Gilbert Simondon: Une pensée de l'individuation et de la technique* (Paris: Albin Michel, 1994), pp. 55–6; Muriel Combes, *Simondon: Individu et collectivité* (Paris: PUF, 1999), pp. 18–20; Bernard Aspe and Muriel Combes, 'L'acte fou', *Multitudes* 18 (2004); Jean-Hugues Barthélémy, *Penser L'individuation: Simondon et la philosophie de la nature* (Paris: L'Harmattan, 2005), pp. 37–8.

44. On Simondon's 'encyclopedism', see Pascal Chabot, 'L'encyclopédie idéale de Simondon', in Jacques Roux (ed.), *Gilbert Simondon: une pensée operative* (Saint-Etienne: Publications de l'Université de Saint-Etienne, 2002), pp. 149–61.

45. It is in this sense, as Barthélémy notes, that Simondon's 'genetic ontology' is neither a science nor a philosophical Knowledge of the kind claimed by German idealism. In other words, it is not objectivizing. It represents a 'knowledge' of individuation, but this 'knowledge' is inseparable from a process of the individuation of knowledge. See Jean-Hugues Barthélémy, *Simondon ou l'encyclopédisme génétique* (Paris: PUF, 2008), p. 37.

46. See also Didier Debaise, 'Les conditions d'une pensée de la relation selon Simondon', in Pascal Chabot (ed.), *Simondon* (Paris: Vrin, 2002), pp. 53–68; Didier Debaise, 'Qu'est-ce qu'une pensée relationnelle?', *Multitudes* 18 (2004); Barthélémy, *Penser l'individuation*, p. 100.

47. Indeed, for Simondon, a particular relation is only ever an aspect of the '*internal resonance*' of the system (INFI, 28–9), which is to say of the entire set of relations constituting the system.

48. In this sense, the pre-individual does not, strictly speaking, come 'before' the operation of individuation. Barthélémy discusses this question of temporality in *Simondon ou l'encyclopédisme génétique*, pp. 45–9. See also on this: Combes, *Simondon: Individu et collectivité*, p. 37.

49. On this, see Barthélémy, *Penser l'individuation*, p. 103.

50. See Gilles Deleuze, 'On Gilbert Simondon', in *Desert Islands and Other Texts 1953–1974*, p. 87.

51. As Muriel Combes writes, 'a physical system is said to be in metastable equilibrium (or false equilibrium) when the slightest modification of the system's parameters (pressure, temperature, etc.) is sufficient to break this equilibrium. It is in this way that, in supercooled water ... the slightest impurity having a structure which is isomorphic to the structure of ice plays the role of a seed crystal and is capable of causing the water to turn to ice.' See her *Simondon: Individu et collectivité*, p. 11.

52. Deleuze, 'On Gilbert Simondon', p. 87.

53. On singularities, see also Didier Debaise, 'Le langage de l'individuation', *Multitudes* 18 (2004).

54. For useful introductions to Cybernetics and Information Theory, see: W. Ross Ashby, *An Introduction to Cybernetics* (London: Chapman & Hall Ltd, 1957); Francis Heylighen and Cliff Joslyn, 'Cybernetics and Second-Order Cybernetics', in R.A. Meyers (ed.), *Encyclopedia of Physical Science and Technology* (New York: Academic Press, third edition, 2001); John R. Pierce, *An Introduction to Information Theory: Symbols, Signals and Noise* (New York: Dover, second edition, 1980); and Kenneth M. Sayre, *Cybernetics and the Philosophy of Mind* (London: Routledge, 1976).

55. As Simondon writes, 'an information is never relative to a unique and homogeneous reality, but to two orders in a state of *disparation*: . . . it is *the sense* [signification] *which will emerge when an operation of individuation discovers the dimension according to which two disparate realities can become a system* . . . [I]nformation is *this through which the incompatibility of the non-resolved system becomes the organizing dimension in its resolution*; information presupposes a system's change of phase, for it presupposes a primary pre-individual state which is individuated according to the organization which has been discovered' (INFI, 31, emphasis in the original).

56. Gilbert Hottois suggests that Simondon derives the notion of 'transduction' from that of the 'transducer', which is any apparatus capable of transforming energy (for example, a microphone). See his *Simondon et la philosophie de la 'culture technique'* (Bruxelles: De Boeck, 1993), p. 45. See also Barthélemy, *Penser L'individuation*, pp. 131–2. However, it should be noted that the notion of 'transduction' is also used in genetics and physiology in a sense which is analogical to its technological one.

57. '[T]he structure of a complex organism is not only integration and differentiation; it is also this institution of a transductive mediation of interiorities and exteriorities, going from an absolute interiority to an absolute exteriority through different mediating levels of relative interiority and exteriority' (INFI, 226).

58. It is in this way that relational being is said to have unity, not the unity of identity, but rather 'a *transductive unity*' (INFI, 31).

59. This point is attested to in Combes, *Simondon: Individu et collectivité*, pp. 24–8 and Hottois, *Simondon et la philosophie de la 'culture technique'*, p. 39. This is also, though with some reservations, the thesis of Isabelle Stengers in her 'Pour une mise à l'aventure de la transduction', in Chabot (ed.), *Simondon*, pp. 137–59. With regard to the 'problematic' nature of the domains of knowledge where the paradigm of crystallization will play the role of a structural germ, Barthélemy has pointed out certain 'relational' tensions that Simondon effectively exploits: the coexistence and reciprocal limitation of the individuality and interaction of particles in the physical world (following De Broglie's concerns over the definition of 'potential energy'); the opposition between mechanism and vitalism in biology; the problem of the relation between perception and action in the living creature; the opposition of 'psychologism' and 'sociologism' in thinking the 'becoming-transindividual' of the living creature; and the opposition of subject and object in epistemology. See, respectively, his *Penser L'individuation*, pp. 110–11, pp. 151–2, p. 174, p. 187 and p. 224, and p. 235 and pp. 239–40. We could also add to this list: the problematic relation between the physical and the living in bio-chemistry, the

problematic postulation of a neoteny between different species, and the problem of the different levels of individuality applicable to the study of collectivities in biology (INFI, 152, 171, 157–8). It can also be noted that this understanding of Simondon's method also explains his use of scientific notions outside of their usual contexts. For names such as metastability, order of magnitude, potential energy, singularity, information, etc., stand for concepts which must now be understood, not in relation to the scientific domains from which they have been extracted, but from the point of view of an anti-substantialist, relational and transductive conception of being.

60. As Combes explains, 'logical subsequence' here refers to the process of going from the simple to the complex, while 'ontological subsequence' refers to the different levels of being which emerge as ongoing and related resolutions of the pre-individual: from the physical to the biological to psychic and social individuals and finally to the technological (even if higher levels are irreducible to lower ones, since each domain has its own particular characteristics). See her *Simondon: Individu et collectivité*, p. 27. It should also be said that, at each 'ontological' stage, the earlier paradigm does not determine a later process as such. Rather, in accordance with our relational definition of information and singularity, the transposition of the paradigm-germ from level to level is simultaneously a 'construction' of this germ.

61. Barthélémy, *Penser L'individuation*, pp. 176–7.

62. Hottois, *Simondon*, p. 44.

63. See generally on this *Difference and Repetition*, Chapter 2.

64. In his review of Simondon's *L'individu et sa genèse physico-biologique*, published two years before *Difference and Repetition*, Deleuze explicitly notes that Simondon's concept of 'orders of magnitude' is very close to that of 'intensive quantity'. See Deleuze, 'On Gilbert Simondon', p. 87.

65. As Alberto Gualandi puts it, the 'process of individuation actualizes the elements, relations and singular points which constitute the Idea ... It is intensity which determines the Idea to be actualized, for the distinctive feature of intensity is to resolve its differences in a process of individuation which creates new individuals.' See his *Deleuze* (Paris: PUF, 2003), pp. 67–8.

66. Gualandi also makes this point in ibid., p. 66.

67. In Curie's work on symmetry, it is understood that a certain minimal *dissymmetry* is a necessary condition for physical phenomena in general. Simondon also discusses Curie's principle of symmetry (see INFI, 88–90).

68. See also DR, 118: 'words are genuine intensities within certain aesthetic systems'.

69. In fact, Deleuze argues that all intensities are differentially 'implicated'

in one another, to one degree or another depending on the domain in question, and thereby express 'the changing totality of Ideas' (DR, 252, 280–1).

70. Strictly speaking, Deleuze uses the terms 'learning' and 'apprenticeship' rather than 'knowing', in order to emphasize that 'coming to know something' should not be thought, as it traditionally has been, as the grasping of some pre-existing identity (by correctly specifying the criteria of its identity or essence using the 'correct method'). Rather, it should be thought of as a contingent and provisional 'effect' of a differential and open-ended process in which the student or apprentice is implicated (see DR, 164–7, 192).

71. It should be noted that difference is here not so much represented in the concept in accordance with the requirements of establishing the criteria for recognizing pre-given identities. Rather, in its two 'halves' (indi-different/ciation – DR, 246, 279), difference is what drives the progressive development of differentiated systems of concepts corresponding to individuals constituted by intensive processes. As Deleuze writes, '[q]ualities, extensities, forms and matters, species and parts are not primary; they are imprisoned in individuals as though in a crystal. Moreover, the entire world may be read, as though in a crystal ball, in the moving depth of individuating differences or differences in intensity' (DR, 247). The allusion to Simondon's paradigm of both individuation and the thought of individuation – crystallization – should here not go unnoticed.

72. Gualandi puts this same point in more ontological terms when he writes that '[i]f the Idea is the capacity [*puissance*] that Being has to give itself to thought, intensity is the capacity that Being has to exist and affect us'. See his *Deleuze*, p. 70.

73. That the determination of the problem is also 'experimentation' is what Deleuze means when he speaks of 'dice throws' and 'aleatory points'. That these experiments are carried out and determined within the problem is what Deleuze means when he writes that these dice throws are gathered up in a 'single cast'. We shall return to this notion of the throw of the dice below.

74. On 'depth' as a pure intensive 'implex', see DR, 229.

75. DeLanda, *Intensive Science*, p. 15.

76. Ibid., p. 70.

77. We know that Deleuze equates events and singularities. He equates events and 'signs' at LS, 63.

151

4
Structuralism – Structure and the Sense-Event

As noted in the previous chapter, Deleuze's work on the relation between language and the problem is primarily couched in a structuralist vocabulary, and no longer explicitly in terms of 'problems' and 'solutions'. However, as we shall see, Deleuze's concept of structure is, to all intents and purposes, identical to that of the problem. Indeed, in *Difference and Repetition* – the text which formed the basis of our examination of the concept of the problem in *The Logic of Sense*, and published only one year before this latter – Deleuze explicitly aligns the problematic Idea and structure. He writes, for example, that the 'Idea is thus defined as a structure. A structure or an Idea is a "complex theme", an internal multiplicity – in other words, a system of multiple, non-localizable connections between differential elements which is incarnated in real relations and actual terms' (DR, 183; see also DR, 191. On the rapprochement of the 'linguistic Idea' and structuralism in linguistics, see DR, 203–5). It will thus be the task of this chapter to elucidate Deleuze's concept of 'structure' in *The Logic of Sense*, its identity with the concept of the problem, and how it guides Deleuze's thinking about language.

In this chapter, we shall also examine how some of the issues previously examined in relation to the Stoics and Leibniz can be re-described in structuralist terms. In particular, with respect to the Stoics, we shall observe how the 'dualities' inherent in the Stoic system (cause/effect, body/language, thing/incorporeal sense), along with the 'infinite regress of sense', can be dealt with in a structuralist and hence 'problematic' vocabulary. Furthermore, we shall see, with regard to Deleuze's neo-Leibnizianism, how syntheses of singularities-events are most effectively described in structuralist terms and thus, finally, in terms of problems and solutions.

4.1 *Structuralism in* The Logic of Sense *and 'How do We Recognize Structuralism?'*

Deleuze's concept of structure, as found in *The Logic of Sense* (published in 1969), had been elaborated in its entirety two years previous in his 1967 essay 'How do We Recognize Structuralism?'[1] What is more – and importantly for our purposes here – this earlier essay presents the concept of structure in a particularly clear way. In this section, we shall examine point by point Deleuze's earlier exposition of a structure's 'formal criteria of recognition' (HRS, 171). At the same time, we shall correlate these criteria with the relevant passages from *The Logic of Sense*, as well as show how they are reflected in the works of several well-known structuralists, and in particular in the work of the structural linguist, Roman Jakobson.

The first criterion of a structure is the 'Symbolic', or rather, 'the positing of a symbolic order, irreducible to the orders of the real and the imaginary' (HRS, 171, 173). As Deleuze explains, the structure proper to a domain has no relation to 'form, nor signification, nor representation, nor content, nor given empirical reality, nor hypothetical functional model, nor intelligibility behind appearances' (HRS, 173). Rather, structure occupies a 'third order', the symbolic, which is irreducible to the traditional categories of 'realities' and 'images' but is, as will be seen, 'incarnated' in them (HRS, 171, 172). For example, as Deleuze writes,

> Beyond the history of men, and the history of ideas, Michel Foucault discovers a deeper, subterranean ground that forms the object of what he calls the archaeology of thought. Behind real men and their real relations, behind ideologies and their imaginary relations, Louis Althusser discovers a deeper domain as object of science and of philosophy. (HRS, 172)

This three-fold division between the symbolic, the imaginary and the real comes from Lacan.[2] Following one of Lacan's famous definitions of it, 'the real, whatever upheaval we subject it to, is always and in every case in its place; it carries its place stuck to the sole of its shoe'.[3] As opposed to this 'dumb reality', the symbolic is this in relation to which something can be 'missing from its place', like a book which is mislaid according to the terms of a library's cataloguing system. Indeed, in terms of this system of references, 'even if the book were on an adjacent shelf or in the next slot, it would be hidden there, however visible it may seem there'.[4] In contrast to these two orders, the imaginary for Lacan is not so much 'illusory'[5] (indeed, it is an inescapable aspect of the human being's relation to the world), as 'a type of apprehension in which factors such as resemblance and homoeomorphism play a decisive role'.[6] This occurs, for instance, when a relation of 'mirroring' is posited between a term and an object in its 'reality', but without regard for the fact that the term in question is inseparable from an entire system of symbolic relations.[7]

In this respect, 'symbolic' structure can be likened to the 'surface' of sense examined in previous chapters, for both are clearly opposed to the real 'depths' of bodies, as well as to the 'heights' of representational language. Indeed, this latter must now be understood to be 'imaginary' in so far as it would posit a relation of 'copying' or 'picturing' between a true proposition and its corresponding factual state of affairs, but without taking into account the social and linguistic 'symbolic relations' constitutive of sense (static genesis) which are the very condition of possibility for this proposition being true.

But now, of what, precisely, does structure consist? As Deleuze writes, since it is

> [d]istinct from the real and the imaginary, the symbolic cannot be defined either by pre-existing realities to which it would refer and which it would designate, or by the imaginary or conceptual contents which it would implicate, and which would give it a signification. The elements of a structure have neither extrinsic designation, nor intrinsic signification. (HRS, 173)

What the elements of a structure do have, however, is 'a sense which is necessarily and uniquely "positional"' (HRS, 174), that is, a sense which depends on their 'place' in relation to the other elements of the structure.[8] As Deleuze puts it in *The Logic of Sense*, 'each term has sense only by virtue of its position relative to every other term' (LS, 70). This, then, is the second criterion of a structure: 'Local or Positional' (HRS, 173). The notion of 'position' is of course not to be understood spatially, but rather relationally. In other words, an element's place or position in a structure (and thus its sense) will be defined by its relation to all of the other elements in the structure, whatever this relation turns out to be. It is in this manner, for example, that the structural anthropologist, Lévi-Strauss, understands the 'sense' of kinship terms, that is, as a set of contrastive relations integrated into a system. Such a system or structure 'is made up of several elements, none of which can undergo a change without effecting changes in all the other elements'.[9]

Of what, then, do these symbolic elements or 'units of position' consist? In fact, it is at this point that it begins to become clear that the concept of structure coincides with the concept of the problem, for, precisely, both structures and problems consist of 'elements which are held in a differential relationship'. In other words, structure consists of elements which, while having no determined value themselves, 'determine each other reciprocally in the relation' (HRS, 176). Furthermore, corresponding to the determination of these differential relations – that is, to their 'values' – are singularities or distributions of singular points. As Deleuze continues, the *'reciprocal determination* of symbolic elements continues henceforth into *the complete determination* of singular points that constitute a space corresponding to these elements' (HRS, 176–7). The third criterion of a structure is thus named by Deleuze as 'The Differential and the Singular' (HRS, 176).

Let us take an example of a structure in order to concretize the above criteria. Phonology, as defined by the structural linguist Roman Jakobson, has as its object, not the word understood from the point of view of its physiological, physical or psycho-acoustical 'reality', nor the word taken from the point of view of its 'imaginary' semantic or conceptual associations, but the word understood structurally in relation to differential elements called 'phonemes'. The term phoneme, following Jakobson, designates the smallest linguistic unit capable of being 'used in a given language to distinguish words of unlike meaning' (HRS, 176).[10] For example, /b/ and /p/ are two phonemes used in the English language to distinguish between the words '*b*at' and '*p*at'. In other words, phonemes are 'sound differences' which are relative to distinctions of meaning. It should be noted, however, that because not every sound difference distinguishes between words of differing meaning, not every sound difference uttered constitutes a different phoneme. For example, it makes no difference to an English speaker's understanding that another English speaker has said the word 'crown', if the 'r' is pronounced in the standard English fashion /r/, or if it is rolled. On the other hand, should this same person understand the other to have said 'clown' and not 'crown', then what will have been said to have been used is a different phoneme: /l/. Thus, as Deleuze writes, as a contrastive unit, the phoneme does not have a positive value in itself. It is, rather, 'inseparable from the phonemic relation which unites it to other phonemes' (HRS, 176), a relation, that is, which determines each phoneme as a 'pertinent difference' with respect to other pertinent differences. What more can we say about this relation?

Following Jakobson, the phonemic relation of a given language can initially be understood in relation to the presence or absence in a given phoneme of a number of particular 'distinctive features' characteristic of that language. What is more, the distinctive features characteristic of a given language system form a number of 'binary oppositions', the elements of which are either 'compatible' or 'incompatible' with the elements of other oppositions, i.e., capable or incapable of being combined in a single voiced unit. In standard French, for example, the distinctive features are: vocality vs. consonantness, nasality vs. orality, saturation vs. diluteness, gravity vs. acuteness, tenseness vs. laxness and continuousness vs. interception. The opposition tenseness/laxness is then incompatible with nasality but compatible with the oral feature ... and so on.[11] In short, then, for Jakobson, it is because the phonemes of a particular language can be understood to be 'bundles' of the presence and absence of such related distinctive features that that phonemic system can be said to have a structure wherein each phoneme has a well-defined 'position' or 'place'.[12]

In line with Jakobson's understanding of the phoneme, Deleuze argues in *Difference and Repetition* and 'How do We Recognize Structuralism?' that the distinctive features of a phonemic system constitute the differential relations between phonemes, that is, the relations through which phonemes, as the smallest linguistic differential elements, 'reciprocally determine' one another as the pertinent sound differences within a given language system (DR, 203 and HRS, 176). He then goes on to argue that, so determined, phonemes take on the value of singular points which 'completely determine' the phonemic structure (DR, 203 and HRS, 176–7). Here, however, it should be emphasized that by 'complete determination' Deleuze is not simply referring to the way in which phonemes express their constitutive distinctive features, but more particularly to how phonemes are also expressed in relation to a second system of elements having their own particular differential relations, different from the first. In short, phonemes understood as singularities are also necessarily bound up with a system of 'morphemes', that is, the system of the smallest, meaningful units of a given language, considered from the point of view of their grammatical and semantic relations.[13] The reciprocal determination of a particular set of phonemes through their distinctive features will thus be said to be completed with reference to the constituted significations of a particular language. As Deleuze puts it in *Difference and Repetition*, the 'selection of phonemes possessing pertinent value in this or that language is inseparable from that of morphemes as elements of grammatical constructions . . . [bringing] into play the virtual whole of the language' (DR, 205). Jakobson affirms this dual aspect of the phoneme when he writes that, if

> the listener receives a message in a language he knows, he correlates it with the code [i.e., structure] at hand and this code includes all the distinctive features to be manipulated, all their admissible combinations into bundles of concurrent features termed phonemes, and all the rules of concatenating phonemes into sequences.[14]

So, in line with our concept of the problem, we see how structures implicate differential elements, relations and singular points which are caught up in processes of reciprocal and complete determination. As Deleuze puts it in *The Logic of Sense*, a structure

> is constituted by terms which exist only through the relations they maintain with one another. To these relations, or rather to the values of these relations, there correspond very particular events, that is, *singularities* which are assignable within the structure . . . For example, the differential relations among phonemes assign singularities within language, in the 'neighbourhood' of which the sonorities and significations characteristic of language are constituted. Moreover, it seems that the singularities attached to one series [of terms] determine in a complex manner the terms of the other series. (LS, 50, translation modified)[15]

We must be careful, however, not confuse structure and the actual 'things' in which structure is incarnated (HRS, 179). Indeed, even though, in the above example, we spoke in terms of concrete languages, linguistic structure must not, strictly speaking, be confused with the determined phonemes and morphemes of particular languages. Following Deleuze, linguistic structure is 'virtual' as opposed to 'actual'. It consists only of elements called phonemes, which reciprocally determine one another through differential relations (distinctive features), and which are completely determined in relation to elements called morphemes which imply their own differential relations, that is, their own processes of reciprocal and complete determination in relation to other elements and differential relations (lexemes or semantemes, for example, but also series of 'things' to be conceptualized), and so on. For Deleuze, this virtual structure exists and is completely determined by its abstract, constitutive relations before any positive content can be given to any particular phoneme, distinctive feature, morpheme, semanteme, etc. The phonemic and morphological system of a particular language at a given moment in time, then, will be said to be an 'actualization' or 'differenciation' of this virtual structure. This, then, is the fourth criterion of a structure: 'Differenciation' (HRS, 178). As Deleuze writes:

> What is it that coexists in the [virtual] structure? All the elements, the relations and relational values, all the singularities proper to the domain considered. Such a coexistence does not imply any confusion, nor any indetermination, for the relations and differential elements coexist in a completely and perfectly determined whole. Except that this whole is not actualized as such. What is actualized, here and now, are particular relations, relational values, and distributions of singularities; others are actualized elsewhere or at other times. There is not a total language [langue], embodying all the possible [i.e., actual] phonemes and phonemic relations. But the virtual totality of the language system [langage] is actualized following exclusive rules in diverse, specific languages, of which each embodies certain relations, relational values, and singularities . . . Of the structure as virtuality, we must say that it is still undifferenciated, even though it is totally and completely differentiated. Of structures which are embodied in a particular actual form (present or past), we must say that they are differenciated, and that for them to be actualized is precisely to be differenciated. (HRS, 179, translation modified)

Jakobson provides us with an example which illuminates this point. He points out the fact that an audible sound difference (determined in English as /ŋ/ – /n/), reciprocally determined in relation to the same distinctive features (here, the velar vs. the dental), may nevertheless not be actualized in two distinct phonemes in two different languages if the morphological and lexical rules which characterize each language are different. As he writes,

> in Czech, the velar /ŋ/, e.g. in [veŋku], and the dental [n], e.g. in [venek], are variants of one and the same phoneme /n/; the first variant appears before /k/ and /g/, the second in all other positions. In English, however, the dental nasal /n/ and the velar nasal (spelled ng) may occur in identical positions and thus serve to differentiate meanings (e.g., sin, sing); they are, then, two different phonemes.[16]

In other words, following this example, the virtual relations between phonemes and distinctive features, abstractly conceived, have been differenciated into the determined phonemic relation /ŋ/ – /n/ in English, but have been actualized or differenciated in a different way in Czech, precisely in so far as the lexical rules of each language are different. As Deleuze summarizes:

> All differenciation, all actualization is carried out along two paths: species and parts. The differential relations are incarnated in qualitatively distinct

species, while the corresponding singularities are incarnated in the parts and extended figures which characterize each species: hence, the language species [e.g., Czech and English], and the parts [e.g., morphemes and lexemes] of each one in the vicinity of the singularities [e.g., phonemes] of the linguistic structure. (HRS, 179)

It is also clear from the above why the differenciation or actualization of structure can in no way be compared to the 'instantiation' of a general concept. The structure of a particular language, for example, is never the exemplification of a general linguistic structure. The pertinent distinction here is not between the particular and the general, but rather between 'the total structure of a domain as an ensemble of virtual coexistence, and the sub-structures that correspond to diverse actualizations [of that virtual structure] in the domain' (HRS, 179). Indeed, were a particular structure thought of as an instantiation of a more general structure specifying its essence, we would not be able to account for the different forms this particular structure takes at different points in time except with an unsatisfactory reference to 'accidents' or discontinuous 'leaps'. Rather, as Jakobson puts it in relation to phonemic structure, 'no sound change can be comprehended without reference to the [entire] system which undergoes that change'.[17] In other words, the mutations of a particular, actual structure cannot be referred to a 'fortuitous origin' or a 'conglomerate of changes of an accidental nature', but must rather be referred to a 'structure of mutations', that is, to what Deleuze calls the ongoing differenciation or actualization of virtual structure.[18]

In order to head off a possible objection, it should also be noted here that we are not confusing two different things in saying that the structural mutation of a particular language over time is characterized by the same type of process of differenciation as the divergent actualizations of 'virtual' relations and singularities in historically unrelated languages such as Czech and English. Indeed, as Jakobson himself notes, emphasizing structural over historical approaches to the evolution of languages, 'the study of the geographic distribution of different phonological types is not confined to cognate dialects and or languages, but ascertains that the boundaries between different phonological features often do not coincide with the boundaries between languages or language families'.[19] In other words, the 'boundary' between different languages, no matter what their historical relation or evolution, is always a question of the differenciation of virtual structure.

Now, essential for our purposes here, there is a final point to be teased out in relation to the structural criterion of differenciation. It is that 'the process of actualization always implies an internal temporality ... according to which the elements of virtual coexistence are actualized [*s'effectuent*] at diverse rhythms' (HRS, 179–80, translation modified). In other words, it appears that structures are subject not only to reciprocal and complete determination, but also, like problematic Ideas, to a 'progressive determination' which is simultaneously the actualization of the structure (note, however, that Deleuze does not use the term 'progressive determination' as such in the 'Structuralism' essay). As seen in Chapter 3, if the reciprocal determination of one series of elements of the problematic Idea (through their differential relations) is prolonged in a complete determination of these elements in relation to a second series of reciprocally determined elements of the same problem (reciprocally determined elements which are in turn completely determined in relation to a third series, and so on ...), then the determination of the elements of the problem is both entirely internal to the Idea and could only be carried out progressively and experimentally from one series of determinations to another and back again. Or again, as Deleuze puts it in *Difference and Repetition*, explicitly in relation to the concept of structure:

> the essential aspects of sufficient reason – determinability, reciprocal determination, complete determination – find their systematic unity in progressive determination. In effect, the reciprocity of determination ... [signifies] a veritable progression in which the reciprocal terms must be secured step by step, and the relations themselves established between them. The completeness of the determination also implies the progressivity of the adjunct fields. In going from A to B and then B to A, we do not arrive back at the point of departure ... [R]ather, the repetition between A and B and B and A is the progressive tour or description of the whole of a problematic field. In this sense, by virtue of this progressivity, every structure has a purely logical, ideal or dialectical time. However, this virtual time itself determines a time of differenciation, or rather rhythms or different times of actualization which correspond to the relations and singularities of the structure and, for their part, measure the passage from virtual to actual. (DR, 210–11)

Now, it should be noted that in *The Logic of Sense* Deleuze does not speak of 'actualization' or 'progressive determination' in relation to structures (what is more, he does not speak at all of 'differenciation'). As examined in Chapter 3, he speaks rather of actualization and progressive determination in relation to problems. He does, however, explicitly align the concepts of the problem and structure when he writes that 'the problem . . . [refers] to an ideational objectivity or to a structure constitutive of sense' (LS, 120). What is more, it is this problem or structure which, as Deleuze puts it several lines later,

> implies, on the one hand, a space of nomad distribution in which singularities are distributed (*Topos*); on the other hand, it implies a time of decomposition whereby this space is subdivided into sub-spaces. Each one of these sub-spaces is successively defined by the adjunction of new points ensuring the progressive and complete determination of the domain under consideration (Aion) . . . By means of an appropriate process, the problem is determined in space and time and, as it is determined, it determines the solutions in which it persists. (LS, 121)

From this, we can conclude that, even though in *The Logic of Sense* Deleuze does not explicate his philosophical concept of structure in exactly the same way that he does in the 'Structuralism' essay and in *Difference and Repetition*, he nevertheless retains the same concept of structure found in these earlier works and continues to equate this concept of structure with that of the problem in so far as both are comprised of merely determinable elements which are subject to reciprocal, complete and progressive determination (actualization or differenciation).

Returning to the 'Structuralism' essay, Deleuze here explains that the fifth criterion of a structure is its 'serial' nature (HRS, 182). As he writes,

> the symbolic elements that we have previously defined, taken in their differential relations, are organized in series. But so organized, they relate to another series, constituted by other symbolic elements and other relations: this reference to a second series is easily explained by recalling that singularities derive from the terms and relations of the first, but are not limited simply to reproducing or reflecting them. They thus organize themselves in a second series capable of an autonomous development. (HRS, 182)

Now, this concept of series is to all intents and purposes the same as the concept of series examined in Chapter 3 in relation to Deleuze's 'use' of the differential calculus in the construction of his concept of the problem. As was seen, to the extent that a particular curve is defined by its distribution of singular points, the primitive function of this curve can be found by the integration of series of differentiations taken at a singular point and 'analytically continued' into other series generated at other singular points on the curve. The curve will thus be said to be completely determined by a relation between different series of reciprocally determined differences (differentiations) to whose values the singularities constitutive of that particular curve correspond. What is more, it was seen that even in the case where the series diverge at discontinuous points or singular 'poles', the curve of a non-linear function may still be determined by means of a 'composite function' which, in so far as it expresses the differential relation between the power series expansions of the local functions characterizing the poles, is continuous across this group of discontinuous functions. The specific nature of this composite function is then said to be determined by an 'essential singularity' which represents the fluctuations of the values that solutions to the composite function can receive. In other words, once again we have a complete determination of a curve by means of a relation between different series of reciprocally determined differences (power series representing discontinuous local functions at singular poles), to whose values the singularities constitutive of that particular curve (including poles and essential singularities) correspond.

Deleuze now wants to argue that these same conceptual components – symbolic elements (dy, dx), differential relations, singularities and multiple series – define the concept of structure. Indeed, in line with our example, Deleuze explicitly argues that these components hold for phonemic structure, 'for phonemes and morphemes' (HRS, 182). We have seen how this works. Phonemes form a series of differentially related terms to the extent that they reciprocally determine one another through the 'distinctive features' characteristic of a given language. But what is more, they also take on the value of singular points in relation to a series of voiced morphemes which are considered from the point of view of their grammatical and semantic relations (complete determination). Lévi-Strauss' 'serial approach' to 'the problem of totemism' would be another example to which we could refer in this regard. As he writes,

> there are not, first, animals which resemble each other (because they all share animal behaviour), then ancestors which resemble each other (because they all share ancestral behaviour), and lastly an overall resemblance between the two groups; but on the one hand there are animals which differ from each other (in that they belong to distinct species, each of which has its own physical appearance and mode of life), and on the other there are men – among whom the ancestors form a particular case

– who also differ from each other (in that they are distributed among different segments of society, each occupying a particular position in the social structure). The resemblance presupposed by so-called totemic representations is *between these two systems of differences*.[20]

A 'totemic identification' within a given social structure, then, will be a singularity corresponding to the simultaneous determination of the values of the terms of both series (animal and social), but only in so far as each series of terms is understood to be reciprocally determined by very different types of differential relation. To speak generally, therefore, and say that structural elements taken in their differential relations are necessarily organized in series, is simply to say that each term of the structure has a value ('position') which is determined, first of all, by its reciprocal relation to other terms of the same type and, secondly, by the way in which it is related to a second, heterogeneous set of terms (having their own relations and values or positions) through singularities corresponding to the values of all of the terms of the structure. As Deleuze puts it in *The Logic of Sense*,

> the serial form is realized in the simultaneity of at least two series . . . each one of which is constituted by terms of the same type or degree, although these terms differ in nature from those of the other series (they can of course differ also in degree). The serial form is thus essentially multi-serial. This is indeed the case in mathematics, where a series constructed in the vicinity of a point is significant only in relation to another series, constructed around another point, and converging with, or diverging from, the first. (LS, 36–7)

Now, it should also be noted that, in *The Logic of Sense*, Deleuze mentions a characteristic of series – or, rather, of the relation between series – which is not addressed in the 'Structuralism' essay:

> The law governing two simultaneous series is that they are never equal. One represents the *signifier*, the other the *signified*. But thanks to our terminology, these two terms acquire a particular meaning. We call 'signifier' any sign which presents in itself an aspect of sense; we call 'signified', on the contrary, that which serves as the correlative to this aspect of sense, that is, that which is defined in a duality relative to this aspect. What is signified therefore is never sense itself . . . [What is] signified is any thing which may be defined on the basis of the distinction that a certain aspect of sense establishes with this thing. (LS, 37)

We are not yet, however, in a position to fully appreciate these relations of 'signification' between series, and so we shall return to this point when we examine the structural criterion of the 'empty square' or 'paradoxical element', for it is this element which determines the relations of signification between series.

To continue the explication of the structural criterion of series such as it is presented in the 'Structuralism' essay, it should be remarked that a further characteristic of series is that their organization 'supposes a veritable *mise en scène* . . . a true creation' (HRS, 183).

> The determination of a structure occurs not only through a choice of basic symbolic elements and the differential relations into which they enter, nor merely through a distribution of the singular points which correspond to them. The determination also occurs through the constitution of a second series, at least, that maintains complex relations with the first. (HRS, 183)

Now, it can be argued that this serial 'staging' is another way of talking about progressive determination. Indeed, the 'choosing' of the basic symbolic elements and differential relations of a first series (reciprocal determination), as well as the 'constitution' of a second series with its own elements and relations to complete the determination of the first series (and so on), clearly amounts to an experimental and progressive determination of a structure. In fact, it would appear that the construction of multiple series with their terms and corresponding singularities is equivalent to the process described in Chapter 3 as the 'adjunction' and 'transformation' of singularities in the determination of the problematic Idea. In other words, a structure, just like the problem, is characterized by the reciprocal, complete and progressive determination of purely differential elements by means of the adjunction (or 'apprehension') and transformation (or 'condensation') of singularities, where singularities are understood to correspond to the values of relations between differential elements, and where differential elements are in turn determined by syntheses or condensations of adjoined singularities. As Deleuze writes in *Difference and Repetition*, with respect to his concept of problematic Ideas, 'problems are inseparable from a power of decision . . . This power of decision is exercised to the highest degree in the two fundamental procedures of adjunction and condensation' (DR, 197). And again, speaking of the actualization or differenciation of the problem:

> On the one hand, in the *progressive* determination of the conditions [of the problem], we must in effect discover the adjunctions which *complete* the initial field of the problem as such . . . On the other hand, we must condense all the singularities . . . in a sublime occasion, *Kairos*, which makes the solution explode like something abrupt, brutal and revolutionary. (DR, 190, emphasis added)

The objection here, of course, is that Deleuze appears to have made structure dependent upon an agent who 'chooses' the terms and relations of each series of the structure. But we know from Chapters 2 and 3 that he absolutely excludes the idea that such an agent is foundational. What is more, it was affirmed above that progressive determination is always internal to the structure. What exactly is it, then, in relation to which 'the variety of terms and the variation of differential relations are determined in each case' (HRS, 184)? What is it, in other words, in relation to which the progressive determination of elements by the adjunction and transformation of singularities is carried out? This question is answered by Deleuze's sixth criterion of a structure: the 'Empty Square', paradoxical element or object = x which drives the structure (HRS, 184). As he puts it, if the series of the structure

> present relative displacements in relation to each other, this is so because the *relative* places of their terms in the structure depend first of the *absolute* place of each, at each moment, in relation to the object = x that is always circulating, always displaced in relation to itself. It ... allows the structure to be defined as an order of places subject to the variation of relation ... Distributing the differences through the entire structure, making the differential relations vary with its displacements, the object = x constitutes the differenciating element of difference itself. (HRS, 185–6)[21]

Deleuze cites a number of different examples of such a paradoxical element in the work of various structuralists: Lacan's 'phallus' (which will be examined in the following chapter), Lévi-Strauss' '*mana*' and Jakobson's 'zero phoneme'. In line with our linguistic example, then, we shall illustrate some of the characteristics of the paradoxical element by examining the 'zero phoneme'. In their article, 'Notes on the French Phonemic Pattern', Jakobson and Lotz define the zero-phoneme, such as it is manifested in the French language, as

> opposed to all other French phonemes by the absence both of distinctive features and of a constant sound characteristic. On the other hand, the zero phoneme ... is opposed to the absence of any phoneme whatsoever. In the initial prevocalic position this phoneme is know under the name 'h aspiré'; although under emphasis it can be implemented under aspiration, usually it is a lack of sound, which acts in the given sequence as do French consonants. The vocalic variant of the zero phoneme, which appears in other positions, is called 'e caduc' and alternates between the presence and absence of a vowel.[22]

165

It appears that despite this 'absence both of distinctive features and of a constant sound characteristic', the zero phoneme has a very important role to play in the French phonemic system. For example, as *h aspiré*, it permits an audible distinction between phrases such as '*les zéros*' [lezeʀo] (the zeros) and '*les héros*' [le'eʀo] (the heroes). In this and many other cases, the *h aspiré* is manifested as a glottal stop functioning as a 'phantom consonant'. This both prevents a liaison (or, in certain cases, an elision) between the preceding particle and the vowel-sound with which nouns commencing with *h* typically begin, and also aids in the articulation of this vowel-sound in the manner of a consonant. Without such a stop and corresponding absence of a liaison, '*les héros*' would thus have a pronunciation identical to that of '*les zéros*'. A comparable example of such a zero phoneme in English would be the optional glottal stop which serves to distinguish 'a name' from 'an aim'.[23] It can also be noted that the *h aspiré* has permitted the introduction of many non-Latin and non-Greek words into the French language without a modification of the existing phonological system (thus: *héros, harpe, hareng, harem, hamac, haricot,* etc.).[24]

The 'e caduc', or '*e muet*' as it is more commonly known in French, is similarly characterized by the fact that it is undetermined in relation to any phonological rule while nevertheless having a number of certain indispensible functions. On the one hand, its sound freely oscillates between the central [ə], the closed [ø] and the open [œ]; and it disappears quite frequently in the spoken chain without modifying the meaning of the message.[25] On the other hand, it has an important epenthetic function, permitting the distinction of words in short, spoken chains, that is, in the absence of a larger phonemic context (e.g., '*ours blanc*' (white bear), often pronounced [uʀsə'blɑ̃]). It also aids in the distinction of words characterized by consonantal groups which are unknown or infrequently used (such as in the imported words '*gnome*' (gnome) and '*pneu*' (tire), which the French have the tendency to pronounce, respectively, [gə'nɔm] and [pə'nø]). The *e muet* can also often be heard at the end of words terminating with a consonant, even though this final sound should, strictly speaking, be purely consonantal. In this case, its function is to 'support' the final consonant, preventing its disappearance from the chain and thus its confusion with a word of different meaning (this is particularly relevant in distinguishing feminine from masculine forms).

In sum, therefore, the extremely variable zero phoneme, while not a phoneme itself (being determined neither in relation to the network of distinctive features, nor, strictly speaking, in relation to word-units to be distinguished by these means), nevertheless determines the presence of phonemes as the pertinent sound differences capable of distinguishing words of different meaning. In many important respects, therefore, it is due to this element, which is neither a phoneme nor a morpheme or semanteme, that a series phonemes and a series of morphemes/semantemes can form a structure. As Deleuze puts it, Jakobson's zero phoneme 'does not by itself entail any differential character or phonetic value', but it is in relation to this element that 'all the phonemes are situated in their own differential relations', that is, in a differential relation to each other and in a differential relation to series of morphemes/semantemes (HRS, 186).

This highlights a number of important features of the paradoxical element as elaborated by Deleuze in the 'Structuralism' essay, as well as in *The Logic of Sense*. First of all, as has been clearly seen in the case of the zero phoneme, it is in relation to this object = x that the terms, differential relations and singularities of the structure are determined with respect to one another (HRS, 184). Or again, as Deleuze puts it in *The Logic of Sense*, the paradoxical element 'has the function of linking the two series together, of reflecting them in one another, of making them communicate, coexist, and be ramified' (LS, 51, translation modified).

In the second place, if, as has been argued, the series of the structure are in themselves composed of purely differential terms and relations (reciprocal determination), and if the paradoxical element brings these series into a determinate relation (complete and progressive determination), it follows that this object = x essentially functions as the 'differenciator' of these elements and relations, as well as 'the principle of the emission of singularities' corresponding to their values (LS, 51). Indeed, in our example, it is because the zero phoneme brings a series of 'sound differences' into relation with the series of different 'acoustic word-images' corresponding to the semantemes of a given language, that the relations and terms of the first series are differenciated with respect to the second, or, what amounts to the same thing, that phonemes are determined as singularities corresponding to the pertinent values of the sound differences in their relation to the series of semantemes.

Thirdly, as mentioned above, the paradoxical element determines each series either as 'signifying' or as 'signified'. More precisely, it determines as signifying the series in which it is in 'excess' and as signified the series in which it is 'lacking' (LS, 41, 51). Thus, on the one hand, the zero phoneme, while not itself a phoneme, functions as a type of supplementary sound difference at the same level of phonemes. On the other hand, this is a sound difference which does not by itself correspond to any difference of meaning at the level of the series of morphemes and semantemes. Thus, following Deleuze, in so far as it can be said to be in excess in the series of phonemes, but lacking in the series of word units, the zero phoneme determines the former as signifying in relation to the latter which is signified.[26] It is in this way that, as noted above, the signifying series 'presents in itself an aspect of sense' with respect to the signified series (LS, 37). In other words, in so far as it is supplemented by an 'excessive' paradoxical element which brings the two series into differential communication, the signifying series can be said to have a determining role with respect to the terms of the signified series, that is, with respect to their 'relative positions' in the structure. Or again, the signifying series represents the differential conditions of the signified series, while the signified series, once brought into communication with the signifying series by means of the paradoxical element, brings about the differenciation of these conditions or their actualization (we differentiate between words in oral discourse by means of sound differences, but the sound differences which end up being pertinent depend on the words to be distinguished).

Finally, the paradoxical element, despite its determining role, is not strictly speaking assignable within the structure. As Deleuze asserts, it has 'no identity except in order to lack this identity, and has no place except in order to be displaced in relation to all places' (HRS, 188). This is particularly clear in the case of the zero phoneme. For it is at precisely the same instant that the zero phoneme situates the series of phonemes in their reciprocal relations (network of distinctive features), as well as determining them as singularities with respect to the elements and relations constitutive of the series of morphemes and semantemes (pertinent sound differences), that it gives each phoneme an identity and a structural 'position' which it, itself, essentially lacks. It is in this sense, as Deleuze writes, that the paradoxical element 'has the property of being always displaced in relation to itself' (LS, 40). In other words, because the paradoxical element determines the order of positions or 'places' within a structure while not itself being of this structure, it can be said to be dis-placed in relation to these places it determines.

So, as seen in the case of the zero phoneme, the paradoxical element, while not assignable within the structure, nevertheless brings the series of the structure into communication, differenciating their terms and distributing their corresponding singularities in relation to one another, and determining one of the series as signifying and the other as signified.

Deleuze also mentions several other characteristics of this object = x which are less visible in the case of the zero phoneme. In particular, he emphasizes the 'mobility' and 'perpetual circulation' of the paradoxical element (HRS, 186–7; LS, 40, 51, 70). How is this notion of 'mobility' to be understood? In fact, this takes us back to our discussion of the processes of determination of the elements of the structure. Let us recall that the reciprocal determination of the terms of a single series is prolonged in a complete determination in relation to a second series. What is more, this second series has its own reciprocally determined elements and differential relations which are, in turn, completely determined in relation to a third series, and so on, progressively, from one series to another (adjunction and transformation of singularities). If, as has been argued above, such heterogeneous series are brought into communication by paradoxical elements, then these processes of reciprocal, complete and progressive determination necessarily depend on the presence of such paradoxical elements. It appears, therefore, that the 'perpetual circulation' of the paradoxical element refers to the way in which the determination of each particular series or order of the structure refers us to the determining role of all of the objects = x in all of the other series or orders of the structure. As Deleuze relates it, 'for each order of structure the object = x is the empty or perforated site that permits this order to be articulated with the others in a space that entails as many directions as orders. The orders of the structure do not communicate in a common site, but they all communicate through their empty place or respective object = x' (HRS, 188).

How can this notion of 'communication' between the different orders of structure through diverse paradoxical elements be made more comprehensible? Following Deleuze, it appears that the paradoxical element is caught up in complex relations of 'subordination' and actualization between the different orders of the structure. As he writes,

> in each structure, the object = x must be disposed to give an account 1) of the way in which it subordinates within its order the other orders of structure, that then only intervene as dimensions of actualization; 2) of the way in which it is itself subordinated to the other orders in their own order (and no longer intervenes except in their own actualization);

3) of the way in which all the objects = x and all the orders of structure communicate with one another, each order defining a dimension of space in which it is absolutely primary; 4) of the conditions in which, at a given moment in history or in a given case, a particular dimension corresponding to a particular order of the structure is not deployed for itself and remains subordinated to the actualization of another order. (HRS, 188–9)

But what exactly are these relations of subordination and actualization for which the paradoxical element must account? In fact, it appears that they can be described in terms of the signifying relations between series, examined above. In other words, one series subordinates another if it is signifying in relation to this other series which is, in turn, signified. The signified series is then understood to be a dimension of the actualization of the signifying series. However, it must also be understood that, in a structure of multiple orders or series, these relations of signification can be very complex. A series which is signified from the point of view of a particular object = x may be, in turn, signifying in relation to a different object = x. Thus, for example, even though series of morphemes and semantemes are signified in relation to the series of phonemes and the functioning of the zero phoneme, as well as representing a dimension of the differenciation or actualization of the series of phonemes, they must also be held to be signifying from the point of view of the paradoxical element which brings about the (reciprocal, complete and progressive) determination of their elements and singularities in relation to a third series of, for example, bodies or states of affairs to which propositions refer. Such a paradoxical element would be, for example, of the *mana* type, following the work of Lévi-Strauss: a 'supplementary' or 'floating signifier' which brings together series of meaningful words and series of 'things known' in syntheses of knowledge, precisely because it is an 'indeterminate value of signification, in itself devoid of meaning and thus susceptible of receiving any meaning at all'.[27] In this case, a series of phonemes must be held to be signified in relation to this process of the constitution of semantemes in relation to states of affairs and paradoxical elements of the *mana* type, and to intervene only as a particular dimension of the actualization of these semantemes, that is, with regard to the rules of their phonic articulation. On the other hand, of course, at precisely the same time, series of objective things or states of affairs will be determined as signified in relation to this series of semantemes and its 'floating signifiers', and will bear, in their own way, on the differenciation or actualization of these semantemes (in terms of the pertinence of various concepts, for example, or the creation of other, more adequate concepts from the language's virtual 'semantic reserve'). As Deleuze writes, 'it is always the case that one series has the role of the signifier, and the other the role of the signified, even if these roles are interchanged as we change points of view' (LS, 38).

In short, then, the 'perpetual displacement' of the paradoxical element refers to the way in which, in determining the terms and singularities of the structure, we are referred from the functioning of one such element in a particular series or order to another element in another series or order, and the relations of signification and actualization they bring about for each series or order of the structure in relation to all the others. 'Distributing the differences through the entire structure, making the differential relations vary with its displacements, the object = x constitutes the differenciating element of difference itself' (HRS, 186). It is in this way, then, that Deleuze affirms a type of 'structural causality' between different structures or, what ultimately amounts to the same thing, between different orders of the same structure. As he writes:

> All structures are infrastructures. The structural orders – linguistic, familial, economic, sexual, etc. – are characterized by the form of their symbolic elements, the variety of their differential relations, the species of their singularities, finally and, above all, by the nature of the object = x that presides over their functioning ... Between structures, causality can only be a type of structural causality ... The orders of the structure do not communicate in a common site, but they all communicate through their empty place or respective object = x. (HRS, 188)

So we have seen that it is in relation to a paradoxical element or object = x, and not an agent, that the determination of the elements of the structure is carried out. However, in an apparent contradiction, the final criterion of a structure – 'From the Subject to Practice' – concerns quite precisely the role of an agent in relation to structure. Deleuze writes that, while the empty square or object = x must not be 'filled by a term', it is nevertheless 'accompanied [*accompagnée*] by an eminently symbolic instance which follows all of its displacements, accompanied without being occupied or filled ... The *subject* is precisely the agency [*instance*] which follows the empty place' (HRS, 190). How, then, are these two criteria – the 'Empty Square' and 'From the Subject to Practice' – to be reconciled?

The subject, it appears, is a necessary though not sufficient condition for the creation and/or determination of structures. On the one hand, it has been seen, the 'choice' of symbolic terms, as well as the 'constitution' of series in relation to which these terms are differentially determined, refer to a 'creativity' or a 'power of decision' which implies a subject. But on the other hand, it has been seen that this subject cannot be foundational, and that it is rather a paradoxical element which causes the series of the structure to communicate and its terms to be determined. The resolution of this apparent contradiction would thus be to say that the subject is a necessary 'moment' of structure, but that it is itself always derived or produced by structure (be it biological, psychological, social, and so on). In this sense, the agent is thus, following Lacan's term, 'less subject than subjected [*assujetti*] – subjected to the empty square' (HRS, 190). Or again, as Deleuze writes, 'the empty place must be rid of the symbolic events that eclipse it or fill it', but at the same time, it must 'be given over to the subject which must accompany it on new paths, without occupying or deserting it' (HRS, 191). Contrary to impressions, therefore, structuralism is

> not at all a form of thought that suppresses the subject, but one that breaks it up and distributes it systematically, that contests the identity of the subject, that dissipates it and makes it shift from place to place, an always nomad subject, made of individuations, but impersonal ones, or of singularities, but pre-individual ones. (HRS, 190)

It is clear from this, of course, that the structuralist subject is akin to the Stoic sage who 'identifies' with the paradoxical element or aleatory point which traces the line of Aion. Or again, it is the neo-Leibnizian *personne*, an operator which is both derived from and brings about disjunctive syntheses of singularities-events. Or finally, it is the 'divided subject', 'questioner' or 'thrower of the dice' who, dissolved in diverse processes of intensive individuation, experiences the problematic Idea as an 'imperative question' which can only be answered by a 'dice throw' or a distribution of singularities which is only ever a *re*-distribution of singularities. Indeed, Deleuze directly confirms for us this last comparison when he writes that the 'structuralist *hero*' has a 'power to cause relations to vary and to redistribute singularities, *always casting another throw of the dice*' (HRS, 191, emphasis added). And we cannot mistake how this idea of the 'structural hero' is echoed in *The Logic of Sense* when Deleuze claims that the singularities of the problem or structure 'are not imprisoned within individuals and persons' considered as foundational, and that 'the dissolved self, the cracked I, the lost identity . . . liberate the singularities of the surface' (LS, 140–1).

To bring this section to a close, it has been seen that the concept of structure found in the 'How do We Recognize Structuralism?' essay is to all intents and purposes identical to the one found in *The Logic of Sense* (and, indeed, in *Difference and Repetition*). It has also been shown that the concept of structure is identical to the concept of the problem found in both *The Logic of Sense* and *Difference and Repetition*. Indeed, both problems and structures are comprised of series of purely differential elements which are reciprocally, completely and progressively determined by the adjunction and transformation of singularities corresponding to the values of these elements. What is more, these processes of determination are brought about by the circulation of a paradoxical element that is itself accompanied by a 'divided subject' who, whilst being thoroughly 'dissolved' in the structure's or problem's differential network, brings the series of the structure or problem into communication.

4.2 *Structure and the Sense-Event*

We must now return to the following question: what is the relation that Deleuze establishes in *The Logic of Sense* between structure or the problem and language? In answering this question, we shall draw together many of the threads developed throughout the preceding chapters. In the first place, it will be seen how Deleuze uses the notion of structure to organize into a productive system the various dualities that have thus far been employed: corporeal things and incorporeal events, things and propositions, substantives and verbs, and denotations and expressions. Secondly, we shall examine how Deleuze uses the notion of structure to 'serialize' the infinite regress of the expression of sense, examined in Chapter 1, and make it 'productive'. Finally, it will be seen how the disjunctive synthesis, or the affirmation of difference more generally, must be thought of in structuralist terms. We shall then be in a position to attempt an answer to the question: what are the conditions of the event if everything, up to and including the language wherein events are determined, is to be an event?

To turn to the first point, it can be recalled from Chapter 1 that Deleuze's reading of the Stoics involved a number of dualities. As Deleuze writes, the 'first important duality was that of causes and effects, of corporeal things and incorporeal events' (LS, 23). This duality, we can remember, corresponds to the Stoic ontological distinction, affirmed by Deleuze, between bodies which alone exist and incorporeals which do not exist but which are nevertheless 'something'. It was also seen that these incorporeals were at once the effect of causal relations between bodies and the 'sayables' of propositions. Thus, in so far as event-effects do not exist outside of the propositions which express them, Deleuze argues that the first duality between causes and effects 'is prolonged in the duality of things and propositions, of bodies and language' (LS, 23).

Now, as Deleuze continues to explain, each term of this second duality itself involves a duality. On the side of 'things' there are, on the one hand, physical qualities and real relations which constitute the state of affairs; and on the other hand, there are incorporeal events. On the side of the proposition or language, there are, on the one hand, proper names, substantives and general adjectives – 'names of stasis' – which denote the state of affairs; and on the other hand there are verbs which express events or pure becomings, such as 'to grow' in the proposition 'Alice grows' (LS, 24). Furthermore, as was seen in Chapter 1, every name expresses a sense which must be denoted by another name. This was what Deleuze called the 'infinite regress of sense' or 'Frege's paradox'. It thus follows that the duality on the side of the proposition between different types of name (substantives and verbs) must be prolonged in the duality between denotation and the expression of sense. As Deleuze writes, this 'is the final displacement of the duality: it has now moved inside the proposition' (LS, 25).

The main line of argument of the first half of Chapter 1 was that the incorporeal event on the side of 'things' must be determined with respect to the ongoing expression of sense in propositions. Viewed through the lens of the above dualities, the question is thus: what is the relation between the terms comprising each side of the dualities – bodies, events, propositions, and propositions about (the sense of) propositions – such that the event and the expression of sense can be brought together in this way? Analyzing Deleuze's reading of the Stoics, we examined the way in which the ontological distinction between bodies and incorporeals grounded a network of relations between the various parts of Stoic philosophy (physics, logic, epistemology and ethics), thereby permitting the ongoing 'evental' determination of things in general (bodies, concepts, beliefs and desires) within a 'comprehensive representation' enveloping a pure sense-event. As was seen, however, the Stoics ultimately determined the sense-event with reference to Zeus, his body and name creating a totality on both the physical and logical sides of the ontological divide.

We then turned to Deleuze's reading of Leibniz in order to approach an alternative solution to this problem of the purely 'evental' relation between the expression of sense and the event. It was seen in Chapter 2 that, beginning with series of trope-like events making up the lives of worldly things, events called 'processes of triangulation' or 'disjunctive syntheses' brought about the simultaneous and related determination of individuals, persons and general concepts (the so-called static ontological and logical geneses). In order to arrive at this point, however, Deleuze was obliged to extend certain aspects of Leibniz's work, which dealt only with convergent series of events whose existence is guaranteed by an uncreated, underlying substance, namely, God. Deleuze's neo-Leibnizianism was then examined in Chapter 3 through an analysis of his philosophical concept of the problematic Idea, which is constructed in order to spell out the conditions for the internal genesis of the sense and truth of propositions (along with the event-determined object which realizes this truth), up to and including philosophical propositions with regard to the nature of the problematic Idea. It was then seen that the problem or problematic Idea is composed of series of merely determinable, differential elements which are reciprocally, completely and progressively determined by the adjunction and transformation of singularities-events corresponding to the values of the relations between these elements. This fully differential problem was then said to be actualized by diverse processes of intensive individuation in so far as a 'divided subject', in the absence of some underlying substance, must think the relational unity of such differential processes with reference to a 'pre-individual field' having the same form as the problematic Idea. What was lacking from this discussion of the problematic Idea and its actualization, however, was a fully differential account of language and the proposition.

How, then, does Deleuze's account of structure respond to this lack and thereby create a systematic relation between the events making up the lives of things and the expression of sense or sense-event, such that we can speak of the evental-determination of things 'all the way down'? In short, it is by 'serializing' the terms of each side of the dualities examined above in such a way that things, events, propositions and propositions about (the sense of) propositions form a structure which is reciprocally, completely and progressively determined in relation to a paradoxical element (which, as will be seen, is the ontologically primary event).

With regard to this structural solution to the problem of the relation between the event and sense, Deleuze writes in the 'Sixth Series on Serialization' that the series of a structure can be determined in various ways:

> We can consider a series of events and a series of things in which these events are or are not realized; or we can consider a series of denoting propositions and a series of denoted things; or a series of verbs and a series of adjectives and substantives; or a series of expressions and senses and a series of denotation and *denotata*. These variations are unimportant, since they represent solely degrees of freedom in the organization of heterogeneous series. The same duality, we have seen, occurs *outside*, between events and states of affairs; *at the surface*, between propositions and denoted objects; and *inside* the proposition between expressions and denotations. (LS, 37)

What must be understood here is that, by serializing the terms comprising each side of the dualities examined above, Deleuze treats these terms as 'differences' to be determined only with respect to one another. How is this differential determination to be carried out? By precisely the same kinds of processes of reciprocal, complete and progressive determination we examined throughout Chapters 3 and 4. First of all, then, each series of terms must considered to be held in a differential relation through which they *reciprocally* determine one another. In particular, the terms of the two basic series of bodies and language are respectively held together by causal relations on the one hand and, on the other, by the circular or conditioning-conditioned relation between the propositional dimensions of denotation, manifestation and signification, along with phonemic, morphological and semantic relations. In Chapter 1, we discussed causal relations between bodies while examining Deleuze's concept of Chronos. We also discussed the circular relation between denotation, manifestation and signification. Furthermore, it was seen in Chapter 2 that Deleuze affirms an 'expressive causality' or 'law-like' relation between the events truly predicable of the individuals constitutive of a particular world (sufficient reason). Finally, in this chapter, we have discussed the phonemic, morphological and syntactic relations constitutive of language systems.

So, as we have seen, to the 'values' of the causal relations between different bodies correspond series of singularities or, more precisely, as they have been called, singularities-events. As was argued, a body, characterized by various events, is the cause for another body of a singularity-event or 'sayable' being true of this latter, and so on, indefinitely.[28] In other words, singularities-events are at once the 'effect' of causal relations between bodies, whatever their evental-nature turns out to be, and are picked out by verbs in denoting propositions. Yet this is only another way of saying that the reciprocal determination between bodies through their causal relations is prolonged in a *complete* determination of their events-effects in relation to series of propositions, having their own constitutive relations.

It has also been seen that language necessarily involves certain 'sense-events'. In other words, propositions, taken in the circular conditioning-conditioned relation between their various dimensions, also express senses which must themselves be denoted by further propositions expressing their own senses, and so on, indefinitely. The reciprocal and complete determination of bodies must therefore also be *progressively* determined with respect to series of propositions bearing on propositions. It is in this way, therefore, that Deleuze argues that expressed sense engenders both propositions with their various dimensions, and the objective correlates of these dimensions: denoted states of affairs, the manifested beliefs and desires of the subject, and signified concepts (LS, 120).

Now, these relations of determination between various series – bodies, propositions, propositions about propositions, and so on – are also spoken of by Deleuze in terms of the structural relations of 'signification', examined above, which hold between them. As he writes,

The law governing two simultaneous series is that they are never equal. One represents the *signifier*, the other the *signified* . . . We call 'signifier' any sign which presents in itself an aspect of sense; we call 'signified', on the contrary, that which serves as the correlative to this aspect of sense, that is, that which is defined in a duality relative to this aspect. What is signified therefore is never sense itself . . . Thus, the signifier is primarily the event as the ideal logical attribute of a state of affairs, and the signified is the state of affairs together with its qualities and real relations. The signifier is also the entire proposition, in so far as it includes dimensions of denotation, manifestation, and signification in the strict sense. And the signified is the independent term which corresponds to these dimensions, that is, the concept, and also the denoted thing or manifested subject. Finally, the signifier is the sole dimension of expression, which in fact has the privilege of not being relative to an independent term, since sense as expressed does not exist outside of the expression; and the signified, in this case, is the denotation, the manifestation, or even the signification in the strict sense. In other words, the signified is the proposition in so far as sense, or that which is expressed, is distinguished from it. (LS, 37–8)

Following our analyses of the structural signifying-signified relation above, what must be understood here is that, on the one hand, the signifying series represents an aspect of the virtual or differential condition of the signified series and corresponds to something which is itself never signified, namely, sense. On the other hand, the signified series represents a dimension of the actualization or differenciation of this virtual or differential condition.

But now, what can be said of the paradoxical element which brings about the communication of series, and the determination of these signifying and signified, differential and differenciating relations? The paradoxical element here is clearly the event itself, in so far as it is displaced from series to series, causing each series to communicate and all of their terms to be determined. The event is thus, first of all, an incorporeal effect resulting from relations between bodies but also attributed to them. It corresponds, secondly, to the verb of the proposition which expresses a process. Finally, it is the 'sense-event' or ongoing expression of sense in the proposition. This last aspect of the event, then, corresponds precisely to what has been called the evental-determination of the event, that is, the Unique Event or Aion.

So, we have seen in the present chapter that Deleuze's concept of the problem is essentially identical to that of his concept of structure. It has also been seen that structure is capable of accounting for processes of reciprocal, complete and progressive determination bearing on series of things, propositions, and propositions about (the sense of) propositions. Let us then return to some of the issues raised at the conclusion of Chapter 3, in particular with respect to the relation between the problem and language.

First of all, it was argued in Chapter 3 that the concept of the problem was constructed in order to specify the conditions under which the relation between the sense of a proposition and what it designates can be internally established within sense itself. Every designating proposition will have sense, but this sense will be located in a sub-representative problem in relation to which such propositions function as elements of response or cases of solution. Indeed, even philosophical propositions with regard to the objective nature of the problem must obey these conditions. The problem was then defined as the reciprocal, complete and progressive determination of purely differential elements by the adjunction and transformation of singularities corresponding to the values of the relations between these elements. The sense of these philosophical propositions with regard to the nature of the problem was then held to be determined, or 'make sense', in a mutually determining relationship with the propositions constitutive of a theory of intensive individuation, that is, in so far as this latter theory presupposes the existence of a pre-individual field having the same form as the problem. However, the question still remained: how are these considerations with respect to sense and truth supposed to apply to the particular, non-philosophical propositions characteristic of the diverse domains in which intensive individuation occurs (physics, biology, psychology, sociology, linguistics, etc.) and bearing on states of affairs which are supposed to be constituted by events 'all the way down'? In other words, how do propositions in general – constitutive of knowledge and bearing on known things – 'make sense' within the problematic Idea?

In fact, it has just been seen that Deleuze's philosophical concept of the problem is equivalent to that of structure, and also that the concept of structure specifies the conditions necessary for thinking the purely differential determination of series of things, series of propositions, and series of propositions about propositions (the ongoing determination of sense), all in relation to the Event understood as a paradoxical element systematically displaced throughout these heterogeneous series and causing them to communicate. Within the signified/signifying relations which hold between these different series with respect to the displacement of the Event, sense is that which never exists outside of the propositions which express it, but also that which itself is never signified since it must always be distinguished from the proposition. It is in this way, then, that propositions can be said to find their sense and truth value, in relation to their corresponding 'evental' states of affairs, within sense itself.[29] Sense or the Event, in other words, such as this is structurally understood in *The Logic of Sense*, is precisely the sub-representative problematic Idea of *Difference and Repetition*. Indeed, Deleuze confirms this alignment of these concepts when he writes that sense is 'expressed as the problem to which propositions correspond in so far as they indicate particular responses, signify instances of a general solution, and manifest subjective acts of resolution' (LS, 121).

*   *   *

One very important question, however, still remains for us to answer: if everything is an event, what brings about the event of language? Indeed, we have thus far presupposed the existence of language or, more precisely, the separation of the two series of things and propositions which constitute the surface (see, on this, LS, 186). Indeed, this presupposition appears to be entirely necessary for our structural account of the event and sense. The question of the event of language is thus extremely subtle. For, if we are to remain consistent with the above analyses we must ask: how can the event of language be said to result from relations between bodies, yet also be determined in relation to sense, if sense does not exist outside of the language and propositions which express it? In order to account for the event of language, we must turn to Deleuze's relation to psychoanalysis and, in particular, his account of sexuality and the 'phantasm'.

An examination of Deleuze's relation to psychoanalysis will also allow us to address two further points. The first of these is the question of how we are to understand the 'divided subject' in *The Logic of Sense*'s structural characterization of the event and language. Indeed, while we noted above that it is the Event which is the paradoxical element in the structural account of sense, we lost sight of the role of the 'agent' which is both 'subjected' to the paradoxical element (the Event) and necessarily accompanies its perpetual circulation. We will thus argue that Deleuze's account of the phantasm effectively reintroduces the subject in both its passive and active or creative roles in relation to the structural synthesis of events.

The final issue to be addressed concerns the 'static' nature of the above structural account of the ontological priority of the Event. Indeed, despite the important role of 'progressive' determination in structuralism in general, the structure of sense or the Event, such as we have examined it here, has the appearance of a kind of timeless or *a priori* condition for the evental-determination of words, things and the relations between them. This appearance of stasis, however, is in fact only a result of the presupposition of the separation of things and propositions at the surface, and of the lack of an account of the creative role of the 'divided subject'. Once it is seen how language and the subject both emerge as events, even as they condition syntheses of events, we will be in a position to see the dynamism inherent in Deleuze's evental ontology.

In sum, it is the three notions of the event of language, the divided subject and the dynamism of the event, as well as the relations between these notions, which will be the focus of Chapter 5.

Notes

1. Although the original publication of this essay was 1972 – see François Châtelet (ed.), *Histoire de la philosophie vol. VIII: le XXe siècle* (Paris: Hachette, 1972), pp. 299–335 – it was clearly written much earlier: as Deleuze writes in the opening lines, '*This is 1967*' (HRS, 170). Deleuze also sent a copy of this text, with an accompanying letter to be found in the Althusser archives, to Louis Althusser in February 1968. See Dosse, *Gilles Deleuze et Félix Guattari: Biographie Croisée*, p. 273.

2. Lacan does, however, explicitly acknowledge his debt to Lévi-Strauss' and Mauss' formulations with respect to the 'symbolic'. See, for example, Jacques Lacan, 'A Theoretical Introduction to the Functions of Psychoanalysis in Criminology', in *Écrits*, trans. Bruce Fink (New York and London: W.W. Norton & Company, 2006), p. 108: 'Let us thus concur with Marcel Mauss' clear formulations: . . . The structures of society are symbolic; individuals, in so far as they are normal, use them in real behaviours; in so far as they are mentally ill [*psychopathe*], they express them by symbolic behaviours.'

3. Jacques Lacan, 'Seminar on "The Purloined Letter"', in *Écrits*, p. 17.

4. Ibid. Now, it should also be noted that Lacan follows Lévi-Strauss in arguing for the all-embracing nature of the symbolic. As Lévi-Strauss writes, 'culture may be looked upon as an ensemble of symbolic relations, in the front rank of which are to be found language, marriage laws, economic relations, art, science and religion' (cited in Jean Laplanche and Jean-Bertrand Pontalis, *The Language of Psycho-Analysis*, trans. Donald Nicholson-Smith [New York: Norton, 1973], p. 440). As Lacan himself writes: 'Symbols in fact envelop the life of man with a network so total that they join together those who are going to engender him "by bone and flesh" before he comes into the world; so total that they bring to his birth, along with the gifts of the stars, if not with the gifts of the fairies, the shape of his destiny; so total that they provide the words that will make him faithful and renegade, the law of the acts that will follow him right to the very place where he is not yet and beyond his very death; and so total that through them his end finds its meaning in the last judgment, where the Word absolves his being or condemns it.' See Jacques Lacan, 'The Function and Field of Speech and Language in Psychoanalysis', in *Écrits*, p. 231.

5. Jacques Lacan, 'Variations of the Standard Treatment', in *Écrits*, p. 290.

6. Laplanche and Pontalis, *The Language of Psycho-Analysis*, p. 210.

7. Thus Lacan speaks of a '*function of misrecognition*' when the child initially identifies itself with its 'mirror image', that is, at a stage 'prior to its social determination' in the symbolic dimension of language and culture. See generally Jacques Lacan, 'The Mirror Stage as Formative

of the *I* Function', in *Écrits*, pp. 75–81. We shall return to these ideas in Chapter 5.

8. As Lévi-Strauss (who is following the work of Jakobson in phonology) puts it, 'sense always results from the combination of elements which are not themselves signifying'. See Claude Lévi-Strauss, 'Réponses à quelques questions', *Esprit* 33: 11 (1963), p. 637 (my translation).

9. Claude Lévi-Strauss, *Structural Anthropology I*, trans. Claire Jacobson and Brooke Grundfest Schoepf (New York: Basic Books, 1963), p. 34, p. 279.

10. Roman Jakobson, 'Phoneme and Phonology', in *Selected Writings I: Phonological Studies* (The Hague: Mouton & Co., 1962), p. 231.

11. For the full account of the phonemic structure of French, see Roman Jakobson and J. Lotz, 'Notes on the French Phonemic Pattern', in *Selected Writings I: Phonological Studies*, pp. 426–34.

12. See, for example, the diagram of the French phonemic structure in ibid., p. 433.

13. Deleuze's major reference with respect to morphology is the French linguist Gustave Guillaume. See, for example, DR, 205; LS, 184 and 351, n.1.

14. Roman Jakobson and Morris Halle, *Fundamentals of Language* (The Hague: Mouton & Co., 1956), p. 5. Deleuze, however, ultimately criticizes the phonology of the Prague School for taking oppositions between distinctive features as primary in determining phonemic structures, in relation to morphological structures understood as already given and not as having been produced and continuing to evolve. As he writes, following the work of Gustave Guillaume, the 'selection of phonemes possessing pertinent value in this or that language is inseparable from that of morphemes as elements of grammatical constructions. Moreover, the morphemes, which on their own account bring into play the virtual whole of the language, are the object of a progressive determination which proceeds by "differential thresholds" and implies a purely logical time capable of measuring the genesis or actualization. The formal reciprocal determination of the phonemes refers to that progressive determination which expresses the action of the virtual system on the phonic matter; and it is only when the phonemes are considered abstractly – in other words, when the virtual [whole of language] is reduced to a simple possible [i.e., to a system of already constituted, although perhaps not yet realized units] – that their relations take the negative form of an empty opposition, rather than that of filling differential positions around a threshold' (DR, 205). For an example of the genesis or actualization of morphological structures – in this case, verbal systems – see Gustave Guillaume, *Temps et Verbe* (Paris: Champion, 1929).

15. It can be noted that while Deleuze does not here speak explicitly of

'reciprocal' and 'complete' determination, it is certain that he has these processes in mind when he speaks of one series of terms determining 'in a complex manner' the terms of another series.

16. Jakobson, 'Phoneme and Phonology', p. 231.
17. Ibid., p. 233.
18. See on this Roman Jakobson, 'Remarques sur l'évolution phonologique du russe', in *Selected Writings I: Phonological Studies*, p. 110. See also HRS, 180: 'time conceived as a relation of succession of two actual forms merely abstractly expresses the internal times of the structure or structures that are actualized in depth in these two forms, and the differential relations between these times' (translation modified). The internal temporality of structures and its relation to actualization or differenciation is examined further below.
19. Jakobson, 'Phoneme and Phonology', p. 232.
20. See Claude Lévi-Strauss, *Totemism*, trans. Rodney Needham (London: Merlin Press, 1964), p. 77, pp. 85–9.
21. Compare this passage from *The Logic of Sense*: 'If the terms of each series are relatively displaced, *in relation to one another*, it is primarily because they have in themselves an *absolute* place; but this absolute place is always determined by the terms' distance from this [paradoxical] element which is always displaced, in the two series, *in relation to itself*' (LS, 40–1).
22. Jakobson and Lotz, 'French Phonemic Pattern', p. 431.
23. Ibid., p. 431; Roman Jakobson and Linda Waugh, *The Sound Shape of Language* (New York: Mouton, 1987), pp. 153–5.
24. See on this, Adrian Battye and Marie-Anne Hintze, *The French Language Today* (London: Routledge, 1992), p. 134.
25. For this and for what follows, see André Berri, 'Aspects phonétiques et phonologiques du E-muet du français', *Revista Fragmentos* 30 (2006), pp. 199–217.
26. This conforms (albeit for different reasons) to the standard Saussurian definitions of signifier and signified as the 'sound-image' and the 'concept' respectively. See Ferdinand de Saussure, *Course in General Linguistics*, trans. Wade Baskin (New York: McGraw-Hill, 1959), p. 67.
27. Claude Lévi-Strauss, *Introduction to the Work of Marcel Mauss*, trans. Felicity Baker (London: Routledge & Kegan Paul, 1987), p. 55. Lévi-Strauss compares *mana* type words to Jakobson's zero phoneme at p. 72, n.18. Deleuze analyses Lévi-Strauss's work on structure, and the role of *mana* type words therein, at LS, 48–50. See also HRS, 186.
28. This Stoic point could, of course, also be put in terms of Leibnizian 'expressive causality' and 'sufficient reason'.
29. Deleuze's apparent 'idealism' here will appear shocking to some. Perhaps this is only because they are associating 'idealism' with

Berkeley's 'immaterialism', and not with the various brands of idealism characteristic of Kantian and post-Kantian philosophy which were so influential for Deleuze (see, for example, Deleuze's very positive comments on Maïmon's relation to Kantian transcendental idealism at DR, 173–4 and 192–3). In fact, according to Paul Redding's recently published work, all of these German idealisms found their common ancestor in Leibniz, whose influence on Deleuze was the subject of Chapter 2. As Redding has argued, German idealism in its various guises shares a number of general features which can all be traced back to certain developments in Leibniz's thought. These features of idealism include, among others: a revival of a number of Platonic and Aristotelian themes, particularly with regard to the 'ideality' of spatio-temporal and conceptual 'form'; a conception of the 'perspectival' nature of perceptual knowledge; and an appeal to elements from the Platonist and Neo-Platonist tradition such as a prioritizing of concepts and inferences over sense experience, and a holistic and organicist view of knowledge and the cosmos. See Paul Redding, *Continental Idealism: Leibniz to Nietzsche* (London: Routledge, 2009), pp. 3–5. Indeed, much of our work in previous chapters effectively shows how these features of idealism are present in Deleuze's philosophy. Thus, in Chapter 3, we saw how Deleuze understands spatio-temporal and conceptual form in terms of the actualization of 'fully differential problematic Ideas'. In Chapter 2, we saw how Deleuze extended the Leibnizian notion of the 'point of view' with reference to Nietzschean 'perspectivism', in order to argue that the genesis of the known and knowledge are a matter of 'points of view on points of view'. It has also been seen throughout this present work how Deleuze prioritizes the workings of 'sense' over any direct or naïve perceptual realism. And finally, we saw in Chapter 3 how Deleuze essentially follows Simondon in arguing for a holistic view of knowledge and the cosmos, that is, in so far as we must think, in the absence of any given substance, the unity of the intensive processes which constitute us and our world within the problematic Idea.

5

Psychoanalysis – Dynamic Genesis

Deleuze's relation to psychoanalysis in *The Logic of Sense* is ultimately governed by the following problem: how can the surface (that is to say, the metaphysical surface, transcendental field, problem or structure of sense), with its constitutive series of things and propositions, be understood as an event which is itself determined on the surface? In other words, if the above-analyzed structure of sense is supposed to account for the progressive evental-determination of events in general, and if events have ontological priority over fixed things 'all the way down', then Deleuze must show that the structure of sense is not an already given condition like the Kantian transcendental, but rather an event which is immanent to itself. As will be seen in this chapter, Deleuze turns to psychoanalysis because it is capable, through its concepts of infantile sexuality, the phallus, castration and the phantasm, of thinking the genesis of structure in a structural way. Put in psychoanalytic terms, the 'genesis of structure' is thought by means of a structural account of the entry of the real, biological child into what Lacan calls the 'symbolic order', comprising all of the linguistic and cultural structures governing human existence. In other words, psychoanalysis develops a structural account of the 'event' of the symbolic order for the child, the 'symbolic' being, for Deleuze, another name for the metaphysical surface, problem or structure of sense, such as these have been analyzed throughout the preceding chapters in their linguistic and intersubjective aspects.

What is at stake in this immanence of the metaphysical surface to itself is, following Deleuze, the 'dynamic genesis' of sense or the event, which goes directly from real actions and passions (here, the actions and passions of the biological child) to events on the metaphysical surface, that is, *'from depth to the production of surfaces'* (LS, 186, emphasis in original). It is this genesis which involves the event of language – understood as the effective separation of the two series of words endowed with sense and sonorous things 'at the surface' – and, simultaneously, the event of the 'divided subject' (*personne*, questioner, etc.) which accompanies the paradoxical element circulating between these two series of words and things and bringing them into communication. As Deleuze writes, 'from the point of view of the other [static] genesis, we posit eating and speaking by right as two series already separated at the surface' (LS, 186). The task of the 'dynamic genesis', on the contrary, is to show 'how speaking is effectively disengaged from eating, how the surface itself is produced, or how the incorporeal event results from bodily states', beginning with the body of the divided subject (LS, 186–7). In short, Deleuze turns to psychoanalysis in order to give an account of how these two events characterizing the dynamic genesis – the event of language and the event of the divided subject – both produce the metaphysical surface, and are determined on the metaphysical surface.[1]

Now, it should be noted here that, in so far as Deleuze turns to psychoanalytic theory for his account of the dynamic genesis, he is not so much interested in psychoanalysis as a clinical practice as he is in its function, within his own philosophy of events, as 'the science of events' (LS, 211).[2] What is more, not only does Deleuze not treat psychoanalysis as a clinical practice (indeed, he is more interested in 'metapsychology'),[3] he does not limit himself to employing the principles and concepts of a single psychoanalytic school. Rather, he develops a reading of psychoanalysis which cuts across the different strains of psychoanalytic thought, such as these existed at the time of the writing of *The Logic of Sense*. For example, even though Deleuze puts many Lacanian concepts to work, his 1969 account of the 'phantasm' bears little resemblance to the 'Logic' of the phantasm outlined in Lacan's 1966–67 Seminar.[4] Deleuze also criticizes Lacan's definition of psychotic language as the 'endless and panic-stricken sliding of the signifying series over the signified series' (see LS, 90–1, translation modified). What is more, his use of Melanie Klein is also in direct conflict with Lacan's reading of her work. Thus, while Lacan criticizes Klein for speaking about pre-Oedipal experience without reference to the dimension of the 'symbolic' which alone could make sense of such experience (albeit retroactively), for Deleuze, Klein's work supplies 'the early elements of the Oedipus complex' with reference to a completely original and irreducible dimension: the 'depths' (LS, 200).[5] By the same token, however, we disagree with Serge Cottet's argument that, in 1968, psychoanalysis for Deleuze essentially *was* Melanie Klein.[6] Indeed, Deleuze is explicitly critical of her concept of the 'introjected good object' (LS, 188), as well of her neglect of the theme of the 'body without organs' (LS,

351–2, n.3). Finally, while the Freudian approach to infantile sexuality is enormously important for Deleuze, he is nevertheless critical of Freud's 'pronominal model' of the place of the ego in the phantasm (LS, 213).

In short, it would appear that Deleuze feels at liberty to pick and choose his concepts from the psychoanalytic corpus in order to qualify psychoanalysis as a 'science of events', and without regard for the internal, theoretical divisions recognized by practicing French psychoanalysts in and around 1969.[7] Indeed, as will be seen, Deleuze often runs together concepts from different schools. His account and criticisms of these concepts, however, are not, for all that, confused. In fact, Deleuze presents an entirely coherent reading of psychoanalytic theory, that is to say, in so far as it is consistent with his philosophical theory of sense and the event. Thus, for example, he understands the 'phantasm' – the nature of which is disputed among Freudians, Kleinians and Lacanians – with reference to his own notion of the 'dynamic genesis' of sense and the event. As he writes, we must

> determine the phantasm's point of birth and, through this, its real relation to language. This question is nominal or terminological to the extent that it is about the use of the word 'phantasm'. But it engages other things as well, since it fixes this use [of the word 'phantasm'] in relation to a particular moment, allegedly making it necessary in the course of the dynamic genesis ... The phantasm is a surface phenomenon and, moreover, a phenomenon which is formed at a certain moment in the development of surfaces. (LS, 215–16)

We shall return to the concept of the phantasm. It has only been mentioned here to emphasize the fact that Deleuze's approach to psychoanalysis must be understood as following from the philosophical system he is constructing in *The Logic of Sense*, and not from his adherence to this or that school of psychoanalytic thought. Indeed, it is in this manner that we interpret Deleuze's statement that, 'in *The Logic of Sense*, I thought I'd discovered things ... about events, that contradicted psychoanalysis but could be reconciled with it.'[8] It is also in this way that we understand Deleuze's later 'excuse' for his 'complacency' towards psychoanalysis: that he 'rendered it inoffensive' by presenting it as 'an art of surfaces'.[9]

In sum, then, Deleuze couches his formulations with respect to the dynamic genesis of sense in terms of a system of metapsychological concepts which are the subject of ongoing dispute between various schools of psychoanalytic thought. This can make not only the various aspects of the dynamic genesis, but also the conceptual connections between the static and dynamic geneses, particularly difficult to understand. It is thus the task of this chapter to first of all carefully explicate the four 'steps' of the dynamic genesis such as Deleuze formulates them with reference to various psychoanalytic figures and concepts; and secondly, to examine the way in which Deleuze connects the dynamic genesis to the previously examined static genesis in order to affirm the immanence of the metaphysical surface to itself, which is to say the ontological priority of events 'all the way down'.

Now, it should also be remarked that Deleuze's engagement with psychoanalysis is not only extremely complex, both in terms of his unusual approach to its different schools of thought and the connections he makes between the psychoanalytic dynamic genesis and the earlier static genesis; it also represents nearly a quarter of the actual text of *The Logic of Sense*, appendices excluded. There is thus a significant number of issues which must be covered in this chapter. We shall break matters down in the following way. First of all, we shall examine how Deleuze takes up certain Kleinian concepts (while criticizing others from a Lacanian point of view) in order to argue that the child's initially disorganized, bodily experiences and object relations come to be organized in the form of an 'imago' or 'good object'. This good object is in turn signified by a 'Voice' which, while not yet a language (having its determined structure of phonemes, morphemes and semantemes, and its determined dimensions of denotation, manifestation, signification and sense), will be made sense of retrospectively, once the child enters the all-embracing 'symbolic order'. Deleuze calls this 'first step' of the dynamic genesis 'from noise to the voice', in order to emphasize that there appears at this early stage a first differentiation between 'noisy' corporeal things in depth and the 'familial hum' which will come to be endowed with sense.

We shall then turn to the second step of the dynamic genesis, which is essentially an account of Freud's theory of infantile sexuality, coupled with certain Lacanian considerations with respect to the nature of the 'phallus' and the Kleinian concept of 'reparation'. This step of the genesis is designed to show how, in relation to the Voice, the child, who was initially enveloped in full corporeal 'depth', comes to form out of his or her component sexual drives a total 'physical surface' for his or her body.

Our examination of the third step of the dynamic genesis, which has as its focus the Oedipus complex and its resolution, will then show how this dynamic process of the formation and coordination of a total physical surface is an essential step towards the child's entry into the symbolic order, that is, towards what can be called the child's passage to the metaphysical surface. This is because, following certain Lacanian formulations, the resolution of the Oedipus complex comes about when the child is 'castrated' of the 'phallus', the phallus being an essential element in the formation of the total physical surface of his or her body. What occurs in castration is that the child ceases the attempt to *be* what he or she imagines is the total and wholly satisfying object of his or her mother's desire (the 'imaginary phallus'), and comes to 'identify' in various ways with the father who symbolically *has* the phallus in so far as he is a representative of the social law of the mother's desire. In this identification with the father, then, the child effectively situates him or herself in relation to a rule-governed way of organizing the social world, that is, in relation to other persons within the structural-symbolic dimension of language and culture. This 'passage' to the metaphysical surface thus effectively represents the event of the divided subject (*personne*, questioner, thrower of the dice, etc.), that is to say, the subject that is at once dissolved in intensive, corporeal processes, and a form produced on the metaphysical surface.

The fourth and final stage of the dynamic genesis concerns the event of language. We shall examine the way in which Deleuze takes up and extends the psychoanalytic concept of the phantasm in order to account for this event. As will be seen, the phantasm has several characteristics which are essential for Deleuze's account of the dynamic genesis. In the first place, the phantasm is a mental representation corresponding to the satisfaction of the sexual drives. Secondly, the phantasm, like sense, is both inseparable from and irreducible to the propositions in which it is expressed, and thus something which essentially 'results' from the operations of the entire, intersubjective, metaphysical surface. Thirdly, the phantasm finds its origin in castration (and thus the real actions and passions which make castration possible) to the extent that the child denies its original sexual aims and objects (i.e., being the phallus for the mother) at the level of the metaphysical surface. In other words, with castration, the child 'denegates' his or her original sexual aims and objects at precisely the same time that he or she identifies with the 'law of desire' such as this comes to be articulated in the symbolic order of language and culture. This 'reinvestment' and 'articulation' of desire at the metaphysical surface is precisely the process of the phantasm. Furthermore, in so far as this process of the phantasm depends on the operations of the entire metaphysical surface, it must be considered to be a product of the 'static genesis' which therefore determines the denoted individuals, the beliefs and desires of the manifested persons, and the signified concepts belonging to the phantasm.

What, then, does this have to do with the event of language? As has been said, the event of language is the process which separates words endowed with sense from the sounds of bodies in general. The first step of the dynamic genesis showed how the child's early corporeal experiences were organized in the form of a 'good object' signified by a 'Voice' which is not yet a language from the child's point of view (that is, having a determined structure of phonemes, morphemes and semantemes, and having its four determined dimensions of denotation, manifestation, signification and, underpinning these, sense). Around the time of the Oedipus complex, the child undergoes a 'linguistic apprenticeship': he or she extracts phonemic differences from the Voice and begins to 'speak'. Nevertheless, this speech cannot at this stage be equal to language, for the child has not yet acceded to the organizing principle of language, which can only be found at the level of the metaphysical surface (sense or the static genesis: the fourth dimension of the proposition). Now, with castration, the passage to the metaphysical surface and the process of the phantasm, the child is able to gradually connect its speech with the propositions constitutive of the phantasm, that is, with language *per se*. The event of language, therefore, which itself depends on castration and everything that entails, involves these three moments: from noise to the Voice, from the Voice to speech and from speech to language in the phantasm.

It is in this way, then, that psychoanalysis is able to account for the events of the divided subject and of language, that is, for the event of the metaphysical surface *for* each and every subject. But it is also clear that, in so far as these events of language and of the divided subject are inseparable from the process of the phantasm, which is itself coextensive with the products of the metaphysical surface (static genesis), they must also be considered to be determined *on* the metaphysical surface (or, more precisely, these events must be considered to be inseparable from their *ongoing* determination on the metaphysical surface). The metaphysical surface can thus, in this way, be considered to be an event which is immanent only to itself.

So let us now turn to the detail of these arguments, beginning with the first step of the dynamic genesis and Deleuze's 'use' of Melanie Klein in conjunction with the Lacanian concept of the 'imago'.

5.1 First Step of the Dynamic Genesis: From Noise to the Voice (Klein and the Pre-Oedipal)

As argued above, Deleuze appropriates certain aspects of Kleinian theory in order to establish the 'first stage' of this dynamic genesis of sense. That is, Deleuze uses Klein in order to establish how the 'undifferentiated noise' characterizing bodies in depth is organized in the form of a 'good object' which is in turn signified by a 'Voice' belonging to a dimension other than that of bodies, even though it is not yet a language having its determined dimensions and structure. In order to examine Deleuze's treatment of Klein in this regard, it is appropriate to first of all present the broad outlines of her thought.

Melanie Klein always perceived her own work as being based on and consistent with Freud's methods and findings, despite Freud's critical dismissal of her work.[10] She did, however, and in a strikingly original way, extend Freud's work by psychoanalyzing very young children.[11] Her work led her to expand a number of Freudian concepts, related in particular to early 'mechanisms of defence' against anxiety, and to conclude, in short, that 'both the Oedipus complex and the super-ego are well in evidence at a much earlier age than had been assumed'.[12] Indeed, Deleuze's primary interest in Klein lies in the manner in which she characterizes this early development of the Oedipus complex (see LS, 200), even if he views it from a perspective slightly different from Klein's.

The long paragraph on pages 187 to 188 of *The Logic of Sense*'s 'Twenty-Seventh Series of Orality' is a dense statement of some of the basic tenets of Kleinian theory, and even duplicates the kind of 'alimentary and excremental' vocabulary which Klein uses to express her ideas. In short, Klein's work focuses on the way in which the infant, from birth, deals with the anxiety produced both by external factors and by the internal conflict between the life and death drives, whose existence was postulated by Freud in *Beyond the Pleasure Principle*. In particular, Klein focused on the relation between various mechanisms of defence against anxiety (such as introjection, projection, splitting and identification) and the development of both internal and external, as well as part and whole, 'object relations' which are expressed, symbolized and 'worked out' in the pre-linguistic 'phantasies' characterizing the infant's psychic life. In this relation, the particular and evolving natures of phantasies can be said to be both the 'result' of the mechanisms of defence as well as a stimulus for the continued use of these mechanisms. What is more, Klein sees this mutual relation between the defences and phantasy as evolving in relation to an ongoing tension between two 'positions' – the paranoid-schizoid position and the depressive position – each describing a kind of constellation of anxieties, mechanisms and object relations. It is this structured evolution which prepares the way for the development of the super-ego and Oedipus complex, precisely because the object relations which are necessary for these latter developments, particularly with respect to the maternal and paternal figures, are herein elaborated. Let us now unpack these notions further, since this will allow us to appreciate precisely what is going on in Deleuze in his use and critique of Kleinian psychoanalysis.

For Klein, during the first three or four months of life the infant is described as being in the 'paranoid-schizoid position', so called because it is characterized, on the one hand, by persecutory anxiety, and on the other hand, as shall be seen, by processes of 'splitting'.[13] Even at this early stage, for Klein, sufficient ego exists to experience anxiety, to employ defence mechanisms against this anxiety and to form primitive 'phantastical' object relations.[14] Anxiety here derives from both internal and external sources and is experienced as 'persecution'. It originates in the polarity of the internal life and death drives, as well as from the conflict between external frustrations and gratifications. The external frustrations arise particularly with respect to feeding, so it follows that the first, albeit tumultuous, object-relation is to the mother or, more precisely, to the breast. Phantastical defence mechanisms, such as splitting, introjection and projection, then come into play, in a way which shall be examined below, in order to cope with this anxiety from without as well as from within.[15] With respect to phantasy, it should be noted that for Klein, the infant forms unconscious phantasies which, while initially experienced 'more as somatic sensations than as abstract images', make the physical satisfactions, frustrations and other feelings connected with their erogenous zones 'psychologically meaningful' for the infant. Essentially, infantile phantasies convert raw sensation into an experience endowed with a certain quality: good or bad.[16] In phantasy, the mechanism of splitting 'discriminates' between good and bad objects (initially, the good and bad breast), while the mechanisms of introjection and projection generate the psychological sense of the infant's relation to these objects which, at the physical level, is primarily bound up with activity in the oral zone (e.g., swallowing or spitting out), and later with activity in the anal, urethral, genital and other zones identified by Freud. Finally, it should be remarked that, in this complex relation between phantasy and bodily sensation, there is at first no sharp distinction for the infant between its own body and what is outside it. This is because the outside and the inside are here psychically constituted for the infant by its own activity of projection and introjection (corresponding, for example, to physical spitting out and swallowing). In short, while the adult conceives of objects as existing independently, both of him or herself and of each other, the infant's object relations at first always refer in some way to him or herself.[17] Or again, as Deleuze puts it, 'the nursing infant is . . . stage, actor and drama at once. Orality, mouth and breast are initially bottomless depths . . . The entire system of introjection and projection is a communication of bodies in, and through, depth' (LS, 187).

For Klein, then, the relation to the breast should initially be thought of as a relation to a 'part-object', not only because it is not seen as an integral part of a larger whole (the mother), but also because, in order to deal with anxiety, the infant phantastically 'splits' the breast 'into a good and bad object' (LS, 187).[18] In other words, even before perceiving the breast (or indeed the mother) as a whole, the infant, under threat from both inside and outside, must forcibly distinguish between the good and the bad breast, since, precisely, the danger would come from a confusion of the two.[19] Splitting therefore leads to an imaginary differentiation and dispersal of the threatening elements which were formerly mixed up with what is experienced as good.[20] Concomitant with this splitting process, then, on the one hand, the infant 'projects' its internal life impulses and attributes them to the breast which has been experienced as gratifying and good; and he or she also projects his or her destructive impulses and attributes them to the breast which has been experienced as frustrating and bad, persecuting and attacking.[21] It thereby follows that, in this process, the infant also splits his own ego into a libidinal and a destructive part, a good and bad self.[22] On the other hand, the infant 'introjects' or internalizes the good as well as the bad breast, that is, the infant phantasizes that it ingests the breast and that it now resides inside it as an 'internal (part-) object'. For Klein, such internal part-objects will later form the basis of the super-ego. As Hanna Segal puts it:

In the oral-sadistic phase, the child attacks his mother's breast and incorporates it as both destroyed and destructive – 'a bad persecuting internal breast'. This in Melanie Klein's view is the earliest root of the persecuting and sadistic aspect of the super-ego. Parallel with this introjection, in situations of love and gratification the infant introjects an ideal loved and loving breast which becomes the root of the ego-ideal aspect of the super-ego.[23]

We shall return to examine this point, as well as Deleuze's take on it.

Now, because the mechanisms of splitting, projection and introjection are intimately bound up with both phantasy and oral (anal, etc.) activity, they are often expressed in the literature using those phantastical and vivid terms, so characteristic of Klein's work, which Deleuze describes as painting the 'unforgettable picture' of a 'theatre of terror' (LS, 187). Take, for example, the following account of a typical 'phantasy of attack', that is, of the aggressive splitting, projection and corresponding introjection of the bad breast from Klein's 'A Contribution to the Psychogenesis of Manic-Depressive States':

> In the very first months of the baby's existence it has sadistic impulses directed, not only against its mother's breast, but also against the inside of her body: scooping it out, devouring the contents, destroying it by every means which sadism can suggest. The development of the infant is governed by the mechanisms of introjection and projection. From the beginning the ego introjects objects 'good' and 'bad', for both of which the mother's breast is the prototype – for good objects when the child obtains it, for bad ones when it fails him. But it is because the baby projects its own aggression on to these objects that it feels them to be 'bad' and not only in that they frustrate its desires: the child conceives of them as actually dangerous – persecutors who it fears will devour it, scoop out the inside of its body, cut it to pieces, poison it – in short, compassing its destruction by all the means which sadism can devise. These imagos, which are a phantastically distorted picture of the real objects upon which they are based, become installed not only in the outside world but, by the process of incorporation, also within the ego.[24]

This gives us an idea of the kind of vocabulary used by Klein – and repeated by Deleuze – for the expression of infantile phantasies, as well as of the phantastical, anxiety-ridden relation that the infant at this stage maintains to the bad breast. This is, however, only one part of the story. For at the same time, as has been said, the infant 'splits off' and develops a relation to a good breast. In opposition to the bad breast, the infant loves the good breast and has 'phantasies of a pleasant kind in relation to it'.[25] Indeed, in these phantasies, 'the good breast tends to turn into the "ideal" breast which should fulfil the greedy desire for unlimited, immediate and everlasting gratification. Thus feelings arise about a perfect and inexhaustible breast, always available, always gratifying.'[26] This ability to isolate a 'good' object will have important consequences for the developing child. But for the moment, it is clear that depending on the emotional state of the infant – that is, on its level of anxiety and on the way in which the actions of the mother confirm or falsify the infant's phantasies – both the good and the bad breast will tend to be re-split, re-projected and re-introjected.[27]

However, as Klein goes on to explain, even though this activity leads to the ongoing fragmentation of the ego and its objects, and can have a detrimental effect on the child's grasp of reality,[28] the interactions 'between the processes of introjection and projection – re-introjection and re-projection – . . . are essential for the whole development of the ego, for they again and again relieve the young infant's anxieties' and allow the formation of a good object.[29]

So now, what is the importance of this good object or breast? In short, being synonymous with the survival of the ego, filled with the infant's accumulated good experiences, the infant tries to preserve and identify itself (by 'projective identification') with the good breast and, in so far as it does so, the good breast relieves anxiety.[30] It also follows that, when anxiety is diminished in this way, so too are processes of splitting and dispersal, which in turn allow the ego to begin to integrate itself, its objects and its feelings towards them.[31] This situation then leads to what Klein calls the 'depressive position', characterized, as will be seen, by guilt and sorrow. As Deleuze writes, the paranoid-schizoid position

> is succeeded by a depressive position which characterizes a dual progress, since the child strives to reconstitute a complete *good* object and to identify himself with the object. The child strives thus to achieve a corresponding identity, even if in this new drama he has to share the threats, sufferings, and all the passions undergone by the good object. (LS, 187–8)

During the second quarter of the first year of life, a number of important changes take place for the infant. Physiologically, the central nervous system matures and perceptions become better organized, which in turn allows for memory and a better relation to the external world.[32] Sexually as well, in the Freudian sense of this term, urethral, anal and genital trends increase in strength, though oral impulses and desires still predominate.[33] Finally, psychologically, because of the lessening of anxiety due to the relation to the good breast, the ego tends to integrate itself and its objects. These various aspects of development, of course, all impact on one another.

This new stage of life is nevertheless fraught with its own anxieties. Specifically, in so far as the infant begins to integrate its objects, he or she comes to realize that the good and bad breasts or mothers are in fact one and the same. In other words, the infant begins to have an ambivalent relation with one and the same breast, which is seen as the source of both its gratifications and frustrations, which is to say that one and the same breast is both loved and hated. This leads the infant to experience the sorrow of what Klein calls 'the loss of the loved object', that is, the destruction and ruin of the good and ideal breast.[34] What is more, the infant comes to believe that it is itself responsible for this loss, since it realizes that it has been attacking and has even destroyed this loved and life-giving object (which is confirmed, for example, in situations where the breast is taken away from it), and this gives rise to feelings, not only of loss but also of guilt and sorrow: in short, depressive anxiety.[35]

This 'position', then, has two major and related consequences. First of all, faced with this new, depressive anxiety, the infant defends itself by embarking upon a process of what Klein calls 'reparation' whereby, in phantasy, the mother's body or breast, both inside and outside the infant, is somehow put back together and repaired.[36] This process of reparation, aided by the increasing integration of the ego and its objects, leads in turn to the infant's testing of his phantasies against reality, particularly with regard to the breast. For, in its concern for the object, the infant must closely observe the impact of its impulses and phantastical actions on the breast or mother, whose different behaviours can no longer be simply split off from one another.[37]

The second major consequence of depressive anxiety or the loss of the object is that the infant begins to turn to other objects, notably the father, as a means both of securing another life giving object,[38] and of enlisting its help in the phantastical reparation of the mother.[39] Indeed, this turn to other objects is also given impetus by the infant's testing of its phantasy against reality, since, as part of that reality testing, the infant is obliged to take an interest in the objects, like the father, which surround the mother.[40]

In fact, according to Klein, the child already had a relation to the father in the paranoid-schizoid position, or more precisely to the penis understood as a part-object.[41] At this very early stage, when it is frustrated due to the absence of the breast, and in correspondence with its libidinal movements, the infant phantasizes that, using the equation 'breast = penis', the 'father or mother enjoys the desired object of which he is deprived – mother's breast, father's penis – and enjoys it constantly', leading the infant to hate both this bad breast and this bad penis.[42] What is more, according to these early 'sexual theories', 'the father's penis . . . becomes incorporated in the mother during the [sexual] act', from which it follows that, in feeding, both the breast and the penis part-objects will be subject to phantasies of attack and internalization in relation to oral projection and introjection, and will thus be established as both the internal and external, destroyed and destroying, bad breast and penis.[43] Klein also argues that these 'sexual theories are the foundation for combined parent figures such as: the mother containing the father's penis or the whole father; the father containing the mother's breast or the whole mother; the parents fused inseparably in sexual intercourse . . . [O]wing to internalization, the infant establishes such combined parent figures within himself.'[44] This picture of the bad penis becomes even more complicated in so far as clinical material reveals that the infant, in his or her hatred of the breast, sadistically phantasizes that the penis damages and destroys the mother.[45]

On the other hand, and still in the paranoid-schizoid position, when the child is gratified and turns his or her attention to the good breast and its idealization, the penis may be seen as a kind of 'guardian of the maternal space',[46] and thus as a good, external and internal object. To the introjection of the good breast, therefore, corresponds also the introjection of the good penis.[47] These two part-objects, the breast and penis, in both their good and helpful and bad and persecuting aspects, are for Klein the earliest seeds of the super-ego and Oedipus complex.[48]

Now, working through the depressive position, the relation to the father-penis changes to the extent that, due to the infant's increasing powers of integration, as well as its activity of reparation and its turn to the objects beyond the mother, the father comes to be seen as a whole person who helps and supports the mother, who is herself becoming more integrated. The earliest seeds of the super-ego can thus be thought of here as having burgeoned, in so far as the child continues to introject these more and more 'wholesome' objects along with their standards, admonitions and prohibitions: mother and father.[49] Nevertheless, it is important to note that regressions to the paranoid-schizoid position may still occur and that processes of splitting, for example, may be brought to bear on both the mother and the father as a defence against depressive anxiety. In particular (and we shall see below how Deleuze expands upon this idea), the infant may split 'the complete object into an uninjured live object and an injured and endangered one (perhaps dying or dead)'.[50]

The continuing tension between these two positions notwithstanding, everything is, as Deleuze explains, now prepared for the access to a sexual position marked by Oedipus (LS, 188). How does this occur for Klein? In short, in line with Freud's theories, the child's sexual development is at this stage progressing rapidly (if oscillating wildly). Although oral activity still dominates, the infant has already begun to experience anal, urethral and, most importantly here, genital desires. And coupled to this development is, as has just been seen, the growing awareness of an external world and in particular of the mother and father and their relation. It is thus inevitable that, even from the first year of life, sexual desires come to be directed at the mother and father figures, and in a way which coincides with the manner in which these figures have been and continue to be built up by the child's own psychological development as its moves through the paranoid-schizoid and depressive positions.

However, does this progression to the Oedipus complex occur in the same way for Deleuze? In fact, to further continue an examination of the Kleinian reading of the Oedipus complex would be gratuitous, for, at this point, Deleuze radically modifies Klein's position. The first criticism which Deleuze brings to Klein in this regard concerns the status of the 'good object'. As he writes, it

> seems to us that the good object is not introjected as such, because it belongs from the very start to another dimension . . . It belongs to the heights, it holds itself above . . . The superego does not begin with the first introjected objects, as Melanie Klein says, but rather with this good object which holds itself aloft. (LS, 189)

So why does Deleuze hold that the good object is not introjected? It is because the good object, on the one hand, is supposed to be a 'whole' and 'complete' object. As Klein puts it, 'the gratifying breast, taken in under the dominance of the sucking libido, is felt to be complete'.[51] However, if this good object is introjected, and if anxiety is ongoing in the child, this object would have to be re-split, re-projected and re-introjected. This is, of course, incompatible with the good object being whole and complete. As Klein writes, the 'infant's feeling of having inside a good and complete breast may, however, be shaken by frustration and anxiety. As a result, the divorce between the good and bad breast may be difficult to maintain, and the infant may feel that the good breast too is in pieces.'[52] Or again, as Deleuze expresses it: 'Klein herself showed that the splitting of the object into good and bad in the case of introjection is duplicated through a fragmentation which the good object is unable to resist . . . [I]ntrojection, to be precise, does not allow what is wholesome to subsist' (LS, 188). To overcome this contradiction, then, Deleuze affirms that the good, complete object is not introjected as such, and that a revision is therefore required of 'the equilibrium proper to the schizoid position and its relation to the subsequent depressive position' (LS, 188).

Following Deleuze, what the schizoid position initially opposes to bad partial objects is not a good object, but 'an organism without parts, a body without organs, with neither mouth nor anus, having given up all introjection or projection, and being complete, at this price' (LS, 188). What is more, it is in the opposition between the part objects and the body without organs that 'the tension between id and ego is formed' (LS, 188). This notion of a 'body without organs' is taken from the work of Antonin Artaud. Deleuze understands it to represent the schizophrenic's active response to the collapse of meaning into the depth of bodies, that is to say, to the collapse of the frontier between words and things. In this collapse, not only does the word cease being caught up in the production of sense and thereby appear only as a bodily sound, the ideal surfaces of bodies, which are produced on the metaphysical surface in relation to propositions, themselves collapse. On the one hand, then, the entire body is experienced as 'no longer anything but depth' (LS, 87), and is characterized only by actions and passions (LS, 91, 192). And on the other hand, every word is 'physical, and immediately affects the body', invading it by constantly forming 'a mixture and a new state of affairs' with it in depth, instead of being caught up in the infinitely divisible ideal sense-event at the surface (LS, 87–8). In this situation, as Deleuze writes, for the schizophrenic 'it is less a question of recovering meaning than of destroying the word, of conjuring up the affect, and of transforming the painful passion of the body into a triumphant action, obedience into command, always in this depth beneath the fissured surface' (LS, 88). Artaud's 'breath-words (*mots-souffles*) and howl-words (*mots-cris*)' are examples of such actions in so far as they weld together the 'wounding phonetic elements' of language into units which are 'incapable of being decomposed', that is, incapable of forming new mixtures with the body (LS, 88, 90). It can thus be argued that to such indecomposable cries 'a glorious body corresponds . . . an organism without parts . . . (the superior body or body without organs of Antonin Artaud)' (LS, 88).[53] It is a body of this type which, following Deleuze, the infant in the schizoid position opposes to the bad partial objects. But how does he justify this correlation, which at first glance seems rather facile, between the infant and the 'schizophrenic'?

In the first place, Deleuze claims to find in one of Klein's case studies dealing with 'schizoid phenomena' a misrecognition of the theme of the body without organs (LS, 351–2, n.3).[54] Secondly, Deleuze makes a distinction between the infant's anal and urethral sadism, such that 'excrements' correspond to 'hard and solid fragments which change', and 'urine' to 'a liquid principle capable of binding all of the morsels together, and of surmounting such a breaking apart in the full depth of a body (finally) without organs' (LS, 189). He is then in a position to make the link between the infant and the schizophrenic by arguing that, if

> we assume that the schizophrenic, with all the language he has acquired, regresses to this schizoid position [of the child], we should not be surprised to find again in schizophrenic language the duality and complementarity of words-passions, splintered excremental bits, and of words-actions, blocks fused together by a principle of water or fire. (LS, 189)

Whilst these two related arguments may themselves seem far too tenuous to bring about a substantial revision of the Kleinian notion of the schizoid position, it must be remembered that Deleuze's concern here is primarily to resolve a problem in the Kleinian system with reference to certain elements of Klein's thought. As seen, this problem is that the essential role assigned to the 'good object' in the movement from the schizoid through to the depressive and sexual positions has been assigned to something with incompatible characteristics (whole and fragmented). Deleuze thus wants to argue that what the infant in the schizoid position initially opposes to bad partial objects is not a good object but rather a body without organs. As for the good object, Deleuze does indeed have a positive account of it (it belongs, from the start, to the heights, not the depths . . .), but he derives this account from Lacan. Indeed, although Deleuze does not name it as such, his concept of the 'good object' corresponds quite precisely to that of the 'imago of the maternal breast' such as this was analyzed by Lacan in 'Les complexes familiaux' ('The Family Complexes') and 'The Mirror Stage'.[55]

Now, an imago, for Lacan, is a 'subjective determination' of an image, imbued with feeling, which influences 'the way the subject relates to other people, who are perceived through the lens of these various images'.[56] Or again, an imago is an unconscious representation whose content is given by sensation; whose form is retrospectively determined by later psychic activity;[57] and whose power is derived from a complex or structure of interpersonal relationships.[58] The relationship between mother and newborn examined above in Kleinian terms is thus a type of complex, and the good object or breast with which the infant identifies is the imago corresponding to this complex. Indeed, Lacan has analyzed this relationship and this imago as the 'weaning complex' and the 'maternal breast' respectively.[59] The imago of the maternal breast, as will be seen, is both a product of the activities characteristic of the weaning complex and the infant's means of access to this complex in so far as it fixes the feeding relationship to an image in the psyche of the newborn.[60] So the question becomes: what, for Deleuze, are the characteristics of the good object, and how are these reflected in Lacan's analyses of the imago of the maternal breast?

The first characteristic of the good object, following Deleuze, is that in 'opposition to partial introjected objects . . . the good object as such is a complete object' (LS, 189). Lacan, for his part, argues that the imago of the breast for the infant is an unconscious representation of intrauterine life, that is, of a state of *perfect unity or coexistence* with the mother which was cut off by birth, and which the postnatal feeding relationship tends to re-establish, thereby reinforcing and fixing the imago.[61] It is in this sense that the infant '*identifies* with the good object' rather than introjecting or projecting it, as is the case in Klein's work (LS, 190, emphasis added. See also LS, 192). In other words, the infant 'assumes' the imago of the maternal breast and thereby recognizes itself in that image, that is, in the feeding relationship.[62]

The second characteristic of the good object, for Deleuze, is that it takes 'upon itself the two schizoid poles – that of partial objects from which it extracts its force and that of the body without organs from which it extracts its form, that is, its completeness and integrity' (LS, 190). In relation to the first 'pole', Lacan similarly argues that the 'content' of the imago of the breast is given by the initially disorganized sensations and emotions which are typical of the first months of life: e.g., in the vague awareness of a 'presence' which fulfils the maternal function; in the infant's 'oral fusion' with the breast (where the infant 'absorbs' as much as it is completely 'absorbed' in the feeding relation); and in the satisfaction of being rocked in its contrast with the feelings of distress, suffocation and coldness which dominate at birth.[63] It is in this way, therefore, that we can understand Deleuze's assertion that 'the good object is not the successor of the schizoid position [as it is in Klein], but rather forms itself in the course of this position, with borrowings, blockages, and pressures which attest to a constant communication between the two' (LS, 190, translation modified).

Deleuze and Lacan appear to differ, however, as to the origin of the 'form' of the imago. In the above citation, Deleuze appears to understand it to be 'extracted' from the 'body without organs'. Lacan, on the other hand, argues that the form could only be 'revealed' in the structures of subsequent psychic activity, since the infant at this stage has no awareness of object-form.[64] As will be seen, however, Deleuze later clarifies his position and brings it closer to Lacan's by arguing that, being 'necessarily gathered into a voice which speaks', the good object must be 'signified' and thus retroactively made sense of once the infant accedes to the organizing principle of language (LS, 193–4, 352, n. 5). We shall return to this point.

Following Deleuze, the good object's third characteristic is that it 'is by nature a lost object . . . It only shows itself and appears from the start as already lost, as *having been lost*' (LS, 191). Now, it is certain that, for Lacan, in so far as the imago of the maternal breast comes about during the weaning complex and refers to intrauterine life, it refers to something already 'lost'. What is more, it is clear that the loss of this primordial unity is itself a condition of the genesis of the imago, since the content of this latter is given by postnatal sensations and emotions. It is in this sense that, as Deleuze says, the good object is found 'for the first time' as 'found again'.[65] 'Coming about in the course of the schizoid position, the good object posits itself as having always preexisted in this other dimension which now interferes with depth' (LS, 191).

Following this point, Deleuze argues that the good object, as an essentially wholesome but lost object, both 'frustrates' the child and takes on those aspects of the super-ego which Klein understood as resulting from the introjection of both good and bad partial objects. For Deleuze, the good object frustrates the child precisely because of its ambivalent nature, that is, in as much as it can only be found (or formed) as a result of its already being lost. Nevertheless, as lost, the object 'confers its love' or reassuring unity 'on the one who is able to find it for the first time as "found again"'. Yet, by exactly the same token, it 'confers its hate on the one who . . . identifies with the partial objects' which form its content, for it is precisely these disorganized sensations and emotions which signal the loss of the object (LS, 191). As Deleuze puts it:

> Frustration, in view of which the first time can only be a second time, is the common origin of love and hatred. The good object is cruel (the cruelty of the superego) to the extent that it ties together all these moments of love and hate conferred from on high with an instance which turns its face away and offers its gifts (*dons*) only as gifts offered once before (*redonnés*). (LS, 191)

The fourth and final characteristic of the good object, for Deleuze, is that while it can never be recovered as such, it can nevertheless be 'signified' (LS, 352, n.5).[66] Or to put it another way, following Deleuze, if 'we take into consideration the characteristics of the good object (of being found only as lost, of appearing for the first time as already there, etc.) it appears that they are necessarily united in a voice which speaks and comes from on high' (LS, 193, translation modified). What, however, does this mean?

In the first place, it means that from the moment of birth, the child bathes in a familial hum: he or she hears other people speaking and, moreover, speaking about him or her. In other words, because the persons implicated in the weaning complex, accessed by the infant through the imago of the maternal breast, are speakers of a language, the characteristics of this imago or good object will be said to have been united in or signified by this voice.[67] As Deleuze puts it, for

> the child, the first approach to language consists in grasping it as the model of that which preexists, as referring to the entire domain of what is already there, and as the familial voice which conveys tradition, it affects the child as a bearer of a name and demands his insertion even before the child begins to understand. In a certain way, this voice has at its disposal all the dimensions of an organized language: it denotes the good object as such or, on the contrary, the introjected objects; it signifies something, namely, all the concepts and classes which structure the domain of pre-existence; and it manifests the emotional variations of the whole person (the voice that loves or reassures, attacks and scolds, that itself complains about being wounded, or withdraws and keeps quiet). (LS, 193–4)

The problem, of course, concerns how the child at this pre-linguistic stage comes to see in the Voice the characteristics of the good object. Now, it is clear that, for Deleuze as much as for Lacan, the elements of language along with the speakers of this language are ultimately determined as such within a structure of symbolic relations of the type examined throughout the preceding chapters (the structure constitutive of sense which engenders propositions, the dimensions of these propositions, and the objective correlates of these dimensions). But it is equally clear that, for the newborn caught up in its imaginary identification with imagos, these symbolic relations are at first utterly enigmatic. As Deleuze says, the voice 'presents the dimensions of an organized language, but without yet being able to render explicit the organizing principle according to which the voice would itself be a language ... it has the dimensions of a language without having its condition; it awaits the *event* that will make it a language' (LS, 194, translation modified). In other words, while the Voice appears to possess the dimensions of denotation, manifestation and signification, the child at this stage is unable to grasp the 'fourth dimension' of sense or the event (the ongoing sense-event) which engenders these dimensions, the relations between them, and their objective correlates. The question of how the good object comes to be signified will thus depend on the child's full entry into the structural and intersubjective dimension of language. Is this not, however, Lacan's argument that the 'form' of the imago of the breast could only be 'revealed' in the structures of subsequent psychic activity (even though it will always have been 'informed' by the sensations and emotions characteristic of the first few months of life), that is, in the structural or symbolic dimension of linguistic and intersubjective relations? Indeed, as will be seen, this is precisely Lacan's and, following him, Deleuze's argument: the imagos, good objects or 'proto-symbolizations' characteristic of the first months of life will be retroactively made sense of after the resolution of the Oedipus complex, that is, after the infant's entry into the dimension of the 'symbolic'.[68]

We can thus see in what way Deleuze understands the passage from the noise of the depths to the Voice of the heights as the 'first stage of the dynamic genesis' of the metaphysical surface (LS, 193). Let us recall that the dynamic genesis or event of the metaphysical surface, which is coextensive with the event of language and the speaking subject, requires that this surface of sense both emerge from the depths of bodies and come to determine these bodies. It has just been seen, however, how the newborn organizes its early bodily experiences and object relations into an imago or good object which, to the extent that it is signified by the Voice, will be retroactively made sense of after the child's acquisition of language and corresponding entry into the structural-symbolic dimension of language and culture after the resolution of the Oedipus complex. Nevertheless, it has yet to be seen precisely how this entry into the structural and intersubjective dimension of language is to be made. And so we must turn to the 'second step' of the dynamic genesis.

5.2 Second Step: Formation and Coordination of Surfaces (Freud and Infantile Sexuality)

The second step of the dynamic genesis, which is the focus of the 'Twenty-Eighth Series of Sexuality', involves the formation of corporeal surfaces and their coordination. It is described by Deleuze in terms primarily derived from Freud's theory of infantile sexuality, but also Lacan's 'Mirror Stage' and his concept of the 'phallus', as well as the Kleinian notion of 'reparation'. The basic idea is that infantile sexuality is a physical 'surface' phenomenon which is distinct from both the undifferentiated depths of bodies and the heights of the Voice, although also, as will be seen, derived from their relation. What is more, this sexual 'physics of surfaces' establishes the conditions which are necessary for the Oedipus complex and, hence, for the infant's eventual entry into the symbolic dimension of language and culture, that is to say, his or her passage to the metaphysical surface to which the sexual physics of surfaces will be said to 'correspond'. The 'Twenty-Eighth Series of Sexuality' is thus a continuation of Deleuze's appropriation of psychoanalytic theory in order to show how the metaphysical surface is an event which results from bodies even as it determines these bodies, and is coextensive with the events of language (the differentiation of words and things) and the divided subject.

Following Freud, infantile sexuality and the way in which it is dealt with are fundamental causes of the phenomena with which psychoanalysis deals: not only the psychoneuroses and psychoses, but also perversion. However, in order to grasp 'infantile, normal and perverse sexual life as a single whole', it was necessary for Freud to 'enlarge the concept of what was sexual'.[69] He thus argued that the 'sexual drive' is made up of various 'component drives' whose sources 'are the organs of the body and in particular certain specially marked *erotogenic zones*' – the oral, the anal and the genital, for example – which procure a certain amount of pleasure for the infant.[70] Initially, these individual component drives strive for satisfaction in their own way (depending on the nature of their sources) and independently of one another; but they then tend to converge, as the infant passes through several stages or phases of 'sexual organization', under the primacy of one or other of the zones. Thus, as is well known, the infant moves through an oral stage, followed by an anal and finally a phallic stage.[71] As Deleuze puts it, a

> stage is characterized by a type of activity which assimilates other activities and realizes in a certain mode a mixture of drives . . . Zones, on the contrary, represent the isolation of a territory, activities which 'invest' this territory, and drives which now find in it a distinct source. The organization of zones and the organization of stages occur, of course, almost simultaneously, since all positions are elaborated during the first year of life, each one encroaching on the preceding position and intervening in its course. (LS, 196–7)

Now, for Freud, the drives are motor forces which originate in the body and, considered from this point of view, are in themselves without quality.[72] On the other hand, however, they are experienced in mental life by means of 'representatives' (whose nature we shall come to examine). He writes that a drive 'appears to us as a concept on the frontier between the mental and the somatic, as the psychical representative of the stimuli originating from within the organism and reaching the mind, as a measure of the demand made upon the mind for work in consequence of its connection with the body'.[73]

More specifically, according to Freud, a drive is characterized by its 'pressure', its 'aim', its 'object' and its 'source'.[74] The pressure of a drive is its 'motor factor, the amount of force or the measure of the demand for work it represents'. The drive's ultimate aim is always 'satisfaction, which can only be obtained by removing the state of stimulation at the source of the drive'. The object of a drive is 'the thing in regard to which or through which the drive is able to achieve its aim'. And the drive's source is a 'somatic process which occurs in an organ or part of the body'. It should also be remarked that the object of a drive is variable and contingent on the subject's history: it is not originally connected with the drive; it may be an external object or a part of the subject's own body; it may be changed over time; and it may satisfy several drives simultaneously. Likewise, there may be many different 'paths' leading to the ultimate aim of the satisfaction of a drive, from which it follows that a drive may have various nearer or intermediate aims which can be combined or interchanged with one another, particularly depending on the current state of their 'organization' under the primacy of this or that zone.[75]

Let us now examine how Deleuze takes up these various characteristics of the sexual drives and translates them into his own idiosyncratic vocabulary. He argues first of all that each erogenous zone in which a drive finds a source is formed around a 'singularity' constituted by a mucous membrane (LS, 197). Deleuze here refers to Simondon's argument that the orifices of the body function as singularities which bring internal corporeal spaces and the external environment into relation in intensive processes of individuation. He writes that, 'as Simondon said of membranes, "the entire content of internal space is topologically in contact with the content of external space on the limits of the living"' (LS, 197). He is thus signalling with this reference to Simondon that there is an intensive 'physics of surfaces', of the type examined in Chapter 3, at work in infantile sexuality. Indeed, Deleuze also connects the object and the aim (satisfaction) of the sexual drive to this 'physics of surfaces' which, as was seen, is characterized by differential series and singularities. As he writes,

> each zone is the dynamic formation of a surface space around a singularity constituted by the orifice. It is able to be prolonged in all directions up to the vicinity of another zone depending on another singularity. Each erogenous zone is inseparable from one or several singular points, from a serial development articulated around the singularity and from a drive investing this territory. It is inseparable from a partial object 'projected' onto the territory as an object of satisfaction (image), from an observer or an ego bound to the territory and experiencing satisfaction, and from a mode of joining up with other zones. The entire surface is the product of this connection ... [S]exuality in its first (pregenital) aspect must be defined as a veritable production of partial surfaces. The auto-eroticism which corresponds to it must be characterized by the object of satisfaction projected onto the surface and by the little narcissistic ego which contemplates it and indulges in it. (LS, 197)

So let us first of all examine some of the details of the Freudian theory of infantile sexuality and then see how these are reflected in Deleuze's sexual 'physics of surfaces'. Three notions to which we must pay particular attention are: what Freud calls the 'pleasure principle' (also called the 'pleasure-unpleasure *series*'),[76] the 'object of satisfaction', and the role of the 'phallus' in the coordination of the infant's component sexual drives.

Following Freud, to begin with, 'sexual activity attaches itself to functions serving the purpose of self-preservation' and, in particular, the need for nourishment.[77] As he puts it, it 'was the child's first and most vital activity, his sucking at his mother's breast . . . that must have familiarized him with pleasure . . . The satisfaction of the erotogenic zone is associated, in the first instance, with the satisfaction of the need for nourishment.'[78] This initial experience of nutritive satisfaction leaves behind in the infant a need for its repetition which, following Freud, 'reveals itself in two ways: by a peculiar feeling of tension, possessing, rather, the character of unpleasure, and by a sensation of itching or stimulation which is centrally conditioned and projected on to the peripheral erotogenic zone'.[79] Pleasure, then, will be experienced as the reduction of unpleasure or of the quantity of excitation or pressure. Correspondingly, the sexual aim at this early oral stage 'consists in replacing the projected sensation of stimulation in the erotogenic zone by an external stimulus which removes that sensation by producing a feeling of satisfaction'.[80] There is thus, in other words, a 'pleasure principle' governing the infant's relation to the mother's breast, that is, an 'economic' principle working through a correlation between alternating experiences of pleasure and unpleasure, or a 'pleasure-unpleasure *series*'.[81]

Now, what is crucial here is that, once experienced, the pleasurable activity implicated in the reduction of tension may be pursued for its own sake, independently of the satisfaction associated with the vital function of feeding. This new search for pleasure is what is manifested in 'auto-erotic' phenomena such as thumb sucking, that is to say, phenomena where the sexual drive 'is not directed towards other people, but obtains satisfaction from the subject's own body'.[82] Freud then goes on to argue that, having understood the nature of the sexual drive such as this arises at the oral zone, we are in a position to understand the sexual activity of infants in relation to the other zones (anal, genital and so on), for each will be characterized by: a general pressure or tension, the aim of satisfaction or the removal of unpleasure, and auto-erotic behaviour (retaining the stool, infantile masturbation, etc.). The distinction between one zone and another, then, will primarily concern 'the nature of the contrivance necessary for satisfying the drive; in the case of the labial zone it consisted of sucking, and this has to be replaced by other muscular actions according to the position and nature of the other zones'.[83]

Laplanche and Pontalis make the important point that, in auto-erotism, when the sexual drives become detached from the self-preservative drives and find their objects in the infant's own body, not only is the natural mode of apprehending the object of satisfaction effectively split, the object is itself shown to be variable.[84] Deleuze echoes this point when he writes that what occurs in the sexual position is the separation of 'two states of the sexual drives [and] two sorts of objects of these drives' (LS, 353, n.3). In other words, the libidinal drives come to be separated from the life (and death) drives with which they were originally connected in depth, and the 'pellicular objects' of sexuality come to be separated from the part-objects of the depths (see LS, 198–9). Indeed, and we shall see the importance of this, it is because of the liberation of the sexual drives from the drives of conservation, as well as the variability of the object of satisfaction, that the sexual drives will eventually be able to be delivered over to phantasy.[85]

Now, it was noted that Deleuze calls the 'object of satisfaction' in auto-erotism an 'image' projected onto the surface or territory surrounding the zone. What Deleuze here calls an 'image' corresponds to what Freud calls a 'mnemic image' or 'memory-trace', from which the ideational representations of the drives in mental life, mentioned above, will be derived.[86] The idea here is that, when the infant experiences real satisfaction, it retains a number of memory-traces of it. These *Mnems*, as Freud also calls them, correspond to a perceptual image of the object which brought about the satisfaction, as well as to a motor image of the muscular movement which permitted the discharge of unpleasurable tension. Following Freud, when this state of tension recurs, there is a 'wishful activation' (or 'recathexis') of the mnemic image of the object which produces a 'hallucination' that is indistinguishable from perception. Of course, if the remembered muscular action is also reactivated and introduced, the infant will experience disappointment, requiring him or her to learn to discriminate between its imaginary ideas and reality. This learning process, however, is a slow one, and in the meantime the mnemic images come to be connected with auto-erotic activity.[87] Or again, as Deleuze puts it, at this early phase of the infant's existence, 'a series of images is projected over the [erogenous] zone, that is, a series of objects capable of assuring for the zone an auto-erotic satisfaction' (LS, 225). A 'sucked-on finger', for example, is understood to be 'a projection of the breast' (LS, 352, n.3).[88]

Strictly speaking, however, for Freud, the objects-images belonging to the various component drives are only 'pregenital' part-objects, albeit of a different nature from the fragmented part-objects of the depths.[89] For, not only have the component drives yet to converge in a single 'normal' sexual drive, the objects of these drives have yet to be integrated into a whole 'love-object' which would satisfy the aim of a unified sexual drive, that is, 'the union of the genitals in the act known as copulation'.[90] Crucially, however, 'preparations have been made from earliest childhood' for this 'process of finding an object'.[91] In other words, adult object-choice will be modelled on the infant's early experiences of satisfaction and their corresponding memory-traces, particularly with respect to his or her primary caregivers.[92] As Freud writes:

> The characteristics of infantile sexual life which we have hitherto empha-sized are the facts that it is essentially autoerotic (i.e. that it finds its object in the infant's own body) and that its individual component drives are upon the whole disconnected and independent of one another in their search for pleasure. The final outcome of sexual development lies in what is known as the normal sexual life of the adult, in which the pursuit of pleasure comes under the sway of the reproductive function and in which the component drives, under the primacy of a single erotogenic zone [i.e., the genital zone], form a firm organization directed towards a sexual aim attached to some extraneous sexual object ... In order to complete our picture of infantile sexual life, we must also suppose that the choice of an object ... has already frequently or habitually been effected during the years of childhood: that is to say, the whole of the sexual currents have become directed towards a single person in relation to whom they seek to achieve their aims.[93]

Now, for Freud, in the adult sexual organization, the component sexual drives will be subsumed under the dominance of the genital zone in so far as the stimulation of the various other erotogenic zones come to be seen as making possible, 'through the medium of fore-pleasure which can be derived from them (as it was during infantile life), the production of the greater pleasure of [genital] satisfaction'.[94] In other words, the pleasurable-unpleasurable tension generated by the stimulation of the non-genital erotogenic zones leads to a further increase in tension 'which in its turn is responsible for producing the necessary motor energy for the conclusion of the sexual act ... [which is] of the highest intensity' and pleasure.[95] Of course, the infant must wait for the changes which come about at puberty to experience this type of satisfaction in its full intensity. Nevertheless, following Freud, even if a proper combination of the component drives under the primacy of the genitals has not been entirely effected in infancy, 'at the height of the course of development of infantile sexuality, interest in the genitals and in their activity acquires a dominating significance which falls little short of that reached in maturity'.[96]

It is crucial to note, however, that there is a major difference between the adult and the infantile genital organization of the drives. It is that, for infants of 'both sexes, only one genital, namely the male one, comes into account'.[97] In other words, for Freud, the little girl is ignorant of the existence of the vagina, and rather believes that her penis has been castrated. It is a question, therefore, not of a primacy of the genitals, 'but a primacy of the *phallus*',[98] which is thought of as present though castratable for the little boy, and absent or castrated for the little girl.[99] For Freud, it is this early understanding of the genital zone which sets up the 'castration' and 'Oedipus' complexes, in so far as it determines the infant's relation to both the mother and father as particular objects involved in the search for the satisfaction of his or her unified sexual drive.

So how exactly does Deleuze read a 'physics of surfaces' into these various aspects of the Freudian theory of infantile sexuality? He writes that:

> The pregenital erogenous zones or surfaces cannot be separated from the problem of their coordination. It is certain, though, that this coordination is enacted in several ways: by contiguity, to the degree that the series which is developed over one zone is extended in another series; at a distance, to the degree that a zone can be turned inward or projected onto another, furnishing the image by which the other is satisfied; and above all, indirectly, as in Lacan's mirror stage. It is nevertheless true that the direct and global function of integration, or of general coordination, is normally vested in the genital zone. It is this zone which must bind all the other partial zones, thanks to the *phallus*. And the phallus, in this respect, does not play the role of an organ, but rather that of a particular image projected, in the case of the little girl as well as the little boy, onto this privileged (genital) zone . . . [A]s a wholesome and good organ, it confers love and punishment, while at the same time withdrawing in order to form the whole person or the organ corresponding to the voice, that is, the combined idol of both parents. (LS, 200)

It is clear from this passage that Deleuze understands the coordination of the partial surfaces of the component drives to be a consequence of the development both of pleasure-unpleasure series and of the objects-images of satisfaction corresponding to these series. Indeed, a pleasure-unpleasure series which is developed in relation to a particular erogenous zone may be extended in the pleasure-unpleasure series belonging to another zone. This is obviously the case for Freud in the post-pubescent mechanism of 'fore-pleasure', where the pleasurable-unpleasurable tension generated at one erogenous zone is prolonged in the tension, and ultimate discharge of this tension, at the genital zone. It is also the case in the phallic stage of infantile sexuality, where the infant's intense interest in the genital zone involves the subordination of other activities to that zone. As Freud writes, 'it is scarcely possible to avoid the conclusion that the foundations for the future primacy over sexual activity exercised by this erotogenic zone are established by early infantile masturbation, which scarcely a single individual escapes'.[100]

With respect to the objects-images of satisfaction corresponding to the pleasure-unpleasure series, Deleuze emphasizes their role in the coordination of partial surfaces in a number of different ways. First of all, he argues that one zone may provide the image by which this latter is satisfied. This is obviously the case when the component drives are subsumed under the genital zone and the object of satisfaction of this zone – primarily, the infant's caregiver – becomes the privileged object of all the zones. But it is also the case that, for Freud, activity at the anal zone prefigures the object-image by which the genital zone will come to be satisfied. As he writes, the 'relationship between the penis and the passage lined with mucous membrane which it fills and excites already has its prototype in the pregenital, anal-sadistic phase. The faecal mass, or as one patient called it, the faecal "stick", represents as it were the first penis, and the stimulated mucous membrane of the rectum represents that of the vagina.'[101]

Secondly, Deleuze understands the activities typical of Lacan's 'Mirror Stage' as bringing about a convergence of partial surfaces. Indeed, Lacan argues that between six and eighteen months of age the infant comes to recognize his or her reflection in a mirror image and thereby unifies, in an image, 'a libidinal dynamism that has hitherto remained problematic'.[102] In other words, the infant 'assumes' an image of the 'total form of his body' and identifies with it 'in opposition to the turbulent movements with which the subject feels he animates it'.[103] For Lacan, this identification (and corresponding transformation of the 'fragmented image of the body') is at the root of all of the child's subsequent identifications.

Finally, and above all, Deleuze emphasizes the role of the 'phallus' as an image which is projected over the genital zone and which binds the other partial zones. The concept of the phallus here, however, does not coincide with the Freudian concept examined above. It is rather to be taken in its extended Lacanian sense as the imagined object of the mother's desire, which the child wants to 'be' in order to satisfy her desire.[104] What does this mean? Following Lacan, the (imaginary) phallus is a third term which intervenes in the initially dual, feeding relation which exists between the infant and the mother in what Lacan calls the 'dialectic of frustration'.[105] This third term must, however, be seen from two different points of view. On the one hand, the mother finds in her new-born an object of satisfaction which is a substitution – albeit, an imperfect one – for the phallus which she perceived herself at a very early age to lack.[106] On the other hand, the child in the feeding relation attempts to make sense of what keeps the mother busy when she does not answer his or her cries (frustration). The child formulates for itself, in other words, the question of what the mother might desire *beyond* him or her: '"*Chè vuoi?*", "What do you want?"'[107] The answer the infant comes up with, says Lacan, is that what the mother desires is the 'phallus', and he or she will thus seek to identify with or *be* this imagined thing.[108] As Lacan argues, the question 'What do you want?' is effectively taken up in the following form: 'What do you want *from me?*'[109] In this attempt at imaginary identification, the child can thus be said to integrate its partial surfaces or component drives in so far as its various activities come to be dominated by the task of becoming the phallus, that is to say, becoming a total and fully satisfying love-object for the mother.

The question arises, of course, as to when the infant comes to understand that he or she is only the imperfect substitute for the mother's missing phallus. In short, it is by realizing that the mother lacks the phallus or, what amounts to the same thing, that the phallus is the property of the father. Following Lacan, it is at this stage that the infant will start competing with the father in order to *be* the phallus which the father *has* (the object of the mother's desire), thereby fully entering into the Oedipus complex as such. We shall return to these points in detail in the following section.

Now, all of these characteristics of the imaginary phallus are effectively enumerated by Deleuze (see, for what follows, LS, 200). As he writes, first of all, 'it is a wholesome and good organ' in so far as it would make sense of (that is, integrate into a whole) the comings and goings of the mother, as well as provide a single, satisfying outcome for the infant's sexual aims to the extent that he or she is able to become the phallus. Secondly, to the extent that the phallus 'confers both love and punishment', it frustrates the child. Thirdly, it withdraws 'in order to form the whole person or the organ corresponding

213

to the voice', which is to say that the presences and absences of the mother are 'grouped as such' by the phallus in a series of alternating terms, thereby forming the beginnings of the kind of 'symbolic order' belonging to the voice.[110] Finally, it is 'the combined idol of both parents', that is to say, both the imaginary object of desire for the mother and, as will be seen in the following section, the privileged symbolic term in relation to which, as Lacan puts it, the father 'is not without having it'.[111]

So we are at last in a position to see how Deleuze appropriates the Freudian theory of infantile sexuality, along with several Lacanian supplements to this theory, for his physics of surfaces. First of all, as has been seen, the sexual drives are initially intimately connected with the life and death drives in depth. Now, according to Deleuze's physics of surfaces examined in Chapter 3, this depth 'acts in an original way, *by means of its power to organize surfaces and to envelop itself within surfaces*' (LS, 124). And in fact, we have just seen how the infant's component sexual drives emerge from the depths at precisely the same time as they produce a physical surface for the body of the child. As analyzed above, this surface-production has as its conditions the fact that the drives: (1) are regulated by series of differences in intensity of unpleasurable and pleasurable feelings; (2) find original sources in the erogenous zones functioning as singularities; and (3) have various objects capable of discharging the tension accumulated at that zone, thereby producing experiences of satisfaction which are remembered and whose repetition is sought. Understood in this way, each drive originating in corporeal depth is capable of converging with the others, thereby forming the entire surface of the infant's body in so far as the singularities in which each drive finds a source can be connected to the others, either by the prolongation of their pleasure-unpleasure series, or in relation to appropriate objects-images capable of assuring the satisfaction of all of the drives (and in particular, the imaginary phallus). As Deleuze writes, 'the surface does not preexist [the erogenous zones]. In fact, each zone is the dynamic formation of a surface space around a singularity constituted by the orifice. It is able to be prolonged in all directions up to the vicinity of another zone depending on another singularity ... The entire surface is the product of this connection' (LS, 197).

Now, as has been said, to this corporeal surface which is 'haunted' by singularities and differences of intensity, a metaphysical surface corresponds. Let us recall Deleuze's words, examined in Chapter 3: 'Metaphysical surface (*transcendental field*) is the name that will be given to the frontier established, on one hand, between bodies taken together as a whole and inside the limits which envelop them, and on the other, propositions in general' (LS, 125). We have yet to see, however, how psychoanalysis can account for the correspondence of such a metaphysical surface to the physical surface of the infant's body. This will be the subject matter of the following sections, but it can already be intimated that this 'correspondence' will depend upon the infant's entry into the symbolic dimension of language and culture. In particular, we shall see how Deleuze's understanding of the concept of the phantasm is intimately connected with the relation between the physical and metaphysical surfaces, for the phantasm involves the reinvestment and re-articulation of the infant's sexual aims and imaginary sexual objects at the level of the structural-symbolic.

Before turning to examine these concepts, however, we should mention several of Deleuze's other remarks concerning how he understands the relation between Klein's work on the pre-Oedipal depths, the Freudian theory of infantile sexuality, and the several Lacanian concepts we have examined above. In the first place, following Deleuze, the sexual position is formed 'in the reaction of the depressive position to the schizoid position . . . [The] height renders possible a constitution of partial surfaces' (LS, 198). Deleuze does not, however, elaborate on this point in much detail. What appears to be at stake, though, is the substitution in the depressive position of 'introjected and projected partial objects for objects that are out of reach' (LS, 198), such as, in the first place, the *imago* of the breast or the withdrawn object of the heights corresponding to the Voice. This 'good object', let us recall, is the wholesome and complete object which the infant 'assumes' or identifies with in acceding to the intersubjective relationship which is the 'weaning complex'. As an image of primordial (albeit lost) unity, the good object imposes 'an alternative on the ego – to model itself after the good object or to identify itself with bad objects' (LS, 227), that is, with the disorganized sensations, emotions and bad, part-object relations which rather signal the loss of the good object in corporeal depth. It thus follows that in so far as the infant strives to identify with the out of reach good object and to repeat the remembered experience of satisfaction, the possibility arises for a liberation of the sexual drives from the life and death drives with which they were originally connected in depth (whereby, for example, pleasurable suckling would be split off from purely alimentary suction). The sexual drives would then be able, first of all, to 'find new sources in the erogenous zones and new objects in the images projected onto these zones', and secondly to 'get involved in the productive labour of [the coordination of] surfaces and in new relations with these new pellicular objects' (LS, 199). It is in this way, therefore, that Deleuze argues that the 'origin' of the 'pregenital images of partial zones . . . is in the idol, or in the good object lost and withdrawn in the heights' (LS, 227).

Now, concomitant with this liberation of the sexual drives in the depressive position, following Deleuze's reading of Klein, is a process of 'reparation' whereby the breast which was aggressively attacked in the schizoid position is somehow put back together or repaired. And, as was seen above, essential to this Kleinian process of reparation is the enlisting of the father or 'good penis'. Deleuze, however, now understands Klein's 'good penis' to share some of the characteristics of Lacan's imaginary phallus, particularly with respect to its role in coordinating the partial surfaces of the infant's body and in making sense of the mother's mysterious comings and goings. In other words, when Deleuze says that the phallus mends the mother's wounds or repairs her, he is no longer speaking of 'reparation' in the strict Kleinian sense of the term, but rather of the way in which the phallus 'groups' or integrates into a whole the mother's presences and absences. He writes:

> the transition from the bad penis to the good [phallus] is the indispensible condition for the arrival of the Oedipus complex in its strict sense, to genital organization and to the corresponding new problems . . . The phallus, as the image projected on the genital zone, is not at all an aggressive instrument of penetration and eventration. On the contrary, it is an instrument of the surface, meant to *mend* the wounds that the destructive drives, bad internal objects, and the penis of the depths have inflicted on the maternal body, and to reassure the good object, to convince it not to turn its face away. (The processes of 'reparation' on which Melanie Klein insists seem in this sense to belong to the constitution of a surface which is itself restorative.) . . . The phallus should not penetrate, but rather . . . it should trace *a line at the surface.* This line, emanating from the genital zone, is the line which ties together all the erogenous zones . . . bringing all the partial surfaces together into one and the same surface on the body of the child. Moreover, it is supposed to reestablish a surface on the body of the mother. (LS, 200–1)

Finally, in a last twist on this merging of different strains of psychoanalytic thought, Deleuze writes that in this 'phallic stage' the child 'splits' the good object of the heights according to the two disjunctions subsumed under it (unharmed-wounded and present-absent), using them to qualify a mother image and a father image: 'the mother taking on the aspect of an injured body to be mended, and the father taking on the aspect of a good object to be made to return' (LS, 201). What does this mean? As noted in the previous section, for Klein, both parental figures were initially combined: 'the maternal body of the depths comprised a multiplicity of penises as partial internal objects; and especially, the good object of the heights was, as a complete organ, both penis and breast – mother provided with a penis, father provided with a breast' (LS, 204). In Deleuzian-Lacanian terms, however, we would rather say that the maternal breast, mother or good object was originally conceived of as omnipotent, lacking nothing.[112] In other words, the mother was initially conceived of as a 'phallic mother'.[113] Now, for Klein, the splitting of such an imaginary 'combined parent figure' is to be thought of as the result of a regression to the paranoid-schizoid position, or as a defence against depressive anxiety. For Deleuze, however, following Lacan, this splitting is rather a consequence of the child's realization that the mother lacks the (imaginary) phallus. This phallus, which the infant then strives to be, would totalize or make sense of the disconnected aspects of the mother's behaviour (the mother's 'wounds', as we explained above: her inexplicable presences and absences). On the other hand, it signifies something currently out of reach and mysterious, even though it will eventually be found in the possession of the father who 'is not without having' the phallus. It is in this manner, therefore, that Deleuze argues that the good object is split into a mother image and a father image. A full examination of this point, however, requires us to turn to the third step of the dynamic genesis.

5.3 Third Step: From the Physical Surface to the Metaphysical Surface (Lacan, Oedipus and Castration)

Deleuze's third step of the dynamic genesis, which is the subject of the 'Twenty-Ninth Series – Good Intentions are Inevitably Punished', essentially concerns the infant's passage from the physical surface to the metaphysical surface which corresponds to it. It is primarily couched in terms of Lacan's reading of the Oedipus complex and its dissolution, that is, in terms of the infant's 'castration' which marks his or her passage to the symbolic dimension of language and culture.[114]

Although Freud never gave a fully systematic account of the

Oedipus complex in all its various aspects, it can be understood, in very general terms, to be an organized

> body of loving and hostile wishes which the child experiences towards its parents. In its so-called *positive* form, the complex appears as . . . a desire for the death of the rival – the parent of the same sex – and a sexual desire for the parent of the opposite sex. In its *negative* [or *inverted*] form, we find the reverse picture: love for the parent of the same sex, and jealous hatred for the parent of the opposite sex. In fact, the two versions are to be found in varying degrees in what is known as the *complete* form of the complex.[115]

For Lacan, however, whom Deleuze here follows, 'the subject always desires the mother, and the father is always the rival, irrespective of whether the subject is male or female'.[116] As has been examined in the above section, the infant gains access to this complex in so far as its component sexual drives converge and take the mother as the privileged object of sexual satisfaction. Or again, in Deleuzian-Lacanian terms, the child enters the Oedipus complex in so far as he or she creates a surface for its entire body by becoming the phallus, that is, the total and fully satisfying object of the desire of the mother such as this is imagined by the infant. The rivalry with the father, then, as has already been intimated, will commence once the child realizes that it is the father who has the phallus or object of the mother's desire. So how exactly does this occur for Lacan and thus for Deleuze?

Lacan in fact divides the Oedipus complex into three stages, characterized by the infant's relation to three types of 'lack': frustration, privation and castration.[117] 'Frustration', first of all, is defined as an imaginary lack of a real object (the breast) whose agent is symbolic (the mother), but this must be considered as occurring over several related moments.[118] The 'dialectic of frustration', as Lacan calls it, is considered as a set of 'impressions, lived by the subject during a period of development where its relation to the real object is usually centred on the so-called primordial *imago* of the maternal breast', that is, as has been seen, on the image of a lost unity through which the infant recognizes itself in the difficult feeding relationship (weaning complex).[119] That the lack involved in frustration is imaginary, means that it is understood through the lens of this imago of a harmonious but lost totality.[120] That the mother is a 'symbolic agent' of frustration, on the other hand, means that she corresponds to the couple presence-absence or plus-minus, that is, the symbolic terms through which the infant develops its relation to the breast which comes and goes, through its own vocal system of cries. As Lacan puts it, the 'maternal object is exclusively called [*appelé*] when it is absent – and when it is present, rejected, in the same register as the appeal [*l'appel*]'.[121] What happens, however, when the mother does not answer the infant's cries? First of all, following Lacan, the mother comes to be seen as a real, omnipotent 'power', a law unto herself, who responds to the child's cries as she pleases. Correspondingly, the object comes to be seen, not only as providing the real satisfaction of a need, but also as a symbolic 'gift' which may be withheld or, if given, symbolize a 'favourable power'.[122] Finally, in so far as the object becomes a symbolic gift, the child's cries must be seen not so much as relating to biological needs as they are to a demand for the mother's favour or love, to which the infant feels it has a rightful claim.[123] Frustration, properly speaking, occurs against this symbolic background. For Lacan, the 'object of frustration is less the object [of need] than the gift'.[124]

What is crucial here, however, is that the reason behind the mother's giving or withholding of the gift – that is to say, behind the desire of the mother (the phallus) – remains unperceived by the child, this being why the mother is at this stage considered as the 'phallic mother', lacking nothing and sufficient unto herself.[125] The child nevertheless tries to identify with the imagined objects of the mother's essentially unquenchable desire. Or again, more precisely, since the mother lacks nothing, the child attempts to 'deceive' the phallic mother, the giver of gifts, into loving him.[126] At what point, however, does the infant realize that there is a third term involved – the phallus – which the mother desires in so far as she lacks it? Or again (and as has been seen, this amounts to the same question), at what point does the infant realize that he or she is only the imperfect substitute for the mother's missing phallus? As Lacan argues, the child experiences a 'fundamental disappointment' once it realizes that he or she is not the mother's only object of desire, that the mother desires the phallus, and that she is herself lacking this object.[127] But how exactly does this occur?

Lacan calls the second stage of the Oedipus complex 'privation'. Temporally speaking, it corresponds to Freud's 'phallic stage', and is defined as the mother's real lack of a symbolic object (the phallus) whose agent is imaginary (the 'imaginary father').[128] Four interrelated things occur at this stage. First of all, the infant, who had previously been desired by the mother in his or her entirety as a substitute for the phallus, presents his real organ to the mother and comes painfully 'to measure all of the difference there is between what he is loved for [the mother's substitute phallus] and what he can give', that is, his or her real organ.[129] Secondly, the 'imaginary father' appears as the one who both deprives the mother of the phallus and indicates to the infant that he or she is not the only object of the mother's desire. Thirdly, the infant begins to grasp the phallic difference between the sexes. Finally, the child begins to compete with the imaginary father to be the phallus, that is, the object of the mother's desire. Let us more fully examine these points.

The imaginary father of which Lacan here speaks has no necessary relation to the real father. He is rather an integral part of the infant's imaginary relation (*imago*) which is the 'psychological support' of his or her relations with his or her fellows and, more particularly, is behind the child's 'libidinal capture'.[130] Indeed, he is the one who, as will be seen, makes the Oedipus complex possible in so far as he introduces a third term – the imaginary phallus – into the relation between the infant and the mother, this latter having previously been understood as lacking nothing.[131] As one commentator has put it, the 'imaginary phallus is what the child *assumes* someone must have in order for them to be the object of the mother's desire'.[132] This 'someone' is the imaginary father. The idea here is that something 'is articulated bit by bit in the child's experience, which indicates to him that, in the mother's presence to him, he is not alone' in being desired by the mother.[133] But how does this come about?

Key here is the fact that the infant has now progressed to the phallic phase of its development, is displaying an intense interest in his or her genital zone, and is engaged in infantile masturbation. From the child's point of view, the excited organ of this zone becomes an element in his or her games of seduction with the mother. From the mother's point of view, however, nothing essentially changes, for it is the infant in his or her totality who is loved by the mother as a substitute phallus.[134] As Lacan argues, what 'then plays the decisive role is that what the child has to present appears to him . . . as something pitiful. The child is thus placed before this opening to be the captive, the victim, the passive element of a game in which he becomes the prey of the Other's significations.'[135] Or again, in other words, because the mother appears to be indifferent to the organ, she effectively signifies to the child his or her insufficiency or, what amounts to the same thing from the child's point of view, prohibits the child from using his organ as he or she would like.[136] Furthermore, in this gap between what the mother loves the child for in its totality (substitute phallus) and what the child presents (its real organ), the child comes to imagine the one who would be desired by the mother as a total love-object, phallus included. This is the 'imaginary father'. As Chiesa puts it, unlike the child's own body image, the body image of the imaginary father 'is supplied with something supplementary that obtrudes: the phallic *Gestalt*'.[137]

Several consequences follow from this. First of all, the father who imaginarily embodies the desired phallus contradicts the child's belief that he or she is the only object of the mother's desire. Indeed, at this stage, the imaginary father in some sense *is* the imaginary phallus.[138] Secondly, the child begins to 'compete' with this rival which is the imaginary father in order to be the phallus, that is to say, he or she attempts to identify with the imagined, complete object of the mother's desire.[139] Thirdly, in so far as the mother (who was originally conceived of as 'phallic': a real power, not lacking anything) is thought to desire the paternal phallus, she must herself be understood to be really deprived of this object (hence, 'privation'). Finally, in this process, the child arrives at an initial understanding of the symbolic law of sexual difference, in the sense that the phallus is here promoted to the rank of a symbolic object which one either has or does not have; and clearly, the mother does not have it.[140] It is precisely in this manner, therefore, that Lacan understands this stage to be characterized by 'privation', that is, by the mother's real lack of a symbolic object whose agent is imaginary (the imaginary father). As Lacan summarizes it, what is essential in privation

> is that the mother founds the [imaginary] father as the mediator of what is beyond her law and her whims, that is, purely and simply, the [symbolic] law as such . . . At the imaginary level, the father well and truly intervenes to deprive the mother, which means that the demand addressed to the Other [i.e., 'love me!'], if it is properly passed on, is referred to a superior court . . . It is at this level that . . . what comes back to the child is purely and simply the law of the father, such as this is imaginarily conceived by the subject as depriving the mother. It is . . . the first appearance of the law in the form of this fact: that the mother is dependent on an object which is no longer simply the object of her desire, but an object that the Other either has or does not have.[141]

The third and final stage of the Oedipus complex is understood by Lacan to be characterized by 'castration': the child's symbolic lack of an imaginary object (the imaginary phallus) whose agent is real (the real father).[142] As we have just seen, during the second stage of the complex, the child is competing with the imaginary father to be the mother's exclusive object of desire, to be the imaginary phallus. To say, then, with Lacan, that the child is castrated of an imaginary object is to say that he or she is obliged to recognize that he or she is not the mother's imaginary phallus.[143] How does this occur? What is required, following Lacan, is the intervention of the real father, who is revealed as the one who in fact *has* the phallus. Lacan writes: the 'third stage [of the Oedipus complex] is as follows – the father can give the mother what she desires, and can give it because he has it'.[144] From this decisive moment onwards, the phallus is thus 'no longer the imaginary object with which the subject can deceive [the mother], but the object which is always in an Other's power to show that the subject doesn't have it [in the case of the little girl], or has it in an insufficient way [in the case of the little boy]'.[145] The Oedipus complex, then, will be said to be resolved in so far as the child comes to symbolically identify with the father as the one who has the phallus, that is, for the little boy, to identify with the father as the possessor of the penis and, for the little girl, to recognize the man in so far as he possesses it.[146] As a consequence of this identification with the bearer of the symbolic phallus, the boy comes to realize that he has all the prerequisites in order to 'himself one day accede to this problematic and paradoxical position of being a father'.[147] The girl, for her part, comes to know that she will one day be able to find the one who, in fulfilling the role of the father, will be able to give her a child.[148]

There are three further issues to consider here. First of all, it should be remarked that what the real father as the bearer of the phallus represents is not so much a means of differentiating between the sexes, although he most certainly fulfils this function. More generally, what the real father embodies, to a greater or lesser extent, is the law of the mother's desire, that is, the entire 'set of social conventions respected by the mother'.[149] Previously, as has been seen, the infant apprehended the mother's love through the lens of the symbolic couple presence-absence which, to the extent that the infant could not make them correspond to his or her own system of cries, was experienced as frustrating. Consequently, the child attempted to trick the mother into loving him by identifying with the imagined objects of her desire, or by attempting to be the imaginary phallus. What the appearance of the real father now brings about, however, is a law-like 'grouping' of the oppositional sequence presence-absence.[150] In other words, the real father comes to be seen as the one who was effectively occupying the mother during her absence. The father thus 'makes sense' of the mysterious comings and goings of the mother or, what amounts to the same thing, embodies the law of the mother's desire. Of course, what has been occupying the mother involves an entire network of intersubjective relations and obligations (familial, economic, and so on). But for the child, the father is the first representative of this social structure of the mother's desire. Symbolic identification with the real father as the one who has the phallus is thus, at bottom, 'always identification with a rule-governed way of organizing the social world',[151] that is, with 'a preformed symbolic apparatus that institutes the *law in sexuality*'.[152]

A second, crucial point is that no real father could ever fully occupy the paternal position or embody the symbolic law, that is to say, be the symbolic father as such.[153] Rather, following Lacan, the symbolic father is akin to the mythical 'dead father' of Freud's *Totem and Taboo*, whose law, which initially depended only on him, all the real fathers of history took upon themselves to uphold.[154] Or again, more precisely, because no real father could embody the entire set of social conventions respected by the mother (because, in other words, the law of the mother's desire is never entirely reducible to the real father), Freud was obliged to think the symbolic father – the original father – by means of such a myth.[155]

Finally, since this is crucial to Deleuze's use of psychoanalysis in *The Logic of Sense*, it is important to examine in more detail how Lacan views the relation between castration and the intersubjective, structural or symbolic dimension of language. Lacan in fact equates castration with what he calls a 'paternal metaphor', whereby the symbolic father or 'Name-of-the-Father' is understood 'to be a signifier which is substituted for the first signifier introduced in symbolization, the maternal signifier . . . [that is,] the mother who comes and goes'.[156] Now, since the 'signified of these comings and goings is the phallus', it can be said that the symbolic father, by means of this 'metaphoric substitution', comes to signify for the child the meaning of the phallus, which is to say, the law governing the mother's desire.[157] But is not this process of substitution precisely what we have called in previous chapters the serial 'regress of sense', whereby the sense of a given signifier must be denoted by another signifier of a higher degree? And what is more, have we not also seen that this serial production of sense always takes place in an intersubjective context, in relation to always displaced or decentred *personnes* (infant ↔ mother ↔ real father ↔ symbolic father)? Indeed, it appears that for Lacan it is precisely because castration is inseparable in this way from the serial and intersubjective production of sense that it marks the child's entry into the structural-symbolic dimension of language and culture, that is, his or her passage to what Deleuze calls the 'metaphysical surface'. Indeed, for Lacan, the paternal metaphor 'allows the child actually to relate to a *signifying* Other for the first time'.[158] For Lacan, then, all subsequent determinations of sense must be said to be derived from this first one, for this latter marks the child's very entry into the structure of sense.

So how do the above considerations play out in the text of *The Logic of Sense*? As noted at the end of the previous section, for Deleuze, the child in the phallic phase splits the good object of the heights into a mother image and a father image. It was argued, following certain Lacanian formulations, that this splitting coincides with the infant's realization: 1) that the 'phallic mother' is not complete (she is 'wounded', frustratingly present-absent); 2) that she has an object of desire beyond the child (the phallus); and 3) that this object can be found in the possession of the withdrawn, imaginary father 'retired into its height' (LS, 204). As has been seen in this section, the child now begins to compete with this father (by identifying with what he imaginarily embodies) in order to be the complete object of the mother's desire: a totally satisfying love-object which would effectively control her desire, that is, her presences and absences. But now, is this not precisely the situation which Deleuze describes in his hybrid psychoanalytic vocabulary, derived from both Klein and Lacan? He writes:

> As for the wounded body of the mother, the child wishes to repair it with his restorative phallus and make it unharmed. He wishes to recreate a surface to this body at the same time that he creates a surface for his own body. As for the withdrawn object, he wishes to bring about its return, to render it present with his evocative phallus. (LS, 204)

We can thus see in this citation three of the essential elements of Lacan's understanding of frustration and privation: (1) the attempt to group, integrate or 'repair' the mother's presences and absences by (2) being the complete object of her desire and (3) identifying with the out-of-reach imaginary father in so far as he is thought to possess the requisite qualities.

This way of reinterpreting the Freudian Oedipus complex also explains why Deleuze is able to assert that Oedipus is initially 'gay and innocent'. As he continues:

Incest with the mother through restoration and the replacement of the father through evocation are not only good intentions. As intentions, they are inseparable extensions of what is apparently the most innocent activity, which, from the point of view of the child, consists of creating a total surface from all his partial surfaces, making use of the phallus projected from the good penis from above, and causing the parental images to benefit from this projection. (LS, 205)

Why, however, Deleuze asks, does it all turn out so badly? Why is Oedipus a tragedy, that is, 'a tragedy of Semblance [*Apparence*]' (LS, 207). It is because, through castration, the image of a harmonious totality which the child had projected at the physical surface comes to be dissipated on a metaphysical surface of sense, that is, in what Lacan calls the structural or symbolic dimension of language and culture. Let us examine how Deleuze develops this idea.

Deleuze first of all outlines the essential features of the progression from privation to castration such as these were examined above in relation to Lacan. These features can be enumerated as follows: (1) once the child realizes that the mother's comings and goings signify the phallus embodied by the imaginary father, he or she realizes by implication that the mother is herself deprived of this object; (2) the child then begins to compete with the imaginary father in order to be the complete object of the mother's desire; (3) the real father then appears who has the phallus; (4) this real father, who is only ever a partial representative of the symbolic or 'dead' father, then castrates the child by making him or her understand the impossibility of being the phallus for the mother. Deleuze essentially reiterates these 'moments' when he writes that 'what Oedipus saw' once he had differentiated the parental images in the move from frustration to privation is that the mother

> is wounded like a castrated body. The phallus as a projected image, which bestowed a new force on the child's penis, designates, on the contrary, a lack in mother. This discovery threatens the child in an essential manner, for it signifies (on the other side of the cleavage) that the penis is the property of the father ... It becomes therefore true, at this moment, that by wishing to restore the mother, the child has in fact castrated and eventrated her; and that by wishing to bring back the father, the child has betrayed and killed him, transformed him into a cadaver [i.e., into the 'symbolic' or 'dead father']. Castration, death by castration, becomes the child's destiny. (LS, 205–6)

Now, as Deleuze goes on to show, what is essential in the child's castration is that it marks his or her passage from the sexual, physical surface (coordination of component drives, projected images of satisfaction, etc.) to the structural or symbolic dimension of language and culture, that is, to what we have called in previous chapters the metaphysical or transcendental surface. Deleuze, however, describes this passage in his own idiosyncratic way. On the one hand, he speaks of the process of forming a physical surface as a projected 'image of action . . . not at all a particular action, but any action which spreads itself out at the surface and is able to stay there (to restore and to evoke, to restore the surface and to summon to the surface)' (LS, 207). 'Projection' should here be understood in all of its geometrical, intentional and temporal senses. Indeed, the projected image is essentially two things. It is an image on a surface which should 'restore' or 're-present' a physical state of affairs 'point for point' (the child's 'restoration' of the mother's 'wounds' and corresponding creation of a surface for its own uncoordinated body). And it is an intended action which will be realized only in the future (it is the 'evocation' of or attempted identification with the father who, in the child's imagination, embodies the law of the mother's desire).[159]

On the other hand, Deleuze argues that the action which will have been effectively 'accomplished' by the child's imaginary projections (restoration and identification) is 'projected on a surface no less than the other action. This surface, though, is entirely different; it is metaphysical or transcendental' (LS, 207).[160] Now, we have seen that the projected image of action on the physical surface refers to the actions and passions of the child as its real causes (the drives, frustration, etc.). The accomplished action on the metaphysical surface, however, should rather be thought of as 'the necessary result of actions and passions, although of an entirely different nature, and itself neither action nor passion: event, pure event' (LS, 207). In other words, and in accordance with our analyses of the determination of events on the metaphysical surface in previous chapters, the accomplished action, as an incorporeal event-effect, must appear 'as produced and not willed' (LS, 208). Which is to say that the accomplished action or event could only be determined in an intersubjective and linguistic context by disjunctive syntheses of other such singularities-events which are prolonged over series of ordinary events. Or again, the accomplished action or event must be determined by the way in which it is implicated in a structure of purely differential symbolic elements which are reciprocally, completely and progressively determined by means of the adjunction and transformation of series of singularities-events corresponding to the values of the relations between these elements.[161]

Now, in this regard, we should note Deleuze's argument that the accomplished or produced action is essentially 'determined by the forms of murder and castration' (LS, 208). In other words, as an event, the accomplished action has the form of 'to kill the father and castrate the mother, to be castrated and to die' (LS, 207). But in fact, we have just seen what these 'forms' amount to for Deleuze: the castration of the mother refers to the way in which the symbolic elements which represent for the child her desire (presence-absence or $+/-$), come to be grouped or integrated by a real father who could himself only ever partially incarnate an entire structure of social and linguistic relations (the symbolic or dead father, the law-giver). But this is precisely to say that, for the child, the predicates-events or singularities-events characterizing the real father correspond to the values of the relations between the 'ordinary' symbolic terms $+/-$ characterizing the mother, but only as a function of the real father's relation to other persons, characterized by their own predicates-events, in the intersubjective symbolic order. Now, in so far as the child identifies with this real father as a representative of the dead father or open series of *personnes*, he or she assumes his or her own symbolic castration (renunciation of the attempt to be the imaginary phallus) and effectively enters the structural dimension of language and culture as another potential, partial embodiment of the symbolic law. What is effectively accomplished by the projected images of the actions of restoration and evocation on the physical surface must, in other words, be considered to be an event which is determined on the metaphysical surface in relation to syntheses of series of singularities-events bearing on symbolic elements (ordinary points or events) and carried out in relation to persons or divided subjects who are themselves only ever 'produced forms'. This accomplished action or incorporeal event-effect is of course the event of the 'divided subject', that is to say, the event of the child's passage to the metaphysical surface. And the tragedy of this event is that the image of a harmonious totality which the child had attempted to establish at the level of the physical surface (through restoration and evocation) established the very conditions necessary for the dissolution of that image on the metaphysical surface of sense (structural-symbolic dimension of language and culture).

So Deleuze's appropriation of the various psychoanalytic concepts examined above has given us a conception of those 'divided subjects' or *personnes* who populate the metaphysical surface as themselves events, derived from a physical, sexual surface and, beyond or below that, an undifferentiated corporeal 'depth'. But the question now arises: how, if the physical surface and even corporeal depth have temporal priority over the metaphysical surface, can we continue to affirm that things in general are derived from this latter? And further, since this seems to have slipped from our account: what more can be said about the relation of the metaphysical surface, psychoanalytically conceived, and language? We have just come to understand the event of the divided subject on the metaphysical surface (or, what amounts to the same thing, the event of the metaphysical surface for the subject), but what more can be said of the event of language, understood as the separation, at the surface, of words endowed with sense from the sounds of bodies? To answer these questions, we must turn to Deleuze's appropriation and extension of the psychoanalytic concept of the 'phantasm'.

5.4 Fourth Step: from Speech to Language (Phantasm and Metaphysical Surface)

This last step of the dynamic genesis, elaborated around the concept of the phantasm, is examined by Deleuze throughout the Thirtieth, Thirty-First, Thirty-Second and Thirty-Fourth Series. Although Deleuze never explicitly spells this out, he understands the phantasm in a very general way which can be summed up in the words of the Kleinian, Susan Isaacs: 'Phantasy is ... the mental corollary, the psychic representative, of instinct' or the drives.[162] Or again, more specifically, a phantasm is a mental representation corresponding to the satisfaction of the drives or 'the fulfilment of a wish'.[163] It can be recalled that the drives are experienced in mental life by means of certain 'ideational representatives' or 'representations' which are derived from the 'mnemic images' of past satisfactions. A phantasm can thus be considered as a representation or system of such representations which is focused on the satisfaction of the drives,[164] and of which the earliest form is the 'hallucinatory satisfaction of the wish' implicated in auto-erotic activity.[165]

Phantasy, it can be noted, may also be conscious or unconscious. The typical conscious phantasy is the daydream, whose wish-fulfilling function is evident. Such conscious phantasies have a high degree of the type of consistency to be found in waking life. Unconscious phantasies, for their part, are closely associated with the ideational representatives which have, through the mechanism of 'repression', been denied entry into consciousness.[166] The repression of ideational representatives occurs to the extent that the attainment of the represented satisfaction of the drive, while pleasurable in itself, would produce unpleasure in so far as it is 'irreconcilable with other claims and intentions'.[167] And it is of course clear that, being incompatible with the symbolic order of language and culture, pre-Oedipal sexual ideas involving the parental objects-images of satisfaction will be subject to repression at the time of the dissolution of the Oedipus complex.[168] Such repression, however, 'does not hinder the instinctual representative from continuing to exist in the unconscious, from organizing itself further, putting out derivatives and establishing connections'.[169] And these further organizations and derivatives are, precisely, unconscious phantasies.[170]

Now, it must also be noted that unconscious phantasies may become conscious. But in order to do so, they must undergo an appropriate transformation or translation.[171] As Freud states:

> it is not ... correct to suppose that repression withholds from the conscious *all* the derivatives of what was primally repressed. If these derivatives have become sufficiently far removed from the repressed representative, whether owing to the adoption of distortions or by reason of the number of intermediate links inserted, they have free access to the conscious.[172]

Dreams, parapraxes and neurotic symptoms, then, are all different ways in which the organized derivatives of repressed ideational representatives may reach consciousness. These phenomena, which form the majority of the material with which psychoanalysis typically deals, are all 'compromise-formations' between repressed, unconscious wishes and the demands of reality, and incorporate elements from both domains. Thus, for example, in dream-formation, unconscious wishes or phantasies are combined with 'residues' from the previous day's conscious thoughts, and then undergo a complex process called the 'dream-work' (condensation, displacement, considerations of representability and secondary revision) in order to reach consciousness.[173] It is precisely in this way that, for Freud, 'a dream is a (disguised) fulfilment of a (repressed) wish'.[174]

A particular type of unconscious phantasy, which is granted special importance by Deleuze, is known as an 'originary' or 'primal phantasy' (LS, 217). Following Laplanche and Pontalis, as Deleuze does in this regard, a primal phantasy is a '[t]ypical phantasy structure which psycho-analysis reveals to be responsible for the organization of phantasy life, regardless of the personal experiences of different subjects'.[175] For example, phantasies of intrauterine life and castration, the significance of which we have examined above, are understood to be primal phantasies in so far as they are more or less universally met with in human beings and can be seen to organize their phantasy life. From the point of view of the subject, what is essential about these phantasies is that 'they claim to provide a representation and a "solution" to whatever constitutes a major enigma for the child': the origin of the subject, the emergence of sexuality and the origin of the distinction between the sexes, for example.[176] From the point of view of the psychoanalytic theorist and analyst, on the other hand, primal phantasies respond to the conceptual need to think the child's entry into the symbolic without reference to some real event which would transcend the symbolic dimension in which the primal phantasm itself is elaborated, and at which the theorist him or herself is working. As Deleuze writes, the originary phantasm itself 'integrates effortlessly the origin of the phantasm' (LS, 217). We shall return to this point.

Now, in the 'Thirtieth Series of the Phantasm' and the 'Thirty-First Series of Thought', Deleuze outlines five characteristics of the phantasm which are essential to his logic of sense or the event. The most straightforward of these is that 'the phantasm covers the distance between psychic systems with ease, going from consciousness to the unconscious and vice versa, form the nocturnal to the diurnal dream' (LS, 217). This point is derived from Laplanche and Pontalis' reading of Freud, and stands in opposition to the Kleinian approach which sharply distinguishes between conscious *fantasy* or daydreams and unconscious *phantasy*.[177] In particular, Laplanche and Pontalis note that, in Freud's analysis of dreams in *The Interpretation of Dreams*, it is difficult to clearly separate out the different types of phantasy involved. As they write,

> the day-dreams utilized by the secondary revision may be directly connected with the unconscious phantasy which constitutes the 'nucleus of the dream' . . . So, in the dream-work [that is, in the transformation of the dream-thoughts into the manifest content of the dream], phantasy is to be found at both poles of the process: on the one hand, it is bound to the deepest unconscious wishes . . . while at the other extreme it has a part to play in the secondary revision. The two extremities of the dream process and the two corresponding modes of phantasy seem therefore to join up,

or at least to be linked internally with each other – they appear, as it were to symbolize each other.[178]

It appears that what is essential for Deleuze in this 'capacity for "passage"' of the phantasm (LS, 217), is precisely that its different 'modes' symbolize each other. In other words, if unconscious and conscious phantasies are always reflected in one another, there is no way to 'discover' some unconscious 'nucleus of phantasy' (that is, the 'original', repressed, ideational representatives of the drive) beyond the way in which this could be articulated according to the demands of consciousness. Indeed, as we shall see, this point is reflected in two further characteristics of the phantasm: first of all, that the origin of the phantasm is inseparable from the development of the phantasm in the symbolic dimension of language and culture; and secondly, that the existence of the phantasm is inseparable from its expression in the propositions typical of consciousness. Before coming to these points, however, let us examine several other characteristics belonging to the phantasm.

First of all, following Deleuze, the phantasm 'represents neither an action nor a passion, but a result of an action and passion, that is, a pure event' (LS, 210). Now, at the end of the previous section, we saw the nature of this event which is both brought about by corporeal actions and passions, and is the effect of a sense-event. On the one hand, the restoration of the mother and identification with the imaginary father which accompanies the infant's creation of a physical surface for his or her own body (projection of an image of action), refers for its real causes to the infant's passions and actions. On the other hand, the result of these actions and passions (that is, the privation of the mother, the 'death' of the father and the symbolic castration of the subject) is projected on a metaphysical surface which is irreducible to the physical surface, and which produces the result of the child's actions and passions as a sense-effect which follows from the very structural nature of this metaphysical surface (disjunctive syntheses, in an intersubjective context, of singularities-events corresponding to the values of relations between series of ordinary points). What does it mean, however, to say that the phantasm *represents* this 'result' or event?

Following Deleuze, what happens in the passage from the physical to the metaphysical surface is that the original 'willed action has been denied almost, and suppressed by what is really done; and what is really done is *negated* as well by the one who did it and who rejects responsibility for it (it's not me, I didn't want that – "I have killed unwittingly")' (LS, 206). Now, 'negation' here must be understood in its Freudian sense (*Verneinung*, also translatable as 'denial' or 'denegation'). For Freud, negation bears on repressed images or ideas which are incompatible with conscious concerns and, importantly, is also 'a way of taking cognizance of what is repressed'.[179] In other words, negation or denial is a way of bringing repressed material to consciousness in the form of 'I didn't think that', but where the 'that' is precisely the repressed material. By use of this negation, thought is thus able to take up the repressed material while still respecting the demands of consciousness in its relation to social reality. Freud even goes so far as to argue that 'the performance of the function of judgement [of reality] is not made possible until the creation of the symbol of negation has endowed thinking with a first measure of freedom from the consequences of repression and, with it, from the compulsion of the pleasure principle'.[180] In short, negation allows repressed material, which had previously only been subject to the pleasure principle, to be 'sublimated' and come under the sway of the reality principle, that is, under the sway of conscious thought as it responds to the demands of social reality.[181] As Deleuze summarizes, the 'famous mechanism of "denegation" (that's not what I wanted ...), with all its importance with respect to the formation of *thought*, must be interpreted as expressing the passage from one surface to another', that is from the physical to the metaphysical surface (LS, 208).

Now, still following Deleuze, from being subjected solely to the pleasure principle or the differential energy of the intensive pleasure-unpleasure series, the repressed sexual ideas formed around the parental objects-images are through denegation 'sublimated' and reinvested by a 'desexualized energy' which belongs to the 'metaphysical surface, or surface of pure thought' (LS, 208). For Freud, 'desexualization' signifies the transformation of erotic libido into ego-libido which accompanies the shift from the pleasure to the reality principle, that is, from purely sexual aims and objects to social aims and objects.[182] For Deleuze, 'desexualized energy' is the psychoanalytic name for the potential energy of the metaphysical surface which was examined in Chapter 3, that is, the differential energy of the pure event which will be actualized in concrete individuals, persons and concepts. The potential energy of this surface, let us recall, refers to the way in which the differences between its constitutive series are distributed, these series being made up of symbolic terms which are reciprocally, completely and progressively determined by the adjunction and transformation of the singularities-events corresponding to the values of the differential relations between these terms. It thus follows that, if the repressed images and ideas of Oedipus are to be reinvested by the desexualized energy of the metaphysical surface, they must come to be 'symbolized' somehow by the elements or terms which make up the surface. As Deleuze puts it, the process by which desexualized energy reinvests the repressed material 'corresponds in its first aspect to what is called "*sublimation*", and in its second aspect to what is called "*symbolization*"' (LS, 208). Now, even if we have yet to see precisely how this symbolization takes place in the phantasm, it is nevertheless clear that it will be due to sublimation and symbolization that the phantasm will be able to 'represent' the event of the passage from the physical to the metaphysical surface on the metaphysical surface. As Deleuze writes, the

> phantasm, like the event which it represents, is . . . distinguished not only from states of affairs and their qualities, but from the psychological lives and from logical concepts as well. It belongs as such to an ideational surface over which it is produced as an effect. It transcends inside and outside, since its topological property is to bring 'its' internal and external sides into contact, in order for them to unfold onto a single side. This is why the phantasm-event is submitted to a double causality, referring to the external and internal causes whose result in depth it is, and also to a quasi-cause which 'enacts' it at the [metaphysical] surface and brings it into communication with all the other event-phantasms . . . The event is sense itself, in so far as it is disengaged or distinguished from the state of affairs which produce it and in which it is actualized. (LS, 211)

A further characteristic of the phantasm, essential for Deleuze's concept of the event, concerns 'the situation of the ego in the phantasm itself' (LS, 212). Now, it is clear that the phantasm finds its 'author' in the ego which, initially lodged in the depths and then projected on the psychical surface, finally comes to identify with the symbolic father on the metaphysical surface. But the ego also typically appears *in* the phantasm 'as acting, as undergoing an action, or as a third observing party' (LS, 212). Nevertheless, following Deleuze, what is essential is that the ego, such as it appears in the phantasm, is, finally, 'neither active nor passive and does not allow itself at any moment to be fixed in a place' (LS, 212). Citing Laplanche and Pontalis once more, Deleuze argues that the 'originary phantasm "would be characterized by an absence of subjectivation accompanying the presence of the subject in the scene"' (LS, 212).[183] For Laplanche and Pontalis, this lack of subjectivation follows from the idea that, in phantasy understood as the *mise en scène* of desire, the subject does not imagine and aim at some object which would satisfy the sexual drives, 'but rather [at] a *sequence* in which the subject has his own part to play and in which permutations of roles and attributions are possible'.[184] In other words, following these authors, the subject is not strictly speaking the first term of the sequence subject → verb → object, but is rather desubjectivized 'in the very syntax of the sequence in question', and may come to occupy the position of object as much as that of the subject, or even of the action.[185] For Deleuze, however, while this model of desubjectivation no longer understands the ego as entirely active or passive, because the ego may (and, ideally, does) occupy both 'syntactical' positions, the model ultimately remains 'pronominal' and thus still makes an implicit 'appeal to the ego' (LS, 213).[186] Deleuze then argues that what is 'beyond the active and the passive is not the pronominal, but the result – the result of actions and passions, the surface effect or the event' (LS, 213). In other words, for Deleuze, the desubjectivation of the ego in the phantasm follows from the very nature of the impersonal and pre-individual metaphysical surface on which the phantasm unfolds. For, as has been argued, the subject on this surface could only ever be a result, a form produced by disjunctive syntheses of singularities-events or processes of triangulation carried out in relation to an open series of 'divided subjects' or *personnes*. Deleuze describes this situation for us when he writes that what

> appears in the phantasm is the movement by which the ego opens itself to the surface and liberates the a-cosmic, impersonal and pre-individual singularities which it had imprisoned ... Thus, the individuality of the ego merges with the event of the phantasm itself, even if that which the event represents in the phantasm is understood as another individual, or rather as a series of other individuals through which the dissolved ego passes. The phantasm is inseparable therefore from the toss of the dice or from the fortuitous instances which it enacts ... We find once again here an illustration of the principle of positive distance, with the singularities which stake it out, and of an affirmative usage of the disjunctive synthesis. (LS, 213–14)

A fourth characteristic of the phantasm is that, like the event it represents, 'it does not exist outside of a proposition which is at least possible' (LS, 214). This is not to say that the phantasm-event is said or signified by the proposition *per se*. The phantasm-event is rather coextensive with the sense that is produced over the entire metaphysical surface, that is to say, by the way in which the sense of propositions bearing on interrelated events is produced by the structural dimension of language and culture. It can be recalled that this structural co-determination of the event and the sense of the proposition was examined in detail in Chapter 4. In line with these earlier analyses, Deleuze now argues that the phantasm-event 'inheres in a particular element of the proposition ... the *verb* – the infinitive form of the verb' (LS, 214). Indeed, we have seen the way in which the verb of the proposition picks out an event or process (as opposed to nouns and adjectives, which denote fixed and measured things or states of affairs). We have also seen how verbs (such as 'to grow' in 'Alice grows') express pure becomings which are ontologically prior to fixed states of affairs. Finally, we have seen how the duality between verbs and substantives is prolonged, within the relations constitutive of the proposition, in a duality between the denotation of things and the ongoing expression of sense in the proposition, this latter being equivalent to the structural sense-events of the metaphysical surface. When Deleuze thus writes that the phantasm-event inheres in 'the infinitive form of the verb', this must be understood as a shorthand means of referring to the way in which the events constitutive of states of affairs are determined in an ongoing way by these sense-events. For as has been seen, like the infinitive form of the verb, the metaphysical surface is ultimately neutral with respect to the persons, times, voices and moods – that is to say, neutral with respect to the persons, individuals and signified concepts – in which it will be actualized. As Deleuze writes,

> we must conceive of an infinitive which is not yet caught up in the play of grammatical determinations – an infinitive independent not only of all persons but of all time, of every mood and every voice (active, passive, or reflective). This would be a neutral infinitive for the pure event, Distance, Aion, representing the extra-propositional aspect of all possible positions, or the aggregate of ontological problems and questions which correspond to language. From this pure and undetermined infinitive, voices, moods, tenses, and persons will be engendered. Each one of them will be engendered within disjunctions representing in the phantasm a variable combination of singular points, and constructing around these singularities an instance of solution to the specific problem – the problem of birth, of the difference of the sexes, or the problem of death. (LS, 214–15)

What now can be said in a more concrete fashion about the way in which the event of the passage to the metaphysical surface is determined in the phantasm, if this latter is strictly coextensive with the sense produced on the metaphysical surface? This takes us to Deleuze's fifth characteristic of the phantasm which concerns the dual origin of the phantasm, or again, the 'double causality' to which the phantasm is subject. As he writes, 'the phantasm returns easily to its own origin and, as an "originary phantasm", integrates effortlessly the origin of the phantasm (that is, a question, the origin of birth, of sexuality, of the difference of the sexes, or of death . . .). This is because it is inseparable from a displacement, an unfolding, and a development within which it carries along its own origin' (LS, 217). What does this mean?

As has been seen, the origin of the phantasm can be traced back to castration, that is, to the way in which the real father, who is only ever a partial representative of the symbolic or 'dead' father, makes the child understand that he or she must give up the attempt at being the phallus for the mother. What occurs at this point is that the child represses and then denegates his or her original sexual aims and objects (bearing on the parental objects-images) and, through this very denegation, reinvests these sexual ideas with the desexual- ized or 'potential energy' belonging to the metaphysical surface (the entire symbolic dimension of language and culture). The sublimation and symbolization through which this reinvestment occurs is the very process of the phantasm which, as has just been seen, does not exist outside of the propositions which come to express or symbolize it. On the one hand, then, the phantasm finds its real origin in the actions and passions of the child which lead up to castration (the frustration of needs and desire and the attempt to be the phallus – restoration of the mother and identification with the imaginary father). On the other hand, with castration, a result is produced (to castrate the mother and to be castrated, to symbolically kill the father and to be killed) which is irreducible to these real actions and passions, since it is an effect of the very nature of the metaphysical surface to which castration elevates the child. Indeed, to say that the real father is only ever a partial representative of the dead father or law-giver; or again, to say that the mother is deprived not by the imaginary father but by the symbolic law of sexual difference; or, finally, to say that the child is castrated in so far as he or she assumes his or her place in the order which dictates the law of his or her sexual desire, is to say that each of these subjects is a 'divided subject', that is, a form produced by an open linguistic and social structure in which they are obliged to 'phantastically' formulate their desire, that is, to represent to themselves in an ongoing way a socially acceptable satisfaction of the drives.[187] There is thus no contradiction between the idea that the passage to the metaphysical surface (sublimation and symbolization of sexuality in the phantasm) begins with castration, and the notion that the phantasm is coextensive with the entire metaphysical surface. For, while the phantasm begins with castration, castration is also always-already a result of the pre-existing symbolic order in which the phantasm will be developed.[188] As Deleuze writes:

> The paradoxical situation of the beginning, here, is that it is itself a result, and that it remains external to that which it causes to begin. The situation would afford no 'way out', had not castration transformed the narcissistic libido into desexualized energy. This neutral or desexualized energy constitutes the second screen, the cerebral or metaphysical surface on which the phantasm is going to develop, begin anew with a beginning which now accompanies it at each step. (LS, 218)

Now, it should be noted that a crucial consequence follows from the above formulations. Even though the beginning of the phantasm finds its condition in 'external' castration, because castration is always-already the result of the internal mechanisms of the metaphysical surface with which the process of the phantasm is coextensive, then the phantasm must be said to internally determine its external beginning within its very elaboration on the metaphysical surface. In other words, castration and all that it presupposes (the depths, infantile sexuality, etc.) must be considered to be a primal, unconscious phantasy which is inseparable from the individual phantastical formulations of desire to which castration gives rise for each subject on the metaphysical surface. Deleuze recounts:

> The phantasm returns to its beginning which remained external to it (castration); but to the extent that beginning itself was a result, the phantasm also returns to that from which the beginning had resulted (the sexuality of the corporeal surfaces); and finally, little by little, it returns to the absolute origin from which everything proceeds (the depths). One could now say that everything – sexuality, orality, anality – receives a new form on the new [metaphysical] surface, which recovers and integrates not only images but even idols and simulacra ... But what does it mean to recover and to integrate? We gave the name 'sublimation' to the operation through which the trace of castration becomes the line of thought, and thus to the operation through which the sexual surface and the rest are projected at the surface of thought. We gave the name 'symbolization'

to the operation through which thought reinvests with its own energy all that which occurs and is projected over the [metaphysical] surface. (LS, 219)

So the importance for Deleuze of 'originary' or 'primal phantasies', such as the phantasy of castration now becomes clear. In line with Laplanche and Pontalis' formulations examined above, we have now seen how the phantasy of castration must be understood as a more or less 'universal' phantasy structure which organizes phantasy life in general. For the child, given that it implicates elements stretching from earliest infancy to his or her entry into the symbolic dimension of language and culture and beyond, the unconscious phantasy of castration and all it involves provides a representation and solution to some of the fundamental mysteries which confront him or her: the origin of birth (imago of the breast or of intrauterine life), sexuality (the phallic mother or question of the mother's desire), the difference between the sexes (the phallus) and death (symbolic castration). For the psychoanalytic theorist and analyst, the unconscious phantasy of castration responds to the conceptual need to think the analysand's more or less difficult sublimation of his or her infantile sexuality (passage to the symbolic) without referring to some real event transcending the symbolic dimension in which the analyst is working, and in which the analysand's conscious phantasms are elaborated in analysis. Indeed, we have already noted that conscious and unconscious phantasies essentially symbolize each other. It can now be said that conscious phantasy refers to the unconscious primal phantasy of castration as to its origin, as much as it is the privileged – and indeed the only – means of accessing this latter. Conscious phantasy 'makes sense of', as much as it is 'made sense of' by, the unconscious phantasy of castration, which itself refers to a complex of underlying questions and problems: the origin of birth, the mother's presence-absence, sexuality, the difference between the sexes, real father vs. symbolic father, and death.

Sublimating its own origin, symbolizing its conscious and unconscious aspects at the same level, and not existing outside of the possible propositions which express it in an ongoing way in an inter-subjective and linguistic context, the phantasm which is coextensive with the products of the metaphysical surface can thus be said to be immanent only to itself. Or, more precisely, it is immanent to 'all the other event-phantasms' (LS, 211), that is to say 'the variants of one and the same phantasm' (LS, 212), authored by the open series of divided subjects populating the metaphysical surface (parent and child, analyst and analysand, etc.). Following Deleuze, the question 'where does the phantasm begin?' must, therefore, be replaced by the question 'where does the phantasm go, in what direction does it carry its beginning?' (LS, 217). For if the beginning of the phantasm is to be determined in an ongoing and intersubjective way on the meta-physical surface, then it will not be able to escape the various ideal transformations or sense-events which the transcendental field brings about (adjunction and transformation of singularities-events). What this means is that castration and everything it implicates, like all of the other events on the metaphysical surface, are always-already open to 'counter-actualization'. As Deleuze explains,

> to die and to kill, to castrate and to be castrated, to restore and to bring about, to wound and to withdraw, to devour and to be devoured, to introject and to project, become pure events on the metaphysical surface which transforms them, and where their infinitive is drowned out. For the sake of one single language which expresses them, and under a single 'Being' in which they are thought, all the events, verbs, and expressible-attributes communicate as one inside this extraction. The phantasm recovers everything on this new plane of the pure event, and in this sym-bolic and sublimated part of that which cannot [finally] be actualized; similarly it draws from this part the strength to orient its actualization, to duplicate it, and to conduct its concrete counter-actualization. (LS, 221)

The sublimation and symbolization of castration (sexuality, etc.) in the phantasm is thus also the potential for its 'transmutation' (LS, 212, 218). It is clear, however, that this transmutation is in no way analogous to the processes involved in the Freudian 'dream-work', that is, if this latter is to be understood as translating and transform-ing an original, unconscious 'nucleus' of phantasy which itself refers to some real incident in the life of the child. Indeed, it should now be obvious that it is one thing to interpret or uncover the 'real cause' behind the phantasy or neurotic symptom in a Freudian manner, but quite another to 'become masters of actualizations and causes' in a Deleuzian manner (LS, 212). As Deleuze writes, 'psychoanalysis in general is the science of events, on the condition that the event should not be treated as something whose sense is to be sought and disentangled. The event is sense itself' (LS, 211).

So, it is now clear that the process of the phantasm is essentially equivalent to that of the static genesis. In order to arrive at this con-clusion, we were obliged to pass through all of the above-analyzed steps of the dynamic genesis. At this point, however, we must return to one step in the argument yet to be addressed. We must answer the following question: if the phantasm does not exist outside of propositions which are at least possible, if the phantasm is essentially symbolized using the terms of language, what is the phantasm's relation to language at the moment of the phantasm's birth? Indeed, it is incontestable that at the time of the child's castration and entry into the symbolic, he or she will be far from having mastered the language in which his or her phantasm will be articulated. Following Lacan, we have seen that the 'paternal metaphor' allows the child to apprehend a signifying Other for the first time, but there is a great difference between this apprehension and the ability to engage in discourse in a substantial way. So what more can be said about the event of language for the child, and what is the relation of this event to the event of the passage to the metaphysical surface?

In the 'Thirty-Second Series on the Different Kinds of Series', Deleuze tells a rather convoluted story about language acquisition and its relation to sexuality and the phantasm. The essence of this story can, however, be reduced to the following idea: the passage from pre-Oedipal sexuality to the phantasm can be described in structural terms and, what is more, in such a way that it is brought into relation with the development of the type of intersubjective, linguistic 'structure of sense' examined in Chapter 4. Let us recall that this latter structure was not only characterized by differential relations between series of phonemes, morphemes, semantemes, etc., but also by processes of reciprocal, complete and progressive determination bearing on series of things, propositions, and propositions about propositions. What Deleuze poetically describes as 'a new heralding of the [infant's] body founded on phonology' (LS, 231), can thus be re-described in this more prosaic way, the details of which we must now examine.

We have already analyzed the serial or structural organization which belongs to the physics of surfaces of pregenital sexuality. First of all, each erogenous zone (functioning as a singularity) in which a component sexual drive finds a source is inseparable from a pleasure-unpleasure series belonging to that zone. As Deleuze puts it, the 'serial form is founded in the erogenous zone of the surface, in so far as the latter is defined by the extension of a singularity or, what amounts to the same thing, by the distribution of potential or intensity' (LS, 225).

Secondly, each erogenous zone supports a 'series of images

240

[which] is projected over the zone, that is, a series of objects capable of assuring for the zone an auto-erotic satisfaction' (LS, 225). Indeed, it was seen not only how the infant engaging in auto-erotic activity recathects the mnemic images of past pleasures or satisfactions, but also how a given erogenous zone may project the partial objects-images by which another zone is satisfied. Following Deleuze, each one of these images

> becomes coextensive to the entire range of the partial surface [surrounding the zone] and traverses it, as it explores its orifice and field of intensity ... They are organized into series according to the way in which they are made coextensive (a piece of candy, for example, or chewing gum, the surface of which is multiplied by its being crunched, by being stretched respectively); but they are also organized according to their origin, that is, according to the whole from which they are extracted (another region of the body, another person, external object or reproduction of an object, a plaything, etc.), and according to the degree of their distance from the primitive objects of alimentary and destructive drives from which the sexual drives were just released. (LS, 225)

These variations in the types of serial organizations of the images appear to be inessential. What is important at this level of the structure, however, is that whatever the method of organization, the terms of each series of images are homogeneous or of the same type, that is, they can be reciprocally connected or determined in a simple way (LS, 225).

But now, given the importance for Deleuze of the role of the phallus in coordinating the component sexual drives, we must consider a more complicated serial form. This is because, when we consider the convergence of the component drives under the primacy of the genital zone, both through the prolongation of their pleasure-unpleasure series or through the relation of their partial objects-images of satisfaction to a total and fully satisfying love-object (imaginary phallus), we are in fact considering a complex relation between *heterogeneous* series. We might say, in the structuralist vocabulary developed in Chapter 4, that it is a question here of a 'complete determination' of the elements of the reciprocally determined series belonging to each component drive, in the series belonging to each of the other drives, the terms of which have their own reciprocal relations.

What should also be noted at this stage is that the parental images, themselves inseparable from this phallic phase of the development of the Oedipus complex, 'enter into one or several series'. As has been examined, these series can be described as 'heterogeneous series with alternating terms, father and mother, or two coexisting series, maternal and paternal: for example, wounded, restored, castrated, and castrating mother; withdrawn, evoked, killed and killing father' (LS, 226). Now, what coordinates these series of parental images in their heterogeneous relation with the child's pregenital sexual series is the displacement of the phallus throughout all of these series. The phallus must therefore be understood as the paradoxical element or object = x of the structure of sexuality which is always missing from its place.[189] Indeed, as has been analyzed, in the child's sexual relations to its parents, the mother was initially understood as phallic before the appearance of the imaginary father who deprived her of the phallus. The child then attempted to be the phallus for the mother, competing with the father by identifying with his body image, and integrating in the process his or her own component drives in order to become a total love-object for the mother, an object, that is, which would also 'restore' the mother by 'grouping' her presences and absences (symbolic plus-minus). At this point, however, the real father intervenes as the one who has the phallus, thereby making it impossible for the infant to be the imaginary phallus, which is to say that he 'castrates' the child of this phallus. Finally, however, the real father is understood to be only the 'bearer' of the 'symbolic phallus' and, as such, is only a partial representative of the symbolic or 'dead' father whose law the child must identify with if he or she is to assume an appropriate place in the symbolic dimension of language and culture. Thanks to this displacement of the phallus, then, the above analyzed complete determination of the terms of the series belonging to the infant's component sexual drives can now be seen to be itself completed in this larger serial structure. It is also clear, moreover, that the phallus as paradoxical element determines each series as either signifying or signified, as seen in Chapter 4. Indeed, this is entirely in line with our analysis of the 'paternal metaphor' which substitutes the signifier Name-of-the-Father for the Desire-of-the-Mother, this latter originally being the signifier of the imaginary phallus which was to make sense of the mother's comings and goings (the object of her desire) and simultaneously act as the point of convergence for the child's component sexual drives (in so far as he or she was able to be this object). As Deleuze puts it, the phallus as the paradoxical element of the structure of desire is both signified and signifier, deficiency and excess, that is, respectively, in its imaginary and symbolic guises (LS, 228).

What now of the phantasm which finds its 'external origin' in castration and the child's corresponding passage to the symbolic dimension of language and culture, and its 'internal origin' in this same symbolic dimension? Deleuze tells us that the process of the phantasm is nothing other than the resonance, brought about by the displacement of the phallus, between two series, one of them infantile or pregenital and the other Oedipal or post-pubescent. It is a question, in other words, 'of two series of independent images, whereby the Event [of castration] is disengaged only through resonance of these two series in the phantasm . . . The event to be comprehended is no different from the resonance itself' (LS, 226, translation modified). Of course, there is no longer any possibility of a convergence between these series (as there was in the case of the series belonging to the component sexual drives). Rather, these series must be understood to be divergent, firstly in so far as they are discontinuous in time (LS, 226), and secondly to the extent that the paradoxical object, which situates all the terms of a given series in their particular relations, is determined in a different way in each series (lack and excess: LS, 228). Crucially, however, the two series may also be understood to be related to one another as divergent, precisely in so far as we take into account the particular mode of displacement of the phallus in each one. Indeed, even though the two series are temporally divergent, they must also be understood to be simultaneous in relation to the displacement of the phallus. On the one hand, if we consider the sexual, pre-Oedipal partial objects-images of satisfaction, the phallus in relation to this series is what connects them together or causes their corresponding component drives to converge. On the other hand, in the other series, the phallus circulating between the Oedipal, parental objects-images also 'gets involved in Oedipal dissociations' of the type examined above (LS, 227). What the 'resonance' between these two series signifies, then, is that the phallus will be able to integrate the terms of the first series only in so far as its displacements are taken into account in the second series (these displacements being: phallic mother → imaginary father → real father → symbolic father → open series of partial representatives of the symbolic law populating the metaphysical surface). The two series will remain irreducible to one another, but they will also communicate and come to be determined in relation to one another, in an ongoing way, within the phantasm as it is produced over the entire metaphysical surface. The phantasm, then, represents the complete determination of the series constitutive of the structure of desire. But what is more, in so far as the phantasm is coextensive with all of the sense-events of the metaphysical surface, it also represents the progressive determination of all of the terms of this structure. Indeed, it is precisely in this sense that, as has been argued, the phantasm or metaphysical surface can be said to be immanent only to itself: it recovers or incorporates everything by giving it a new form, even and especially its beginning in 'external' castration and all this implies (pregenital sexuality, the depths, etc.).

Now, however, as Deleuze asks, 'is it not the case that the serial organization presupposes a certain state of language' (LS, 229)? Indeed, it has been said that the phantasm does not exist outside of the propositions which symbolize and express it. But at the same time, the infant initially 'comes to a language that she cannot yet understand as a language, but only as a voice, or as a familial hum of voices which already speaks of her' (LS, 229). It was seen in the first section of this chapter how, to the extent that it accesses the intersubjective weaning complex, the child organizes its 'noisy' bodily experiences and object relations into a good object (imago of the maternal breast) which is in turn signified by this familial hum or Voice. For the parents, of course, this Voice is already structured by various linguistic and social symbolic relations, but for the infant these relations are utterly enigmatic. From the point of view of the child, the Voice presents all of the dimensions of an organized language: it denotes the good object as well as the introjected objects, it signifies the concepts and classes structuring the domain of preexistence, and it manifests the emotional variations of the whole person. However, the infant has yet to accede to the surface organization on which these dimensions mutually presuppose and determine one another in an ongoing and related way (the fourth dimension of sense or the static genesis).

Deleuze now turns to the Lacanians Robert Pujol and Serge Leclaire in order to argue that if 'the child comes to a preexisting language which she cannot yet understand, perhaps conversely, she grasps that which we no longer know how to grasp in our own language, namely, the phonemic relations, the differential relations of phonemes' (LS, 230).[190] The infant's extreme sensitivity to the basic phonemic differences constitutive of its mother tongue has often been remarked. Indeed, even Freud noted this phenomenon in his analysis of children's play in *Beyond the Pleasure Principle* (the famous *Fort!-Da!*).[191] It thus appears that prior to Oedipus and castration, the child undertakes a 'phonemic apprenticeship' of the formative elements of language, before it comes to an understanding of the formed linguistic units (morphemes and semantemes) from which phonemic differences are inseparable. What is of crucial importance here, for Deleuze, is that the apprehension of phonemic difference is free to enter into a relation with the differential series of pregenital sexuality. As he puts it, it is 'a question of phonemic difference in relation to the difference of intensity which characterizes the erogenous zone' (LS, 230). This relation is not at all arbitrary, however, for it is clear that the determination of the terms of both the phonemic series and sexual series will be completed in relation to the symbolic dimension of language and culture wherein one finds formed linguistic units, the privileged signifiers of a culture, and this culture's laws of sexual desire between subjects. In other words, the event of language for the child – understood as the separation, at the surface, of words endowed with sense from the noise of corporeal things in general – depends on the event of the child's passage to the metaphysical surface. This is the meaning of Deleuze's assertion that 'the oral zone would pursue its liberation [from the depths] and its progress in the acquisition of language only to the extent that a global integration of [erogenous] zones could be produced, or even an alignment of clusters and an entry of phonemes into more complex elements' (LS, 231).

The first stage of the dynamic genesis thus went from noise to the Voice. The second stage of the genesis, described as the formation and coordination of corporeal surfaces, can now be re-described as the passage from Voice to speech, speech beginning *'when the formative elements of language are extracted at the surface, from the current of voice which comes from above'* (LS, 232, emphasis in original). The third step of the dynamic genesis was characterized in terms of the child's passage to the metaphysical surface. Finally, having this third step as its condition, the fourth and last step of the genesis can be described as the structural passage from speech to language, from the point of view of which it can be seen that the child's acquisition of language is inseparable from the development of the phantasm over the entire metaphysical surface. In fact, Deleuze calls this passage from speech to language the passage 'from speech to the verb', since the verb in its infinitive form is, like the metaphysical surface, ultimately neutral with respect to the times, persons, voice and mood – that is, the individuals, states of affairs, persons and signified concepts – which brought the phantasm about and in which it will be actualized. In a passage which may serve as a conclusion to this section, Deleuze explains that

Speaking, in the complete sense of the word, presupposes the verb and passes through the verb, which projects the mouth onto the metaphysical surface, filling it with the ideal events of this surface. The verb is the 'verbal representation' in its entirety, as well as the highest affirmative power of the disjunction (univocity, with respect to that which diverges). The verb, however, is silent . . . In the verb, the secondary organization is brought about, and from this organization the entire ordering of language proceeds . . . We have seen the way in which the order of language with its formed units comes about – that is, with denotations and their fulfilments in things, manifestations and their actualizations in persons, significations and their accomplishments in concepts; it was precisely the entire subject matter of the static genesis. But in order to get to that point, it was necessary to go through all the stages of the dynamic genesis . . . In order that there be language, together with the full use of speech conforming to the three dimensions of language, it was necessary to pass through the verb and its silence, and through the entire organization of sense and nonsense on the metaphysical surface – the last stage of the dynamic genesis. (LS, 241)

* * *

Finally, we see how Deleuze resolves the problem with which we began this chapter, namely, how can the metaphysical surface be understood as an event which is itself determined on the metaphysical surface? For we have now seen how Deleuze sets out, in relation to a reading of several of psychoanalysis' more central concepts, a 'dynamic genesis of sense' leading to a phantasm whose 'process' is essentially coextensive with the operations of the metaphysical surface or static genesis. In so far as this phantasm, by its very nature, reintegrates its own origin, it can be said that it is immanent only to itself.

Corresponding to this dynamic genesis and 'immanent event' of the metaphysical surface, we have also seen the event of language, understood as the process which separates words endowed with sense from the noises of corporeal things. Indeed, we have seen this process unfold throughout the dynamic genesis which went from noise to the Voice, from the Voice to speech, and from speech to language or the verb. Finally, we have examined the event of the 'divided subject' which populates the metaphysical surface. It is from the body of this subject, its corporeal and interpersonal relations, that the phantasm in which the subject is essentially dissolved is produced.

Let us now turn to the task of drawing together the various threads which have been developed over the preceding chapters and of attempting a definitive statement of Deleuze's philosophy of the event.

Notes

1. Joe Hughes gives a very good account of the relation between the static and dynamic geneses in his *Deleuze and the Genesis of Representation* (London and New York: Continuum, 2008), pp. 20–47. Contrary to the reading presented in this present work, however, Hughes does not treat the dynamic genesis as an event which is determined on the metaphysical surface, and thus gives it an ontological status which is very different from all of the other events composing Aion (the Unique Event, etc.).

2. For a clear introduction to some of the clinical aspects of psychoanalysis, particularly in its Lacanian variety, see Bruce Fink, *A Clinical Introduction to Lacanian Psychoanalysis: Theory and Technique* (Cambridge and London: Harvard University Press, 1997).

3. 'Metapsychology' is a term 'invented by Freud to refer to the psychology of which he was the founder when it is viewed in its most theoretical dimension. Metapsychology constructs an ensemble of conceptual models which are more or less far-removed from empirical reality. Examples are the function of a psychical apparatus divided up into agencies, the theory of the drives, the hypothetical process of repression, and so on.' See Laplanche and Pontalis, *The Language of Psycho-Analysis*, p. 249.

4. Indeed, in the Thirtieth Series of *The Logic of Sense*, Deleuze appears to follow, at least to a certain extent, Laplanche and Pontalis' reading of Freud's concept of phantasy, which sees phantasy as the *mise en scène* of unconscious desire and emphasizes the 'desubjectivized' place of the subject *in* the phantasized scene. See Jean Laplanche and Jean-Bertrand Pontalis, 'Fantasy and the Origins of Sexuality', in Victor Burgin, James Donald and Cora Kaplan (eds), *Formations of Fantasy* (London and New York: Methuen, 1986). Lacan, on the other hand, emphasizes the defensive or 'protective function of phantasy' with respect to the trauma of castration. On this difference between Freud's and Lacan's concepts of phantasy, see Dylan Evans, *An Introductory Dictionary of Lacanian Psychoanalysis* (London and New York: Routledge, 1996), pp. 59–61. On Lacan's concept of phantasy and its 'defensive' aspect, see also Lorenzo Chiesa, *Subjectivity and Otherness: A Philosophical Reading of Lacan* (Cambridge and London: MIT Press, 2007), pp. 149–50.

5. On this Lacanian criticism of Klein, see, for example, Jacques Lacan, 'Guiding Remarks for a Convention of Female Sexuality', in *Écrits*, p. 613: 'I am referring to Melanie Klein's lack of concern for the

fact that the earliest Oedipal fantasies, which she includes in the maternal body, actually derive from the reality presupposed by the Name-of-the-Father.'

6. See Serge Cottet, 'Les machines psychanalytiques de Gilles Deleuze', *La cause freudienne – Revue de psychanalyse*, 32 (1996), p. 16. Cottet appears to project the subsequent importance of Artaud for Deleuze, in texts such as *Anti-Oedipus* and *A Thousand Plateaus*, onto his use of Klein in *The Logic of Sense*, since, to a certain extent, Klein is critically read through Artaud in *The Logic of Sense* (see, for example, LS, 351–2, n.3). Our alternative reading is that Deleuze's use of Klein, affirmative or otherwise, as much as his use of Freud or Lacan and the relations established between various elements of their theories, is dictated by their role in the argument of *The Logic of Sense* as a whole.

7. For a detailed account of the complex history of psychoanalysis in France, see Elisabeth Roudinesco, *Jacques Lacan & Co.: A History of Psychoanalysis in France, 1925–1985*, trans. Jeffrey Mehlman (Chicago: University of Chicago Press, 1990).

8. See Gilles Deleuze, 'On Philosophy', in *Negotiations*, p. 144.

9. See Gilles Deleuze, 'Note for the Italian Edition of *The Logic of Sense*', in *Two Regimes of Madness*, trans. Ames Hodges and Mike Taormina, ed. David Lapoujade (New York: Semiotexte, 2006), pp. 63–6.

10. See, for example, her 'Preface to the First Edition', in *The Psycho-Analysis of Children: The Writings of Melanie Klein, Volume I*, trans. Alix Strachey and H.A. Thorner (London: The Hogarth Press, 1986), p. x. On Freud's view of Klein, see Robert Caper, *Immaterial Facts: Freud's Discovery of Psychic Reality and Klein's Development of his Work* (London and New York: Routledge, 2000), pp. 76–7.

11. Freud's characterization of the mental features of children's lives was rather derived from what could be reconstructed from his work with adults, or as in the case of 'Little Hans', from the testimony of adults. See on this, Juliet Mitchell, 'Introduction to Melanie Klein', in Lyndsey Stonebridge and John Phillips (eds), *Reading Melanie Klein* (London and New York: Routledge, 1998), p. 19.

12. Hanna Segal, *Introduction to the Work of Melanie Klein* (London: Karnac Books, 1988), p. viii. See also Melanie Klein, 'Early Stages of the Oedipus Complex (1928)', and 'The Oedipus Complex in Light of Early Anxieties (1945)', in *Love, Guilt and Reparation and Other Works 1921–1945* (London: The Hogarth Press, 1975), pp. 186–98 and pp. 370–419.

13. We are here reconstructing the broad outlines Melanie Klein's, 'Some Theoretical Conclusions Regarding the Emotional Life of the Infant', and 'Notes on Some Schizoid Mechanisms', in Joan Riviere (ed.), *Developments in Psycho-Analysis* (London: The Hogarth Press, 1952), pp. 198–236 and pp. 292–320.

14. See on this, Klein, 'The Emotional Life of the Infant', p. 210. See also Segal, *Introduction to the Work of Melanie Klein*, p. 24.
15. For Klein, the mechanisms of splitting, projection and introjection are all 'staged' in phantasy. In other words, what the psychoanalyst or outside 'observer can describe as a mechanism is experienced and described by the person himself as a detailed phantasy'. See Segal, *Introduction to the Work of Melanie Klein*, p. 17.
16. Caper, *Immaterial Facts*, pp. 95–6. See also Paula Heimann, 'Certain Functions of Introjection and Projection in Early Infancy', in Riviere (ed.), *Developments in Psycho-Analysis*, p. 155.
17. See also on this, Heimann, ibid., pp. 142–3.
18. See Hanna Segal, *Klein* (London: Karnac, 1989), pp. 123–4. Because such part-objects are not integrated within a larger whole and are endowed with a moral value, Deleuze calls them '*simulacra*', after the 'bad' ungrounded images of the Platonic Ideas (LS, 187).
19. Julia Segal, *Melanie Klein* (London: Sage, second edition, 2004), p. 33.
20. Klein, 'Notes on Some Schizoid Mechanisms', p. 297.
21. Klein, 'The Emotional Life of the Infant', p. 200.
22. Ibid., pp. 204–5.
23. Segal, *Introduction to the Work of Melanie Klein*, p. 4.
24. Melanie Klein, 'A Contribution to the Psychogenesis of Manic-Depressive States (1935)', in *Love, Guilt and Reparation*, p. 262. See also 'The Emotional Life of the Infant', pp. 200–1: 'If we consider the picture which exists in the infant's mind – as we can see it retrospectively in the analyses of children and adults – we find that the hated breast has acquired the oral-destructive qualities of the infant's own impulses when he is in states of frustration and hatred. In his destructive phantasies he bites and tears up the breast, devours it, annihilates it; and he feels that the breast will attack him in the same way. As urethral- and anal-sadistic impulses gain in strength, the infant in his mind attacks the breast with poisonous urine and explosive faeces, and therefore expects it to be poisonous and explosive towards him. The details of his sadistic phantasies determine the content of his fear of internal and external persecutors, primarily of the retaliating (bad) breast.'
25. Melanie Klein, 'Love, Guilt and Reparation (1937)', in *Love, Guilt and Reparation*, p. 308.
26. Klein, 'The Emotional Life of the Infant', p. 202.
27. Deleuze, in line with Kleinian theory, describes this ongoing process of re-projection and re-introjection in the following way, emphasizing the role of the 'bad breast': 'Not only are the breast and the entire body of the mother split apart into a good and a bad object, but they are aggressively emptied, slashed to pieces, broken into crumbs and alimentary morsels. The introjection of these partial objects into the

body of the infant is accompanied by a projection of aggressiveness onto these internal objects, and by a re-projection of these objects into the maternal body. Thus, introjected morsels are like poisonous, persecuting, explosive, and toxic substances threatening the child's body from within and being endlessly reconstituted inside the mother's body. The necessity of a perpetual re-introjection is the result of this' (LS, 187).

28. Klein, 'Notes on Some Schizoid Mechanisms', p. 298 and p. 304.
29. Klein, 'The Emotional Life of the Infant', p. 209.
30. Klein, 'Psychogenesis of Manic-Depressive States', p. 264. See also Segal, *Introduction to the Work of Melanie Klein*, pp. 67–8.
31. See generally on this Klein, 'The Emotional Life of the Infant', pp. 203–4.
32. Segal, *Introduction to the Work of Melanie Klein*, p. 69.
33. Klein, 'The Emotional Life of the Infant', p. 211.
34. Klein, 'A Contribution to the Psychogenesis of Manic-Depressive States', p. 264 and pp. 266–7.
35. See Klein, 'The Emotional Life of the Infant', pp. 211–12; 'Notes on Some Schizoid Mechanisms', pp. 307–8; 'A Contribution to the Psychogenesis of Manic-Depressive States (1935)', pp. 285–7.
36. See Klein, 'The Emotional Life of the Infant', p. 214; 'Love, Guilt and Reparation (1937)', p. 308. Deleuze will speak of 'reparation' as a process which belongs to the constitution of a surface (see LS, 201). We shall return to this point.
37. See Klein, 'The Emotional Life of the Infant', p. 215. See also Segal, *Introduction to the Work of Melanie Klein*, p. 73.
38. See Klein, 'The Emotional Life of the Infant', p. 220. See also Melanie Klein, 'On Observing the Behavior of Young Infants', in Riviere (ed.), *Developments in Psycho-Analysis*, pp. 256–7.
39. See Melanie Klein, 'The Oedipus Complex in Light of Early Anxieties (1945)', in *Love, Guilt and Reparation*, p. 401 and p. 410.
40. See Klein, 'The Emotional Life of the Infant', p. 224.
41. With regards to the problematic status of this 'penis', as Paula Heimann writes, while the case of the infant's relation to the breast may be relatively clear, since this is involved in feeding, '[h]ow the infant arrives at any notion of the father's penis may still be regarded as an open question'. See her 'Certain Functions of Introjection and Projection in Early Infancy', pp. 164–5. Melanie Klein assumes, however, that there is an 'inherent unconscious knowledge of the existence of the penis and of the vagina'. See her 'The Oedipus Complex in Light of Early Anxieties (1945)', in *Love, Guilt and Reparation*, p. 409. R.D. Hinshelwood, it seems to us, clarifies the situation by making the point that, at this stage, the penis as part object is not so much understood as belonging to a real father, as simply that which 'occupies' the

mother, corresponding to the way in which the infant phantasizes the situation in relation to its own oral, anal and genital desires. See the entry 'Father', in *A Dictionary Of Kleinian Thought* (London: Free Association Books, 1991), pp. 308–9.

42. Klein, 'The Emotional Life of the Infant', p. 219. On the equation 'breast = penis', see Klein, 'The Oedipus Complex in Light of Early Anxieties (1945)', p. 409.

43. Melanie Klein, 'The Importance of Symbol-Formation in the Development of the Ego (1930)', in *Love, Guilt and Reparation*, p. 219.

44. Klein, 'The Emotional Life of the Infant', pp. 219–20.

45. See Klein, 'The Oedipus Complex', p. 410.

46. Hinshelwood, *A Dictionary Of Kleinian Thought*, p. 308.

47. Klein, 'The Oedipus Complex', p. 409 and p. 417.

48. Ibid., p. 409: 'The imagos of his mother's breast and of his father's penis are established within his ego and form the nucleus of his super-ego. To the introjection of the good and bad breast and mother corresponds the introjection of the good and bad penis and father. They become the first representatives on the one hand of protective and helpful internal figures, on the other of retaliating and persecuting internal figures, and are the first identifications which the ego develops.'

49. See Klein, 'The Emotional Life of the Infant', p. 229.

50. Ibid., p. 213.

51. Klein, 'Notes on Some Schizoid Mechanisms', p. 297.

52. Ibid., pp. 297–8.

53. For the full account of the issues involved here, as well as for Deleuze's analyses of such 'schizophrenic' procedures, see the 'Thirteenth Series of the Schizophrenic and the Little Girl' (LS, 82–93). It is clear from this that Deleuze's understanding of the schizophrenic's relation to language is very different from that of both Freud and Lacan. For Freud, in schizophrenia, words are not treated from the point of view of their physical or sonorous nature. Rather, the schizophrenic treats concrete things as abstract and then reconstructs his or her relation to the external world by means of words and 'figures of speech' which have been subjected to unconscious processes of condensation and displacement. See Sigmund Freud, 'The Unconscious', in *The Standard Edition of the Complete Psychological Work of Sigmund Freud* [henceforth SE], volume XIV, trans. James Strachey (London: The Hogarth Press, 1957), Ch. VII. For Lacan, schizophrenic language is defined as the 'endless and panic-stricken sliding of the signifying series over the signified series', while for Deleuze, in schizophrenia, *'there are no longer any series at all'* (LS, 91, translation modified).

54. Deleuze is referring to the following passage in Klein's 'Notes on Some

Schizoid Mechanisms', p. 311: '[The patient] reported the following dream: there was a blind man who was very worried about being blind; but he seemed to comfort himself by touching the patient's dress and finding out how it was fastened. The dress in the dream reminded her of one her frocks which was buttoned high up to the throat. The patient gave two further associations to this dream. She said, with some resistance, that the blind man was herself; and when referring to the dress fastened up to the throat, she remarked that she had again gone into her "hide". I suggested to the patient that she unconsciously expressed in the dream that she was blind to her own difficulties, and that her decisions with regard to the analysis as well as to various circumstances in her life were not in accordance with her unconscious knowledge . . . Actually, the interpretation of this dream did not produce any effect and did not alter the patient's decision to bring the analysis to an end in that particular hour.'

55. See Jacques Lacan, 'Les complexes familiaux dans la formation de l'individu – Essai d'analyse d'une fonction en psychologie', in *Autres Écrits* (Paris: Seuil, 2001); 'The Mirror Stage as Formative of the *I* Function as Revealed in Psychoanalytic Experience', in *Écrits*.

56. Evans, *Dictionary*, p. 85.

57. See Lacan, 'Les complexes familiaux', pp. 31–2.

58. Chiesa, *Subjectivity and Otherness*, p. 27.

59. See Lacan, 'Les complexes familiaux', pp. 30–6.

60. Ibid., p. 30.

61. Ibid., p. 31: 'it is the refusal of weaning that founds the positivity of the complex, that is to say, the *imago* of the feeding relationship which [the complex] tends to reestablish' (my translation). See also Chiesa, *Subjectivity and Otherness*, p. 198, n.63.

62. On identification as the 'assumption' of an image and corresponding formation of the subject, see Evans, *Dictionary*, p. 82; Chiesa, *Subjectivity and Otherness*, p. 28; and Lacan, 'The Mirror Stage', p. 76. As Lacan puts it elsewhere, 'the imago is the form, which is definable in the imaginary spatiotemporal complex, whose function is to bring about the identification that resolves a psychical phase – in other words, a metamorphosis in the individual's relationships with his semblables'. See Jacques Lacan, 'Presentation of Psychical Causality', in *Écrits*, pp. 153–4.

63. Lacan, 'Les complexes familiaux', pp. 32–3.

64. Ibid., pp. 31–2.

65. This notion of the object which is 'found only as lost' also echoes Freud's argument in the 'Three Essays on Sexuality', with respect to the long process of finding an appropriate sexual or love-object. As he writes, at 'a time at which the first beginnings of sexual satisfaction are still linked with the taking of nourishment, the sexual drive has a

sexual object outside the infant's own body in the shape of his mother's breast. It is only later that the drive loses that object . . . There are thus good reasons why a child suckling at his mother's breast has become the prototype of every relation of love. The finding of an object is in fact a refinding of it.' See Sigmund Freud, 'Three Essays on the Theory of Sexuality', in SE VII, trans. James Strachey (London: The Hogarth Press, 1953), p. 222. It is clear, however, that for Freud the 'refinding' of the lost object occurs only after the resolution of the Oedipus complex. For Lacan, on the contrary, even though such objects-images will be made sense of retrospectively as they are for Freud, the imago of the maternal breast will nevertheless be made sense of as a *pre*-Oedipal 'refinding' of an intrauterine life which had been lost. It can thus be said that, while Deleuze cites neither Freud nor Lacan in this matter, because he is here focusing on the pre-Oedipal, he is almost certainly referring to the Lacanian imago of the breast when he speaks of the 'lost object'.

66. Deleuze is here following the Lacanian Robert Pujol. See his 'Approche théorique du fantasme', *La Psychanalyse* 8 (1964), p. 15.

67. Indeed, for Lacan, 'the imaginary [dimension] is always already structured by the symbolic order'. See Evans, *Dictionary*, p. 84.

68. See also on this point, Chiesa, *Subjectivity and Otherness*, pp. 61–2.

69. Sigmund Freud, 'Two Encyclopedia Articles – (A) Psychoanalysis', in SE XVIII, trans. James Strachey (London: The Hogarth Press, 1955), p. 244.

70. Ibid., pp. 244–5. The eye and the skin can also function as erotogenic zones. Most generally, it 'is a part of the skin or mucous membrane in which stimuli of a certain sort evoke a feeling of pleasure possessing a particular quality'. See Freud, 'Three Essays on Sexuality', p. 169 and p. 183. It should also be noted that the Standard Edition of Freud's works in English translate both *Instinkt* (instinct) and *Trieb* (drive) as 'instinct'. However, whereas an instinct is genetically transmitted and independent of individual experience, a drive is closely related to the subject's individual history and is inseparable from how it is represented in his or her psychic life. We have thus chosen to modify the Standard Edition translation to reflect this conceptual distinction and to remain consistent with Deleuze's original French text of *The Logic of Sense*, where the German *Trieb* is always translated by the French *pulsion* (drive).

71. See on this, Freud, 'Three Essays on Sexuality', pp. 197–9. On the 'phallic' stage, see also Sigmund Freud, 'The Infantile Genital Organization (an Interpolation into the Theory of Sexuality)', in SE XIX, trans. James Strachey (London: The Hogarth Press, 1961), p. 142.

72. On this last point, see Freud, 'Three Essays on Sexuality', p. 168.

73. Sigmund Freud, 'Instincts and Their Vicissitudes', in SE XIV, trans. James Strachey (London: The Hogarth Press, 1957), pp. 121–2.

74. For what follows, see ibid., pp. 122–3.

75. Freud shows that 'the object is variable, contingent and only chosen in its definitive form in consequence of the vicissitudes of the subject's history. He shows too how aims are many and fragmented . . . and closely dependent on somatic sources which are themselves manifold.' See Laplanche and Pontalis, *The Language of Psycho-Analysis*, p. 215.

76. See Freud, 'Instincts and Their Vicissitudes', p. 120.

77. Freud, 'Three Essays on Sexuality', p. 182. Freud uses the term 'anaclisis' 'to designate the early relationship of the sexual drives to the self-preservative ones: the sexual drives, which become autonomous only secondarily, depend at first on those vital functions which furnish them with an organic source, an orientation and an object'. See Laplanche and Pontalis, *The Language of Psycho-Analysis*, p. 29. As Deleuze puts in *The Logic of Sense*, the 'sexual drives are fashioned very much after the drives of conservation, being born together with them and substituting introjected and projected partial objects for objects that are out of reach' (LS, 198).

78. Freud, 'Three Essays on Sexuality', p. 181.

79. Ibid., p. 184.

80. Ibid., p. 184.

81. See also on this, Laplanche and Pontalis, *The Language of Psycho-Analysis*, p. 322: 'Inasmuch as unpleasure is related to the increase of quantities of excitation, and pleasure to their reduction, the principle in question [i.e., the 'pleasure principle'] may be said to be an economic one.'

82. Freud, 'Three Essays on Sexuality', p. 181.

83. Ibid., p. 185.

84. See on this, Laplanche and Pontalis, *The Language of Psycho-Analysis*, pp. 45–6.

85. As Laplanche and Pontalis write, the 'origin of phantasy cannot be isolated from the origin of the drive (*Trieb*) itself. The authors [i.e., Laplanche and Pontalis], reinterpreting the Freudian concept of the *experience of satisfaction*, locate this origin in auto-erotism, which they define not as a stage of evolution but as a moment of a repeated disjunction of sexual desire and non-sexual functions: sexuality is detached from any natural object, and is handed over to phantasy, and, by this very fact, starts existing as sexuality.' See Laplanche and Pontalis, 'Fantasy and the Origins of Sexuality', pp. 27–8 (translation modified).

86. For what follows, see Sigmund Freud, 'Project for a Scientific Psychology', in SE I, trans. James Strachey (London: The Hogarth

Press, 1966), pp. 318–19; and Sigmund Freud, 'The Interpretation of Dreams (Second Part)', in SE V, trans. James Strachey (London: The Hogarth Press, 1958), pp. 536–40.

87. See Sigmund Freud, 'Some General Remarks on Hysterical Attacks (1909)', in SE IX, trans. James Strachey (London: The Hogarth Press, 1959), p. 233. See also Sigmund Freud, 'Two Principles of Mental Functioning', in SE XII, trans. James Strachey (London: The Hogarth Press, 1958), p. 223: 'The continuance of auto-erotism is what makes it possible to retain for so long the easier momentary and imaginary satisfaction in relation to the sexual object in place of real satisfaction.'

88. Freud writes that 'it is clear that the behaviour of a child who indulges in thumb-sucking is determined by a search for some pleasure which has already been experienced and is now remembered . . . It is also easy to guess the occasions on which the child had his first experiences of the pleasure which he is now striving to renew . . . his sucking on his mother's breast'. See Freud, 'Three Essays on Sexuality', p. 181.

89. On this last point, see LS, 199: it is important to distinguish 'between the introjected and projected internal partial object (simulacrum) and the object of the surface, projected over a zone in accordance with an entirely different mechanism (image)'.

90. Freud, 'Three Essays on Sexuality', p. 149.

91. Ibid., p. 222.

92. Ibid., p. 223: There are 'good reasons why a child sucking at his mother's breast has become the prototype of every relation of love . . . A child's intercourse with anyone responsible for his care affords him an unending source of sexual excitation and satisfaction from his erotogenic zones. This is especially so since the person in charge of him, who after all, is as a rule his mother, herself regards him with feelings that are derived from her own sexual life: she strokes him, kisses him, rocks him and quite clearly treats him as a substitute for a complete sexual object.' See also Laplanche and Pontalis, *Language of Psycho-Analysis*, p. 156: 'The image of the satisfying object . . . may be recathected in the absence of the real object (hallucinatory satisfaction of the wish). And it will always guide the later search for the satisfying object.'

93. Freud, 'Three Essays on Sexuality', p. 197 and p. 199. Laplanche and Pontalis, however, caution against a too simplistic reading of the integration of part objects into a whole object. See their *Language of Psycho-Analysis*, p. 276.

94. Freud, 'Three Essays on Sexuality', p. 211.

95. Ibid., p. 210.

96. Freud, 'The Infantile Genital Organization (an Interpolation into the Theory of Sexuality)', p. 142.

97. Ibid., p. 142.

98. Ibid., p. 142.
99. See also on this, Sigmund Freud, 'Some Psychical Consequences of the Anatomical Distinction Between the Sexes', in SE XIX, trans. James Strachey (London: The Hogarth Press, 1961), pp. 248–58.
100. Freud, 'Three Essays on Sexuality', p. 188.
101. Sigmund Freud, 'On Transformations of Instinct as Exemplified in Anal Erotism', in SE XVII, trans. James Strachey (London: The Hogarth Press, 1955), p. 131.
102. Lacan, 'The Mirror Stage', p. 76.
103. Ibid., p. 76.
104. 'If the mother's desire *is* for the phallus, the child wants to be the phallus in order to satisfy her desire.' Jacques Lacan, 'The Signification of the Phallus', in *Écrits*, p. 582.
105. Although it is not clear that Deleuze was familiar with this material at the time of writing *The Logic of Sense* (see our discussion of this at n. 114 below), for what follows, see generally: Jacques Lacan, *Le séminaire livre IV: La relation d'objet, 1956–1957* (Paris: Seuil, 1994), pp. 59–75. For a detailed examination of the dialectic of frustration and its relation to the Oedipus complex, see Chiesa, *Subjectivity and Otherness*, pp. 65–75.
106. Lacan derives this point from Freud. See, for example, Sigmund Freud, 'The Dissolution of the Oedipus Complex', in SE XIX, pp. 178–9: 'Renunciation of the penis is not tolerated by the girl without some attempt at compensation. She slips – along the line of symbolic equation, one might say – from the penis to a baby . . . The two wishes – to possess a penis and a child – remain strongly cathected in the unconscious and help to prepare the female creature for her later sexual role.'
107. Jacques Lacan, 'The Subversion of the Subject and the Dialectic of Desire in the Freudian Unconscious', in *Écrits*, p. 690.
108. The 'child, in its relationship with its mother – a relationship that is constituted in analysis not by the child's biological dependence, but by its dependence on her love, that is, by its desire for her desire – identifies with the imaginary object of her desire in so far as the mother herself symbolizes it in the phallus'. Jacques Lacan, 'On a Question Prior to Any Possible Treatment of Psychosis', in *Écrits*, pp. 462–3.
109. Lacan, 'The Subversion of the Subject', p. 690.
110. See also on this Lacan, *Le séminaire livre IV*, p. 68.
111. See on this Jacques Lacan, 'Le Désir et son interprétation', *Bulletin de Psychologie* 13 (1959–1960): pp. 329–35.
112. Lacan, *Le séminaire livre IV*, p. 69, p. 187. As Chiesa notes, 'the mother is [initially] experienced as a desiring Other (the Desire-of-the-Mother), but this desiring Other is not thought to lack anything (the imaginary phallus). This distinction is central: at first, *the*

Desire-of-the-Mother is not associated with lack. How else could we justify the fact that Lacan continuously maintains that the child considers his mother to be omnipotent?' See his *Subjectivity and Otherness*, p. 70.

113. Lacan, 'The Signification of the Phallus', p. 576. Of course, this belief that the mother is phallic is a supposition which can only be formed *retroactively*, once the infant perceives the mother to lack and thus to desire the phallus. On this point, see Chiesa, *Subjectivity and Otherness*, p. 70.

114. The Lacanian reading of the Oedipus complex – which, to all evidence, Deleuze is here following – was delivered at Lacan's *Séminaire* between the years 1956 and 1958. It remains a question, however, as to whether Deleuze in 1969 could have been aware of this material. Indeed, he never cites any of Lacan's seminars, and the official edited transcripts for these years were only published in 1994 (*Le séminaire, livre IV: La relation d'objet, 1956–1957*) and 1998 (*Le séminaire, livre V: Les formations de l'inconscient, 1957–1958*). It can be noted, however, that summaries of these seminars, approved by Lacan, appeared in the *Bulletin de psychologie* between 1956 and 1959. As Roudinesco relates: 'In 1953, [Lacan] hired a stenographer to transcribe his seminar. The transcriptions were deposited with Granoff . . . and were generally available to all members of the SFP. Three years later, and until 1959, J.-B. Pontalis, working with Lacan's approval, produced excellent summaries of the seminars on "Object Relations", "Formations of the Unconscious", and "Desire and Its Interpretation", all of which were published in the *Bulletin de psychologie*'. See Roudinesco, *Jacques Lacan & Co*, p. 566. The relevant references are: Jacques Lacan, 'La relation d'objet et les structures freudiennes', *Bulletin de Psychologie* 10: 7 (1956–7), pp. 426–30; 10: 10 (1956–7), pp. 602–5; 10: 12 (1956–7), pp. 742–3; 10: 14 (1956–7), pp. 851–54; 11: 1 (1956–7), pp. 31–5. And Jacques Lacan, 'Les formations de l'inconscient', *Bulletin de Psychologie* 11: 4–5 (1957–8), pp. 293–6; 12: 2–3 (1958–9), pp. 182–92; 12: 4 (1958–9), pp. 250–6.

115. Laplanche and Pontalis, *Language of Psycho-Analysis*, p. 282.

116. Evans, *Dictionary*, p. 130. Indeed, although Deleuze does not cite Lacan at all in this 'Twenty-Ninth Series', it is clear from the fact that he does not mention any differences between the Oedipus complex for the little boy and for the little girl that he is following the Lacanian and not the Freudian account of Oedipus.

117. See the table in Lacan, *Le séminaire livre IV*, p. 269.

118. Ibid., pp. 66–8.

119. Ibid., p. 62.

120. See on this Chiesa, *Subjectivity and Otherness*, p. 67.

121. Lacan, *Le séminaire livre IV*, p. 67 (my translation).
122. Ibid., pp. 68–9.
123. Ibid., p. 101.
124. Ibid., p. 101 (my translation).
125. At this stage, 'the question of the phallus is already posed somewhere in the mother, where the infant must locate it'. See Jacques Lacan, *Le séminaire livre V: Les formations de l'inconscient*, 1957–1958 (Paris: Seuil, 1998), p. 194 (my translation).
126. Lacan, *Le séminaire livre IV*, p. 101, p. 194, p. 224.
127. Ibid., pp. 81–2.
128. Ibid., p. 269.
129. Ibid., p. 243.
130. Ibid., p. 220.
131. Ibid., p. 208.
132. Sean Homer, *Jacques Lacan* (London: Routledge, 2004), p. 55.
133. Lacan, *Le séminaire livre IV*, p. 224.
134. As Lacan puts it elsewhere, somewhat more elliptically, 'what [the infant] has is no better than what he does not have, from the point of view of his demands for love, which would like him to be the phallus'. See Lacan, 'The Signification of the Phallus', in *Écrits*, p. 582.
135. Lacan, *Le séminaire livre IV*, p. 227.
136. For Lacan, it is thus not the imaginary father but the mother who initially pronounces the 'incest taboo'. As he writes, the 'mother is herself fully capable of showing the child that what he or she offers her is insufficient and also of pronouncing the prohibition against using the new instrument'. Or again, it is in fact the mother 'who posits [the father] as the one who makes her law'. See Lacan, *Le séminaire livre V*, p. 187 and p. 194 (my translations).
137. Chiesa, *Subjectivity and Otherness*, p. 69.
138. See Lacan, *Le séminaire livre V*, p. 193.
139. Ibid., p. 185. See also Jacques Lacan, 'Les formations de l'inconscient', *Bulletin de Psychologie* 12: 2–3 (1958–9), p. 185.
140. Lacan, *Le séminaire livre IV*, p. 153, pp. 218–19. As seen above, for Freud, the couple having–not having the phallus is a symbolic distinction, as opposed to the couple having a penis–having a vagina which is a real distinction.
141. Lacan, *Le séminaire livre V*, pp. 191–2 (my translation).
142. Lacan, *Le séminaire livre IV*, p. 269.
143. Jacques Lacan, 'Les formations de l'inconscient', *Bulletin de Psychologie* 12: 4 (1958–9), p. 256.
144. Lacan, *Le séminaire livre V*, p. 194 (my translation).
145. Lacan, *Le séminaire livre IV*, p. 209 (my translation). In so far as the little girl at this stage realizes that she does not have the phallus, she must be considered to be both castrated *and* deprived of the phallus.

146. Lacan, *Le séminaire livre V*, p. 194, p. 196.

147. Lacan, *Le séminaire livre IV*, p. 204 (my translation).

148. Ibid., p. 203.

149. Matthew Sharpe and Joanne Faulkner, *Understanding Psychoanalysis* (Stocksfield: Acumen, 2008), p. 111.

150. Chiesa, *Subjectivity and Otherness*, p. 81.

151. Sharpe and Faulkner, *Understanding Psychoanalysis*, p. 112.

152. Jacques Lacan, *The Seminar, Book III: The Psychoses*, 1955–1956, trans. Russell Grigg (New York: W.W. Norton, 1993), p. 170.

153. Lacan, *Le séminaire livre IV*, p. 205.

154. See on this, Sigmund Freud, 'Totem and Taboo', in SE XIII, trans. James Strachey (London: The Hogarth Press, 1955), p. 143.

155. Lacan, *Le séminaire livre IV*, pp. 210–11.

156. Lacan, *Le séminaire livre V*, p. 175 (my translation).

157. Ibid., pp. 175–6.

158. Chiesa, *Subjectivity and Otherness*, p. 91.

159. As Deleuze puts it, 'the entire image of action is projected on a physical surface, where the action itself appears as willed and is found determined in the forms of restoration and evocation' (LS, 207). It should, however, be remarked that Deleuze cautions us against understanding this 'willed action' as 'a psychological project of the will', for, strictly speaking, it is the projected image with which the child is passively driven to identify by its familial relations, biological needs and initially uncoordinated sexual drives, which 'renders it [the will] possible' in the first place (LS, 207).

160. Deleuze also calls it a '"cerebral" surface' (LS, 207).

161. As has been seen, it amounts to the same thing to say that an event is determined, in relation to '*personnes*', by processes of triangulation or disjunctive syntheses, as it does to say that it is reciprocally, completely and progressively determined in intersubjective and linguistic contexts.

162. Susan Isaacs, 'The Nature and Function of Phantasy', in Riviere (ed.), *Developments in Psycho-Analysis*, p. 83. It should, however, be noted that, this general definition aside, Deleuze is at pains to distance himself from most of the details of the Kleinian school's understanding of phantasy (see LS, 215–16).

163. Laplanche and Pontalis, *The Language of Psycho-Analysis*, p. 314.

164. See on this, Roger Perron, 'Idea/Representation', in Alain de Mijolla (ed.), *International Dictionary of Psychoanalysis* (Detroit: Thomson Gale, 2005), pp. 780–3.

165. Sigmund Freud, 'A Metapsychological Supplement to the Theory of Dreams', in SE XIV, p. 231.

166. Sigmund Freud, 'Repression', in SE XIV, pp. 148–9.

167. Ibid., p. 147.

168. Sigmund Freud, 'The Ego and the Id', in SE XIX, pp. 34–35; 'An Outline of Psycho-Analysis (1940 [1938])', SE XXIII, trans. James Strachey (London: The Hogarth Press, 1964), p. 155; 'The Dissolution of the Oedipus Complex', p. 173 and p. 177.
169. Freud, 'Repression', p. 149.
170. See Freud, 'The Unconscious', pp. 190–1.
171. Ibid., p. 166.
172. Freud, 'Repression', p. 149.
173. See Freud's summary of this process in 'A Metapsychological Supplement to the Theory of Dreams', pp. 226–9.
174. Sigmund Freud, 'A Short Account of Psycho-Analysis', in SE XIX, p. 200
175. Laplanche and Pontalis, *The Language of Psycho-Analysis*, p. 331.
176. Ibid., p. 332.
177. Ibid., p. 318. See also Laplanche and Pontalis, 'Fantasy and the Origins of Sexuality', pp. 19–20.
178. See Laplanche and Pontalis, *The Language of Psycho-Analysis*, p. 316. See also their 'Fantasy and the Origins of Sexuality', pp. 20–1.
179. Sigmund Freud, 'Negation', in SE XIX, p. 235.
180. Ibid., p. 239.
181. Jean Hyppolite, in his commentary on Freud's *Verneinung*, makes the link between Freud's *Verneinung* and Hegel's *Aufhebung* or 'sublimation'. As he writes, when Freud writes that 'negation is an *Aufhebung* of the repression', it 'is Hegel's dialectical word [which is used], which means simultaneously to deny, to suppress, and to conserve, and fundamentally to lift [*soulever*]'. See 'A Spoken Commentary on Freud's "Verneinung" by Jean Hyppolite', in *Écrits*, pp. 747–8.
182. See Freud, 'The Ego and the Id', pp. 45–6.
183. See Laplanche and Pontalis, 'Fantasy and the Origins of Sexuality', p. 22 (translation modified).
184. Laplanche and Pontalis, *The Language of Psycho-Analysis*, p. 318.
185. Laplanche and Pontalis, 'Fantasy and the Origins of Sexuality', p. 26 and pp. 22–3.
186. As Deleuze writes, the 'value of the pronominal – to punish oneself, to punish, or to be punished, or better yet, to see oneself, rather than to see or to be seen – is well attested to in Freud's writings' (LS, 213). On these phantastical pronominal reversals between sadism and masochism, as well as between scopophilia and exhibitionism, see Freud, 'Instincts and Their Vicissitudes', pp. 127–30. See also the famous 'grammatical transformations' in beating-phantasies, examined in Freud, 'A Child is Being Beaten', in SE XVII, pp. 179–204.
187. As Lacan puts it 'man must traverse the entire forest of the signifier in order to return to his original and instinctively valid objects'. Lacan, *Le séminaire livre V*, p. 206 (my translation).

188. Deleuze writes: 'As [the phantasm] returns to its external beginning (deadly castration), it is always beginning again its internal beginning (the movement of desexualization)' (LS, 220).
189. For an analysis of the phallus as the quasi-cause or paradoxical element *par excellence* in *The Logic of Sense*, see also Žižek, *Organs without Bodies*, pp. 87–93.
190. The texts in question are Robert Pujol, 'Approche théorique du fantasme', and Serge Leclaire, *Psychoanalyzing: On the Order of the Unconscious and the Practice of the Letter*, trans. Peggy Kamuf (Stanford: Stanford University Press, 1998).
191. See on this Sigmund Freud, 'Beyond the Pleasure Principle', in SE XVIII, pp. 14–16.

Conclusion

The task set at the beginning of this study was to understand the precise way in which Deleuze asserts the ontological priority of events over substances in his 1969 publication, *The Logic of Sense*. This assertion, it has been seen, takes a very particular and complex form. Indeed, it has been shown throughout the preceding chapters how Deleuze constructs a concept of the ontologically primitive event – the event which ontologically depends on no underlying substance, but on which all substantial things ontologically depend – with reference to the way in which various figures and intellectual movements in the history of thought collectively pose and resolve what can be called the 'problem' of the event. In other words, Deleuze extracts from the work of the above-examined thinkers a number of event-related problems and a hybrid family of event-related concepts which, with certain important qualifications, can be said to resolve these problems. Let us therefore review the various stages of the way in which Deleuze constructs his concept of the event, spelling out how the event is to be understood if everything is ultimately to be thought of as ontologically dependent on events. We shall then be in a position to make some evaluative comments with regard to Deleuze's project as a whole in *The Logic of Sense*.

First of all, Deleuze analyzes the way in which the 'verbs of becoming' in denoting propositions express 'ideal events' which are ontologically prior to determined states of affairs. These events are held to be ideal in so far as they are not themselves objectively 'present' in the same way as fixed things and states of affairs (in themselves, they are the 'infinite identity' of the two directions implicated in the change), but are nevertheless the necessary conditions for thinking the constitution of new states of affairs, as well as for thinking the constitution of the states of affairs which will be understood as past in relation to these latter. Thus, it was seen how the verb 'to grow' in the proposition 'Alice grows' expresses a paradoxical process in which Alice simultaneously becomes larger than she was but also smaller than she will become. But at the same time, it was seen that it is necessary to posit such a process in order to account for the passage and relation between, as well as the constitution of, the two determined states: Alice having been smaller at t_1 and Alice being now larger at t_2.

Now, for Deleuze, the relation between events and language goes well beyond the way in which verbs of becoming express ideal changes. For if determined things and states of affairs are ontologically dependent on events, then our knowledge of these things will in turn depend on the way in which their constitutive events can themselves be determined – that is, ordered and related – in language. This should not, however, mislead us into thinking that we can finally establish the order of events underlying all things with reference to some stated 'image of eternity', for language itself is an event which is endlessly coming about. The 'problem of the event', for Deleuze, can thus be expressed in the following way: 'given the ontological priority of events and their relation to language, what are the evental conditions of the event if everything, including the very language in which events are ordered and related, is ultimately to be a well determined event?' In order to answer this question or resolve this problem, Deleuze turns first of all to the Stoics.

Taking up the Stoic ontological division between bodies and incorporeals, Deleuze compares events with Stoic incorporeal 'sayables' or *lekta*, which are at once the effects of causal relations between bodies and the sense of propositions. Understanding the event in this way allows Deleuze to affirm that events occurring in and bringing about determined states of affairs are themselves determined in relation to an incorporeal 'sense-event'. This sense-event, it was then seen, is nothing other than the ongoing and systematically related articulation of the causal analyses of bodies, conceptual construction, and the development of the wise person's beliefs and desires.

Deleuze also uses the Stoics in order to resolve two further problems. As was seen in relation to Deleuze's analysis of the contemporary, tri-dimensional model of the proposition, sense cannot be isolated in any of the dimensions of denotation, manifestation or signification. Rather, because each of these dimensions is called upon to ground the others in various ways, sense is constantly displaced between them in a circular manner. Connected with this first problem is a second one which was described as follows. On the one hand, the dimension of signification shares an important characteristic of sense in so far as it appears as the condition of possibility for a proposition being true in relation to an objective state of affairs.

Indeed, a proposition devoid of sense or signification can be neither true nor false. On the other hand, however, it is generally held that the truth or falsity of a proposition is ultimately not a matter of its signification or sense, but only of its correspondence (or lack of correspondence) with a factual state of affairs. In response to the first problem, Deleuze argues that the ongoing determination of sense or the event in Stoic philosophy should be seen as a 'fourth dimension' of the proposition which determines the other three: the causal analysis of bodies being aligned with denotation, the wise person's beliefs and desires with manifestation, and conceptual construction with signification. But now, turning to the second problem, it can also be seen that in so far as the ongoing sense-event grounds the relation between the dimensions of signification and denotation, a relation is established within sense between the condition of truth and the truth of propositions in relation to determined states of affairs.

A difficulty with Stoic philosophy, however, at least from the point of view of Deleuze's philosophy of events, is that it ultimately reduces the ongoing sense-event to an underlying, substantial instance: the body and name of Zeus. This Stoic reduction is, therefore, incompatible with the assertion that events are ontologically prior to substances all the way down. While nevertheless retaining certain aspects of Stoic philosophy, Deleuze thus turns to Leibniz in order to develop conceptual tools which will be more appropriate to the resolution of the problem of the event.

Taking up in his own way the Leibnizian notions of compossibility and incompossibility, Deleuze now argues that relations of convergence and divergence between series of singularities-events preside over the 'static ontological and logical geneses' of individuals, persons and general concepts. It was seen that individuals and persons are initially considered to be determined within a world in so far as the trope-like events which define them converge, that is, in so far as there is an expressive or law-like relation between the events that can be truly predicated of one individual and of another. But at the same time, because divergences between series of events are inevitably perceived from one person to another (depending on their particular, finite 'points of view'), these persons' knowledge of worldly individuals depends upon 'disjunctive syntheses' of divergent events in an intersubjective and linguistic context. Such syntheses, it was argued, can be thought of in terms of a 'process of triangulation' involving the simultaneous and related determination of the beliefs of a knowing subject, the beliefs of another such subject or *personne*, and a world of individuals (which will be said to have been 'common' to the initially divergent worlds) corresponding to these beliefs. For Leibniz, of course, such syntheses are, ideally at least, carried out in relation to the person of God, with the aim of reducing 'merely apparent' divergences to God's coherent view of things. Deleuze, however, denies the existence of such an original substantial instance and thus argues that individuals and persons must be considered to be generated from real underlying divergences and their syntheses. What is more, because there is no given substance to which the ideal play of events is reducible, persons will always remain open to divergences or differences which must be affirmed as such in the determination of any particular identity (individual or person). Finally, in relation to the genesis of general concepts, it was seen how, in order to determine within a disjunctive synthesis a world of individuals 'common' to divergent worlds, relations must be sought between the trope-like events which characterize these individuals. These relations were then said to be embodied in variable and overlapping classes of tropes – that is, in concepts of increasing and decreasing generality – which individuals and persons will be said to exemplify precisely in so far as they are common to the world disjunctively synthesized out of the divergent worlds.

With reference to Leibniz, then – or rather, with reference to a certain neo-Leibnizianism without God – Deleuze is able to re-describe the various aspects of the ongoing sense-event for the Stoics (causal analysis, beliefs and desires of the sage, and conceptual development) in terms of the ideal play of singularities-events whose relations of convergence and divergence bear on the determination of individuals, persons and general concepts. In other words, the neo-Leibnizian static ontological and logical geneses are a re-description in strictly evental terms of the 'fourth dimension' of the proposition, examined in relation to the Stoics, which makes the tri-dimensional model function entirely from within by generating the relations between these dimensions as well as their objective correlates. What is more, the static ontological and logical geneses overcome the divide between the dimensions of signification and denotation – that is to say, between the condition of truth and the truth of the conditioned proposition in relation to the world – for within disjunctive syntheses or processes of triangulation the logical proposition (signification) both conditions and is conditioned by individuals and persons acting as ontological propositions (denotation and manifestation). Finally, in so far as this ideal play of converging and diverging events depends on no unproduced substance, it should be seen as a crucial component of Deleuze's philosophy of events 'all the way down'.

In Chapters 3 and 4, it was seen how Deleuze re-describes Chapter 2's neo-Leibnizian 'processes of triangulation' with reference to his own concepts of the 'problem' (or 'structure') and 'singularity'. In particular, the philosophical concept of the problem sets out how one can think the relation between the sense and the truth of a proposition, along with the determined object which realizes this truth, as being internally generated within sense itself, that is, without reference to anything transcending this dimension and determining it from the outside. For Deleuze, every true denoting proposition expresses a sense or singularity-event, but this sense or singularity-event will itself be determined in relation to a sub-representative problem for which related series of such propositions collectively function as elements of response or cases of solution. It thus amounts to the same thing to say that singularities-events collectively define the problem as well as generate its 'solutions' (in the form of determined individuals, persons and concepts), as it does to say that a proposition which is true in relation to its corresponding 'evental' state of affairs 'makes sense', in both the active and passive senses of this phrase, in relation to a sub-representative problem (it will be made sense of by the elements of the problem, just as it will contribute to making sense of these elements).

The focus of Chapter 3 was primarily to show how even philosophical propositions with regard to the objective nature of the problem must both make sense of, and be made sense of by, the problem. It was in this way that I spoke of the problem of the problem. It was seen how, with reference to certain interpretations of the differential calculus (as well as group theory and Riemannian differential geometry) and the meta-mathematical theses of Albert Lautman, Deleuze elaborates a theory of the 'problematic Idea' as the reciprocal, complete and progressive determination of purely differential elements (ordinary points or events) by the adjunction and transformation of singularities-events corresponding to values of the relations between these elements. These propositions with respect to the nature of the problem were then held to 'make sense' in relation to the propositions constitutive of a theory, inspired by the work of Gilbert Simondon, of the intensive individuation of 'things' in diverse scientific domains (physics, biology, sociology, psychology, and so on). The complete, philosophical concept of the problem was then held to embrace both of these theories. On the one hand, intensive individuation necessarily presupposes a 'pre-individual field' which takes the same form as the problematic Idea. On the other hand, the theory of intensive individuation shows how the problematic Idea is the problem for its various solutions, that is, for the determined individuals, persons and concepts characteristic of diverse scientific domains. In other words, the theory of intensive individuation makes sense of, and is made sense of by, the theory of problematic Ideas. Finally, it was seen how, 'between' these two halves of the problem, there is a 'divided subject' (or rather an open series of such subjects) who, while entirely dissolved in (biological, psycho-social, etc.) intensive processes, must in the absence of any subtending substance think itself, its world, and the relations between them, in purely differential terms.

Chapter 4 then addressed one of the issues left over from Chapter 3, namely, that of providing a fully differential account of language and the proposition, that is, in terms of the type of differential series and singularities constitutive of the problem. We thus examined Deleuze's concept of 'structure' and saw that it is essentially identical to the concept of the 'problem', as well as fully compatible with an account of the differential determination of a relation between series of 'things', series of propositions, and series of propositions about (the sense of) propositions. The event, then, was said to be a 'paradoxical element' which circulates throughout the different series of the structure of sense, bringing their elements into relation, and which is always accompanied by a 'divided subject' who is both creative and a structurally produced form. With respect to series of bodies, the event corresponds to values of their causal relations. With respect to series of propositions, the event is both what is picked out by the verb in the denoting proposition and the ongoing and intersubjective determination of sense or the sense-event (disjunctive synthesis, static genesis, etc.). This is also the manner in which Deleuze speaks of the intensive processes of individuation examined in Chapter 3 as constituting a 'physics of surfaces' to which corresponds a 'metaphysical surface' which, precisely like the problem or structure of sense, is the ongoing articulation of a relation between, on the one hand, bodies taken together as a whole and inside the limits of their physical surfaces, and on the other hand, propositions in general.

The concepts of the problem (or structure), singularity and the divided subject thus effectively re-describe the static ontological and logical geneses, which were themselves re-descriptions of the way in which, for the Stoics, events occurring in and for states of affairs are determined in relation to an ongoing sense-event on the line of Aion, bringing about determined individuals, persons and signified concepts. What is more, it is in terms of these concepts that propositions can be said to find their sense and truth value in relation to 'evental' states of affairs within sense itself, that is, within the problem or structure constitutive of sense; and that such propositions collectively define the conditions of the problem and generate its solutions in the form of event-determined individuals, persons and concepts. Finally, then, it is in terms of the problem, structure of sense or metaphysical surface that Deleuze will be able to affirm the ontological priority of events 'all the way down', for the problem (structure of sense, metaphysical surface, etc.) is nothing other than the ongoing evental-determination of the events characterizing 'things' in general.

Chapter 5 then addressed a final issue, namely, that of accounting for the metaphysical surface of sense as an event which is produced on the metaphysical surface. This immanent event of the metaphysical surface was analyzed into two related events: (1) the event of language, understood as the separation of the two series constitutive of the metaphysical surface, namely, words and propositions endowed with sense, and noisy corporeal things; and (2) the event of the 'divided subject' (*personne*, questioner, dice-thrower, etc.) which circulates between these two series of words and things and brings them into communication. The question thus became: how do these two events emerge from bodies, produce the metaphysical surface of sense, and come to be determined on this very surface? Taking up in his own way the Kleinian pre-Oedipal 'depths' as well as Freudian and Lacanian approaches to infantile sexuality, the phallus, castration and the phantasm, Deleuze argues that the events of language and the divided subject are produced in the following way. First of all, the child organizes its initially disorganized bodily experiences and object relations into the form of an imaginary 'good object' (imago of the maternal breast) which is in turn signified by a Voice or familial hum surrounding the child. This Voice is not yet a language for the child, although it will become so, and thus be retrospectively made sense of once the child accedes to its organizing principle (static genesis or fourth dimension of sense). The relation to the 'wholesome' good object then makes it possible for the child to extract itself from its confused corporeal relations in depth in order to form, from his or her component sexual drives, a total 'physical surface' for his or her body, as well as for the mother who is alternatively present and absent. Key to this process is the 'phallus' which is embodied by the 'imaginary father'. The phallus both integrates the mother's mysterious presences and absences (the phallus is what occupies the mother during her absences), and is a total and wholly satisfying love-object which the child strives to be in order to control the mother's desire. The child thus competes with the imaginary father in order to be the phallus up to the moment when the real father intervenes as the one who in fact has the phallus (that is, who partially represents the social-symbolic law of the mother's desire), and who thus 'castrates' the child of the imaginary phallus. 'Castration' here means that the child abandons the attempt to be the phallus for the mother and identifies with the real father in various ways, positioning him or herself with respect to a rule-governed way of organizing social relationships. In other words, the child positions him or herself with respect to the structural-symbolic dimension of language and culture which, for Deleuze, is nothing other than what we have called the intersubjective, metaphysical surface. Castration, then, effectively represents the event of the divided subject on the metaphysical surface or, what amounts to the same thing, the event of the metaphysical surface for this subject who is both dissolved in intensive, corporeal processes (physical or biological depth, sexuality) and a form produced by the intersubjective and linguistic operations of the metaphysical surface (processes of triangulation, etc.).

We then saw how the event of language is essentially simultaneous with this event of the divided subject. In particular, we saw that the 'phantasm' is a representation of the satisfaction of the sexual drives and whose 'process' is coextensive with the intersubjective and linguistic practices characterizing the metaphysical surface. The phantasm, finding its origin in castration or the child's passage to the metaphysical surface, is thus a reinvestment and articulation (sublimation and symbolization) of the infant's desire on the metaphysical surface. Prior to castration, the infant had organized its corporeal experiences in depth into the form of a 'good object' signified by a Voice or confused familial hum. The child then began to extract phonemic differences from this Voice and to speak. Now, with castration and the corresponding release of a phantasm, the child accedes to the organizing principle of language, that is, to the metaphysical surface or 'fourth dimension' of sense which grounds the tri-dimensional model of the proposition and makes it function from within (static genesis, process of triangulation). At this point, the child is able to gradually connect its speech with the propositions constitutive of the phantasm representing the satisfaction of its desire. This process, going from 'noise' to the Voice, from the Voice to speech, and then from speech to the neutrality of the metaphysical surface, is the event of language as such, that is, the separation 'at the surface' of words endowed with sense and noisy corporeal 'things'.

So it is clear that the events of the divided subject and of language both represent the event of the metaphysical surface for each and every subject, and themselves presuppose the metaphysical surface. We can thus say that the metaphysical surface is an event which is immanent to itself. Indeed, it was seen how the process of the phantasm, being essentially coextensive with the structural operations of the metaphysical surface, internally determines its own 'external' origin (castration). The metaphysical surface thus represents not only the evental-determination of the events characterizing things in general, but is itself an event.

Putting these technical details aside, let us now restate in point form Deleuze's philosophy of the event, such as this is presented in *The Logic of Sense*, in the most prosaic terms possible:

1. Events are what characterize things in general. Ontologically, relations between events of all types, orders, magnitudes and durations make the 'thing' what it is, whatever it is.

2. As human beings, we talk about events. The verbs of denoting propositions pick out events. Indeed, we come to know things through the way in which we combine, order, and so on, their constitutive events. We try to discover law-like relations between events, and we develop concepts which spell out what structure or combinations of events must characterize a particular thing in order for it to be a thing of a certain general type.

3. The process of combining and ordering events, of discovering law-like relations between things and creating general concepts for them, is itself an ongoing event which comes about in an intersubjective and linguistic context. This process is best described with reference to a complex and shifting structure of relations between events, wherein events of different types and at different levels are said to determine each other, and to determine things in general, and without reference to some already given thing which could fix this structure from the outside. Events are thus said to determine each other 'reciprocally' in so far as there is a homogeneous or law-like relation between the series of event-determined things they characterize. Events are said to determine each other 'completely'

in so far as the reason why a reciprocal determination of events holds for a particular, homogeneous series of event-determined things is said to be found in another such reciprocally determined series of event-determined things of a different 'type', either within the same 'order', or belonging to another such 'order' (physical, biological, social, psychological, linguistic, etc.). Finally, events are said to determine each other 'progressively' in so far as these relations between different series can never finally be reduced to some given 'thing' or static 'image' of the cosmic order of events, and so refer to an ongoing and creative process of varying the relations of reciprocal and complete determination between events, and thus transforming them. Events are thus perfectly individual and 'trope-like' in their characterization of things, but in so far as they may be determined and transformed in the above-mentioned ways, they must be held to be the purely differential elements of an entire, moving structure of events bearing on things.

4. To say that events are combined and ordered in an intersubjective and linguistic context – that is, in a structure which presupposes a shared language and culture – is not, however, to say that events are ultimately reducible to a pre-given language, or to a human subject understood as ultimately determinant. Rather, both language and the human subject are themselves event-determined things within this structure. The subject comes to be identified, and to identify itself, as being caught up in the structural process of combining and ordering events in intersubjective discourse only in so far as the events which characterize it in its worldly, social, psychological and linguistic relations can be determined to be of a socially appropriate type within the structure.[1] And language is determined by the way in which the speech-events of this subject, in so far as it is an identifiable subject of the structure, come to both make sense of, and be made sense of by, the speech-events of all the other subjects within the structure, where by 'speech-event' is meant a spoken or written proposition bearing on individuals, other persons, or other propositions.

5. The ongoing process of the reciprocal, complete and progressive determination of events thus constitutes the evental-determination of the events characterizing things in general, 'through and through' and 'all the way down'. It is this process or event which ultimately holds together all of the different series of events and event-determined things of different orders. Finally, it is the event which we human beings collectively bring about in discourse, but

also the event which ultimately determines us as the corporeal, social, speaking and knowing 'things' we are.

Armed with this summary, we can now consider several issues concerning *The Logic of Sense* as a whole and round out our examination of this work. In particular, we are now in a position to return to one of the issues raised in the Introduction, namely, the way in which the very form of the text of *The Logic of Sense* reflects the concept of 'structure' through which Deleuze thinks the ontological priority of events. Indeed, in the first place, the text is constructed, not in the form of chapters, but rather in the form of 'series' which, on the one hand, can be viewed as more or less self-contained examinations of various event-related problems and conceptual solutions. The propositions making up these studies are, of course, the 'terms' of the chapters-series. On the other hand, it is clear that each of these series comes to complement and 'complete' the others in various ways. Furthermore, as we move from one series to another, we find that the concepts developed in the earlier series, as well as the relations between them, are 'progressively' being modulated, that is, refined, re-described and even re-determined. Thus we saw, for example, how the early studies of what was called the Stoic 'sense-event' (initially found in Series 1–3, but then also in Series 20–21 and 23–24) were progressively completed, re-articulated and extended with reference to the series of studies devoted to the neo-Leibnizian static ontological and logical geneses (Series 16–17 and 24–25), as well as with reference to the concepts of structure, the problem, singularity and the divided subject (examined in Series 6, 8–9, 15 and 17). What is more, all these analyses were themselves completed in the later series dealing with the psychoanalytic, dynamic genesis of sense (Series 27–34). By calling the chapters of *The Logic of Sense* 'series', Deleuze is thus doing much more than paying lip-service to the structural concept of series analyzed therein. Indeed, it appears that we must understand Deleuze's philosophy of events, such as this was summarized above, as itself an 'event of thought' produced by the serial structure of his text.

In the second place, it should be noted that in so far as the series which form the text of *The Logic of Sense* can be said to function as a structure or underlying 'problem', the serialized propositions of this text (which are 'serially constitutive' of the family of concepts making up Deleuze's philosophy of events) must be understood to both condition this problem and generate its solutions, that is, in so far as these propositions both make sense of, and are made sense of by, this underlying problem. What is more, as has been shown, the series of studies forming the problematic structure of *The Logic of Sense* are run through and united by a 'paradoxical element' or 'fundamental question' which was formulated as: 'what are the evental conditions of the event if everything, including the very language in which events are ordered and related, is ultimately to be a well determined event?'

Finally, it should be noted that the family of concepts making up Deleuze's philosophy of events can also be said to emerge as an event within a 'process of triangulation' or 'disjunctive synthesis' in an intersubjective and linguistic context. Indeed, each of the philosophers or thinkers analyzed by Deleuze can be considered to be a 'person', 'divided subject' or 'thrower of the dice' in the above-examined technical senses of these terms. Within the structure of the text of *The Logic of Sense*, these persons all experience the question of the ontological priority of events 'all the way down' as a problem or imperative question and, correspondingly, their philosophies or systems of thought can be considered to be responses to this imperative question. Their philosophies are 'throws of the dice', as it were. On the one hand, they partially determine the conditions of the problem expressed throughout the series making up *The Logic of Sense*, and on the other hand, they generate the solutions to this problem. Or again, in other words, each person or thinker is caught up in a process of triangulation which brings about a three-fold determination of: the particular beliefs of each thinker with regard to the ontological priority of events over substances; a world of individuals which can be said to be common to their synthesized points of view (these individuals being understood at an abstract philosophical level to be determined by events 'all the way down'); and a system of concepts (divided subject, singularity, problem-structure, etc.) which characterizes this world of individuals as determined by events through and through, and these persons as philosophers of the event in this or that respect, or to this or that degree.[2] In sum, we can say that the series constitutive of the structure of *The Logic of Sense* are brought into communication – thereby allowing their elements to be reciprocally, completely and progressively determined – by a 'paradoxical element' which is nothing other than the fundamental question of the ontological priority of events over substances, and which is itself accompanied by a series of 'divided subjects' who actualize, in their own particular ways, the problematic structure this question envelops into determined individuals, persons and concepts (in so far as these are understood to be determined by events 'all the way down'). As Deleuze writes in the preface, 'to each series [of *The Logic of Sense*] there correspond figures which are not only historical but topological and logical as well. As on a pure surface, certain points of one figure in a series refer to the points of another figure: an entire galaxy of problems with their corresponding dice-throws, stories, and places, a complex place' (LS, xiv).

Now, however, the question arises: is Deleuze himself caught up in this process of triangulation? Is he, in other words, one of the philosopher-persons in relation to which the synthesis of the series of the text is carried out, or does he stage this synthesis, as it were, from the outside? As noted in the Introduction, this is one of the most difficult questions to address in Deleuze scholarship in general: who is speaking in Deleuze's work?

It is true that the concepts which form the core of Deleuze's philosophy of events – that is, of the problem (with its serial processes of determination), singularity and the divided subject – are unique to Deleuze. Although he develops these concepts in relation to Lautman's and Simondon's work, they are not identical to anything found in these latter works. Indeed, each of these thinkers' works only characterizes one particular aspect of the concept of the problem, and Deleuze's contribution is precisely to introduce certain original propositions with regard to the relations between Lautmanian 'problematic Ideas' and Simondonian processes of 'intensive individuation'. It was then seen that it is ultimately with reference to these propositions and the corresponding concepts of the problem, singularity and the divided subject that Deleuze constructs his neo-Leibnizian 'static geneses', which are themselves a re-description of the Stoic ongoing sense-event. It was also seen that it is in terms of these concepts that Deleuze develops his idiosyncratic version of structuralism. Finally, it is clear that the process of the phantasm, examined in relation to various psychoanalyst theorists, must be understood through the lens of these concepts.

At the same time, however, what makes Deleuze's own concepts so compelling is precisely the way in which they are expressed in the details of these other thinkers' works, that is, the way in which they appear to resolve the various problems each these thinkers faces when their works are forced to confront the question of the ontological priority of events. This forceful confrontation is what was called, in the Introduction, Deleuze's contingent, 'canon-forming reconstruction' of the history of philosophy around the problem of the event. Indeed, one of the fundamental aims of this work has been to examine the finer points of the ways in which Deleuze's affirmation of the ontological priority of events is expressed in the work of the historical figures and intellectual movements he examines in *The Logic of Sense*. By the same token, however, it is clear that Deleuze does not bring about this canon-forming reconstruction from outside, as it were. Rather, Deleuze's own thought is inseparable from the complex conversation analyzed throughout this present work.

We are thus confronted with a curious situation. Deleuze's concepts of the problem, singularity and the divided subject are his own, but they are also 'results', that is, conceptual events produced within the disjunctive synthesis of the series of analyses, propositions and philosophical points of view which make up the problematic structure of *The Logic of Sense*. This should, however, come as no surprise, for we know that differential problems such as the one formed by the text of *The Logic of Sense* are only ever internally determined by the adjunction and transformation of singularities-events (senses) corresponding to the values of the relations between the elements (propositions) making up the problem. In so far, then, as Deleuze's own propositions bearing on the concepts of the problem, singularity and the divided subject 'make sense of' the propositions in which the rest of the intersubjective, problematic structure of *The Logic of Sense* is expressed, these concepts can be said to be his own creation. But at the same time, in so far as these propositions are 'made sense of by' their underlying problematic structure, Deleuze's creative activity must also be said to be the result of the particular way in which he 'accompanies' the imperative question of the ontological priority of events (paradoxical element) such as this circulates between the intellectual figures and series which make up *The Logic of Sense*.

So who is speaking in *The Logic of Sense*? It has been said that the diverse propositions bearing on Deleuze's concepts of the problem, singularity and the divided subject collectively 'make sense of', as much as they are 'made sense of by', the rest of the propositions forming the intersubjective and problematic structure of the text itself. Though the sense (or sense-event) of these propositions is produced in such an intersubjective context, this should nevertheless not prevent us from being able to separate out which philosophical propositions are attributable to which thinker. As has been argued, the sense which insists in propositions is irreducible to the dimension of personal manifestation, but at the same time, sense does not exist outside of the way in which the particular personal beliefs manifested in these propositions can be determined in a process of triangulation. This is the reason why some effort has been taken, throughout this work, to analyze precisely which thinker says what, and to prevent the collapse of the distinctions characterizing each thinker's specific point of view on a world in which events have ontological priority over substances 'all the way down'.

But now, does this mean that Deleuze's philosophy of events – built, as it is, on 'points of view only on other points of view' or the 'affirmation of difference' – is always-already open to further transformations? This conclusion is inescapable. Indeed, it is tempting to read Deleuze's subsequent works as carrying out such transformations, in other contexts, guided by different questions, and in relation to other thinkers, be they philosophers, scientists or artists. Perhaps the way in which certain concepts from *The Logic of Sense* – the 'body without organs', for example, but also 'intensity' and 'multiplicity' – are taken up again in apparently altered forms in *Anti-Oedipus* and *A Thousand Plateaus* can be seen as an indication of this ongoing determination of the sense-event. In fact, one has the impression that Deleuze's concepts are always produced in a complex relation with the many different thinkers with whom he deals. Is this to say, then, that Deleuze continues to use the serial or structural 'method' devised in *The Logic of Sense* in his subsequent works? Such a conclusion would perhaps be too hastily drawn, for even though all of Deleuze's works appear to take the form of a productive but complex 'conversation', 'method' is clearly, and often, one of the topics of this conversation: the method of 'plateaus that communicate with one another across microfissures', for example, developed in relation to the work of the anthropologist Gregory Bateson in *A Thousand Plateaus*.[3] Or again, the philosophical method outlined in *What is Philosophy?*, couched in terms of 'concepts', 'planes of immanence' and 'conceptual personae', and produced in relation to the work of François Laruelle and Etienne Souriau, among others.[4]

A number of questions now follow from this line of reasoning: How can we account for these differences in Deleuze's concepts and method from one text to another? Does Deleuze abruptly change his concepts and method, or, more subtly, are they transformed and modulated by his entering into different conversations, with different thinkers and different sets of problems and questions? And finally, if we agree with the latter position, with reference to which set of concepts and which method, developed in which of Deleuze's works, should we understand such transformations and modulations? If questions such as these cannot be answered with any definiteness, perhaps we should rather argue that there is in fact no 'master text' in Deleuze's oeuvre, that is, no privileged conversation or set of thinkers through whose work we could come to understand the 'real Deleuze'. Indeed, if this is case, there is no justifiable reason why *The Logic of Sense* has for so long been neglected in the secondary literature. In particular, there is no good reason why, as noted in the Introduction, the structuralist and psychoanalytic Deleuze should be overlooked in favour of Deleuze the vitalist, the philosopher of difference, of becomings and of haecceities. It is in fact hoped that this present work will be seen, not only as a contribution to the secondary literature on Deleuze, but also as a work aimed at liberating Deleuze's thought, in some small way, from these latter, overly restrictive images.

But now, leaving to one side this problem of the relation between *The Logic of Sense* and the rest of Deleuze's philosophical oeuvre, we must ask ourselves: with what other philosophies, and with which other thinkers, can we bring Deleuze's 1969 philosophy of events into relation and thereby produce something new? What original propositions can we ourselves bring to such a synthesis? It was suggested in the Introduction that contemporary interest in events is manifested in the work of continental European philosophers as diverse as Alain Badiou, Michel Serres, Bruno Latour and Bernard Stiegler, as well as in the work of various Anglo-American philosophers such as Donald Davidson, Jaegwon Kim, Jonathan Bennett and Nicholas Rescher. It is certain that, with the present clarification of his philosophy of events in hand, Deleuze could be brought into a productive dialogue with these thinkers. However, it is also the case that, armed with the above understanding of events, Deleuze could also be productively exposed to the criticisms of those philosophers who defend substance-based ontologies, or even called upon to shed a new light on some of the contentious issues to be found in such approaches. Finally, even beyond these metaphysical issues, several studies have already shown how Deleuze's philosophy of events can be brought into a fruitful conversation with political and aesthetic thought.[5]

This work is not, however, the place to examine these further connections. The aim here has been the rather more modest one of explicating the precise way in which Deleuze thinks the ontological priority of events. In so far as Deleuze's philosophy of events has been read in relation to its sources, this present study can be considered to be a work in the history of philosophy. In so far as it has been devoted to elucidating the oft-neglected *Logic of Sense*, this book is a contribution to the secondary literature surrounding Deleuze's philosophy. Finally, in so far as I have managed to give a clear statement of how Deleuze understands the ontological primacy of events, I have, it is hoped, opened the way for the kinds of dialogues mentioned above. The different directions in which the present work can be taken are, however, like all events, highly uncertain. And yet we can at least make the following observation. Because Deleuze's philosophy of events is always-already open to further transformations, both within philosophy and external to philosophy, if we are to remain faithful the Deleuzian event, there is no choice for the future but to go beyond Deleuze. But then the question remains: will this very event of 'going beyond' remain Deleuzian? We would have to reply, paradoxically: it will if it does not, and will not if it does.

Notes

1. This is not, of course, to say that a subject, in order to be a discoursing and knowing subject, must be recognized as possessing certain necessary or essential qualities. It is rather to say that different subjects may enter into 'processes of triangulation' only in so far as they recognize each other as possessing something minimally, if contingently, 'in common', which would allow for the mutual translation and determination of their respective beliefs about worldly things. In other words, a minimal criterion for a process of triangulation is that there must be some recognizable perceptual, social and linguistic 'overlap', however small, between the subjects who collectively carry out such a process. This 'overlap' is not pre-given, but is determined within the process of triangulation precisely to the extent that this latter 'works', that is to say, manages to bring about a three-fold determination: of the beliefs of the subjects involved, of a world of 'things' common to these subjects' different points of view, and of a set of concepts characterizing these things. To translate this argument back into Deleuzian terms, we can say that the 'psychoanalytic' events of the divided subject and of language make processes of triangulation possible (in so far as these processes take place on the structural-symbolic metaphysical surface), as much as these processes of triangulation make the evental-determination of the subject and language possible within the process of the phantasm (which is developed over the entire metaphysical surface).

2. Of course, the Stoics and Leibniz are not, strictly speaking, philosophers

of the event, since they affirm the existence of an underlying substance to which the play of events is reducible. Nevertheless, it is precisely from the point of view of the philosophy of events generated by the structure of *The Logic of Sense* as a whole that their 'philosophical beliefs' can be said to have gone a long way towards, but without finally reaching the point of, establishing the ontological priority of events over substances.

3. Gilles Deleuze and Félix Guattari, *A Thousand Plateaus*, trans. Brian Massumi (London: Athlone Press, 1987), p. 22.

4. Gilles Deleuze and Félix Guattari, *What is Philosophy?* trans. Hugh Tomlinson and Graham Burchill (London and New York: Verso, 1994).

5. Paul Patton in particular has already brought a number of Deleuze's formulations with regard to events into a productive relation with various ideas to be found in political philosophy. See his *Deleuze and the Political* (London and New York: Routledge, 2000) and 'The Event of Colonization', in Ian Buchanan and Adrian Parr (eds), *Deleuze and the Contemporary World* (Edinburgh: Edinburgh University Press, 2006), pp. 108–24.

Bibliography

Alunni, Charles, 'Continental Genealogies: Mathematical Confrontations in Albert Lautman and Gaston Bachelard', in Simon Duffy (ed.), *Virtual Mathematics: The Logic of Difference* (Manchester: Clinamen, 2006), pp. 65–99.

Arnim, Herman von, *Stoicorum Veterum Fragmenta*, 3 Volumes (Leipzig: Teubner, 1903–1905).

Ashby, W. Ross, *An Introduction to Cybernetics* (London: Chapman & Hall Ltd, 1957).

Aspe, Barnard and Muriel Combes, 'L'acte fou', *Multitudes* 18 (2004), http://multitudes.samizdat.net/L-acte-fou

Aurelius, Marcus, *Meditations*, trans. A.D.L. Farquharson (Oxford: Oxford University Press, 1944).

Bacon, John, *Universals and Property Instances* (Oxford and Cambridge: Blackwell, 1995).

Badiou, Alain, 'G. Deleuze, Leibniz: Le Pli et le baroque', *Annuaire philosophique 1988–1989* (Paris: Seuil, 1989), pp. 161–84.

Badiou, Alain, *Being and Event*, trans. Oliver Feltham (London and New York: Continuum, 2005).

Badiou, Alain, *Logics of Worlds: Being and Event II*, trans. Alberto Toscano (London and New York: Continuum, 2009).

Baker, Lang, 'The Cry of the Identicals: The Problem of Inclusion in Deleuze's Reading of Leibniz', *Philosophy Today* 39: 2 (1995), pp. 198–211.

Barnes, Jonathan, *Early Greek Philosophy* (London: Penguin, 2001).

Barrow-Green, June, *Poincaré and the Three Body Problem* (Rhode Island: The American Mathematical Society, 1997).

Barthélemy, Jean-Hugues, *Penser L'individuation: Simondon et la philosophie de la nature* (Paris: L'Harmattan, 2005).

Barthélemy, Jean-Hugues, *Simondon ou l'encyclopédisme génétique* (Paris: PUF, 2008).

Battye, Adrian and Marie-Anne Hintze, *The French Language Today* (London: Routledge, 1992).

Beaney, Michael, 'Introduction', in Michael Beaney (ed.), *The Frege Reader* (Oxford: Blackwell Publishers, 1997), pp. 1–46.

Bibliography

Benveniste, Émile, *Problems in General Linguistics*, trans. Mary Elizabeth Smith (Coral Gables, FL: University of Miami Press, 1971).

Berri, André, 'Aspects phonétiques et phonologiques du E-muet du français', *Revista Fragmentos* 30 (2006), pp. 199–217.

Bobzien, Susanne, 'Logic', in Brad Inwood (ed.), *The Cambridge Companion to the Stoics* (Cambridge: Cambridge University Press, 2003), pp. 85–123.

Bordas-Demoulin, Jean, *Le Cartésianisme ou la véritable rénovation des sciences* (Paris: Hetzel, 1843).

Bouquiaux, Laurence, 'La notion de *point de vue* dans l'élaboration de la métaphysique leibnizienne', in Benoît Timmermans (ed.), *Perspective Leibniz, Whitehead, Deleuze* (Paris: Vrin, 2006), pp. 23–54.

Bowden, Sean, 'Deleuze et les Stoïciens: une logique de l'événement', *Le Bulletin de la société américaine de philosophie de langue française* 15: 1 (2005), pp. 72–97.

Bowden, Sean, 'Deleuze, Leibniz and the Jurisprudence of Being', *Pli (The Warwick Journal of Philosophy)* 17 (2006), pp. 98–120.

Boyer, Carl B., *The History of the Calculus and its Conceptual Development* (New York: Dover, 1959).

Bréhier, Émile, *La théorie des incorporels dans l'ancien stoïcisme* (Paris: Vrin, 1928).

Brun, Jean, *Le stoïcisme* (Paris: PUF, 1958).

Brunschwig, Jacques, 'Le modèle conjonctif', in *Études sur les philosophies hellénistiques: Épicurisme, stoïcisme, scepticisme* (Paris: PUF, 1995), pp. 161–88.

Campbell, Keith, *Abstract Particulars* (Oxford and Cambridge: Blackwell, 1990).

Caper, Robert, *Immaterial Facts: Freud's Discovery of Psychic Reality and Klein's Development of his Work* (London and New York: Routledge, 2000).

Carnap, Rudolf, *Meaning and Necessity: A Study in Semantics and Modal Logic* (Chicago and London: University of Chicago Press, 1947).

Carroll, Lewis, 'What the Tortoise said to Achilles', *Mind* 4: 14 (1895), pp. 278–80.

Casati, Roberto and Achille Varzi, 'Events', in Edward N. Zalta (ed.), *The Stanford Encyclopedia of Philosophy* (Summer 2006 Edition), http://plato.stanford.edu/archives/sum2006/entries/events

Chabot, Pascal, 'L'encyclopédie idéale de Simondon', in Jacques Roux (ed.), *Gilbert Simondon: une pensée opérative* (Saint-Etienne: Publications de l'Université de Saint-Etienne, 2002), pp. 149–61.

Châtelet, François (ed.), *Histoire de la philosophie vol. VIII: le XXe siècle* (Paris: Hachette, 1972).

Chevalley, Catherine, 'Albert Lautman et le souci logique', *Revue d'histoire des sciences* 40: 1 (1987), pp. 49–77.

Chiesa, Lorenzo, *Subjectivity and Otherness: A Philosophical Reading of Lacan* (Cambridge and London: The MIT Press, 2007).

Combes, Muriel, *Simondon: Individu et collectivité* (Paris: PUF, 1999).

Cottet, Serge, 'Les machines psychanalytiques de Gilles Deleuze', *La cause freudienne – Revue de psychanalyse* 32 (1996), pp. 15–19.

Davidson, Donald, 'Three Varieties of Knowledge', in *Subjective, Intersubjective, Objective* (Oxford: Clarendon Press, 2001), pp. 205–37.

Debaise, Didier, 'Les conditions d'une pensée de la relation selon Simondon', in Pascal Chabot (ed.), *Simondon* (Paris: Vrin, 2002), pp. 53–68.

Debaise, Didier, 'Le langage de l'individuation', *Multitudes* 18 (2004), http://multitudes.samizdat.net/Le-langage-de-l-individuation

Debaise, Didier, 'Qu'est-ce qu'une pensée relationnelle?' *Multitudes* 18 (2004), http://multitudes.samizdat.net/Qu-est-ce-qu-une-pensee

DeLanda, Manuel, *Intensive Science and Virtual Philosophy* (London and New York: Continuum, 2002).

Deleuze, Gilles, *The Logic of Sense*, trans. Mark Lester with Charles Stivale, ed. Constantin V. Boundas (New York: Colombia University Press, 1990).

Deleuze, Gilles, *Expressionism in Philosophy: Spinoza*, trans. Martin Joughin (New York: Zone Books, 1990).

Deleuze, Gilles, *The Fold: Leibniz and the Baroque*, trans. Tom Conley (London: Athlone Press, 1993).

Deleuze, Gilles, *Difference and Repetition*, trans. Paul Patton (London: Athlone Press, 1994).

Deleuze, Gilles, *Negotiations 1972–1990*, trans. Martin Joughin (New York: Columbia University Press, 1995).

Deleuze, Gilles, 'On Gilbert Simondon', in *Desert Islands and Other Texts 1953–1974*, trans. Michael Taormina, ed. David Lapoujade (New York: Semiotexte, 2004), pp. 86–9.

Deleuze, Gilles, 'How do We Recognize Structuralism?' in *Desert Islands and Other Texts 1953–1974*, trans. Michael Taormina, ed. David Lapoujade (New York: Semiotexte, 2004), pp. 170–92.

Deleuze, Gilles, 'The Method of Dramatization', in *Desert Islands and Other Texts 1953–1974*, trans. Michael Taormina, ed. David Lapoujade (New York: Semiotexte, 2004), pp. 94–116.

Deleuze, Gilles, 'Note for the Italian Edition of The Logic of Sense', in *Two Regimes of Madness*, trans. Ames Hodges and Mike Taormina, ed. David Lapoujade (New York: Semiotexte, 2006), pp. 63–6.

Deleuze, Gilles and Félix Guattari, *A Thousand Plateaus*, trans. Brian Massumi (London: Athlone Press, 1987).

Deleuze, Gilles and Félix Guattari, *What is Philosophy?*, trans. Hugh Tomlinson and Graham Burchell (London and New York: Verso, 1994).

Dosse, François, *Gilles Deleuze et Félix Guattari: Biographie Croisée* (Paris: La Découverte, 2007).

Bibliography

Duffy, Simon, 'Schizo-Math: The Logic of Different/ciation and the Philosophy of Difference', *Angelaki* 9: 3 (2004), pp. 199–215.

Duffy, Simon, *The Logic of Expression: Quality, Quantity and Intensity in Spinoza, Hegel and Deleuze* (Aldershot: Ashgate, 2006).

Duffy, Simon, 'The Mathematics of Deleuze's Differential Logic and Metaphysics', in Simon Duffy (ed.), *Virtual Mathematics: The Logic of Difference* (Manchester: Clinamen, 2006), pp. 118–44.

Duffy, Simon, 'Albert Lautman', in Graham Jones and Jon Roffe (eds), *Deleuze's Philosophical Lineage* (Edinburgh: Edinburgh University Press, 2009), pp. 356–79.

Duffy, Simon, 'Leibniz, Mathematics and the Monad', in Niamh McDonnell and Sjoerd van Tuinen (eds), *Deleuze and The Fold: A Critical Reader* (Hampshire: Palgrave Macmillan, 2010), pp. 89–111.

Duhot, Jean-Joël, *La conception stoïcienne de la causalité* (Paris: Vrin, 1989).

During, Elie, 'Leibniz selon Deleuze: une folle création de concepts', *Magazine Littéraire* 416 (2003), pp. 36–7.

Evans, Dylan, *An Introductory Dictionary of Lacanian Psychoanalysis* (London and New York: Routledge, 1996).

Evens, Aden, 'Math Anxiety', *Angelaki* 5: 3 (2000), pp. 105–15.

Fink, Bruce, *A Clinical Introduction to Lacanian Psychoanalysis: Theory and Technique* (Cambridge and London: Harvard University Press, 1997).

Foucault, Michel, 'Theatrum Philosophicum', in *Language, Counter-Memory, Practice*, trans. Donald F. Bouchard and Sherry Simon, ed. Donald F. Bouchard (Oxford: Basil Blackwell, 1977), pp. 165–96.

Frede, Michael, 'The Original Notion of Cause', in *Essays in Ancient Philosophy* (Minneapolis: University of Minnesota Press, 1987), pp. 125–50.

Frede, Michael, 'Stoic Epistemology', in Keimpe Algra, Jonathan Barnes, Jaap Mansfeld and Malcolm Schofield (eds), *The Cambridge History of Hellenistic Philosophy* (Cambridge: Cambridge University Press, 1999), pp. 295–322.

Frege, Gottlob, 'Comments on *Sinn* and *Bedeutung* [1892]', in *The Frege Reader*, ed. Michael Beaney (Oxford: Blackwell Publishers, 1997), pp. 172–80.

Frege, Gottlob, 'On *Sinn* and *Bedeutung* [1892]', in *The Frege Reader*, ed. Michael Beaney (Oxford: Blackwell Publishers, 1997), pp. 151–71.

Frémont, Christiane, 'Complication et Singularité', *Revue de métaphysique et de morale* 1 (1991), pp. 105–20.

Frémont, Christiane, *Singularités, individus et relations dans le système de Leibniz* (Paris: Vrin, 2003).

Freud, Sigmund, *The Standard Edition of the Complete Psychological Works of Sigmund Freud*, 24 Volumes, trans. and ed. James Strachey, in collaboration with Anna Freud and assisted by Alix Strachey and Alan Tyson (London: The Hogarth Press, 1953–74).

Gareli, Jacques, 'Transduction et information', in Gilles Châtelet (ed.), *Gilbert Simondon: une pensée de l'individuation et de la technique* (Paris: Albin Michel, 1994), pp. 55–68.

Goldschmidt, Victor, *Le système stoïcien et l'idée du temps* (Paris: Vrin, 1953).

Grosholz, Emily R., 'Studies for the Infinitesimal Calculus', in *Representation and Productive Ambiguity in Mathematics and the Sciences* (Oxford: Oxford University Press, 2007), pp. 207–12.

Gualandi, Alberto, *Deleuze* (Paris: Les Belles Lettres, 1998).

Guillaume, Gustave, *Temps et Verbe* (Paris: Champion, 1929).

Hardt, Michael, *Gilles Deleuze: An Apprenticeship in Philosophy* (Minneapolis: University of Minnesota Press, 1993).

Heimann, Paula, 'Certain Functions of Introjection and Projection in Early Infancy', in Joan Riviere (ed.), *Developments in Psycho-Analysis* (London: The Hogarth Press, 1952), pp. 122–68.

Heylighen, Francis and Cliff Joslyn, 'Cybernetics and Second-Order Cybernetics', in R.A. Meyers (ed.), *Encyclopedia of Physical Science and Technology*, 3rd Edition (New York: Academic Press, 2001), pp. 1–23.

Hinshelwood, R.D., *A Dictionary Of Kleinian Thought* (London: Free Association Books, 1991).

Homer, Sean, *Jacques Lacan* (London: Routledge, 2004).

Hottois, Gilbert, *Simondon et la philosophie de la 'culture technique'* (Bruxelles: De Boeck, 1993).

Hughes, Joe, *Deleuze and the Genesis of Representation* (London and New York: Continuum, 2008).

Hyppolite, Jean, 'A Spoken Commentary on Freud's "Verneinung"', in Jacques Lacan, *Écrits*, trans. Bruce Fink (New York and London: W.W. Norton & Company, 2006), pp. 746–54.

Ildefonce, Frédérique, *Les Stoïciens I: Zénon, Cléanthe, Chrysippse* (Paris: Les Belles Lettres, 2000).

Inwood, Brad, *The Poem of Empedocles: A Text and Translation* (Toronto: University of Toronto Press, 1992).

Inwood, Brad and L.P. Gerson, *Hellenistic Philosophy: Introductory Readings*, 2nd Edition (Indianapolis and Cambridge: Hackett Publishing Company, 1997).

Isaacs, Susan, 'The Nature and Function of Phantasy', in Joan Riviere (ed.), *Developments in Psycho-Analysis* (London: The Hogarth Press, 1952), pp. 67–121.

Jakobson, Roman, 'Phoneme and Phonology', in *Selected Writings I: Phonological Studies*, ed. Stephen Rudy (The Hague: Mouton & Co., 1962), pp. 231–3.

Jakobson, Roman, 'Remarques sur l'évolution phonologique du russe', in

Bibliography

Selected Writings I: Phonological Studies, ed. Stephen Rudy (The Hague: Mouton & Co., 1962), pp. 7–116.

Jakobson, Roman and J. Lotz, 'Notes on the French Phonemic Pattern', in *Selected Writings I: Phonological Studies*, ed. Stephen Rudy (The Hague: Mouton & Co., 1962), pp. 426–34.

Jakobson, Roman and Linda Waugh, *The Sound Shape of Language* (New York: Mouton, 1987).

Jakobson, Roman and Morris Halle, *Fundamentals of Language* (The Hague: Mouton & Co., 1956).

Kant, Immanuel, 'What is Orientation in Thinking?' in *Kant: Political Writings*, trans. H.B. Nisbet, ed. H.S. Reiss (Cambridge: Cambridge University Press, 1991), pp. 237–49.

Klein, Melanie, 'On Observing the Behavior of Young Infants', in Joan Riviere (ed.), *Developments in Psycho-Analysis* (London: The Hogarth Press, 1952), pp. 237–70.

Klein, Melanie, 'Notes on Some Schizoid Mechanisms', in Joan Riviere (ed.), *Developments in Psycho-Analysis* (London: The Hogarth Press, 1952), pp. 292–320.

Klein, Melanie, 'Some Theoretical Conclusions Regarding the Emotional Life of the Infant', in Joan Riviere (ed.), *Developments in Psycho-Analysis* (London: The Hogarth Press, 1952), pp. 198–236.

Klein, Melanie, *Love, Guilt and Reparation and Other Works 1921–1945* (London: The Hogarth Press, 1975).

Klein, Melanie, *The Psycho-Analysis of Children: The Writings of Melanie Klein, Volume I*, trans. Alix Strachey and H.A. Thorner (London: The Hogarth Press, 1986).

Kline, Morris, *Mathematical Thought from Ancient to Modern Times* (New York: Oxford University Press, 1972).

Lacan, Jacques, 'La relation d'objet et les structures freudiennes', *Bulletin de Psychologie* 10: 7 (1956–7), pp. 426–30; 10: 10 (1956–7), pp. 602–5; 10: 12 (1956–7), pp. 742–3; 10: 14 (1956–7), pp. 851–4; 11: 1 (1956–7), pp. 31–5.

Lacan, Jacques, 'Les formations de l'inconscient', *Bulletin de Psychologie* 11: 4–5 (1957–8), pp. 293–6; 12: 2–3 (1958–9), pp. 182–92; 12: 4 (1958–9), pp. 250–6.

Lacan, Jacques, 'Le Désir et son interprétation', *Bulletin de Psychologie* 13 (1959–60), pp. 329–35.

Lacan, Jacques, *The Seminar, Book III: The Psychoses, 1955–1956*, trans. Russell Grigg (New York: W.W. Norton, 1993).

Lacan, Jacques, *Le séminaire livre IV: La relation d'objet, 1956–1957* (Paris: Seuil, 1994).

Lacan, Jacques, *Le séminaire livre V: Les formations de l'inconscient, 1957–1958* (Paris: Seuil, 1998).

Lacan, Jacques, 'Les complexes familiaux dans la formation de l'individu

– Essai d'analyse d'une fonction en psychologie', in *Autres Écrits* (Paris: Seuil, 2001).

Lacan, Jacques, *Écrits*, trans. Bruce Fink (New York and London: W.W. Norton & Company, 2006).

Ladrière, Jean, 'Préface', in Anne Crahay, *Michel Serres: La mutation du cogito* (Bruxelles: De Boeck, 1988).

Laplanche, Jean and Jean-Bertrand Pontalis, *The Language of Psycho-Analysis*, trans. Donald Nicholson-Smith (New York: Norton, 1973).

Laplanche, Jean and Jean-Bertrand Pontalis, 'Fantasy and the Origins of Sexuality', in Victor Burgin, James Donald and Cora Kaplan (eds), *Formations of Fantasy* (London and New York: Methuen, 1986), pp. 5–34.

Lautman, Albert, *Les mathématiques, les idées et le réel physique* (Paris: Vrin, 2006).

Lawlor, Leonard, *Thinking Through French Philosophy: The Being of the Question* (Bloomington and Indianapolis: Indiana University Press, 2003).

Lecercle, Jean-Jacques, *Philosophy Through the Looking-Glass: Language, Nonsense, Desire* (La Salle: Open Court, 1985).

Lecercle, Jean-Jacques, *Deleuze and Language* (Basingstoke: Palgrave Macmillan, 2002).

Lecercle, Jean-Jacques, 'Preface', in James Williams, *Gilles Deleuze's* Logic of Sense: *A Critical Introduction and Guide* (Edinburgh: Edinburgh University Press, 2008), pp. vii–viii.

Leclaire, Serge, *Psychoanalyzing: On the Order of the Unconscious and the Practice of the Letter*, trans. Peggy Kamuf (Stanford: Stanford University Press, 1998).

Leibniz, G.W., *Die philosophischen Schriften von G.W. Leibniz*, 7 Volumes, ed. C.I. Gerhardt (Berlin: Weidmann, 1850–1863).

Leibniz, G.W., *Textes inédits d'après de la bibliothèque provinciale de Hanover*, 2 Volumes, trans. and ed. Gaston Grua (Paris: PUF, 1948).

Leibniz, G.W., *Leibniz: Selections*, ed. Philip P. Wiener (New York: Charles Scribner's Sons, 1951).

Leibniz, G.W., *Theodicy: Essays on the Goodness of God, the Freedom of Man and the Origin of Evil*, trans. E.M. Huggard (London: Routledge and Kegan Paul, 1951).

Leibniz, G.W., *Opuscules et fragments inédits de Leibniz*, ed. Louis Couturat (Hildesheim: Georg Olms, 1961).

Leibniz, G.W., *Leibniz: Logical Papers*, trans. and ed. G.H.R. Parkinson (Oxford: Clarendon Press, 1966).

Leibniz, G.W., *Gottfried Wilhelm Leibniz: Philosophical Papers and Letters*, trans. and ed. Leroy E. Loemker (Dordrecht: D. Reidel Publishing, 1969).

Leibniz, G.W., *Leibniz: Philosophical Writings*, trans. Mary Morris and

Bibliography

G.H.R. Parkinson, ed. G.H.R. Parkinson (London and Toronto: J.M. Dent and Sons, 1973).

Leibniz, G.W., *G.W. Leibniz: Philosophical Essays*, trans. and ed. Roger Ariew and Daniel Garber (Indianapolis and Cambridge: Hackett Publishing Company, 1989).

Leibniz, G.W., *New Essays on Human Understanding*, trans. and ed. Peter Remnant and Jonathan Bennett (Cambridge: Cambridge University Press, 1996).

Lévi-Strauss, Claude, 'Réponses à quelques questions', *Esprit* 33: 11 (1963), pp. 628–53.

Lévi-Strauss, Claude, *Structural Anthropology I*, trans. Claire Jacobson and Brooke Grundfest Schoepf (New York: Basic Books, 1963).

Lévi-Strauss, Claude, *Totemism*, trans. Rodney Needham (London: Merlin Press, 1964).

Lévi-Strauss, Claude, *Introduction to the Work of Marcel Mauss*, trans. Felicity Baker (London: Routledge and Kegan Paul, 1987).

Lombard, Lawrence Brian, 'Ontologies of Events', in Stephen Laurence and Cynthia Macdonald (eds), *Contemporary Readings in the Foundations of Metaphysics* (Oxford: Blackwell Publishers, 1998), pp. 277–94.

Long, A.A. and D.N. Sedley, *The Hellenistic Philosophers: Volume 1: Translations of the Principal Sources, with Philosophical Commentary* (Cambridge: Cambridge University Press, 1987).

Macdonald, Cynthia, 'Tropes and Other Things', in Stephen Laurance and Cynthia Macdonald (eds), *Contemporary Readings in the Foundations of Metaphysics* (Oxford: Blackwell, 1998), pp. 329–50.

McDonnell, Niamh and van Tuinen Sjoerd (eds), *Deleuze and The Fold: A Critical Reader* (Hampshire: Palgrave Macmillan, 2010).

Mates, Benson, *Stoic Logic* (Berkeley and Los Angeles: University of California Press, 1961).

Mates, Benson, *The Philosophy of Leibniz: Metaphysics and Language* (Oxford: Oxford University Press, 1986).

May, Todd, *Gilles Deleuze: An Introduction* (Cambridge: Cambridge University Press, 2005).

Mitchell, Juliet, 'Introduction to Melanie Klein', in Lyndsey Stonebridge and John Phillips (eds), *Reading Melanie Klein* (London and New York: Routledge, 1998), pp. 11–30.

Patton, Paul, 'Introduction', in Paul Patton (ed.), *Deleuze: A Critical Reader* (Oxford: Blackwell, 1996), pp. 1–17.

Patton, Paul, *Deleuze and the Political* (London and New York: Routledge, 2000).

Patton, Paul, 'The Event of Colonization', in Ian Buchanan and Adrian Parr (eds), *Deleuze and the Contemporary World* (Edinburgh: Edinburgh University Press, 2006), pp. 108–24.

Perron, Roger, 'Idea/Representation', in Alain de Mijolla (ed.),

International Dictionary of Psychoanalysis (Detroit: Thomson Gale, 2005), pp. 780–3.

Petitot, Jean, *Morphogenèse du sens* (Paris: PUF, 1985).

Petitot, Jean, 'Refaire le "Timée" – Introduction à la philosophie mathématique d'Albert Lautman', *Revue d'histoire des sciences* 40: 1 (1987), pp. 79–115.

Pierce, John R., *An Introduction to Information Theory: Symbols, Signals and Noise*, 2nd edn (New York: Dover, 1980).

Plato, *The Collected Dialogues*, ed. E. Hamilton and H. Cairns (Princeton: Princeton University Press, 1961).

Plotnitsky, Arkady, 'Manifolds: On the Concept of Space in Riemann and Deleuze', in Simon Duffy (ed.), *Virtual Mathematics: The Logic of Difference* (Manchester: Clinamen, 2006), pp. 187–208.

Pujol, Robert, 'Approche théorique du fantasme', *La Psychanalyse* 8 (1964), pp. 11–46.

Redding, Paul, *Continental Idealism: Leibniz to Nietzsche* (London: Routledge, 2009).

Rescher, Nicholas, *The Philosophy of Leibniz* (Englewood Cliffs, NJ: Prentice-Hall, 1967).

Rescher, Nicholas, *Leibniz, An Introduction to his Philosophy* (Oxford: Basil Blackwell, 1979).

Rescher, Nicholas, *Process Metaphysics: An Introduction to Process Philosophy* (New York: SUNY, 1996).

Robinson, Keith, 'Events of Difference: The Fold in Between Deleuze's Reading of Leibniz', *Epoché* 8: 1 (2003), pp. 141–64.

Rorty, Richard, 'The Historiography of Philosophy', in *Truth and Progress: Philosophical Papers, Volume 3* (Cambridge: Cambridge University Press, 1998), pp. 247–73.

Roudinesco, Elisabeth, *Jacques Lacan & Co.: A History of Psychoanalysis in France, 1925–1985*, trans. Jeffrey Mehlman (Chicago: University of Chicago Press, 1990).

Russell, Bertrand, *The Principles of Mathematics* (Cambridge: Cambridge University Press, 1903).

Russell, Bertrand, *An Inquiry into Meaning and Truth* (Harmondsworth: Penguin, 1962).

Salanskis, Jean-Michel, 'Idea and Destination', in Paul Patton (ed.), *Deleuze: A Critical Reader* (Oxford: Blackwell, 1996), pp. 57–80.

Salanskis, Jean-Michel, 'Pour une épistémologie de la lecture', *Alliage* 35–36 (1998), http://www.tribunes.com/tribune/alliage/accueil.htm

Salanskis, Jean-Michel, 'Mathematics, Metaphysics, Philosophy', in Simon Duffy (ed.), *Virtual Mathematics: The Logic of Difference* (Manchester: Clinamen, 2006), pp. 46–64.

Saussure, Ferdinand de, *Course in General Linguistics*, trans. Wade Baskin (New York: McGraw-Hill, 1959).

Sayre, Kenneth M., *Cybernetics and the Philosophy of Mind* (London: Routledge, 1976).

Segal, Hanna, *Introduction to the Work of Melanie Klein* (London: Karnac Books, 1988).

Segal, Hanna, *Klein* (London: Karnac, 1989).

Segal, Julia, *Melanie Klein*, 2nd Edition (London: Sage, 2004).

Sellars, John, 'An Ethics of the Event: Deleuze's Stoicism', *Angelaki* 11: 3 (2006), pp. 157–71.

Sellars, John, *Stoicism* (Berkeley and Los Angeles: University of California Press, 2006).

Seneca, *Letters from a Roman Stoic*, trans. Robin Campbell (London: Penguin, 1969).

Sharpe, Matthew and Joanne Faulkner, *Understanding Psychoanalysis* (Stocksfield: Acumen, 2008).

Simondon, Gilbert, *L'individuation à la lumière des notions de forme et d'information* (Grenoble: Millon, 2005).

Smith, Daniel W., 'Mathematics and the Theory of Multiplicities', *The Southern Journal of Philosophy* 45: 3 (2003), pp. 411–49.

Smith, Daniel W., 'Axiomatics and Problematics as Two Modes of Formalization: Deleuze's Epistemology of Mathematics', in Simon Duffy (ed.), *Virtual Mathematics: The Logic of Difference* (Manchester: Clinamen, 2006), pp. 145–68.

Smith, Daniel W., 'The Conditions of the New', *Deleuze Studies* 1: 1 (2007), pp. 1–21.

Stengers, Isabelle, 'Pour une mise à l'aventure de la transduction', in Pascal Chabot (ed.), *Simondon* (Paris: Vrin, 2002), pp. 137–59.

Stewart, Ian and Martin Golubitsky, *Fearful Symmetry* (Oxford: Blackwell, 1992).

Williams, Donald C., 'On the Elements of Being', *Review of Metaphysics* 7 (1953–1954), pp. 3–18 and pp. 171–92.

Williams, James, *Gilles Deleuze's* Difference and Repetition: *A Critical Introduction and Guide* (Edinburgh: Edinburgh University Press, 2003).

Williams, James, *Gilles Deleuze's* Logic of Sense: *A Critical Introduction and Guide* (Edinburgh: Edinburgh University Press, 2008).

Žižek, Slavoj, *Organs without Bodies: On Deleuze and Consequences* (New York: Routledge, 2004).

Zourabichvili, François, *Deleuze: Une philosophie de l'événement* (Paris: PUF, 1994).

Index

Index

Index